NEW ENGLAND
CABINS &
COTTAGES

NEW ENGLAND
CABINS &
COTTAGES

Great Lodgings with Easy Access
to Outdoor Recreation

FIRST EDITION

Bethany Ericson

AVALON
TRAVEL

**FOGHORN OUTDOORS
NEW ENGLAND CABINS & COTTAGES**
Great Lodgings with Easy Access to
Outdoor Recreation

First Edition

Bethany Ericson

Text © 2004 by Bethany Ericson.
All rights reserved.
Illustrations and maps © 2004 by
Avalon Travel Publishing.
All rights reserved.

Avalon Travel Publishing is a division of
Avalon Publishing Group, Inc.

Some photos are used by permission
and are the property of the original copyright owners.

ISBN: 1-56691-636-4
ISSN: 1545-5408

Please send all feedback about this book to:

**⑤OGHORN OUTDOORS®
New England Cabins & Cottages**
Avalon Travel Publishing
1400 65th Street, Suite 250
Emeryville, CA 94608, USA
atpfeedback@avalonpub.com
www.foghorn.com

Printing History
1st edition—March 2004
5 4 3 2 1

Editor: Marisa Solís
Series Manager: Marisa Solís
Copy Editor: Kate Willis
Proofreader: Wendy Taylor
Production and Graphics Coordinator: Justin Marler
Illustrator: Bob Race
Cover and Interior Designer: Darren Alessi
Map Editors: Olivia Solís, Naomi Adler Dancis
Cartographers: Mike Morgenfeld, Kat Kalamaras, Olivia Solís
Indexer: Kevin Millham

Front cover photo: Sterling Ridge Resort, Vermont © Susan Peterson

Printed in the United States of America by Malloy Inc.

In loving memory of Walter B. Nye

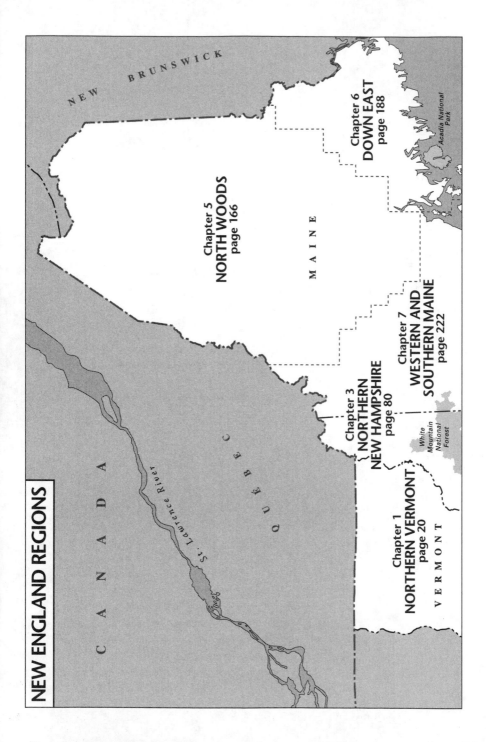

NEW ENGLAND REGIONS

NEW BRUNSWICK

NEW

CANADA

QUEBEC

St. Lawrence River

River

MAINE

VERMONT

Chapter 6
DOWN EAST
page 188

Acadia National Park

Acadia National Park

Chapter 5
NORTH WOODS
page 166

Chapter 7
WESTERN AND SOUTHERN MAINE
page 222

Chapter 3
NORTHERN NEW HAMPSHIRE
page 80

White Mountain National Forest

Chapter 1
NORTHERN VERMONT
page 20

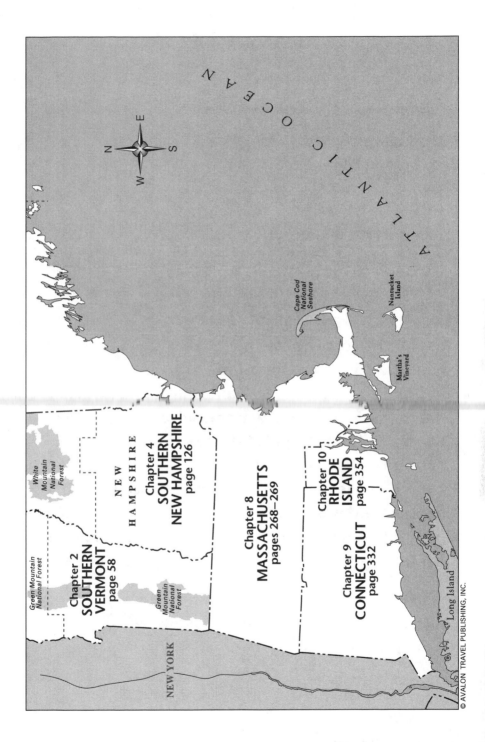

ATLANTIC OCEAN

Cape Cod
National
Seashore

Nantucket
Island

Martha's
Vineyard

White
Mountain
National
Forest

NEW
HAMPSHIRE

Chapter 4
SOUTHERN
NEW HAMPSHIRE
page 126

Green Mountain National Forest

Chapter 2
SOUTHERN
VERMONT
page 58

Green
Mountain
National
Forest

Chapter 8
MASSACHUSETTS
pages 268–269

Chapter 10
RHODE
ISLAND
page 354

Chapter 9
CONNECTICUT
page 332

NEW YORK

Long Island

© AVALON TRAVEL PUBLISHING, INC.

CONTENTS

HOW TO USE THIS BOOK

Foghorn Outdoors New England Cabins & Cottages covers the six New England states—Vermont, New Hampshire, Maine, Massachusetts, Connecticut, and Rhode Island—and is divided into 10 chapters. Although that is a lot of territory to cover in one book, navigating this guide can be done easily in two ways:

1. If you know the name of the lodging facility you want to stay at, or the name of the surrounding geographical area or nearby feature (town, national or state park or forest, mountain, lake, river, etc.), look it up in the index and turn to the corresponding page.

2. If you know the general area you want to visit, turn to the map at the beginning of that chapter. You can then determine which cabins are in or near your destination by their corresponding numbers. Opposite the map will be a chapter table of contents listing each lodging in the chapter by map number and the page number it's profiled on. Then turn to the corresponding page for the cabin you're interested in.

About the Cabin Profiles

Each featured cabin profile includes an introduction to the lodging facility and what it has to offer. This usually includes an overview of the grounds, units, facilities, and amenities. There is also a discussion of the recreation opportunities available on-site or within a short drive. These range from cross-country skiing to kayaking and from hiking to fishing. The practical information you need to have an enjoyable trip is broken down further into the following categories:

Facilities — This section conveys the number of cabins or cottages available, whether kitchen facilities are available, and whether private or communal bathrooms and showers are available. Amenities inside the cabins (such as fireplace, hot tub, and air-conditioning) as well as on the property (such as swimming pool, restaurant, and picnic area) are also mentioned here.

Bedding — This section tells whether linens and towels are provided, and if not, what you should bring to sleep comfortably.

Reservations and rates — This section notes whether reservations are required or recommended. It also discusses the rates for each cabin, which often range due to cabin size, amenities, time of week, and time of year. If there are additional fees for extra persons or pets, that will also be noted here. If there are package deals, that will also be noted. If a cabin is open during part of the year, those dates will be mentioned.

Directions — This section provides mile-by-mile driving directions from the nearest major town.

Contact — This section provides an address, phone number, and Internet address, if available, for the featured cabin.

About the Icons

The icons in this book are designed to provide at-a-glance information on activities that are available on-site or nearby a cabin. Some icons have been selected to also represent facilities available or services provided. They are not meant to represent every activity or service, only the ones that the majority of our readers would be interested in.

 — Hiking trails are available.

 — Biking trails or routes are available. Usually this refers to mountain biking, although it may represent road cycling as well. Refer to the text for that cabin for more detail.

 — Swimming opportunities are available.

 — Fishing opportunities are available.

 — Boating opportunities are available. Various types of vessels apply under this umbrella activity, including motorboats, canoes, kayaks, sailboats, personal watercraft, and rowboats. Refer to the text for that cabin for more detail, including mph restrictions and boat ramp availability.

 — Beach activities are available. This general category may include activities such as beachcombing, surfing, and volleyball. Refer to the text for that cabin for more detail on what's allowed.

 — Winter sports are available. This general category may include activities such as downhill skiing, cross-country skiing, snowshoeing, snowmobiling, snowboarding, and ice skating. Refer to the text for that cabin for more detail on which sports are available.

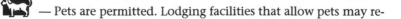 — Pets are permitted. Lodging facilities that allow pets may re-

quire a deposit, nightly fee, or for the pet to be on a leash. Cabins
may also restrict pet size. Always call ahead and discuss the pet
regulations with the cabin owner before making your reservation.

— The cabin or cottage is especially popular with families. Typically that is because it has activities nearby that are suitable for
children. These include a playground or play area, swimming
pool, ocean beach, lake with a wading or swimming beach, or
family-oriented skiing or snow play. At these kid-friendly cabins, you won't have to travel far to keep the kids entertained.

— Wheelchair access is provided. Not all cabins at a facility
may be wheelchair accessible, but if at least one is, the cabin
will receive this icon. Refer to the text for that cabin for more
detail or call the cabin in advance.

About the Ratings

Every lodging option in this book is rated on two scales.

Luxury rating — This scale of ★☆☆☆☆ to ★★★★★ rates the comfort
level of the cabin. We expect that users of this guidebook will have different requirements for cushy living, but in general, a place with more
amenities will get a higher ranking. For example, a tent cabin without
bathrooms or running water may receive a ★☆☆☆☆ or ★★☆☆☆. That
doesn't mean that you can't have the perfect vacation here. All it means is
you might have to carry your water from a nearby fountain and be prepared to use chemical toilets. Likewise, a cottage with fireplace, hot tub,
king-size bed, and down comforters will probably rank ★★★★☆ or
★★★★★. But that doesn't guarantee the perfect vacation; the cabin may
be close to a noisy highway, the management may not be friendly, or the
recreation options may be an hour's drive away.

Recreation rating — This scale of ★☆☆☆☆ to ★★★★★ rates the accessibility of on-site or nearby activities. We expect that users of this guidebook are interested in the outdoors and seek a cabin experience that is
coupled with recreation opportunities. This scale does not rate the number of activities available, nor the level of expertise needed to participate
in them. Rather, it rates how *accessible* they are. For example, if you can
access a trailhead or launch your boat within a two-minute walk of your
cabin, the recreation rating will likely be a ★★★★★. On the other hand,
if fishing or downhill skiing requires a one-hour drive, the cabin may be
rated a ★☆☆☆☆. That doesn't mean you can't have the same quality vacation . . . it just means you'll need more than your feet for transportation.

Rank — Each cabin and cottage that appears in this guide is carefully selected from myriad options, so we like to think that each of the cabins profiled in this book are special. But those places that are extra-special may receive a ranking on one or more of the "Best Cabins and Cottages" categories. For the complete list of the categories and the cabins that have made it to the top ranks, turn to page 5.

About the Maps

Each chapter in this book begins with a map of the area. Every cabin profile in the chapter is noted by a number on the map. These points are placed as precisely as possible, but the scale of these maps often makes it difficult to pinpoint a cabin's exact location. We advise that you purchase a detailed map of the area, especially if it is new to you.

DEFINING CABINS AND COTTAGES IN NEW ENGLAND

For the purposes of this book, a cabin or cottage is a self-contained, stand-alone lodging where you will not share walls with any neighbors and are not required to be a member of any organization. As a result, places that only offer duplex cabins were omitted. As a benefit, this means that places that offer lodging on a boat, above the boat slips of a boathouse, in a single-unit lighthouse, or in a yurt are included.

There are thousands of lodgings that fit this definition in New England, and nearly everyone who grew up in the area has either frequented one, has one in their family, or will rent you one for a small sum. This book focuses on cabins and cottages with a wide range of rates and amenities located near outdoor recreation—and this is truly just the tip of the iceberg.

Cabins in this region were often built on sites that were once tenting areas, and they are often referred to as *camps*. Many a New Englander will refer to going to "the camp" in their family. This term is often used for a lakeside or North Woods cabin. In northern New England, and most notably in Maine, camps are the term generally used for communities of fairly rustic cabins where the main focus is on fishing and hunting. These days, many of the Maine camps are diversifying their focus and attracting all kinds of outdoors-oriented visitors.

The term *lodge* is often used for the main building at a cabin or cottage colony. It may offer other rooms, contain the dining hall, or be simply the owner's house where you check in. This term gets used loosely throughout the region to mean many things, and a number of places use the term *lodges* to indicate the individual cabins on-site.

Warming huts were built in the mountains and backcountry for skiers and other adventurers, and the term *hut* has a wider use in the area now. Huts are sometimes converted warming huts, but they are often bunkhouses and are typically found on mountains.

In New England, the word *cottage* poses a problem for would-be Internet vacation researchers. Due to the great influx of money into the Berkshires, Newport, and southwestern coastal Connecticut in the Gilded Age, many grand summer cottages were constructed. In these areas, the term is typically synonymous with the word mansion. Some of these structures have been converted into hotels, inns, and bed-and-breakfasts, and occasionally the old carriage house or other outbuildings were renovated into the kinds of cabins and cottages this book covers.

A *housekeeping cottage* is one where you clean up after yourself. You cook, you wash your dishes, and you should also clean the place before you leave. If your cabin or cottage comes with housekeeping services, that means you will have daily maid service like you would at a hotel. The American Plan (AP) provides you with all three meals; a Modified American Plan (MAP) means you're on your own for lunch.

And finally, a *grinder* is a sub-style sandwich; a *frappe,* not a milkshake, includes ice cream; and Moxie is *tonic,* which is a soft drink (although seltzer is *soda water*). Also, you *can* get thar from heah—you just might have to use a boat.

© BETHANY ERICSON

Introduction

INTRODUCTION

I grew up a bike ride away from the site of Thoreau's tiny cabin on Walden Pond, near the homes of Emerson and Alcott, Revolutionary War sites, and references to Native American and homesteading history. This environment, combined with an outdoors-oriented family, taught me that the real lessons in living are those learned from self-sufficiency and nature.

We summered in a lakeside cabin that my father's father had built for his family in New Hampshire in the 1940s. "It's a great life, my dearest, and I know you will enjoy it," he wrote in his loopy script in a 1928 love letter to my grandmother, which I found. He was writing by candlelight at Lake of the Clouds, an Appalachian Mountain Club hut near the summit of New Hampshire's Mount Washington. After he died, my grandmother spent every summer in the cabin he had built, watching the loons on the lake. We took her to see the movie *On Golden Pond* in a converted Victorian train station that once had brought city folk to summer by the lake.

My other grandparents were Mainers. They canoed the Allagash and throughout the North Woods. They took me canoe camping, hiking, and blueberry picking, and told me stories about their remote cottage where moose escaped the black flies by swimming in the lake. My grandmother took me swimming in the icy ocean, and my grandfather named the birds and the trees for me.

It's not surprising that I'm drawn to the cabins of New England, just like members of my family. The cabins in New England represent more than industrial-era vacationers "taking the airs." In many cases, the cabins represent a culture of people in touch with, and invested in, the Earth, and who take an interest in their environment and each other. These are places where you can adventure out into the largeness of the woods or water and be warmly welcomed back by camp communities who are gathered around cozy fires.

Whether you seek a cabin or cottage retreat to simply rejuvenate your spirit, rest after a tough winter hike or ski, shower after kayaking the rocky shores, share a romantic leaf-peeping weekend, bike the back roads, canoe with moose, learn to fly-fish, connect with your family, or pen your thoughts on the inseparability of wilderness and the soul, I hope this book will not only guide you to lodging that meets your needs, but welcome you to a lifestyle that has persisted here for centuries.

QUESTIONS TO ASK WHEN RESERVING A CABIN

No matter how much detail this book includes, resort owners, policies, and times change. Although it's convenient that many places allow you to make reservations online, it's generally a good policy to call and ask in-depth questions. Most owners would rather match you to your expectations than have you be disappointed. Tell them the kind of place and vacation you are imagining, so that you can have the best experience possible.

In New England, many cabins (particularly those on the water) are rented to the same families for the same week every single year. Be aware that reservations are almost always mandatory, and (particularly in beach areas) be flexible with your dates and work your way from the shoulder seasons up to "returning guest" status. Deposits are standard fare. Some are returned after your stay, some are applied to the last days of your stay, and most are partially or completely nonrefundable if you arrive more than a day late or leave more than a day early.

Here are some of the things you may want to ask:

- What size beds are in the bedrooms, does the cabin accommodate extra people, and is there a charge for additional people? Are visitors permitted?
- Do you take credit cards? Personal checks?
- What is the cancellation policy?
- Are pets allowed in the cabin? What is the pet policy, and is there an extra charge?
- Does the cabin have heat? If it has a fireplace or woodstove, should I bring my own firewood?
- If the cabin has a kitchen, what kinds of pots and utensils are provided? Does it include paper goods, soap, and cleaning supplies?
- Does the cabin have a barbecue or fire grill for outdoor cooking?
- Are any meals included with the rates or available on-site? Are there restaurants or markets nearby?
- How close is it to other cabins or to the road?
- Does the cabin have a view?
- Is there dock or mooring space for private boats? If so, is there a charge?
- Is personal watercraft riding permissible there?
- Are motorcycles welcomed there?
- If the cabin is in a remote location, is there airport pickup, gear transport, or other services?
- If traveling by car in the backwoods, where is the closest gas station?
- Are there boat rentals or equipment on-site or on the way?

ABOUT THE APPALACHIAN
MOUNTAIN CLUB

Although many of its lodgings do not fit the definitions set forth in this book, the Appalachian Mountain Club (AMC) is a Northeastern institution that bears mentioning here. The AMC is the country's oldest conservation and recreation organization and was founded in the late 19th century when an M.I.T. professor invited some peers to a regular salon of sorts to discuss mountain exploration. The AMC, the Randolph Mountain Club (RMC), and the outdoor clubs of M.I.T., Dartmouth, and Harvard maintain many of the hiking trails in the region to this day. In addition, these organizations, most notably the AMC, maintain lodging facilities in prime outdoor recreation areas.

The AMC runs a number of convenient and charming lodges that are accessible by car, mostly in beautiful areas of the White Mountains of New Hampshire. These places have bunkrooms or private rooms and often serve meals. Outdoor workshops and guided hikes are common offerings. Members also have access to some stand-alone cabins.

The most famous of the AMC's lodgings is the mountain hut system. The AMC has maintained these huts for more than a century. Each is located about a day's hike apart along the Appalachian Trail and is accessible only by foot. These bunkroom-style lodgings are staffed, all have water, and what's most unusual—most of them serve meals. For more information on the AMC, visit the website www.outdoors.org.

BEST CABINS AND COTTAGES

Can't decide where to stay during your next outdoor getaway? Of the hundreds of cabins and cottages in this book, here are my favorites (in alphabetical order) in 14 categories:

Top 10 for Hiking

Virtually any place in the Green Mountains of Vermont or White Mountains of New Hampshire is readily accessible to hiking trails. Here are some of the most notable:

1. **Brass Heart Inn,** Northern New Hampshire, p. 121. These pastoral cottages lie behind the inn at the base of popular Mount Chocoura.
2. **Christmas Farm Inn,** Northern New Hampshire, p. 108. There are many levels of hikes in the Mount Washington Valley that can be enjoyed from this inn.
3. **Grünberg Haus,** Northern Vermont, p. 48. These cozy cabins are on walking trails and have easy access to Long Trail, Camel's Hump, Hunger Mountain, and the Worcester Range.
4. **Josselyn's Getaways,** Northern New Hampshire, p. 91. Stay in a log cabin before ascending the northern Presidentials or discovering Mounts Starr King and Waumbek.
5. **Little Lyford Pond Lodge,** North Woods, p. 180. Hike from your cabin door to Gulf Hagas, "New England's Grand Canyon."
6. **New England Inn & Resort,** Northern New Hampshire, p. 117. Soak in a whirpool tub after risking possibly the worst weather in the world on Mount Washington, New England's highest peak.
7. **Ramblewood Cabins,** Northern New Hampshire, p. 84. Explore New Hampshire's growing Cohos Trail, planned to become the longest foot-trail system in the state.
8. **White Rocks Inn,** Southern Vermont, p. 63. Stay in a converted milk house with easy access to White Rocks National Recreation Area, the Applachian Trail, and the Long Trail.
9. **Wilderness Inn and Café,** Northern New Hampshire, p. 106. Spend your days atop the high peaks of Franconia Notch.
10. **WilloughVale Inn,** Northern Vermont, p. 36. These cabins are near trails that lead to the lakeside cliffs on Mounts Pisgah and Hor, the fire tower atop Bald Mountain, and the new trails of Burke Mountain.

Top 10 for Fishing

New England offers a great variety of fishing and is home to the famous Orvis fly-fishing store. Meanwhile, all of the coastal cabins profiled are near charter boats that offer ocean fishing. Here are some fishing-oriented cabins worth noting:

Bosebuck Mountain Camps

1. **Bosebuck Mountain Camps**, Western and Southern Maine, p. 224. Some of the great innovations of fly-fishing started in this region, with its world-class trout and salmon fishing in sparkling lakes.
2. **Clearwater Lodges**, Southern New Hampshire, p. 141. Lake Winnipesaukee is New Hampshire's largest lake. It offers brook, lake, and rainbow trout; salmon; large and smallmouth bass; pickerel; horned pout; white perch; black crappie; and bluegill.
3. **Eagle Lake Sporting Camp**, North Woods p. 168. Aroostook County offers splendid fishing spots, including the easily accessible Eagle Lake.
4. **Henry's Sportsman's Cottages**, Northern Vermont, p. 23. A 90 percent repeat guest list indicates that this fishing hole has something going on. Fish for bass, northern pike, sunfish, and perch, as well as walleye, salmon, lake trout, and crappie in Lake Champlain.
5. **Leen's Lodge**, Down East, p. 216. West Grand Lake and Grand Lake Stream are world famous for landlocked salmon, lake trout, and smallmouth bass fishing.
6. **Libby Camps**, North Woods, p. 171. Libby Camps is a well-known backwoods, Orvis-endorsed facility that focuses on fly-fishing for salmon and trout.
7. **Robinsons Cottages**, Down East, p. 210. Large cabins in fishing and hunting country offer trout and bass in Denny's River, while Cathance Lake has landlocked salmon, bass, and perch.
8. **Sebago Lake Lodge & Cottages**, Western and Southern Maine, p. 227. Maine's second largest lake is in the south, providing fishing enthusiasts with an earlier ice-out—and record-breaking landlocked salmon.
9. **Tall Timber Lodge**, Northern New Hampshire, p. 83. The Connecticut Lakes offer lake trout and salmon fishing.
10. **Weatherby's**, Down East, p. 212. This is a high-end fishing camp near some of the best landlocked salmon, lake trout, and smallmouth bass fishing in Maine.

Top 10 for Romance

Romance is what you make it, but many of these cabins make it easier. Some offer great privacy or amenities such as two-person whirlpool tubs and fireplaces.

1. **Cedarholm Garden Bay**, Western and Southern Maine, p. 232. Here you will find a blue-tiled whirlpool tub, a stone fireplace, a dramatic sleeping loft, decks facing the ocean, and views of the Owls Head light in Rockland.

2. **Cornucopia of Dorset**, Southern Vermont, p. 66. Tucked behind the inn is a private getaway cottage that is supplied with champagne and chocolate.

3. **Ellis River House**, Northern New Hampshire, p. 110. This inn caters to couples only. You won't need one of their "Do Not Disturb, Romance in Progress" doorknob signs if you stay in the lovely private cottage with a whirlpool tub—and mountain views from the tub itself.

4. **Grünberg Haus**, Northern Vermont, p. 48. Romantic hideaway cabins are concealed by the forest and accessed by walking trails on a small ridge above the inn.

5. **Inn at Covered Bridge Green**, Southern Vermont, p. 72. The Honeymoon Cottage is private and charming, with exposed beams, a spiral staircase, and a romantic loft bed. The bathroom has a giant showerhead made for sharing.

6. **The Inn at Richmond**, Massachusetts, p. 279. This cabin has antique furnishings, luxurious bedding, and wonderful views in the beautiful Berkshires.

7. **The Inn at Sunrise Point**, Western and Southern Maine, p. 234. Spend an evening in the whirlpool tub, with the moonlit waves lapping the rocks beneath your window in the Fitz Hugh Lane cottage.

8. **New England Inn & Resort**, Northern New Hampshire, p. 117. Rent a log cabin with a fireplace and whirlpool tub for two in the White Mountains.

9. **The Summer House Inns & Cottages**, Massachusetts, p. 305. These are some of Nantucket's famous little rose-covered cottages, where you can find antique furnishings, marble whirlpool tubs, skylights, and fireplaces.

10. **Three Mountain Inn**, Southern Vermont, p. 73. This luxurious cottage offers remote-controlled lighting, fireplace, and music. There is a two-person hot tub and a stained-glass window visible only from the sleigh bed.

Top 10 for Viewing Fall Foliage

The famous bright colors of New England's foliage are everywhere in autumn, and their brilliance depends on a number of factors, including the weather. For one of the most popular leaf-peeping routes, drive from Route 7 in western Connecticut up through the Berkshire Hills of Massachusetts to southern Vermont. Foliage season is also an excellent time to visit some of the areas along the Maine Coast that are too crowded in the summer, such as Mount Desert Island or the Camden Hills. Here is just a sampling of fall favorites:

1. **Blue Heron Farm**, Massachusetts, p. 275. Stay where there is a sugaring house, and the maples will reliably impress your eyes.
2. **Grünberg Haus**, Northern Vermont, p. 48. Enjoy this hideaway in the woods on a ridge that looks out on a colorful hillside.
3. **Jericho Valley Inn**, Massachusetts, p. 272. Relax by the fire after a crisp fall day of leaf-peeping on Route 2 (the Mohawk Trail).
4. **The Merck Forest and Farmland Center**, Southern Vermont, p. 64. Maple trees provide some of the best colors, so why not hike into the woods to a site where syrup is produced?
5. **Mohawk Trail State Forest**, Massachusetts, p. 276. Rent a camping cabin in the woods for true immersion into autumn.
6. **Molly Stark Inn**, Southern Vermont, p. 75. Tucked behind the inn, the rustic-looking cottages facing the colorful woods are surprisingly romantic gems.
7. **Old Stone School**, Massachusetts, p. 273. Take in the colors from the top of the state's tallest mountain, Mount Greylock, or from the outdoor photography in the art gallery in this schoolhouse cottage.
8. **Sterling Ridge Inn & Cabins**, Northern Vermont, p. 39. These lovely cabins have astonishing mountain views made more vivid by the changing autumn leaves.
9. **Wilburton Inn**, Southern Vermont, p. 67. This magnificent, sprawling hilltop of creativity offers spectacular fall views.

10. **WilloughVale Inn**, Northern Vermont, p. 36. As if Lake Willoughby isn't scenic enough, the fall colors of the surrounding hills are reflected in the water.

Old Stone School

Top 10 for Boating

New England is a boater's paradise, with Lake Champlain, the Lakes Region of New Hampshire, backcountry paddling and rowing, lake and river fishing, and the glorious coastline. Here are a few of the many fine establishments that cater to keeping you afloat:

1. **The Cottages at the Boat Basin**, Massachusetts, p. 304. The cottages out on wooden docks are right in the middle of the boat action, but they are also private, casually elegant lodgings. You can also launch canoes and kayaks from here.
2. **Craftsbury Outdoor Center**, Northern Vermont, p. 41. On Lake Hosmer, in the idyllic countryside, is this world-class sculling instructional center, complete with cottages.
3. **Harborfields on the Shore**, Western and Southern Maine, p. 242. These Boothbay cottages are home to a master wooden-boat builder and are also a fine place to launch a kayak from.
4. **Hiram Blake Camp**, Down East, p. 192. On the famous sailing waters of Penobscot Bay, these cabins are a short drive to the WoodenBoat School in Brooklin.
5. **North Hero Marina**, Northern Vermont, p. 28. Enjoy the tongue-and-groove log cabins set in the flower fields behind the full-service marina.
6. **Saybrook Point Inn and Spa**, Connecticut, p. 345. Dock your boat and stay in the lighthouse apartment out on the docks.
7. **Sebago Lake Lodge & Cottages**, Western and Southern Maine, p. 227. Rent boats or launch your own at the adjoining marina.
8. **Silver Sands Resort**, Southern New Hampshire, p. 147. Make your reservations well in advance for a beachside cottage by the marina.
9. **Sullivan Harbor**, Down East, p. 206. You're in good company with the Maine Guide owners if you enjoy rowing, kayaking, canoeing, or generally messing about in boats.
10. **Wolfe's Neck Farm Recompence Shore Campsites**, Western and Southern Maine, p. 253. Make a camping cabin your home after a day of kayaking, and perhaps participate in an L.L. Bean workshop.

Top 10 for Biking

There are countless great areas for biking in New England. Here are a few places, and some specific cottages, that keep you in great scenery and away from the cars:

1. **Blue Dory Inn**, Rhode Island, p. 361. Here you can ride the dirt roads that are suited for off-road biking on Block Island.
2. **The Cape Cod Rail Trail**, Massachusetts. All the cottages in Brewster, Orleans, Eastham, and Welfleet have decent access to this trail.

3. **Craftsbury Outdoor Center,** Northern Vermont, p. 41. Rent a mountain bike at this outdoor center on the Vermont end-to-end bike route currently in development.
4. **Even'tide Resort,** Massachusetts, p. 317. The Even'tide is located directly on the 25-mile Cape Cod Rail Trail.
5. **Lake Champlain Islands,** Northern Vermont, p. 23–32. All of the cabins profiled here are within pedaling distance of the bikeway.
6. **Mount Desert Island,** Down East, p. 196–206. All of the cottages listed on Mount Desert Island can access the carriage paths of Acadia National Park.
7. **Phillips Brook Backcountry Recreation Area,** Northern New Hampshire, p. 89. Pedal through the maintained paths of the backwoods to sleep in a yurt.
8. **The Summer House Inns & Cottages,** Massachusetts, p. 305. Paths for pedaling traverse the island of Nantucket.
9. **Timberland Trails Green Valley Lodge and Galusha Cabin,** Southern Vermont, p. 60. Here you will find lovely log cabins with backcountry mountain biking trails.
10. **The Tyler Place,** Northern Vermont, p. 22. What you can't see from the swarms of kids on bikes is that a mile of pedaling will bring you to 700 acres of backcountry land owned by The Tyler Place.

Best for Skiing and Snowmobiling

Carroll Motel and Cottages, Northern New Hampshire, p. 96. State snowmobile trails lead right from your cottage door, and tours can be arranged.

Christmas Farm Inn, Northern New Hampshire, p. 108. This is a romantic spot to stay while enjoying a weekend of skiing at Attitash Bear Peak or cross-country skiing in Jackson.

Craftsbury Outdoor Center, Northern Vermont, p. 41. The facility offers cross-country ski rentals and instruction for experiencing its more than 50 miles of groomed ski trails.

Highland Lodge, Northern Vermont, p. 42. The Greensboro area is well-known for cross-country skiing. The ski shop provides rental skis and snowshoes.

Johnny Seesaw's, Southern Vermont, p. 68. Once known more as love shacks, these cottages today are all about skiing Bromley Mountain with your family.

Josselyn's Getaways, Northern New Hampshire, p. 91. Corridor 5 is the main trail to connect to by snowmobile from these cute log cabins.

Lopstick Lodge and Cabins, Northern New Hampshire, p. 86. Rent a

snowmobile for the day, then relax in a hot tub in one of these cabins.
Moosehead Hills, North Woods, p. 178. From here you can snowmobile
from your cabin onto the Interconnecting Trail System. The Moosehead
Trail circumnavigates Moosehead Lake for 160 miles, with gas and food
along the way. Cross-country skiing trails abound, and Big Squaw Mountain Ski Resort is nearby.
New England Inn & Resort, Northern New Hampshire, p. 117. This is
prime skiing territory just minutes from the many trails and ski resorts in
the White Mountain National Forest area and the cross-country skiing
trails in Jackson.
Sky Valley Motel & Cottages, Northern New Hampshire, p. 114. These cottages are located directly across the street from Attitash Bear Peak Resort.
Tall Timber Lodge, Northern New Hampshire, p. 83. Basing yourself at
one of these northern cottages, try sledding this winter or rent a snowmobile at the lodge.
The Whitney Inn at Jackson, Northern New Hampshire, p. 111. These
cottages are located at the base of Black Mountain, a family-oriented ski
slope, and they are also connected to the popular Jackson ski-touring trails.
Wilderness Inn and Café, Northern New Hampshire, p. 106. Skiing at
Loon Mountain (three miles away) and Cannon Mountain (eight miles
away) is the popular activity for guests who stay here.

Top 10 for Backcountry Winter Adventures

1. **Beaver Cove Camps**, North Woods, p. 177. Take advantage of the year-
round status here to ski or snowmobile around Moosehead Lake.
2. **The Birches Resort**, North Woods, p. 175. These year-round backcountry yurts with woodstoves offer cross-country skiing opportunities.
3. **Indian Rock Camps**, Down East, p. 213. Unlike most camps in the area,
these are open year-round; enjoy a fire after skiing or ice fishing.
4. **Little Lyford Pond Lodge**, North Woods, p. 180. Little Lyford is a top-
notch place to cross-country ski or mush.
5. **The Merck Forest and Farmland Center**, Southern Vermont, p. 64.
Hike, backcountry ski, or snowshoe to your secluded cabin.
6. **Mohawk Trail State Forest**, Massachusetts, p. 276. Woodstoves provide
good heat after your return from winter hiking, snowshoeing, and skiing.
7. **Phillips Brook Backcountry Recreation Area**, Northern New Hampshire, p. 89. Ski the mountainside or into the woods and stay in a yurt.
8. **Ramblewood Cabins**, Northern New Hampshire, p. 84. Enjoy private
cross-country ski trails, great backcountry snowshoeing, and free use of
a heated workshop for snowmobile repairs. Ice fishing is also popular
on the lake.

9. **The Stone Hut,** Northern Vermont, p. 45. The historic Stone Hut, atop Mount Mansfield, is accessible by chairlift during Stowe Mountain's ski season.
10. **Timberland Trails Green Valley Lodge and Galusha Cabin,** Southern Vermont, p. 60. Wilderness trails and bushwhacking abound.

Top 10 for Family Activities

1. **Blue Heron Farm,** Massachusetts, p. 275. The kids can pitch in on farm activities here, from milking goats to picking blueberries for the breakfast pancakes.
2. **Even'Tide Resort,** Massachusetts, p. 317. This cozy place is located on the Cape Cod Rail Trail bike path, and it's a short walk from Marconi Beach, on the National Seashore.
3. **Highland Lodge,** Northern Vermont, p. 42. This family resort has a beach, woods, fields, and environmental-education programs in a setting that oozes with pastoral charm.
4. **Kalmar Village,** Massachusetts, p. 325. This is Cape Cod beach living, with the additional perks of a pool and regular buses to Provincetown and other beaches.
5. **Ocean View Park Campground,** Western and Southern Maine, p. 250. Located on sandy Popham Beach, this place is great for lying in the sun, collecting shells, and swimming.
6. **Quimby Country,** Northern Vermont, p. 35. This is a family summercamp experience with organized activities for the little ones.
7. **Rockywold–Deephaven Camps,** Southern New Hampshire, p. 128. This old-style, family vacation camp on Squam Lake offers endless activities and family fun.
8. **Sebasco Harbor Resort,** Western and Southern Maine, p. 248. Let the kids swim in the saltwater pool, take sailing or kayak lessons, or paddle in the freshwater lake while you play tennis or golf. Popham Beach is nearby, and bikes are available to rent. There's even a bowling alley on-site.
9. **Sunrise Resort,** Connecticut, p. 340. This family-run camping resort is the kind of activity-filled place where parents play with their kids rather than dropping them off with counselors.
10. **The Tyler Place,** Northern Vermont, p. 22. This place is known for its fabulous kids' programs and sports facilities.

Top 10 Most Unusual

1. **A Victorian Village,** Connecticut, p. 343. This neighborhood of little Victorian cottages with homemade gingerbread trim is sure to make you smile.

2. **Blue Heron Farm**, Massachusetts, p. 275. Get involved in the daily activities of running the farm while you visit.
3. **The Cottages at the Boat Basin**, Massachusetts, p. 304. Here you can stay right on the docks of Nantucket Sound.

Loon Hollow

4. **Club Getaway**, Connecticut, p. 335. This is a sporty singles paradise.
5. **Inn at Covered Bridge Green**, Southern Vermont, p. 72. Here you can sleep in Norman Rockwell's former art studio.
6. **Josselyn's Getaways**, Northern New Hampshire, p. 91. Like your creative log cabin? They'll build one for you.
7. **Loon Hollow**, Down East, p. 190. Creativity and caring run deep in these eclectic cottages.
8. **Saybrook Point Inn and Spa**, Connecticut, p. 345. Here you can stay in a lighthouse way out on the docks.
9. **Three Mountain Inn**, Southern Vermont, p. 73. Everything in this den of romance has a remote-control device.
10. **Wilburton Inn**, Southern Vermont, p. 67. The art installations here rival the mountain views for your attention.

Top 10 for Value

There are many affordable lodgings in this book. Here are some that offer an exceptional experience without emptying your wallet:

1. **Castine Cottages**, Down East, p. 191. Perched above the ocean in quaint Castine, these cabins offer great views.
2. **Days' Cottages**, Massachusetts, p. 322. This famous row of white cottages near the tip of Cape Cod continues to offer good rates.
3. **The Driftwood Inn**, Western and Southern Maine, p. 251. A place within sound range of great waves crashing on the rocky shore often costs much more than this.
4. **Fish River Lodge**, North Woods, p. 169. Travel across the lake to take advantage of some newly refurbished cabins with character.
5. **The Glen**, Northern New Hampshire, p. 87. The Glen offers a wilderness experience for a low price that includes meals.
6. **Harvey's Lake Cabins & Campground**, Northern Vermont, p. 51.

These eclectically decorated, fun cottages sit right on a lake.

7. **Leen's Lodge,** Down East, p. 216. This is a gorgeous spot, with meals included in your stay.
8. **Robinsons Cottages,** Down East, p. 210. Here you have spacious, woodland, fishing-and-camping lodges for a great price.
9. **Sunrise Resort,** Connecticut, p. 340. This family-oriented camping resort is very reasonable, especially when you consider it provides three meals a day.
10. **Timberland Trails Green Valley Lodge and Galusha Cabin,** Southern Vermont, p. 60. For the best value, stay at one these great log-cabin homes with a group of people.

Top 10 for Ocean Beach Activities

1. **Chatham Bars Inn,** Massachusetts, p. 307. The sandy beach at this resort is dotted with striped cabanas.
2. **Dennis Seashores,** Massachusetts, p. 300. These cabins are either directly on the water or in the woods across from the beach.
3. **The Dunes on the Waterfront,** Western and  Southern Maine, p. 261. Wade *The Dunes on the Waterfront* or row across the river from the cottages to the protected, wide, white-sand Ogunquit Beach peninsula.
4. **Kalmar Village,** Massachusetts, p. 325. This expansive family cottage resort has landscaped lawns leading to a big, private, sandy beach.
5. **Menemsha Inn and Cottages,** Massachusetts, p. 295. On Menemsha Bite, Martha's Vineyard, these cottages are all about the beach.
6. **Nauset Beach-side,** Massachusetts, p. 311. Stay one minute from one of the best beaches on the Atlantic coast, with good surf, swimming, and surf casting.
7. **Ocean View Park Campground,** Western and Southern Maine, p. 250. These cottages are right on Popham Beach and offer good surf casting.
8. **The Seaside Motor Inn and Cottages,** Western and Southern Maine, p. 257. These cottages are on private, sandy Gooch's Beach in Kennebunkport.
9. **The Summer House Inns & Cottages,** Massachusetts, p. 305. This is in Nantucket, and there is nothing between you and Portugal.

10. **Wallis Sands Place,** Southern New Hampshire, p. 158. These cute cottages are directly across the street from Wallis Sands State Park.

Top 10 Most Luxurious

1. **Bufflehead Cove,** Western and Southern Maine, p. 255. This is the most luxurious honeymoon cottage in the book. And it isn't pretentious.
2. **Cedarholm Garden Bay,** Western and Southern Maine, p. 232. Enjoy the fine craftsmanship and luxury detail of these seaside cottages.
3. **Chatham Bars Inn,** Massachusetts, p. 307. The Bayview cottage is one of the inn's "master suites," with fine furnishings, a wet bar, and a fireplace.
4. **The Inn at Sunrise Point,** Western and Southern Maine, p. 234. Stay directly over the lapping waves, and take advantage of all the amenities.
5. **The Inn at Richmond,** Massachusetts, p. 279. The Kenilworth is the most luxurious of the three cottages, with a whirlpool tub, two cast-iron gas stoves, and delightful breakfasts.
6. **New England Inn & Resort,** Northern New Hampshire, p. 117. Pamper yourself with a fireplace and whirlpool tub after skiing.
7. **The Summer House Inns & Cottages,** Massachusetts, p. 305. These rose-covered Nantucket showpieces offer amenities like marble bathrooms.
8. **Three Mountain Inn,** Southern Vermont, p. 73. Step from the deluxe romantic cottage into the pool with a fieldstone fountain, and float, looking at views of the mountains.
9. **Whalewalk Inn,** Massachusetts, p. 313. If you seek privacy in an upscale setting while exploring the Cape, the Salt Box Cottage here may be for you.
10. **Wilburton Inn,** Southern Vermont, p. 67. Play piano while enjoying your mountain views.

Top 10 for Weddings

1. **The Bradley Inn,** Western and Southern Maine, p. 241. Sitting at the tip of the Pemaquid Peninsula, this location offers great lighthouse photo opportunities and a romantic setting.
2. **Brass Heart Inn,** Northern New Hampshire, p. 121. The barn here has been transformed into one of the largest banquet facilities in Mount Washington Valley. It offers a full service bar.
3. **Christmas Farm Inn,** Northern New Hampshire, p. 108. The on-site wedding consultant helps you plan a ceremony in the Carriage House, a garden, or at nearby Jackson Falls. Receptions can be in the antique barn or in a tent.
4. **Migis Lodge,** Western and Southern Maine, p. 225. Sebago Lake is a pretty location for weddings, and the dining room at Migis is very elegant.

5. **Oakland House Seaside Resort,** Down East, p. 194. Oakland House designs custom wedding packages that might include lobster picnics, wedding-party lodging, dancing, and more—all by the sea.
6. **Sebasco Harbor Resort,** Western and Southern Maine, p. 248. This is a gorgeous seaside location with plenty of lodging choices. The diverse facilities allow for lobster bakes, candlepin bowling parties, and boat trips.
7. **Sterling Ridge Inn & Cabins,** Northern Vermont, p. 39. Mount Mansfield is the backdrop here, and with an inn and several log cabins, there is plenty of room for a lot of guests.
8. **Turning Point Inn,** Massachusetts, p. 283. Minutes from Tanglewood, this charming, chef-owned, 200-year-old tavern with converted barn cottage is truly a delicious location for a wedding.
9. **White Rocks Inn,** Southern Vermont, p. 63. The gothic barn is a good wedding location, and the honeymoon cottage is delightful. There is also an antique limousine available.
10. **Wilburton Inn,** Southern Vermont, p. 67. The handsome Tudor mansion has a terrace with views of the Battenkill Valley.

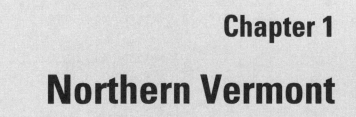

© BETHANY ERICSON

Chapter 1

Northern Vermont

CHAPTER 1—NORTHERN VERMONT

Vermont's less-populated northern forests, lakes, and fields remain relatively unspoiled. If you've ever dreamed of watching your children run through sunny fields of wildflowers with the dog bounding alongside or of lying on a dock and counting the stars, come here. Or perhaps you've dreamed of swimming in a clean lake ringed by mountains or of skiing for miles from cabin to cabin? If you have, then this is the place for you.

You won't find traffic jams here unless there is a drawbridge up, a tractor ahead of you, or cows crossing the road. Through the car's windows you will see lush farmland, great forests, covered bridges, and mighty mountains.

Come in the spring to the sugarhouses in St. Johnsbury or Barton. Spend your summer by Lake Willoughby, swimming and boating. Hike Camel's Hump or bike the trails from Burlington to the Champlain Islands and soak in the splendor of the fall colors. Return in the winter to ski at Stowe, Killington, Sugarbush, or Mad River Glen. Tour the Catamount Trail, try dogsledding, or ice fish on Lake Champlain.

Abenaki people once thrived on this land before French trappers and traders arrived. The ensuing wars resulted in years of marauding riders traveling throughout the north; the good news for us today is that this helped slow settlement. For about four years of its history, this area was part of the Independent Republic of Vermont, a sovereign country that then became part of the Union in 1791.

Railroads arrived, and once-autonomous farms found a wider market for milk, lumber, and maple syrup that has endured the years. Tourists traveled north by train, and thus began a vacationing tradition. People came to cross-country ski near Highland Lodge, cycle through picture-perfect Peacham, picnic atop Owl's Head, and wind through Smugglers Notch, which was guarded by peregrine falcons. Searching for the catamount (a supposedly extinct cougar), Memphre (the monster of Lake Memphremagog), and Champ (the serpent of Lake Champlain) was a popular pastime.

The Long Trail—the hiking trail that inspired the creation of the Appalachian Trail—passes through the west on its way to the Canadian border; the renowned mountain biking Kingdom Trails network winds through the eastern section; the Catamount Trail cuts northward, with its 280 miles of cross-country ski trails; and the Vermont Association of Snow Travelers (VAST) clubs tend to more than 3,500 miles of snowmobiling trails.

There is no lack of public boat launch sites, and there are still remote and wild waters for canoeing, rowing, and kayaking. The fish here include pike, pickerel, bass, freshwater salmon, trout, and perch. To the east, the Connecticut River forms the border with New Hampshire, and to the west, Lake Champlain forms the border with New York. Summer vacationers have always adored the summer cottages that dot the islands of Grand Isle, North Hero, and Isle la Motte.

In fact, the oldest log cabin in the country can be found on the Champlain Islands, where black marble was quarried to make the Brooklyn and Victoria (Montreal) Bridges. And the oldest coral reef in the world (Chazgan Coral Reef) peeks out of a threadbare pasture on Isle la Motte.

In the late 20th century, there was a back-to-the-land movement and a great wave of writers, artists, and musicians moved to northern Vermont. Still, even today, the land is lightly populated, and there is plenty of exploring to do in the woods, lakes, and rivers. And where else can you find a miniature golf course that operates on the honor system?

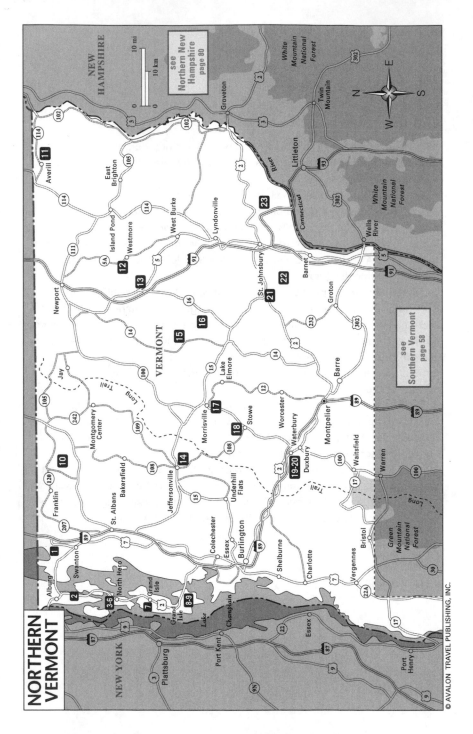

CHAPTER 1
NORTHERN VERMONT

1. THE TYLER PLACE

on Lake Champlain

Luxury rating: ★ ★ ★ ☆ ☆   **Recreation rating:** ★ ★ ★ ★ ★

Rank: Top 10 for Biking, Top 10 for Family Activities

For more than 150 years, families have flocked to Missisquoi Bay on Lake Champlain to camp, fish, and relax. Four generations of the Tyler family have grown up enjoying summers here, and the Tylers have owned this resort for families since 1933.

The Tyler Place is known for its fabulous kids programs, as well as for its great sports facilities and excellent dining rooms. The whole atmosphere is immediately apparent as you drive in past droves of children on bikes and skateboards: "Full-steam kid and adult fun and leisurely private time for parents."

While the Tylers' reputation may be built on making kids happy, with a strong emphasis on family time, there is ample time provided for parents to have a good time with each other as well. After all, the kids are awfully well occupied.

There are nine programs for infants to teens in the morning and evenings, and family activities and free time in the afternoons. The smallest of tykes have a good time here with toys, crafts, playgrounds, heated wading pools, nature walks, gardening projects, storytelling, boat rides, cooking, a petting farm, and more. Evening fun includes parties, campfires, and games.

Teens are not overlooked or condescended to here. In fact, many teens love The Tyler Place so much they end up later returning from college in the summers to be counselors. Overnight camping trips and giant Capture the Flag games may be elements of your stay.

Tyler Place has bike trails, sailboats, canoes, kayaks, tennis courts, hiking, nearby golf, and even aerobic and yoga instruction. You can fish for bass, northern pike, and perch. There are plenty of sitters available, and the Inn offers dancing, concerts, games, and more. French Canadian villages just minutes away await your exploration, and a mile of pedaling will bring you to the 700-acre backcountry land owned by Tyler Place. The Long Trail is less than an hour away.

The cottages have fireplaces and are country casual with a scattering of antiques. The accommodations at Tyler are spread out like a residential neighborhood; you're sure to feel at home. All of them are within a short walk of the main Inn, the kids' centers and playgrounds, the fitness center, craft studio, pools, and waterfront. Meals are buffet style and health-conscious. Kids often dine with the other kids in their age grouping, though there is also a family breakfast room. Adults dine separately at dinner, with the kids off with their counselors. Picnic lunches are available.

Facilities: There are 28 fireplace cottages, as well as lodging in an inn, and family suites in larger houses. All range in sizes and have 1–5 bedrooms. Rates include daily housekeeping, all meals, sports, entertainment, kids programs, and infant and toddler care.

Bedding: All bedding and linens provided.

Reservations and rates: The cottages range in price by size and season $117–264 per person per night. Daily rates for more than two people are much lower. Open May 24–September 7.

Directions: Take I-89 to the Highgate Springs Exit 22 to Route 7 and drive for three miles south. From Northway 87, take the Champlain/NY Exit 42 and drive east via Rouses Point Bridge on Route 2. At the Route 78 intersection, just outside of Alburg, turn onto Route 78 to Swanton, Vermont, and then take Route 7 north to Highgate Springs. (Tyler Place is about 30 miles from the exit off of Northway 87.)

Contact: The Tyler Place, Old Dock Road, Highgate Springs, VT 05460, 802/868-4000 or 802/868-3301, website: www.tylerplace.com.

2. HENRY'S SPORTSMAN'S COTTAGES

on Lake Champlain

Luxury rating: ★ ★ ☆ ☆ ☆   **Recreation rating:** ★ ★ ★ ★ ★

Rank: Top 10 for Fishing

The cottages at Henry's are set up in a row on 1,100 feet of Lake Champlain water frontage. Each faces the lake, and the docks are set up for fishing. This is a popular place for fishing for bass, northern pike, sunfish and perch, as well as for the more elusive walleye, salmon, lake trout, and crappie.

Henry's sees a whopping 90 percent of guests returning each summer. Gwen and Bob Brown used to be dairy farmers and bought the cottages from friends. They rent fishing motorboats, small rowboats up to bass boats, and truly enjoy seeing new generations of repeat guests meeting each other.

© BETHANY ERICSON

Located at the end of a dead-end road, the cottages feel out-of-the-way and private, and the kids' playground is safe from car traffic. The cottages are rustic knotty pine with screened porches, bathrooms with fairly new shower stalls, and simply set-up full kitchens. Nice pots and pans and dishes are on hand for your fish dinners.

Swimming, tubing, water-skiing, and boating on Lake Champlain are mere steps from your door. Personal watercraft (such as Jet Skis) are prohibited, in order to maintain a sense of serenity. If all this quiet starts to be just too relaxing for you, or if the fish are not being cooperative, the bustle and restaurants of Burlington, Vermont and Montreal, Quebec are 45 minutes and 1.5 hours away, respectively.

Facilities: There are 14 housekeeping cottages with basic kitchen facilities and heat. They each accommodate 4–6 people, including children.

Bedding: Check when you call for the current policy on linens. Towels are not provided.

Reservations and rates: Daily rates range $85–115 a night. Weekly rates run from $450 a week to $550 a week. Cottages are rented nightly, with a three-night minimum prior to June, then it's a weekly minimum. Boat slips are $50 per week with a $15 gas credit, or $10 a day with a $3 gas credit. All boats that are not docked will be charged $5 per day or $30 per week for yard parking. There is a lunch fee of $10 daily or $50 per season. The high percentage of returning guests may require new visitors to try for the wait list. Call by January to reserve. Open May–mid-October. One well-behaved pet per cottage is permitted. Pets must be leashed at all times while on the grounds.

Directions: From Vermont, take I-89 north to Exit 17, and then Route 2 north. Immediately after crossing the Alburg Passage Bridge (the third bridge across Lake Champlain), turn left on Poor Farm Road and drive for two miles along the lake to Henry's.

From New York, take I-87 north to Exit 42, and then Route 11 east to Rouse's Point. Turn left at the T intersection, onto Route 9B. Drive one mile through town, and turn right on Route 2, driving across the bridge to Vermont. Continue driving for 11 miles on Route 2. Immediately before crossing the first bridge (Alburg Passage), turn right on Poor Farm Road, and continue driving for two miles along the lake to Henry's.

Contact: Gwen and Bob Brown, **Henry's Sportsman's Cottages**, 218 Poor Farm Road, South Alburg, VT 05440, 802/796-3616.

3. WEST SHORE COTTAGES

by Lake Champlain

Luxury rating: ★ ★ ☆ ☆ ☆   **Recreation rating:** ★ ★ ★ ★ ☆

Norma and Donald Mashtare love to match people correctly to the cabin that will best meet their expectations. Norma grew up here on the Champlain Islands, left for a while, and came home again in 1963. This is a place to return to in the evening and to enjoy the beautiful sunset views after a day spent boating and fishing on Lake Champlain.

These clean cottages vary in dimensions, but the majority are small in size, with vintage wood paneling and linoleum flooring. They have televisions, but no telephones. Some have kitchenettes, though in these units the couch may share space with the kitchen area. Weekly visitors tend to get to know each other, and returning visitors book their cottages for the same time each year.

Mainly couples stay at West Shore; the location right on the main road is not very good for kids, and the on-site swimming is rocky and reedy. Fishing and boating are the big draws, with a marina conveniently down the street. Another attraction is the peaceful summer nights. "This isn't Cape Cod, or somewhere touristy," says Norma. "It's very quiet here. You either like it, or you don't."

West Shore Cottages are a short drive from one of the longest beaches on the lake, at Alburg Dunes State Park. The "beach road" here is closed to motor vehicles and is a great place to bike and walk between the sand dunes and the wetland behind the beach. Another sand beach is nearby, at Knight Point State Park.

Facilities: There are six cottages that can each accommodate 2–5 people.

Bedding: Linens and towels provided.

Reservations and rates: The rates range $45–75 nightly, and weekly rates are also available. Open May–mid-October. One pet is allowed per cabin (kept on a leash and not left alone in the cabin) with a $5 fee per night or $25 per week. Be sure to ask about other pet restrictions when reserving—and be prepared to clean up after your animal.

Directions: Drive north on I-89 to Exit 17, Champlain Islands. Then drive northwest on Route 2. Drive through South Hero, Grand Isle, and across the bridge to North Hero.

Contact: Donald and Norma Mashtare, **West Shore Cottages**, 8888 U.S. Route 2, North Hero, VT 05474, 802/372-8832, website: www.westshorecabinsvt.com.

4. PARKER LODGE
on Lakeview Drive

Luxury rating: ★★☆☆☆   **Recreation rating:** ★★★★☆

Parker Lodge is located across from King Bay Access Area, a Fish and Wildlife–sponsored boat launch on the east shore of Route 2. Next to the house, owned by Ruth and Edwin Saint Marie, there are three very cute cottages: red, green, and blue, each decorated with paddling, golf, or fishing paraphernalia.

The Saint Maries are a very friendly couple of former teachers who are constantly fixing and refurbishing the property, much to the delight of the many returning families and anglers who are wise to these comfortable and convenient cottages with panoramic lake views.

The cottages have grills, screened porches, recliners or rockers, fully

equipped kitchens with all appliances, clean stoves, and tablecloths. The 1950s live on here in the fabulous vintage lamps and period linoleum flooring. The living rooms are spacious, and the layout is suitable for two couples traveling together.

While they are located on the main road, the cottages

maintain a sense of solitude. They are next to fields and have a very calming, friendly, country atmosphere. In the middle of the front lawn is a giant cottonwood poplar tree, its deep diamond-pattern ridges bearing witness to many summers of welcome shade after a day of lakeside sun.

Facilities: There are three two-bedroom cottages, and each can accommodate up to four people.

Bedding: Bedding is provided, but not towels.

Reservations and rates: The cottages are rented weekly (Saturday–Saturday) during June, July, and August for $450–475 a week. Nightly rentals are offered in May and October for $80 per day. Open May –mid-October.

Directions: From Vermont, take I-89 to the Lake Champlain Islands (U.S. 7) exit toward Milton, which is Exit 17. Drive for 24.8 miles on Route 2 and bear right on Lakeview Drive. Drive for about one mile, and Parker Lodge will be on the left.

Contact: Ruth and Edwin Saint Marie, **Parker Lodge**, 31 Parker Lodge Drive (on Lakeview Drive), North Hero, VT 05474, 802/372-8792 or 561/547-0687 (off-season).

5. AQUA VISTA

views of Lake Champlain

Luxury rating: ★ ★ ☆ ☆ ☆   **Recreation rating:** ★ ★ ★ ★ ☆

These 11 white cottages are small but rather sweet, with their small decks, green trim, and striped awnings. They stand in a tidy row on a little hill that overlooks the main road.

These are clean, motel-like cottages intended more for people passing through or visiting for a short stay, as they have small refrigerators but no

© BETHANY ERICSON

cooking capabilities. Inside, you'll find wood paneling, carpeting, a television, telephone, fan, and heat. The bathrooms have shower stalls.

Outside, each cabin has a small porch with metal chairs looking across the lawn and road toward the bay. This is pleasant meadow and farmland, where Route 2 was once the most popular route to Montreal, but it is now a relatively quiet road lined with hay bales. From here you can see Mount Mansfield.

Aqua Vista is a fine base for exploring the Champlain Islands. Isle La Motte is a particularly good place to bike for the day. Aqua Vista is on North Hero, home to some of the best swimming beaches on the lake, as well as nearby marinas. Ira and Ethan Allen proudly named the Hero Islands for their own participation in the Revolutionary War.

Facilities: There are 11 cottages, each accommodating two people, and one housekeeping cottage for four.

Bedding: Linens are provided.

Reservations and rates: The cabins rent for $80 per night. Open June–August. Credit cards are not accepted. Pets and smoking are not allowed.

Directions: From Vermont, take I-89 to Exit 17, Lake Champlain Islands, and drive on Route 2.

Contact: Aqua Vista Cottages, Route 2, Box 72, North Hero, VT 05474, 802/372-6628.

6. NORTH HERO MARINA

on Lake Champlain

Luxury rating: ★ ★ ★ ★ ☆   **Recreation rating:** ★ ★ ★ ★ ★

Rank: Top 10 for Boating

Diana and Bret Kernoff are the proud co-owners of this marina, restaurant, heliport, and cottage-rental establishment. The marina came with two cottages, and they were able to acquire a third. The accommodations

© BETHANY ERICSON

are luxury log cabins with tongue-and-groove pine interiors that are immaculately maintained.

The marina is located in well-sheltered Carry Bay, and boats up to 50 feet in length can be kept at the floating dock slips. Set back behind the marina and a volleyball court, the cabins look out over the water from across a field that flutters with butterflies and flowers with chicory, yellow Indian paintbrushes, and Queen Anne's lace.

The log cabins are for families or couples looking to get away to an idyllic, quiet setting that is luxurious. The cabins are somewhat like hotel suites, and offer everything you need, whether you're arriving by boat or helicopter. One has a woodstove, and all have showers and tubs, washers and dryers, and full kitchens. The larger cabin has a sleeping loft with two queen beds.

Also inquire about renting a unique floating cottage by captaining the *Sunadee I* for a weekend. This is a cheery blue houseboat that holds 2–10 people and includes a kitchen and water slide.

At the marina, all sizes and shapes of boats and personal watercraft can be rented, and there is a pool, an ice cream stand, and a restaurant (with a full bar) that claims to have the best hamburgers on the lake.

Facilities: The large cabin accommodates up to 10 people, while the smaller cabin holds up to 6. There is also a houseboat that holds 2–10 people.

Bedding: All bedding and towels are provided in the cabins.

Reservations and rates: The cabins rent $900–1,200 per week. For August rentals, book as early as possible. Open year-round.

Directions: From Vermont, drive north on I-89 to Exit 17, Champlain Islands. Head northwest on Route 2. Drive through South Hero, Grand Isle, and across the bridge to North Hero. The second paved left turn is Station Road. Turn left here, drive 1.9 miles to the end, and turn right on Pelots Point Road. Drive for 2.4 miles to the end.

Contact: Diana and Bret Kernoff, **North Hero Marina**, 165 Crescent Road, Burlington, VT 05401, summer office: 802/372-5953, winter office: 802/865-2747, cellular: 802/734-1112, website: www.northhero.com.

7. GRAND ISLE STATE PARK

on Lake Champlain

Luxury rating: ★ ☆ ☆ ☆ ☆   **Recreation rating:** ★ ★ ★ ★ ★

Wake up to hear birds chirping and kids whizzing by on bikes. Grand Isle is the largest island on Lake Champlain and is made up of the towns of Grand Isle and South Hero. The park was opened in the late 1950s on the grounds of a former summer resort. The Nature Center is all that remains of the original resort buildings. Further acquisitions helped the park to grow to its current 226-acre size. It's a very popular campground, conveniently located on Route 2, with nearly a mile of Lake Champlain shoreline.

© BETHANY ERICSON

There is only one basic camping cabin on the property. It faces the lake but is right behind the main office, so there is some noise from cars as campers pull in to register. It has beds and a futon in it, as well as a table and chairs, electric lights and outlets. Running water and hot showers are located in the restrooms area.

Here there is swimming, shore fishing, and a boat-launching ramp, plus rowboats and kayaks for rent. There are interpretive programs, games, and special events offered through the Nature Center. Campers at Grand Isle are allowed free day-use entry to the many other state parks in the islands. Knight Point State Park, with a sand beach, extensive lawns, and some nice short trails for walking, is seven miles away.

Back at Grand Isle, there are a sand volleyball court, a fitness trail, and more. Lake Champlain's great waters and bikeway offer endless recreational opportunities.

Facilities: There is one camping cabin, accommodating up to four people.

Bedding: Bring your own bedding and towels.

Reservations and rates: The cabin is $44 per night, with a two-night minimum.

Directions: From Vermont, take I-89 to Exit 17, Lake Champlain Islands, and drive along Route 2. The State Park is one mile south of Grand Isle.

Contact: Grand Isle State Park, 36 East Shore Road South, Grand Isle, VT 05458, 802/372-4300 (summer), 800/252-2363 (January–May), website: www.vtstateparks.com.

8. CAMP SKYLAND

on Lake Champlain

Luxury rating: ★ ☆ ☆ ☆ ☆   **Recreation rating:** ★ ★ ★ ★ ★

Camp Skyland has absolutely stunning views from its private peninsula in South Hero. It sits right where Mallets Bay joins Lake Champlain, and the panoramic view encompasses Mount Mansfield to Camel's Hump in Vermont's Green Mountains and across to the Adirondacks in New York. One guest calls the view "an automatic muscle relaxant."

© BETHANY ERICSON

The line of little green cabins sit in a row, like Monopoly houses, behind a large, open campsite. They are very rustic and small but look over a bluff toward the water and provide a very charming experience. The housekeeping cabins are larger than the regular cabins, but both have single rooms with small bathrooms with shower stalls. Dishes, utensils, and cookware are only provided in the housekeeping cottages.

The property has been in the same family for its entire existence, and the sense of friendly welcome is palpable. "It feels like coming home when you arrive here," another guest said. Meals are not served—and in fact have not been served since desperate travelers offered to stay without being fed during the Montreal Exposition. There is a recreation hall with old rockers and table tennis.

As is the case for much of Lake Champlain, the beach area is smooth shale, and water shoes are a good idea. There are swimming and boat docking areas, and the aging view of what was once known as Profile Point, due to the face seen in the Cliffside. The lawn and camping areas are filled with children getting to know each other and playing. You can try your luck fishing for salmon, lake trout, bass and walleye.

Facilities: There are four housekeeping cabins and eight slightly smaller cabins, all of which have some kind of limited kitchenette. The cabins can accommodate 4–6 people.

Bedding: Bedding is provided, but you'd be wise to bring larger bath and beach towels than are provided.

Reservations and rates: The housekeeping cabins rent for $350 per week and the smaller cabins are $300 a week. Call early to reserve, since 80 percent of the summer is booked a year in advance. Credit cards are not accepted. Smoking is permitted. Call ahead to inquire about the pet policy.

Directions: From Vermont, take I-89 to Exit 17, Lake Champlain Islands, and drive for 6.8 miles on Route 2. Turn left on Landon Road and drive for 1.7 miles. Turn left on South Street and drive for 2.2 miles.

Contact: Jack and Priscilla Arnold, **Camp Skyland**, 398 South Street, South Hero, VT 05486, 802/372-4200.

9. APPLE ISLAND RESORT
by Lake Champlain

Luxury rating: ★☆☆☆☆   **Recreation rating:** ★★★★★

There are five rustic, log camping cabins in Apple Island Resort, which is part of a 188-acre RV resort. The Apple Island Resort also has a full-service marina, a nine-hole golf course at Barcomb Hill Country Club, a general store and deli, and more.

The resort is kept private and requires passes for entry. Apple Island offers you space and fun while you explore the Lake Champlain Islands. Many campers and cabin dwellers stay for the whole season. In fact, the resort is planning a number of additional, seasonal log cabins.

There are picnic tables in the sun and plenty of table space in the shade by the nearby laundry house. There is an Olympic-sized pool nearby, as well as a playground with a geodesic dome to climb.

Also on the grounds are badminton, golf, horseshoes, volleyball, and shuffleboard, as well as a recreation hall with table tennis, a pool, a television, and video games. And should you just want to relax, Cabin Four has a rather soothing porch swing.

Apple Island also offers a marina with seasonal mooring, overnight docking, and launch passes. The marina rents powerboats, fishing skiffs, canoes, small sailboats, and kayaks. There is also gas and a bait and tackle shop on hand. Boat rentals are done by the day, by the half day, or in some cases hourly.

A full recreation schedule is offered throughout the summer, with bingo, barbecues, dancing by the pool or in the barn, fishing derbies, fireworks, tournaments, and more.

Facilities: There are five log camping cabins that can accommodate 2–4 people. It is also possible to extend the space by pitching a tent next to a cabin.

Bedding: Bring your own bedding.

Reservations and rates: Cabins are rented from $49 per day to $294 per week. Call to inquire about seasonal rentals. Open May 1–October 19.

Directions: From Vermont, take Exit 17 off I-89. Bear right toward the Champlain Islands. You're just six miles from Apple Island.

Contact: Apple Island Resort, P.O. Box 183, South Hero, VT 05486, 802/372-5398 (marina) or 802/372-3922, website: www.appleislandresort.com.

10. LAKE CARMI STATE PARK

on Lake Carmi

Luxury rating: ★ ☆ ☆ ☆ ☆   **Recreation rating:** ★ ★ ★ ★ ★

Lake Carmi is a warm-water lake, only 33 feet at its deepest point. It's also the fourth-largest natural lake that is entirely in Vermont. At one point in time the lake was even larger, and where it has filled in, there is a fascinating wetland forest ecology. It has the third-largest peat bog in the state, which is considered to be a State Natural Area.

There are two cabins here, in the state's largest campground. One is in camping area A, and the other is in camping area B, which is on the more appealing part of the water. The road to camping area B cuts through the bog. This camping area would likely be an island were it not for the growth of the bog.

The cabins are surrounded by black spruce and tamarack. They are simple, one-room pine camping cabins with twin bunks and a futon, a small table, and two chairs. The ceiling is painted white and there is a linoleum tile floor. They are small but do offer some sense of space. Restrooms offer running water and hot showers.

The cabins are a peaceful place; you can sit on the porch, pause next to the lake and listen to the crickets, watch great blue herons or kingfishers fish, or entertain ducks that get spooked up on shore by the buzz of personal watercraft. There is a grilling area by the lake for the big walleye you'll land from the boat you'll rent later—when you've sat for a little while longer.

The park includes over two miles of frontage on the south and east shore of Lake Carmi. Both camping areas have swimming beaches. There is also a public day-use area with a beach and cheap rowboat, canoe, and paddleboat rentals. You'll find excellent fly-fishing, hiking, and biking in the area. The park is not far from the Long Trail, Jay Peak, Smugglers Notch and Stowe, nor from Swanton's Missisquoi National Wildlife Refuge and the Missisquoi Valley Rail Trail.

Facilities: There is a snack bar at the day-use area. Stores and laundry are in nearby towns.

Bedding: Bring your own bedding and towels.

Reservations and rates: Call in January to reserve one of the cabins for $44 a night. Open May–Labor Day.

Directions: From Enosburg Falls, drive three miles west on Highway 105, then continue three miles north on Vermont 236.

Contact: Lake Carmi State Park, 460 Marsh Farm Road, Enosburg Falls, VT 05450, 802/933-8383 (summer) or 800/252-2363 (winter), website: www.vtstateparks.com.

11. QUIMBY COUNTRY

on the Averill Lakes

Luxury rating: ★ ★ ★ ☆ ☆   **Recreation rating:** ★ ★ ★ ★ ★

Rank: Top 10 for Family Activities

Quimby Country has continued to offer a family summer-camp experience for more than a century, with its more than 600 acres around the Averill Lakes on the Canadian border. Step into the Main Lodge, with its crackling fireplace, old hickory furniture, and row of rocking chairs overlooking the lake and tennis court, and breathe in the sweet smell of fresh baked goods that radiate from the kitchen.

The cottages, all named after fishing flies, stretch out beside the Main Lodge, facing Forest Lake. They are immaculate, rustic, and calm, with painted walls, birchwood floors, old Ethan Allen furniture, claw-foot tubs, and woodstoves. Each has a porch with rocking chairs. Maid service is

provided, breakfast can be delivered, and picnic lunches are offered. There is no need for lock and key here.

Out front, canoes and rowboats are available on Forest Lake. A short walk through the berry- and bird-filled forest brings you to Big Averill Lake, where there are two beaches to choose from, rocks to scramble

on, and sailboats bobbing in their moorings. There is a ridge to hike, and an outdoor fireplace by the water, where lobster bakes and cookouts are held. Trout, salmon, smallmouth bass, and pike all swim in the five lakes where Quimby boats are licensed. Golf is nearby.

A wonderful young staff lives here to keep Quimby clean and fun. Counselors will organize activities, free of charge, for children who are five years and older. The resident staff and returning guests help create the friendly character of a Quimby experience. Like Rockywold–Deephaven Camps in New Hampshire, longtime guests became stockholders in 1965 in order to preserve this casual, comfortable retreat in its untouched state as long as possible. Their mandate is that "Vacations should bring you three measures of happiness and benefits: *Full enjoyment* in anticipation, *Deep pleasure* in daily realization, and *Glowing memories* to last always."

Facilities: There are 20 different one- to four-bedroom cottages. Seven of the cottages include kitchens. There is a 70-guest limit. The cottages are furnished with full bathrooms and Franklin fireplace stoves, and do not have televisions or phones. During the summer, some cottages are available for partial housekeeping and for full housekeeping during the off-season. Early- to mid-season guests are on a full American Plan (three meals a day), and daily maid service. Picnic lunches can be arranged. Canoes, small sailboats, and rowboats are available.

Bedding: Linens are provided.

Reservations and rates: Rates range $121–151 per night, less in the spring and fall, and less for teenagers and children. Call early to reserve, certainly no later than March. Stockholders and repeat guests (coming three times within five years) begin booking on January 2 at 8 A.M. for the following year. Other reservations for the following year will be accepted after May 1. The cottages are open May–October. Pets are allowed.

Directions: From St. Johnsbury, Vermont, take I-91 north to Exit 23 for Island Pond. Drive on Route 5 North a short way to Route 114 North. Drive about 40 miles on 114 North, past Norton to Averill. You'll see the Lake View Store on your left, and then .1 mile farther on, there's a dirt road on the right called Forest Lake Road. Turn right here and drive for two miles to Quimby Country.

Contact: Quimby Country, P.O. Box 20, Averill, VT 05901, 802/822-5533, website: www.quimbycountry.com.

12. WILLOUGHVALE INN

on Lake Willoughby

Luxury rating: ★★★★☆   **Recreation rating:** ★★★★★

Rank: Top 10 for Hiking, Top 10 for Viewing Fall Foliage

Your first glimpse of Lake Willoughby may take your breath away. It is fittingly called the "Lucerne of America," with fjordlike granite cliffs jutting up from the lake to wooded mountaintops. Perched on the edge of this spectacular scenery is the WilloughVale Inn.

The biggest and brightest of the four lakeside cottages is named after Robert Frost, who wrote the poem *A Servant to Servants* while staying at the WilloughVale in 1909. All the cottages have special touches, like natural-stick furniture or fly-fishing wallpaper. The kitchens are fully equipped, right down to muffin tins and spacious counters. The porches are on the lake, with docks and magnificent mountain views. Each cottage has a fireplace and ceiling fans. Two more new cottages, with whirlpool tubs, are planned and will be next to the inn.

© BETHANY ERICSON

In the warmer months, fish for trout or perch, hike any one of the local mountains, mountain bike, kayak, canoe, sail, or swim. In winter, ice fish, snowmobile on a Vermont Association of Snow Travellers (VAST) trail right from the door, cross-country ski, ice climb, or ski nearby. Fall brings Vermont's famous explosion of color to the surroundings, and this is an unbeatable location for leaf-peeping.

The National Park Service has designated the Lake Willoughby area of the Northeast Kingdom as a registered natural landmark, "Possessing exceptional value in illustrating the natural history of the United States." Don't miss the view of the lake (or the great food) from the Inn's Main Dining Room.

Facilities: There are four cottages that can accommodate 2–4 people. Weekly rentals are offered in July and August; a two-night minimum is required all other dates. Bicycle, canoe, and kayak reservations can be made in advance.

Bedding: All linens provided.

Reservations and rates: The cottages are rented weekly in the summer months for about $1,478. Other dates require a two-night minimum, and prices range $149–249 per night. Look for special packages (Romantic Escape, anyone?) and Internet specials on the WilloughVale website. Closed in April. One pet under 50 pounds may be considered.

Directions: Take I-91 to Barton (Exit 25), and drive north on Route 16 to 5A south.

Contact: WilloughVale Inn, 793 VT Route 5A, Orleans, VT 05860, 802/525-4123, website: www.willoughvale.com.

Other Cabins and Cottages Nearby

- Green Acres Cabins, 1051 VT Route 5A, Orleans, VT 05860, 802/525-3722.

13. PINECREST MOTEL & CABINS

on Barton River

Luxury rating: ★★☆☆☆   **Recreation rating:** ★★★★★

Popular with anglers and hunters, as well as with families, these small, very basic cabins are set just off the road by Barton River. Owner Karin Ehrisman adds to the real character of this friendly place. She pulls no punches, but she just might hug you. If you're at Pinecrest, you're family; don't argue about it.

© BETHANY ERICSON

Forget something? You aren't going to buy a new one, you're going to borrow it from her.

The pine cabins are decorated with plants, skis, and snowshoes, and are kept very clean. They include cable TV and aging furniture, and private bathrooms with shower stalls. The two-bedroom cabins have tiny kitchenettes with dishes, microwaves, and refrigerators. The tall ceilings help add a sense of space, and most have decks or picnic tables out front. You can hear traffic on Route 5, but it isn't intrusive.

Barton is situated in a valley on Crystal Lake. The village is on a slope of land and is split into an upper village on the shore of the lake and a lower village that runs along the river. Fishing licenses, tackle, and restaurants are all found here. Barton River is safe to swim in, though Karin recommends wearing an old pair of tennis shoes.

Mountain biking, hiking, rock climbing, and snowmobiling on a Vermont Association of Snow Travellers (VAST) trail are all within a short walk or drive. The area is known for its water sports, and Pinecrest is just down the street from Crystal Lake, six miles from Shadow Lake, eight miles from Lake Willoughby, and 15 miles from Lake Memphremagog. There are golf courses in the vicinity, and Burke Mountain and Jay Peak are about 40 minutes away for skiing.

Facilities: There are five one-bedroom and five two-bedroom cabins accommodating 2–4 people. Cabin No. 4 has two double beds, while most two-bedroom cabins have a double and two twin beds. The larger cabins have limited kitchenettes.

Bedding: Linens and towels are provided.

Reservations and rates: Cabins rent $50–75 a night or $250–350 a week. Pinecrest receives about 70 percent repeat guests, some booking three or four times a year, so call early. Open year-round. Call ahead to inquire about the pet policy and wheelchair accessibility.

Directions: Pinecrest is located off I-91, Exit 25. Go east on Route 16 and drive into the village of Barton. Turn left onto Route 5 north, and drive two miles. Pinecrest will be on the right.

Contact: Karin Ehrisman, **Pinecrest Motel & Cabins**, Rt. 5 1288 Barton Orleans Road, Barton, VT 05822, 802/525-3472, website: www.virtualvermont.com/pinecrest.

14. STERLING RIDGE INN & CABINS

views of Mount Mansfield and Smugglers Notch

Luxury rating: ★ ★ ★ ★ ☆   **Recreation rating:** ★ ★ ★ ★ ☆

Rank: Top 10 for Weddings, Top 10 for Viewing Fall Foliage

You're guaranteed to smile as you drive up the dirt road to the 360 flowered pastures and woods of Sterling Ridge. The cabins are all private, winterized, modern constructions with a small country-home feel. There is also now a small house that can be rented, called The Pond House. The views of Mount Mansfield (Vermont's tallest peak), and Smugglers Notch are spectacular. Not surprisingly, this is a popular spot for weddings.

A deluxe cabin is very spacious (640 square feet), with a lovely stone fireplace, new furniture, full kitchen, television, two bedrooms with cozy quilts and comforters, a tub with jets, and a cathedral ceiling with fan. The smaller, 540-square-foot cabins are still large by cabin standards. These include gas log fireplaces.

The porches for all cabins are covered, and most have great views and a large picnic table, Adirondack chairs, and a grill. The two companion cottages, Nos. 7 and 8, have a stone path to their doors that traverses a lit bridge over a brook. While all of the cabins are built for privacy, No. 6 sits by itself at the end of the road.

Here in this pleasant, warm atmosphere, there are lawn games, board games, and ponds for swimming and rowing. A VAST trail connects to Sterling Ridge for snowmobiling. Nearby there is fabulous skiing, hiking, golfing, mountain biking, and horse riding, and Lamoille River offers fishing, canoeing, and kayaking. Sterling Ridge has purchased the Green River Canoe and Kayak Company and offers rentals and tours. Stowe Village also has a five-mile recreation path, gondola rides, an alpine slide, and an in-line skate park.

Work is under way on 10 additional cabins at Sterling Ridge. The plan is to include some economical one-room cabins for couples, as well as a couple of new one-bedroom and deluxe cabins. Some will be built around the pond that was recently acquired with the Pond House land, and some will be built up the hill behind Cabin 1 in the woods.

This is a very relaxing atmosphere full of beauty, and the Vermont lifestyle will most likely hook you. The kids catching crawdads in the brook are most likely to be planning a crawdad sanctuary than a mid-afternoon snack, and the family reunions at the Pond House find endless laughter bubbling over the water.

Facilities: There are 10 cabins, and 10 more in the works, each holding 2–6 people.

Bedding: All linens are provided.

Reservations and rates: The nightly rate for two people ranges $75–175 with a two-night minimum stay. Weekly rates range $440–1,100. Smoking is not allowed.

Directions: From Jeffersonville, drive 1.2 miles east on VT 15, then turn right on Junction Hill Road (a dirt road) and drive for 1.1 mile. Or, drive three miles south on VT 108, turn left on Edwards Road, bear left on Cliff Reynolds Road and drive for 2 miles, and at the Y, keep right on Junction Hill Road for .1 mile. (Route 108 is closed from Smugglers Notch to Stowe from November to May each winter.)

Contact: Scott and Susan Peterson, **Sterling Ridge Inn & Cabins**, 155 Sterling Ridge Drive, Jeffersonville, VT 05464, 802/644-8265 or 800/347-8266, website: www.vermont-cabins.com.

15. CRAFTSBURY OUTDOOR CENTER

Craftsbury Common

Luxury rating: ★★☆☆☆   **Recreation rating:** ★★★★★

Rank: Top 10 for Boating, Top 10 for Biking, Best for Skiing and Snowmobiling

---

Secluded Craftsbury Outdoor Center's 140 acres are well known to athletes, due to its world-class running and sculling instructional centers and cross-country skiing trails. You can also rent a mountain bike and ride the trails or country roads. The Center is located on the Vermont end-to-end bike route currently being developed by Vermont Mountain Bike Advocates.

Winter provides legendary snow conditions at Craftsbury, and the facility offers cross-country ski rentals and instruction for experiencing its more than 50 miles of groomed ski trails. Marathons and gentle touring events have been held over the years on the rolling hills between Craftsbury and Highland Lodge. The Center also rents snowshoes and offers night skating on a lit pond. Hot chocolate by the fire in the touring center rounds off the evening. Craftsbury is in a class with the Trapp Family Lodge in Vermont, and Jackson in New Hampshire.

There are also guided nature hikes and yoga classes, as well as tennis, volleyball, and basketball courts. The Center is on Lake Hosmer, a perfect spot to swim or paddle a kayak or canoe. You can also have a guided ride or boat trip, a personal sculling lesson, or guided bird or nature walks, or you can register for a weeklong Elderhostel program on natural sciences.

Accommodations are fairly basic, but with a friendly summer camp feel. Most guests are in dormitories, and there are four basic cabins by the lake for families or people wanting privacy. Cabin D has two levels, with kitchen windows on the lake. All have woodstoves.

The Center was founded by Janet and Russell Spring. They had spent two summers as fire-tower observers, watching the Northeast Kingdom, and Russell sold out of a share of a tennis camp down the street when he envisioned the Craftsbury Outdoor Center. A generation later, Russell Jr. smiles while relaying this history. "Dad said if I was going to come take over for him, I'd better do it soon, as he was about to return. That was 10 years ago. He hasn't yet."

Facilities: There are four cabins accommodating 2–6 people. The included all-you-can-eat meals, including vegetarian options, use fresh local produce. The food is well regarded in the athletic realm and has even spawned a cookbook. Microbrews, wine, juice, first aid, Ben & Jerry's ice cream, and other basics are available in the store. The kitchen may be in limited operation in shoulder seasons; inquire when you call. A weight room with training equipment and sauna, and an educational indoor play area for kids are also on the grounds.

Bedding: Linens are provided.

Reservations and rates: Cabin rates run $75–377 per night, depending on cabin size and time of year. Call ahead to inquire about the pet policy.

Directions: Detailed maps are sent with confirmation packages. Pick-up service from your arrival point to the Center may be arranged.

Contact: Craftsbury Outdoor Center, PO Box 31, Lost Nation Rd., Craftsbury Common, VT 05827, 802/586-7767 or 800/729-7751, website: www.craftsbury.com.

16. HIGHLAND LODGE
Caspian Lake

Luxury rating: ★ ★ ★ ☆ ☆ **Recreation rating:** ★ ★ ★ ★ ★

Rank: Best for Skiing and Snowmobiling, Top 10 for Family Activities

The Highland Lodge is a family resort that starts soothing you with pastoral charm the minute you step from your car. Breathe in the clean air, and rock a spell on the Queen Anne porch. Then tromp off into the woods or pasture, or paddle out onto the lake for the day.

David and Wilhelmina Smith are the third generation of the Smith family to be innkeepers of what was once the Simpson farmhouse, built in the 1860s. Back then the Simpsons supplemented the family income by taking in summer boarders at $12 per week. (This, and other Greensboro tidbits, can be found in *The History of Greensboro*, sold in the lodge gift shop.)

Up the hill behind the main lodge, overlooking Caspian Lake, are the six white cottages. Another four winterized cottages are located on the hillside or in the nearby woods. All of the cottages are clean and very well maintained, with flower boxes and little porches. Most have kitchenettes and gas- or wood-burning stoves. They all have electric heat. There are no phones in the cottages, but there is a telephone room in the main inn, and other office needs can be arranged.

Down on the sandy beach, a "beach person" (not a lifeguard) will show you the facilities, which include rowboats, paddleboats, canoes, kayaks, small sailboats, swimming raft, changing booths, beach towels, kids' beach toys, and sodas.

Environmental education is a priority at Highland Lodge, where the owners have created the Porter Brook Envronmental Center, a nonprofit nature center that runs science courses for elementary-school students. There are also walking trails across the 120 acres and into the Barr Hill Nature Preserve, including self-guided nature trails that are also good for snowshoeing. There are also a clay tennis court, lawn sports, golf in the village, and cycling on pastoral back roads. Dirt-road bikes are available to rent.

The Greensboro area is well known for cross-country skiing. Trails are laid out for views and meander through maple rows, pastures, and woodlands, and across frozen lakes. Schedule your trip on a full-moon night and ski for a memorable experience. The ski shop provides rental skis and snowshoes.

In the main lodge, there is a living room, library, parlor with grand piano, and a playroom with foosball, table tennis, and toys. There is one television in the living room.

The lodge is known for its delicious meals, which mix traditional New England offerings with some innovative cuisine. The lodge makes a point of using Vermont-grown products whenever possible, and you'll dine amidst work by local artists.

Facilities: There are 11 cottages; four are winterized. They can accommodate 4–8 people. Fishing licenses are available at Smith's store in the Bend, the Town Clerk's office in Greensboro, and the Rite-Way Sport Shop in Hardwick.

Bedding: All linens are provided.

Reservations and rates: Cottages with MAP range $117–140 per night. Ask about specials and rates for cottages without meal plans. Call up to a year ahead for August dates. You are invited to reserve the same cottage for the same period of time the next year on your way out. The Lodge is closed mid-October–mid-December.

Directions: From the south, take I-91 to St. Johnsbury. Exit onto VT 15 and Route 2 west, and drive 10 miles to West Danville. Continue driving northwest on VT 15 for 11 miles to VT 16, then drive two miles to East Hardwick. There, turn west, drive downhill to cross Lamoille River, and turn north again and continue driving for four miles to Greensboro.

Contact: Highland Lodge, Greensboro, VT 05841, 802/533-2647, website: www.highlandlodge.com.

17. MOUNTAIN VIEW CAMPGROUND AND CABINS

on Lamoille River

Luxury rating: ★ ★ ☆ ☆ ☆   **Recreation rating:** ★ ★ ★ ★ ★

Mountain View Campground and Cabins is an easygoing destination for relaxing by Lamoille River, and an excellent place to fish in the river in spring and fall. The Lamoille is full of famous holes where rainbow, brown, and brook trout gather. Licenses are available in nearby Morrisville.

© BETHANY ERICSON

It's also a popular river for kayaking and rafting, and you can swim or get in an inner tube at Mountain View's little beach area and meander a couple of miles downriver to Oxbow Park in town, where you'll hopefully have arranged for someone to pick you up.

The cabins appear to be basic camping cabins from the outside, and until they are redone, the largest family-sized cabin and the one with two twin beds are somewhat rustic. However, the other three cabins are a step above—clean and more modern, with covered back porches and picnic tables. Apparently, even the governor of Delaware has stayed here for a week.

Nearby Stowe is a popular hiking destination, and golf, an alpine slide, a gondola, train and glider rides, mountain biking, and more are within a short drive. On the grounds, lawn sports and raspberry and blackberry bushes offer further distraction. By a festively lit pavilion and a bath house sit a hot tub and two swimming pools; the larger pool is kept heated until Labor Day.

Facilities: There are five cabins. Three renovated cabins hold two people each in queen beds, one cabin has two twin beds, and a larger cabin is set up for families with two bedrooms. Tents can be pitched next to the cabins. Laundry, ice, wood, and a snack bar are on the premises.

Bedding: Linens are provided.

Reservations and rates: Rates $75–85 per night. For seven-day stays, subtract $10 per night. Call in April for reservations. Open May 6–October 15. Leashed pets are allowed on the campground, but pets are not allowed in cabins.

Directions: From Morrisville, drive three miles east on Route 15.

Contact: Marceau Family, **Mountain View Campground and Cabins**, 3154 Route 15E, Morrisville, VT 05661, 802/888-2178.

18. THE STONE HUT

atop Mount Mansfield

Luxury rating: ★☆☆☆☆   **Recreation rating:** ★★★★★

Rank: Top 10 for Backcountry Winter Adventures

Vermont is known for its skiing at Stowe and Smugglers Notch, and for its hiking on Mount Mansfield, Vermont's highest mountain. The mountain has dramatic views and steep terrain. Hikers may know of the Mount Mansfield Hostel, the bunkhouse on the slopes of the mountain, but you may not know that the historic Stone Hut atop Mansfield is open November to April for lodging (by lottery). It's accessible by chairlift in ski season, but only by foot otherwise.

The rustic hut is a nice retreat from the business of the downhill slopes, as it is set off from the peak and surrounded by big pines. The hut was built as a warming hut in the 1930s by the Civilian Conservation Corps and has undergone renovations in recent years. There are four bunks with full-size mattresses and two twin bunks. It has a good woodstove that keeps the place extra warm and toasty. If you overdo it with the wood, you'll find your top-bunk dwellers sleeping on the floor before long. Firewood is provided in a woodshed outside, but kindling is not provided.

You should pack as though you are winter camping, except for the tent. Bring all cooking, lighting, and sleeping gear. Also be prepared to pack out anything you pack in. The hut is run by a partnership between the Vermont Department of Forests, Parks, and Recreation and the Mount Mansfield Company (Stowe Mountain Resort). As a result, you can use the restrooms, hot water, and pay phone in the Octagon up top.

One of the best features of staying in the hut is waking early and cutting the first tracks down the mountain, or doing some backcountry skiing on the backside.

Facilities: The Hut sleeps up to 12 people and is accessible by chairlift during the Stowe Mountain Resort ski season. Lift tickets are not included, but single-ride lift tickets can be purchased from the resort. The quad chairlift to reach the Hut operates 7:30 A.M.–4:00 P.M. There are no special baggage services, so anything you want to bring you must be able to carry on your lap on the lift.

Bedding: Bring all of your winter camping gear.

Reservations and rates: The Stone Hut reservations are run on a lottery system. Call and request a form, or download a reservation form from the website. Then submit your reservation request with a payment of $109 per night mid-September–late October, when the lottery results are mailed. The reservations are separated into groups based on the number of nights requested and are selected at random from the group with the longest stays to the shortest stay. If the request can be filled, the payment is processed. Otherwise, your money is returned. To increase your odds, list as many alternate dates as possible. After the lottery you can call and find out about some remaining open dates that will be run on a first-come, first-served basis. The Hut is open mid-November–mid-April.

Directions: Take I-89 to Exit 10 (Waterbury–Route 100). Drive on Route 100 North into the village of Stowe (about 10 miles). In Stowe, turn left onto Route 108 (also called the Mountain Road) and drive for seven miles. The Vermont State Ski Dorm (Mount Mansfield Hostel) will be on your right.

Contact: The Stone Hut, 6992 Mountain Road, Stowe, Vermont 05672, pre-season reservations: 802-253-4014, winter reservations: 802-253-4010, website: www.vtstateparks.com/htm/stonehut.cfm.

19. 1836 CABINS

near Stowe

Luxury rating: ★★★☆☆   **Recreation rating:** ★★★★☆

The 1836 Cabins are secluded in the woods south of Stowe, on property adjoining the Green Mountain Club (GMC), the protector of Vermont's Long Trail System. The area is a popular destination for hikers, skiers, and families splitting time between outdoors fun and tours of Ben & Jerry's,

© BETHANY ERICSON

Cabot Cheese, and Vermont Teddy Bear. At the GMC's Marvin B. Gameroff Hiker's Center there are educational displays, a bookstore, fleece products, hats, T-shirts, and a staff that can help you plan hikes.

Up the road and into the woods are the well-spaced 1836 Cabins. A standard cabin has two small bedrooms, one with a double bed and one with bunks, a living room with a television and sofa bed, a kitchen, and a bath. Deluxe cabins have larger kitchens and just one king bed, and semi-deluxe cabins are the same size as standard cabins, but the large bedroom has a queen bed. Pots, pans, and dishes are provided in all.

The cabins are fairly basic, though they have decent furniture with some nice antique touches, like an old sewing-machine table used as a television stand. They have wall-to-wall carpeting. There are games, books, magazines, and a grill, but no phones. None of the cabins face another one directly, and there is a very good sense of privacy.

Hiking in the area ranges from easy to rough. There is swimming nearby at Waterbury Lake State Park, as well as boating. You can snowshoe (snowshoes are provided) or cross-country ski right from your cabin. Nearby are bicycle rentals, recreation paths, gondola rides, an alpine slide, glider rides, miniature golf, sleigh rides, snowmobiling trails, and much more.

Facilities: There are seven one- and two-bedroom cabins sleeping 4–6 people.

Bedding: Linens and towels are provided.

Reservations and rates: Rates for two people range $79–159 a night depending on the size of cabin and the season. Weekly rates range $475–955; additional occupants are an extra charge. Kids are welcome; there is no charge for two-year-olds and under. There is a minimum two-night stay on weekends. Open year-round.

Directions: From Stowe, drive five miles south on Route 100.

Contact: 1836 Cabins, Route 100, Box 128, Waterbury Center, VT 05677, 802/244-8533, website: www.1836cabins.com.

Other Cabins and Cottages Nearby

- Millbrook Inn Octagon House, Route 117, 533 McCullough Road, Waitsfield, VT 05673, 802/496-2405 or 800/477-2809, website: www.millbrookinn.com.

20. GRÜNBERG HAUS

in the woods of Waterbury

Luxury rating: ★ ★ ★ ☆ ☆   Recreation rating: ★ ★ ★ ★ ★

Rank: Top 10 for Hiking, Top 10 for Romance, Top 10 for Viewing Fall Foliage

---

The Grünberg Haus is a three-story Austrian chalet hidden in the woods of Waterbury. You may arrive in front of this magnificent Tyrolean building, complete with carved balconies and decorative antique snowshoes, and wonder if you've taken a wrong turn and ended up in the Alps.

In the summer, the 30-year-old inn opens the doors to its newer additions: three small, romantic hideaway cabins much like A-frames and concealed by the forest on a small ridge above the inn. Each cabin offers a woodstove, a queen bed with cozy wildlife-themed quilt, braided rugs, wide-pine floors, a vaulted ceiling, paddle fan, antique furnishings, and a small sitting area. A private open porch faces a beautiful view of Crossett Hill.

The two-minute walk up the ridge to the cabins is on a natural trail and is notably steep. The owners compare it to climbing six flights of stairs; it's not for those with weak lungs. Flashlights are provided for returning home in the evening. The inn has a hot tub and sauna facilities.

From here you can canoe Winooski, Lamoille, and Mad Rivers, or sea kayak on Lake Champlain. Hiking trails are abundant here. Besides the Long Trail, there is also Camel's Hump (the third-highest peak in Vermont after Killington and Mansfield), Hunger Mountain, and the Worcester Range. There are also hiking trails right from the cabins on paths that were once a cross-country ski center. Biking, fishing, horseback riding, and more are nearby.

There are no cooking facilities in the cabins, but you are welcome to bring your own cooler or small charcoal grill. Don't miss the sumptuous breakfasts provided in the inn though. Enjoy glazed banana French toast or lemon ricotta pancakes near a large fieldstone fireplace opposite a 20-foot picture window. The pub room in the inn also offers a cozy setting for popping popcorn in a microwave or making a cup of cocoa, and has a refrigerator you can use.

Facilities: There are three cottages that sleep two people.

Bedding: All linens are provided.

Reservations and rates: The rates range $125–175 (depending on the season), for two people and include breakfast. Call ahead at least a month for weekends. There is a 10 percent discount for stays of four nights or more. Pets are accepted with permission and a small fee.

Directions: Take Exit 10 from I-89, and drive south on Route 100 through Waterbury. Watch for the right turn that Route 100 takes just past the bridge, after you've driven through town. The inn is three miles from that turn, on the left.

Contact: Grünberg Haus, 94 Pine Street, Waterbury, VT 05676, 802/244-7726, website: www.grunberghaus.com.

21. POINT COMFORT

on Joe's Pond

Luxury rating: ★ ☆ ☆ ☆   **Recreation rating:** ★ ★ ★ ★ ★

Point Comfort is an aging cottage colony on a peninsula in Joe's Pond, in West Danville. It dates back to the early 20th century. Back then, summer cottage dwellers would get their dry goods, millinery, hardware, and pond-cut ice from the historic Hastings Store, still in operation today and located around the corner from Joe's Pond.

© BETHANY ERICSON

These days the cottages could use some updating, but they are in good hands with Oregon transplants Dana and Angie Turner. All of the cottages have covered porches facing the water. Cottages 2–6 have their own pebble-rock swimming area. Joe's Pond is stocked with brook, brown, lake, and rainbow trout.

Part of the Point Comfort business is boat rentals, and you can dock your boat rentals right at your cottage. Boats available to rent include 12- to 14-foot motorboats, pontoon boats, rowboats, small sailboats, paddleboats, kayaks, and canoes.

Joe's Pond is named after a Native American from Nova Scotia known as Captain Joe, and the pond is known today as the area's harbinger of spring. A cement block is set on the ice each winter, and spring officially begins when ice-out allows the block to sink. Various contests are associated with correctly guessing the date and time of the block sinking.

Joe's Pond spans about 1,000 acres and is about 1,500 feet in altitude. Point Comfort is a favorite spot for families to get out on the lake for a weekend and enjoy the views and pure air here, in one of the highest-elevation towns in Vermont.

Facilities: There are 14 different cottages that can accommodate 2–6 people. The three-bedroom cottages have a kitchen and living room; only half of the cottages have kitchens. The kitschy, 1950s-style Point Comfort Diner is on the property.

Bedding: Linens are provided. Weekly renters should bring towels.

Reservations and rates: Cottage pricing ranges $55–125 a night to $330–750 a week. Open May–October 15. Call ahead to inquire about the pet policy and wheelchair accessibility.

Directions: From St. Johnsbury, drive west for about nine miles on Route 2. Point Comfort Cottages & Diner will be on your right.

Contact: Point Comfort Cottages & Diner, 3182 Route 2, P.O. Box 68, West Danville, VT 05873, 802/684-3379.

Other Cabins and Cottages Nearby
- Injunjoe's Court, U.S. Route 2, PO Box 27, West Danville, VT 05873, 802/684-3430, website: www.injunjoe-court.com.

22. HARVEY'S LAKE CABINS & CAMPGROUND

on Harvey's Lake

Luxury rating: ★ ★ ★ ☆ ☆   **Recreation rating:** ★ ★ ★ ★ ★

Rank: Top 10 for Value

Harvey's Lake Campground is known as the oldest private campground in Vermont. The eight wood-frame cabins with hand-hewn beams and cedar posts from the property are a more recent addition.

© BETHANY ERICSON

Marybeth and Michael Vereline own the property. Michael is the "business visionary," and Marybeth manages the property day to day. She is an incredibly friendly auction addict and has decorated the cabins individually with truly funky antique themes and a general sense of upscale fun. The cabins are private and set well apart in the woods. They are all insulated and offer outdoor fire pits, picnic tables, and Adirondack chairs. The handicapped-accessible honeymoon cottage sits right on the shore, with six large windows facing Harvey's Mountain across the lake, as well as double showerheads.

Most of the focus of the location is on the 409-acre lake, where Jacques Cousteau is said to have taken his first dive. Fishing for rainbow and lake trout is popular; the 148-foot-deep glacial trout lake is far south for such a lake, and at a lower altitude than many others. This means it typically experiences ice-out in mid-April, and anglers can get an early start searching for rainbows.

Rowboats, canoes, paddleboats and bicycles are available to rent per day or week. Next to the cabins is a very clean public beach with a lifeguard. The 1,515-acre Roy Mountain Wildlife Management Area, a popular hunting site, borders the lake on the southeast side.

Facilities: There are 10 cabins in a campground setting. Two more cabins are planned. All cabins include kitchen facilities. Weddings for a maximum of 125 guests can be arranged. Recovery retreats are welcome.

Bedding: Pillows and blankets are provided; sheets and towels are not provided, but are available for a small fee.

Reservations and rates: Cabin rates range $55–120 per night and $395–725 per week. Extra adults are $60 per person; extra children under 12 are $30 per child. Repeat guests make up half the renters, and reserving a year ahead is advisable. Weddings should be reserved one to two years ahead. Open May 15–October 15. One car is allowed per cabin site. One dog is allowed in Cabins 18 and 52.

Directions: Take I-91 to Exit 18W if you're coming from the south and 18E if you're coming from the north. Drive onto Barnet–West Barnet Road. Continue driving on the paved road for five miles, and go into West Barnet. As you approach the village, a campground sign and Paula's Place (a general store on your left) will signal you to slow down for the upcoming sharp left-hand turn across a little bridge next to the white church. Drive across the bridge, and immediately in front of you will be a campground sign. Turn onto the dirt road that will bring you to the Verelines' big gray house and office.

Contact: Marybeth Vereline, **Harvey's Lake Cabins & Campground**, 190 Campers Lane, West Barnet, VT 05821, 802/623-2213, website: www.harveyslake-cabins.com.

23. RICKER POND STATE PARK

in Groton State Forest

Luxury rating: ★★☆☆☆   **Recreation rating:** ★★★★★

Ricker State Park is one of five campgrounds located in the nine state lands that make up 26,154-acre Groton State Forest. This state forest is Vermont's second-biggest contiguous public landholding. The state park offers a boat launch and rental, and the single private camping cabin at the end of a campground road, in Ricker State Park, also has a canoe available.

This area was once a hub of logging activity. Ricker State Park is a nice example of the 1930s Civilian Conservation Corps building-and-replanting skills, and of the beginnings of the Vermont State Park system. The roofed open-air shelter, with a large fireplace for use by all, dates from the 1930s as well.

Ricker Pond and nearby Lake Groton are known for fishing and hiking. Common catches include yellow perch, chain pickerel, smallmouth bass, largemouth bass, bullhead, and panfish. The park offers guides to the 22 miles of hiking trails, including one trail along the former tracks of the

Montpelier to Wells River Railroad that is particularly fine for mountain biking. Hiking through the forest here may provide you with some good opportunities to spot the wildlife, so keep your eyes open for loons, herons, fisher, otter, beaver, mink, grouse, deer, moose, and bear.

© BETHANY ERICSON

The state forest contains a wide variety of ecosystems. Kettle Pond is a secluded area with creeping snowberry, wintergreen, and high-bush blueberries. Peacham Bog is a unique peat wetland. At Owls Head Mountain, the Corps built stone steps to preserve the ecology.

The single camping cabin is on the shore of 92-acre Ricker Pond. It offers basic, rustic accommodations, but the amenities are a step above a typical camping cabin. There are skylights, two bunk beds, a kitchen with cookware, a bureau, a shower, electric heat, and a screened porch that looks toward the pond. For a camping cabin, it has some nice little touches, like flowers in window boxes and a small lawn.

Facilities: There is one cottage with two bunk beds, and it can accommodate up to four people. There's a kitchen with cookware, and electric heating is provided. There is use of a canoe.

Bedding: Bring your own bedding.

Reservations and rates: The cabin is $65 per night. Ask about pets when making reservations. Though all facilities are closed in winter, you can cross-country ski here by walking around the gate. Open mid-May–October 15.

Directions: From Groton, drive two miles west on U.S. 302. Turn right (northwest) on VT 232 and drive for 2.5 miles.

Contact: Ricker Pond State Park, 526 State Forest Rd, Groton, VT 05046, 802/584-3821, website: vtparks.anr.state.vt.us/htm/ricker.cfm.

© BETHANY ERICSON

Chapter 2

Southern Vermont

CHAPTER 2—SOUTHERN VERMONT

Most of southern Vermont is split down the middle by the two ranges of the evergreen-covered mountains that inspired French settlers to give the state its name (Verd Mont). The lower section of hills divides the state's waters into those that connect with Connecticut River and those that flow into Lakes Champlain and Memphremagog.

The land has inspired many writers and artists, including Robert Frost, Rudyard Kipling, and Norman Rockwell. In fact, sleeping pasture-side near a covered bridge in a cottage renovated from Rockwell's art studio may be as Vermont as you can get. Early-morning fishing trips, cycling next to rocky streams, and picnicking by observation towers high in the hills are all commonplace activities here.

Much of Vermont has an atmosphere of a caring, accepting community, and of bucolic charm, and the state is a popular destination for a wide range of vacationers. Whether you want to golf, take off-road Land Rover or falconry lessons at the Equinox, cross-country ski from inn to inn, hike the Long Trail, fly fish, downhill ski, or white-water kayak, make your reservations early.

While tourists leave the cities for the cooler air of beautiful Vermont in the summer, and in winter for its celebrated ski resorts, fall is the bumper-to-bumper travel time. It takes around 40 gallons of sap to make a gallon of maple syrup; if you consider Vermont's famous maple industry, you may begin to get an idea of just how many maple trees there are.

The country's oldest long-distance hiking trail is the Long Trail, which follows the ridge of the Green Mountains. This southern portion shares 100 miles with the Appalachian Trail. It is less arduous here than in the state's northern portions, but no less beautiful, with its clear streams and abundant wildlife. There are hundreds of miles to hike in southern Vermont. Bring your boots, your bug repellent, and a camera.

In the northern section of the Green Mountains is a gorgeous, untouched area called Granville Gulf. Much of the year it is a good place to see moose dipping their heads into ponds, rummaging for snacks. In winter, beautiful Moss Glen Falls, on Mad River, freeze—which is impressive to see, but it's a notoriously treacherous place to drive.

This is prime skiing territory. There is famed ski touring from a mansion belonging to the eldest son of Abe Lincoln in the valley between the Taconic Mountains and the Green Mountains, and serious back country skiing at the Merck Forest. Some of the first Nordic skis in the state are said to have been owned by Rudyard Kipling, who was reportedly given them as a gift from his visiting friend, Sir Arthur Conan Doyle. The downhill snow sports need little introduction with names like Killington, Stratton, Bromley, Okemo, Ascutney, Sugarbush, Suicide Six, and more.

River sports, from kayaking to fishing on the Battenkill, Mad, Connecticut, West, and White Rivers, are longtime Vermont pastimes. Orvis, the famous fly-fishing superstore, is located in Manchester, Vermont. Numerous swimming holes are around by waterfalls and in old marble quarries.

Popular ways to tour Vermont include hiking, cycling, and skiing from one lodging to another. However you get around, from the gorges to the mountain peaks, you'll be sure to find impressive beauty and welcoming hospitality.

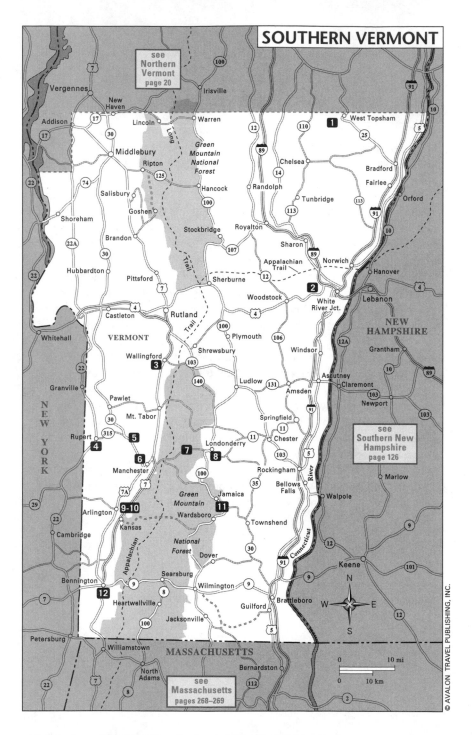

SOUTHERN VERMONT

see Northern Vermont page 20

see Southern New Hampshire page 126

see Massachusetts pages 268–269

NEW HAMPSHIRE

VERMONT

NEW YORK

MASSACHUSETTS

Green Mountain National Forest

Green Mountain National Forest

Appalachian Trail

Long Trail

Trail

Appalachian Trail

Connecticut River

© AVALON TRAVEL PUBLISHING, INC.

Vergennes
New Haven
Addison
Lincoln
Warren
Irisville
West Topsham
Middlebury
Ripton
Chelsea
Bradford
Fairlee
Orford
Salisbury
Hancock
Randolph
Tunbridge
Goshen
Shoreham
Brandon
Stockbridge
Royalton
Sharon
Norwich
Hanover
Hubbardton
Pittsford
Sherburne
Woodstock
White River Jct.
Lebanon
Castleton
Rutland
Whitehall
Plymouth
Windsor
Grantham
Wallingford
Shrewsbury
Granville
Ludlow
Amsden
Claremont
Ascutney
Newport
Pawlet
Springfield
Mt. Tabor
Rupert
Chester
Londonderry
Rockingham
Marlow
Manchester
Jamaica
Bellows Falls
Walpole
Arlington
Wardsboro
Townshend
Cambridge
Kansas
Dover
Keene
Searsburg
Bennington
Wilmington
Brattleboro
Heartwellville
Guilford
Jacksonville
Petersburg
Williamstown
North Adams
Bernardston

N
W   E
S
0   10 mi
0   10 km

CHAPTER 2
SOUTHERN VERMONT

1. TIMBERLAND TRAILS GREEN VALLEY LODGE AND GALUSHA CABIN

Green Valley and Galusha Hill
Backcountry Recreation Areas

Luxury rating: ★ ★ ★ ☆ ☆   **Recreation rating:** ★ ★ ★ ★ ★

Rank: Top 10 for Biking, Top 10 for Backcountry Winter Adventures, Top 10 for Value

Timberland Trails leases land in New England from paper companies and the like to provide low-cost backcountry recreation as one part of the forest's sustainability effort. Its best-known experiment is the yurts at Phillips Brook Backcountry Recreation Area, in New Hampshire. (The other, somewhat similarly managed, backcountry area in New England is the Merck

© BETHANY ERICSON

Forest and Farmland Center in southwestern Vermont.) Here in Vermont, Timberland Trails also manages two wonderful log cabins.

Green Valley Lodge is a spacious gambrel-style log cabin on 1,250 acres of land that are managed as sustainable forest in Washington. The Galusha Cabin is a cozy cabin in nearby Topsham, bordering Groton State Park and the Pine Mountain Wildlife Management Area.

Both cabins have wonderful wilderness views and are prime areas for all backcountry winter sports, mountain biking, and hiking. Bring maps and your compass. The area is also great for canoeing, kayaking, and fishing. If you would enjoy breaking trail on snowshoes, past fisher tracks and beech trees clawed by bears; or backcountry skiing or biking from scenic ridges through pristine forest, make your reservation now.

The cabins are country rustic, but quite comfortable, with fully equipped kitchens. The living rooms have fireplaces. Green Valley Lodge has two floors with four bedrooms and two baths, while Galusha Cabin has two bedrooms and a bunkroom. Green Valley has a basement entrance that is helpful for dealing with your gear on subzero days.

Facilities: Green Valley Lodge sleeps eight people in four bedrooms, and Galusha Cabin sleeps nine people in three bedrooms.

Bedding: Bring your own bedding and linens.

Reservations and rates: Both cabins are rented for $350 per night for exclusive use, or $165 per four guests per night. Winter rates for Green Valley may be up to $50 higher. Weekly rates are available.

Directions: From White River Junction to Green Valley, take I-91 north to the West Bradford Exit (Route 25). Continue driving on Route 25 through Waits River (keep going uphill and to the left at the fork for .5 mile) to East Orange Road. Continue driving on East Orange Road until you pass a church in East Orange. The road will turn to dirt, and you'll continue for 1.5 miles on East Orange Road to the Green Road (on the left with a gate and bridge). Open the gate and follow the Green Road up the drive to the lodge.

From White River Junction to Galusha Cabin, take I-91 to the Wells River Exit and drive on Route 302 West. Continue driving through Barre, and in about 8.4 miles you will be in the middle of the small village of Groton. Turn left at the small square, in front of the United Methodist Church, onto the only paved road, Powder Spring Road. From here, continue driving uphill for 3.8 miles, under the power lines, to the top of the ridge. You will cross the bridge over the Wells River and pass the Quarry Road on your left. On the ridge, turn left (east) onto the plowed dirt road (Clark Road). Drive .5 mile until you come to the power line. At the top of the hill look for the "Tree Farm" sign on the left and the "No ATV" signs. Turn into the drive and follow it north for about 300 yards to the gate. The parking area is just on the other side of the gate, and the cabin is to your right and uphill about 200 feet.

Contact: Green Valley Lodge is on East Orange Road in Washington, and Galusha Cabin is on Clark Road in Topsham. All inquiries and reservations should be directed to **Timberland Trails**, Inc., P.O. Box 1076, Conway, NH 03818, 603/449-9900 or 800/TRAILS-8, website: www.phillipsbrook.org.

2. THE HERRIN HOUSE INN

on Quechee River

Luxury rating: ★ ★ ★ ★ ★   **Recreation rating:** ★ ★ ★ ★ ☆

Hiding behind the Herrin House Inn, in the lovely village of Quechee, is the Enchanted Cottage, a spacious, romantic couples' getaway. The Herrin House is an attractively renovated country residence filled with fine artwork. Owner Joe Herrin describes his transformation with the inn: He retired, recovered, and relaxed in a big house—and then decided to share.

The Enchanted Cottage has exposed beams, wood floors, antique furniture and family heirlooms, a television, a radio and phone, a large bathroom with a claw-foot tub, a gas fireplace, air-conditioning, and a giant four-poster king Rice bed, the kind you have to step up into.

This private retreat does not have kitchen facilities, but breakfast is served in the great room of the inn. The room has wonderful views and a grand piano, and the menu is enticing, with things like vanilla French toast and fresh squeezed juice.

© BETHANY ERICSON

If the weather has thwarted your plans to go fly-fishing, play golf or tennis, ski, or walk the trails through the 16 acres to the river, you are still in luck. Downstairs in the inn is an exercise room, and the luxurious Quechee Club welcomes guests to its courts, exercise rooms, and pools.

Let the Inn set you up with your own fishing guide, or just relax by the fire with a glass of wine, or out on the wraparound porch with a book in your lap, gazing at the undulating green hills of the Vermont countryside.

Facilities: There is one cottage than can accommodate two people.

Bedding: All linens and towels provided.

Reservations and rates: The cottage rates range $210–280 per night, double occupancy, and include use of the Quechee Club. Call at least six months ahead for reservations during fall-foliage season.

Directions: From White River Junction, take I-89 and drive for four miles north of the intersection with I-91 to Exit 1. Turn left (west) onto Route 4. When you reach the blinking traffic light (after approximately 3.5 miles), turn left onto Quechee-Hartland Road. Continue driving one mile south. The inn will be on your left.

Contact: Joe Herrin, **The Herrin House Inn**, P.O. Box 312, Quechee-Hartland Road, Quechee, VT 05059, 802/296-7512 or 800/616-4415, website: www.herrinhouseinn.com.

3. WHITE ROCKS INN

Wallingford

Luxury rating: ★★★★☆   **Recreation rating:** ★★★★☆

Rank: Top 10 for Weddings, Top 10 for Hiking

White Rocks Inn is a great old dairy farm with a slate roof. It was a working farm until 1972. Years ago, blocks of ice were cut from Otter Creek across the street and stored in sawdust to cool the tanks of milk in the little red clapboard milk house.

The milk house has been recently renovated into a cottage but retains its original plank floors. It has a small kitchen with an under-the-counter fridge, two-burner range, microwave, and toaster. The dining area has an antique oak table. The living room has a queen sleeper sofa, a cast-iron woodstove, and an armoire with a television and DVD player. The bathroom contains a whirlpool tub, and the king bed is in the loft. The whole cottage is about 700 square feet.

The cottage overlooks a field, and your closest neighbor is .25 mile away. Hiking is found nearby in White Rocks National Recreation Area, and the Applachian Trail and Long Trail are close to you too. There is swimming in Elfin Lake, fishing in Otter Creek, plenty of skiing, snowshoeing, and a great sledding hill in winter. Rita and Malcolm Swogger are very friendly hosts, and they can recommend easy hikes to beautiful lakes or to the ice caves of White Rock.

The cottage can be rented by the day as a bed-and-breakfast, or by the week as a housekeeping unit. It's popular with honeymooners, romantic couples, and families. Breakfast is served in the inn and could include French toast stuffed with cranberry-orange cream cheese or potato latkes with bacon bits and goat cheese.

White Rock's gothic barn is listed on the National Register of Historic Places and is a popular place for weddings and dinners. It's one of the largest barns in the area, with more than 15,000 square feet of space, and 4,500 square feet of it is available for your event. The large doors open to the meadows. Rita and Malcolm are happy to arrange romantic getaway packages with limo rides to nearby restaurants or to your own private picnic in the meadows.

Facilities: There is one cottage that sleeps 2–4 people. Rollaway beds can be added.

Bedding: Linens are provided.

Reservations and rates: The rates ranges $170–230 a day, and $750–1,100 a week. Fall is the busiest season. Call up to a year ahead. Open year-round.

Directions: The inn is located on Route 7, about 16 miles north of Manchester, Vermont, and 10 miles south of Rutland, Vermont.

Contact: Rita and Malcolm Swogger, **White Rocks Inn Bed & Breakfast**, 1774 U.S. 7 south, Wallingford, VT 05773, 802/446-2077 or 866/446-2077 (toll free), website: www.whiterocksinn.com.

4. THE MERCK FOREST AND FARMLAND CENTER

near the New York border in Rupert

Luxury rating: ★☆☆☆☆   **Recreation rating:** ★★★★★

Rank: Top 10 for Backcountry Winter Adventures, Top 10 for Viewing Fall Foliage

Merck Forest is a nonprofit, educational organization that teaches sustainable forest and farmland management. Here you'll find 60 acres of organic farmland with rare livestock breeds and 3,100 acres of forest managed for rare habitats, maple syrup, wildlife, timber products, and recreation.

A variety of cabins, no more than two miles from the main parking area, are provided for those looking for a rustic wilderness experience or an educational weekend field trip. The cabins offer woodstoves, firewood, outhouses, a water source within a mile, and spectacular views. Some have porches.

This forest was abandoned farmland in the 1800s, and as a result there are gorgeous stands of white birch trees and old stone walls, and maple trees with diameters of 2–3 feet are not uncommon. What is uncommon is to find such accessible beautiful stands of forest without finding great numbers of people everywhere. Escape here to a secret getaway cabin and explore the undisturbed woods, climb Mount Antoine, visit the cows and pigs, or count endless stars at night.

Two of the more distant cabins, Ned's Place and Nenarod, are particularly beautiful and feel very remote. Dunc's Place has a stream and is an old farm site with a plan for a swimming hole. (This and other sites near streams are best avoided during black-fly season, in May.)

Open year-round, Merck Forest is a favorite with hikers and people snowshoeing. Cars don't go any farther than the visitors center. The terrain is suited for backcountry skiers only. Beginners trying to cross-country ski would be frustrated here, particularly with the 400-foot gain in elevation from the visitors center up the hill. Anglers will find trout in the pond and in the streams, though they are on the smaller side. Mountain biking is prohibited here.

Make sure you arrive with plenty of time to hike into your cabin location. You'll head out past the farm and its many exhibits, on a hillside with a view of nearly 100 miles across the field. To the west you may catch a spectacular sunset over the southern Adirondacks.

Facilities: There are six cottages that can accommodate 6–16 people. Snowshoes can be rented on-site; ski equipment can be rented in Manchester. You cannot drive to your site. Merck Forest syrup, potatoes, and eggs may be available in the visitors center.

Bedding: No linens provided.

Reservations and rates: The cabins range in price $45–80 per night. Reservations are required, and payment is due by credit card when you call. For New Years reservations, call up to three years ahead. Typically, you will find some openings for weekdays. Availability can be checked online. Most visitors stay one or two nights. Saturday is the most popular night. Members receive a 20 percent discount on camping fees. Pets are permitted, but must be leashed in the farm part of the property.

Directions: From Boston, take Route 2 west to I-91. Take Exit 2 in Brattleboro, VT, and follow the signs for Vermont Route 30. Drive for approximately 40 miles on Route 30 through Manchester Center. From Manchester, continue to follow Route 30 and drive for 8.2 miles to Vermont 315. Turn left on Vermont 315, and continue 2.6 miles to the top of the hill. The driveway will be on the left. The parking area and visitors center is .5 mile up the driveway.

Contact: Merck Forest and Farmland Center, Route 315, Rupert Mountain Road, P.O. Box 86, Rupert, VT 05768, 802/394-7836, website: www.merckforest.org.

5. CORNUCOPIA OF DORSET

Dorset

Luxury rating: ★ ★ ★ ★ ☆   **Recreation rating:** ★ ★ ★ ☆ ☆

Rank: Top 10 for Romance

Set behind the 1880 colonial home now known as Cornucopia of Dorset is a lovely romantic getaway cottage for couples. Owner Donna Butman keeps the cottage immaculate and adds champagne, cookies, and chocolate for your stay.

The cottage is sunny and pleasant, with a contemporary feel accented by antique touches. There are fabulous wood floors, a small full kitchen, a wood-burning fireplace, a television, a VCR, air-conditioning, a CD player in the cathedral-ceiling living room, a tub in the bathroom, and a private patio. The cozy queen bed is in an upstairs loft with a skylight that provides views of the stars at night.

Dorset is the original marble town of Vermont. As you explore the town, you'll note marble patios, steps, and even sidewalks. The local swimming hole is an old marble quarry, and "quarry towels" are provided by the inn.

Also in the area are nature trails and hiking trails, fly-fishing, biking, golf, horseback riding, cross-country skiing, snowshoeing and tennis. The inn is a short drive from Merck Forest (see The Merck Forest and Farmland Center entry).

Your stay in the cottage comes with breakfast in the solarium. You might have maple-swirled French toast, orange croissants, or breakfast enchiladas with corn muffins. And in the common rooms of the inn, you're welcome to relax ,play a game, or curl up by the fire with Donna's dog or your loved one.

Facilities: There is one cottage suitable for a couple.
Bedding: All linens are provided.

6. WILBURTON INN

Manchester Village

Luxury rating: ★ ★ ★ ★ ☆   **Recreation rating:** ★ ★ ★ ★ ☆

Rank: Top 10 Most Unusual, Top 10 Most Luxurious, Top 10 for Weddings, Top 10 for Viewing Fall Foliage

A regal driveway winds up Strawberry Hill to these impressive mansion and cottages, which were built by Adison Gilbert to go with those of his friend Robert Todd Lincoln (son of Abe). Later, Gilbert's banker, James Wilbur, bought the estate. During World War II, it was leased to a school for the children of European artists and diplomats who had fled the Nazis.

In 1945, Wilburton became an invitation-only inn for gentlemen. This lasted until the 1970s, when the General Tire/RKO conglomerate sold the Equinox Hotel and bought the Wilburton for corporate uses. In 1987 Dr. Albert Levis visited for his birthday, and he purchased it three months later. Albert and Georgette Levis (known as Gorgeous in her sister Wendy Wasserstein's play *The Sisters Rosensweig*) are not only incredibly warm and welcoming hosts, but are committed to supporting the arts. An exploration of the grounds will reveal some rather extraordinary outdoor sculpture, ranging from Easter Island heads to a golden Egyptian tomb.

Most of the cottages are actually large buildings housing various rooms of the inn. However, there is a two-bedroom single unit originally built as the innkeeper's home, and a seven-bedroom, five-bath cottage suitable for a weekend ski house or family reunion. The cottages are more casual than the richly appointed inn but are very comfortable. The two-bedroom cottage contains two baths, a piano room, and views of Mount Equinox, the highest peak in the Taconic mountain range.

The inn offers discount lift tickets to local ski resorts, and there is cross-country skiing in the area, as well as golf and excellent fly-fishing. Orvis, the well-known fly-fishing store, is located in Manchester. Numerous trails leave Manchester to Mount Equinox, as well as into the Green Mountains, with some connecting to the Long Trail.

After all this exercise, relax in the opulent common rooms of the inn. Breakfast is served on glass tables in the sunny Terrace room. If you don't take advantage of your own kitchen in the cottages, you'll find an impressive menu served in front of an immense hearth.

Facilities: There are two self-contained cottages: a two-bedroom, two-bath; and a seven-bedroom with five bathrooms.

Bedding: All linens provided.

Reservations and rates: The reunion-house rate runs up to $850 per night in the high season. Call for cottage rates. Reserve early, the cottages have a high rate of repeat guests.

Directions: From Boston, drive on Route 2 west to I-91 north. Take Exit 2 in Brattleboro, then drive on Route 30 north to 7A south to Manchester. Drive past the Equinox Hotel, which will be on your right. Take the first left turn onto River Road. The inn is .9 mile down River Road, on the left side.

Contact: Wilburton Inn, River Road, Manchester Village, VT 05254, 802/362-2500 or 800/648-4944, website: www.wilburton.com.

7. JOHNNY SEESAW'S

on Bromley Mountain

Luxury rating: ★ ★ ☆ ☆ ☆   **Recreation rating:** ★ ★ ★ ★ ★

Rank: Best for Skiing and Snowmobiling

Johnny Seesaw's is all about skiing Bromley Mountain with your family. But it wasn't always.

In 1920, a Russian logger named Ivan Sesow created the Wonderview Log Pavilion, a Saturday night dance-and-moonshine mainstay that is rumored to have provided what were known as "sin cabins" out back.

According to local lore, Sesow bet the roadhouse in a poker game in 1930—and lost.

Over the next decade, brewery heir Fred Pabst turned the mountainside into the Bromley ski area. Bill and Mary Parrish bought the Wonderview in 1938 and renovated it, renaming it Johnny Seesaw's. A referral-only Ivy

League-ish winter escape, it was one of the first ski lodges in Vermont.

Gary Okun, the present owner, bought the place in 1980, and you no longer need to know someone who has stayed here in order to get a reservation. Johnny Seesaw's is literally within walking distance of the ski slopes, and the licensed pub is a wonderful place to escape the cold. It has "Yankee cuisine dinners" and one of the state's first circular fireplaces, which is rather like dining by a giant indoor campfire.

The cottages cater to families and small groups; they each have two bedrooms and two baths. They are private and comfortably distributed around the property. In winter you'll find a shoveled path to your festive icicle-fringed cottage, with marble steps leading inside to your knotty-pine-walled and fully carpeted living room with a fireplace. In summer, there is a red-clay tennis court and an Olympic-sized pool, and the ski resorts hold concerts and offer golf courses. Bromley also has an alpine slide. The Long and Appalachian Trails are nearby, as is fishing on Battenkill River. The lodge itself has a wraparound porch, a game room, and a pool table.

Facilities: There are four cottages with two bedrooms and two baths.

Bedding: Linens are provided.

Reservations and rates: The cottages rent for $40–99 per adult. Open year-round. Pets are welcome, but "unattended children may be towed."

Directions: From Boston, drive on Route 2 west to I-91 north and take the second exit in Vermont. Follow Route 30 north to Route 11 east (driving for approximately 40 miles). Turn right. Johnny Seesaw's is two miles down on the left-hand side.

Contact: Gary Okun, **Johnny Seesaw's**, P.O. Box 68, Peru, VT 05152, 802/824-5533 or 800/424-CSAW, website: www.jseesaw.com.

8. FROG'S LEAP INN

in Londonderry

Luxury rating: ★ ★ ★ ☆ ☆   **Recreation rating:** ★ ★ ★ ★ ★

In winter, the Frog's Leap Inn, with its poolside TadPool House cottage, is a remote country escape, and there is skiing and snowmobiling nearby. However, Frog's Leap is truly at its most glorious in midsummer. That's when the stone walkway on the other side of the heated pool will lead you (and many a bride) through an astounding array of more than 300 flowering bushes.

Set back behind the main inn, the TadPool House is an apartment cottage above the table tennis, bathroom, and vending machine of the pool house. This gives it a bird's-eye view of the pool and some of the lovely grounds, which stretch across 32 acres of garden, field, and forest.

The cottage is a reasonably spacious two-bedroom with a sofa bed in the living room. It has a television, VCR, and fully equipped kitchen (including a dishwasher), and you'll be surrounded in warm yellow pine and comfortable country furnishings.

In the height of summer, be sure to ask what's planned for poolside. You might find yourself enjoying a barbecue while a live band plays by your pool, or you might prefer to reserve a quieter weekend.

Whether you bask by the pool, wander on the hiking trails, or head off to bike, play tennis, ski, or fish, you'll be well fueled by the breakfast that is included. Swedish pancakes, perhaps? Homegrown herbs and tomatoes are often included, as is cheese from local farms. Owners Dorenna and Kraig have more than 30 years in the hospitality business, and it shows.

Facilities: There is one cottage that can accommodate 2–5 people.
Bedding: Linens are provided.

Reservations and rates: The cottage is $260 per night with breakfast. Ask about weekly rates and special packages. Call at least a month in advance. Open year-round.

Directions: From Boston, take Route 2 west to I-91 north to Exit 6 (Rockingham). Turn left on Route 5 for approximately one mile to Route 103 north to Chester, VT, to Route 11 west to Londonderry (approximately 20 minutes). In Londonderry, on Route 11, take a right (at blinking light) at Route 100 north. The inn is approximately 1.5 miles on the left on Route 100 north (it is 25 miles from I-91, Exit 6).

Contact: Kraig and Dorenna Hart, **Frog's Leap Inn**, RR #1 Box 107 Route 100, Londonderry, VT 05148, 802/824-3019 or 877/FROGSLEAP, website: www.frogsleapinn.com.

9. HILL FARM INN

on Battenkill River

Luxury rating: ★ ★ ☆ ☆ ☆   **Recreation rating:** ★ ★ ★ ★ ☆

For more than 90 years, Hill Farm Inn has offered peaceful country hospitality on 50 acres of farmland and a mile of Battenkill River frontage. It has a warm, old-fashioned, safe feeling, and it's a place where you'd be comfortable letting the kids wander the conservation land paths, gather fiddleheads, or play on the shore of the river.

This is a true 1830s New England farm, with a big red barn and silo. The kids are welcome to visit the farmyard animals, and the air is filled with the scent of hay. The four small basic white cabins with light blue trim are all different from each other, but all are set in the field with great views of the Green and Taconic Mountains.

The Battenkill River is famous for fly-fishing, and is also a good river for canoeing. The inn is not far from access to the Appalachian Trail and other hiking areas. The country roads are nice for biking, and there are streams and a quarry to swim in. At the end of a day out in the country, cabin dwellers are also welcome to unwind in the common rooms of the inn, where there is a parlor with a fireplace.

Facilities: There are four heated cabins accommodating 2–4 people.

Bedding: Linens are provided.

Reservations and rates: The inn is open year-round. Rates run $80–143 per night, double occupancy. The cabins are open May 20–October 20. Pets are not permitted.

Directions: From Boston, drive on Route 2 west to I-91 north. Take Exit 2 into Brattleboro. Take Vermont Route 9 west to U.S. 7 north. Follow U.S. 7 north to Exit 3; turn left onto Route 313. Drive for two miles and turn right onto 7A north. Drive five miles north (through the town of Arlington and into Sunderland). Turn right onto Hill Farm Road, just in front of Battenkill Canoe Rental. The inn is located .5 mile down on the right.

Contact: Kathleen and Craig Yanez, **Hill Farm Inn**, 458 Hill Farm Road, Arlington, VT 05250, 802/375-2269 or 800/882-2545, website: www.hillfarminn.com.

10. INN AT COVERED BRIDGE GREEN

on Battenkill River

Luxury rating: ★★★★☆   **Recreation rating:** ★★★★★

Rank: Top 10 for Romance, Top 10 Most Unusual

© BETHANY ERICSON

You won't find a more picture-perfect, Norman Rockwell Vermont setting than this. Go out into the countryside, cross famous Battenkill River by the covered bridge, and you'll arrive at the Arlington Village green by a chapel; look straight ahead and you'll see a charming 18th-century Colonial inn. The Rockwell-like atmosphere is no coincidence, as this house really was Rockwell's home from 1942 to 1954. Hidden behind the inn are some incredible treasures: a honeymoon cottage and a cottage that was once Rockwell's art studio.

The Honeymoon Cottage was built in the 1940s for Rockwell's son, Jarvis, as a studio. It's small, in a private and charming way. It has old exposed log beams, a kitchenette, an enameled gas woodstove, and a spiral staircase that leads to a romantic loft bed. The bathroom has a wonderful shower stall with a glass-cube wall and a giant showerhead made for sharing.

The Norman Rockwell studio is where the artist did many of his famous *Saturday Evening Post* illustrations. Next to a field of grazing cows and horses, you enter the front door to find a spacious living area with television and VCR, an antique sleigh serving as a coffee table in front of the fire, fabulous furnishings, photos of Rockwell working here, and a long wooden seat under a 10-foot window.

You get a good view of the wagon-wheel chandelier as you take the stairs past a hanging antique bicycle to the sunny floral bedroom with private balcony. The upstairs bathroom has a skylight that looks at the hills. Downstairs is a full kitchen with a baking table and a second bedroom. The rear door opens onto a deck with views of the apple orchard and pastures. These bedrooms can be rented together or separately.

Arlington has been home to numerous New England historic figures and today offers swimming, canoeing, and fly-fishing in the Battenkill River, just a few hundred feet from the inn. Breakfast is included and is considered a formal event.

Facilities: There are two cottages accommodating 2–4 people.

Bedding: All linens provided.

Reservations and rates: Cottage rates range $150–250. Open year-round.

Directions: From Boston, take Route 2 west to Greenfield and drive on I-91 north to Brattleboro, Exit 2. Then follow Route 9 west to Bennington, Vermont. In Bennington, drive on U.S. 7 north to Exit 3 (Arlington & Route 313). Follow Route 313 (and Route 7A north) into Arlington. In Arlington, turn left and follow Route 313 west for 4.5 miles to Covered Bridge Road, on the left. Turn left through the Covered Bridge. The inn is directly ahead, on the right.

Contact: Clint and Julia Dickens, Innkeepers, **The Inn at Covered Bridge Green**, 3587 River Road, Arlington, VT 05250, 802/375-9489 or 800/726-9480, website: www.coveredbridgegreen.com.

11. THREE MOUNTAIN INN

near Jamaica State Park

Luxury rating: ★ ★ ★ ★ ★   **Recreation rating:** ★ ★ ★ ★ ★

Rank: Top 10 for Romance, Top 10 Most Unusual, Top 10 Most Luxurious

The Sage Hill Cottage at Three Mountain Inn takes the cake for combining romance and technology successfully in a humble cottage setting. The cottage has more remote controls than one person should reasonably have, and your welcome introduction will explain the options, from the book-friendly "reading" lights setting to "romance," which will dim the lights and start the gas fireplace. Even the skylights are automated. It's terribly fun.

However, you might have some trouble concentrating on the instructions as you begin to take in your surroundings, which include a luxurious bed facing the fireplace, a two-person hot tub, and a stained-glass window visible only from the sleigh bed. Your ears will perk up as you hear the demonstration of the sound system (its speakers are built right into the beams), but your mind may wander as you note that the bathroom has a two-head shower and a heated-tile floor. An antique armoire conceals a television, VCR, and stereo.

The cottage overlooks a swimming pool with a fieldstone fountain and encourages midnight dips or afternoons floating on your back contemplating the views of Shatterack, Ball, and Turkey Mountains. The cottage's location near Jamaica State Park offers fabulous cross-country skiing, snowshoeing, mountain biking, hiking, waterfalls, and some very large kayaking events. Alpine skiing is close by at Stratton, Magic, and Bromley. The inn provides free snowshoes, bikes, and a canoe.

The inn itself is a 1797 building, with wide king boards and a fabulous array of flowers and artwork arranged by innkeeper David Hiler's mother, Heide. Local glassblowers even make the Three Mountain Inn key chains. You enter the inn through the back into the cozy pub and can relax in the "keeping room" in front of an enormous fireplace.

No cooking facilities are provided in this cabin. It's meant for other means of escape. There are packages available that include dinner in the inn, and the restaurants of Manchester are a short drive away.

If all these settings have you flummoxed, there is also a control setting for "nothing" (it once controlled a heater). And if all the controls excite you, you'll be happy to know you can book this cottage online.

Facilities: There is one cottage that can accommodate two people.

Bedding: Linens are provided.

Reservations and rates: The cottage rate ranges $275–325 per night. Call a year ahead to reserve for popular weekends in October and February. Ski and dinner discounts are offered in special packages. Open year-round. Dogs are welcome with permission, and you may find a welcome basket just for them.

Directions: From Boston, take Route 2 west to I-91 north to Exit 2 in Brattleboro. Follow the signs carefully for Route 30, and drive for about 25 miles. Three Mountain Inn is on the right, just across from Town Hall in Jamaica.

Contact: Three Mountain Inn, Route 30, P.O. Box 180, Jamaica, VT 05343, 802/874-4140 or 800/532-9399, website: www.threemountaininn.com.

12. MOLLY STARK INN

in downtown Bennington

Luxury rating: ★★★★☆   **Recreation rating:** ★★★★☆

Rank: Top 10 for Viewing Fall Foliage

The Molly Stark Inn is a 19th-century Victorian on Route 9 (Main Street) in Bennington. Tucked behind the inn is a very rustic-looking, board-sided cottage facing the woods. In its winter decor of skis and wreaths, it looks like a common ski bunkhouse. Don't be fooled.

© BETHANY ERICSON

Inside the rough boards of this custom-built cottage is a very quiet and elegant romantic hideaway for two. It has a loft with a brass king-sized bed covered in a quilt, a corner whirlpool tub with a woodland view, and a woodstove. The cottage was built with an eye for detail, and there are many amenities, including a stereo, television, telephone, and skylights.

Southern Vermont is a visually stunning place to be during fall foliage. For some excellent hiking, follow Route 9 (the Molly Stark Trail) east to the Appalachian Mountain Trail, or keep going further east for an easy hike to the tower at Molly Stark State Park. You can ski, swim, mountain bike, and fish to your heart's content in southern Vermont. And whatever you do, you'll be fueled by a hearty country breakfast from the inn.

The second cottage behind the inn is known as the Sugarhouse Suites. This is basically a duplex cottage, but it is a new construction, and each side has been soundproofed. These two suites have double-sided fireplaces and whirlpool tubs. You can have continental breakfast delivered to your door and be as private as you like.

Facilities: There is one separate cottage and one duplex cottage behind the main inn. They are meant for couples. Breakfast is included.

Bedding: Bedding is provided.

Reservations and rates: The rates for the cottage range $150–175. The Sugarhouse Suites range $135–160. Extra guests are $20. There is a two-night minimum on weekends, and higher rates may apply during foliage season, holidays, and weekends.

Directions: From Bennington, drive one mile east on Route 9. The inn will be on your right.

Contact: Reed Fendler, **Molly Stark Inn**, 1067 East Main Street, Bennington, VT 05201, 802/442-9631 or 800/356-3076, website: www.mollystarkinn.com.

© BETHANY ERICSON

Chapter 3

Northern New Hampshire

CHAPTER 3—NORTHERN NEW HAMPSHIRE

Now Hampshire gets its nickname, the Granite State, from the northern part of the state. With all there is to do—activities in the towering White Mountains; family attractions in the Notches; hunting, fishing, and hiking in the wilds of the Great North Woods—you'll probably be too busy to see much of your cabin or cottage in the daytime.

Much of this terrain north of the state's central plateau has become part of the White Mountains National Forest. Spring attracts fishing enthusiasts to the many streams and rivers, winter brings lovers of all winter sports to the snowmobile corridors and ski resorts, summer attracts hikers and bikers to the hundreds of trails, and fall brings the leaf-peepers.

The White Mountains National Forest covers 750,000 acres of this area and includes several state parks, most notably Franconia Notch State Park, Crawford Notch State Park, and Mount Washington State Park. It is a managed and multiple-use forest. The White Mountains stretch from Maine into New Hampshire and are part of the Appalachian Mountains system. The famed Appalachian Trail traverses the White Mountains. In fact, its longest section above tree line is in the Presidential Range.

The Presidential Range is the most well known of the numerous ranges in the White Mountains. It includes Mount Washington, the highest peak in the Northeast. A goal of many outdoorsy New Englanders is to see how many of the 48 mountains higher than 4,000 feet they can climb. Some people aim to attempt the entire Presidential Range in one day, while others dream of skiing Tuckerman's Ravine on Mount Washington. A big draw for hikers is the AMC High Huts, a chain of eight mountaintop bunkhouses that offers lodging and food for hikers.

Do not underestimate the hikes in the White Mountains. The trails are rugged, and the weather is unpredictable. At a bit more than 6,000 feet, Mount Washington is known for having "the worst weather in the world." The observatory on top has logged the highest wind speeds on the planet, and hikers regularly die there. But perhaps the danger is the appeal. The famed 1826 avalanche in the White Mountains that killed the Willey family (as they fled from their house) but left their house untouched preceded a wave of tourism to the north.

Never fear, there are mountain and wood trails for all abilities; some even lead to lovely waterfalls. Most of the major downhill ski areas are in the vicinity of the outlet store–filled town of North Conway, while nearby Jackson is a paradise for cross-country skiers. Heading north toward Franconia Notch will bring you to family attractions such as tramways up mountains and The Flume. The Kancamagus Highway offers spectacular scenery. There is rock and ice climbing at Cathedral and White Horse Ledges, as well as at Frankenstein Cliffs. Meanwhile, you can take the old cog railroad or drive up Mount Washington.

Some of New England's important rivers originate in New Hampshire, offering swimming, boating, and fishing opportunities galore. The northern lands are the origin of the Androscoggin and Saco Rivers, as well as the mighty Connecticut River, which forms the Connecticut Lakes before winding for many miles as the western border of the state. The Pemigewasset River starts in Franconia Notch, joins the Winnipesaukee River, and then forms the famed energy source of many a mill, the Merrimack. The Cocheco and Salmon Falls Rivers join in the southeastern part of the state and make up the Piscataqua.

Ethan Allen Crawford was probably the most famous guide to the wilds of the Whites, and his parents turned their log cabin into an inn in the early 1800s. The railroads north brought more tourism, and as a result some of New England's Grand Hotels were built. One of these, The Mount Washington, still sees many visitors. Henry David Thoreau, Nathaniel Hawthorne, and Henry James, as well as many a famed botanist and artist, have made the trek north. When cars replaced train travel, motor inns and cabins sprung up across the land, dotting the mountains, snowmobile routes, and new ski resort trails.

Up in the Great North Woods, the Connecticut Lakes are deep, cold-water lakes that are home to many trout and salmon. Remote ponds dot the wilderness logging roads, and dams on the river keep the cold-water fishing going into the summer. Route 3 is prime moose-viewing territory.

There are miles of groomed snowmobile trails up north. And Garfield Falls, Magalloway Mountain, and the trail into Fourth Connecticut Lake are beloved hiking areas. Meanwhile, work continues to progress on the Cohos Trail, a 162-mile trail through truly remote areas. There are now maps to this trail. Imagine walking from Jefferson to Pittsburg and not seeing a town for 90 miles. (Better make that cabin reservation; you're going to need a shower.)

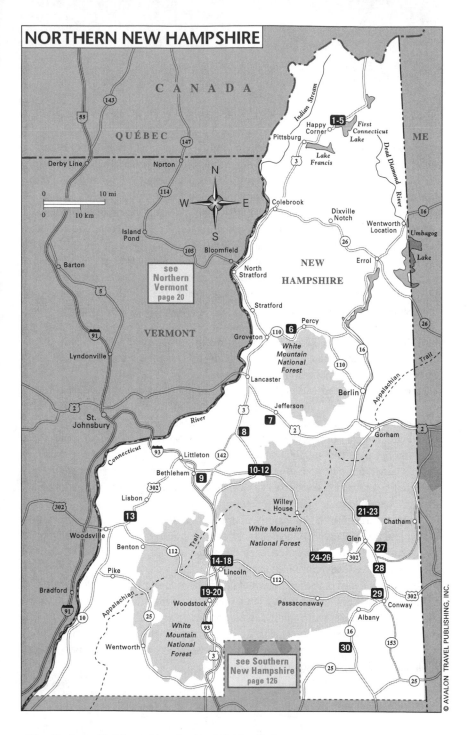

CHAPTER 3
NORTHERN NEW HAMPSHIRE

1. TALL TIMBER LODGE

on First Connecticut Lake

Luxury rating: ★★★★☆   **Recreation rating:** ★★★★★

Rank: Top 10 for Fishing, Best for Skiing and Snowmobiling

Tall Timber is a well known, casual resort with compelling log cabins and unparalleled fishing. The lake is quite shallow and warm, and you can swim from the boat launch or lawn. The resort has an extensive fly-fishing school and offers boating, mountain biking, hunting, snowmobiling, and more. It also has delicious food and a lakeside bar.

© TALL TIMBER LODGE

Some of the log cabins here were built in the late 1940s, and they retain their rustic charm while constantly being updated with appliances and other conveniences. Josselyn's in Jackson built some of the cabins here. Many of the cabins include nice touches like cathedral ceilings, log beds, whirlpool tubs, and gas or wood fireplaces. Fully equipped kitchens, VCRs, stereos, porches, and decks are also among the available conveniences. Bess and Angler's Cove are located a short distance from Tall Timber and are the two most high-end cabins.

The fly-fishing school is offered by Broadside's International angling team. There are three weekend courses: Spring Fly Fling, Simplified Fly-Fishing and the Classical Approach to Fly-Fishing. These workshops include a lodge room or basic cabin as well as meals. Participants bring their own tackle and tools. The lodge has a new conference room for groups and the Fly-Fishing School.

In winter, there are snowmobile rentals. If you stay two midweek nights or more, you may qualify for a sledding-and-lodging combo rate. Sled and Stay is for those doing their own cooking, and Ride and Relax is for those receiving maid service and eating at the lodge.

Jon Howe is the registered New Hampshire Guide on staff, and other guides can be arranged in advance. Tall Timber has boats located on other lakes and outer ponds. There is also a fly shop on-site, with fishing licenses, tackle, and flies.

> **Facilities:** There are 14 cabins with 1–4 bedrooms accommodating up to nine people.
>
> **Bedding:** Bedding is provided.
>
> **Reservations and rates:** Peak season rates range $720–1,425 for a weekly family rate, $97–298 nightly for midweek, and $107–330 nightly on weekends. Fishing weekend workshop fees are about $435. Call early for fishing season, July and August. Reduced rates are available in shoulder seasons and winter. Housekeeping, meal, and activity packages are available. Open year-round. No pets in four of the cabins, but otherwise they are allowed for a $10 fee.
>
> **Directions:** From Boston (takes about 4.5 hours), take I-93 north and drive through Franconia Notch. Take Exit 35 onto Route 3 north, and drive all the way to Pittsburg. In Pittsburg, you have two ways to travel to Tall Timber. Shortly after a church and across from the town's park, you will see a "Top Gas" sign at the Trading Post Country Store. From this point, you can: 1) turn left on Back Lake Road, drive for approximately 2.5 miles until you see the Tall Timber sign on the corner of Beach Road, bear right, and continue a short distance to Tall Timber, or 2) continue driving on Route 3 north for approximately 3.5 miles until you see the Tall Timber sign on the corner of Beach Road, turn left, and continue driving on Beach Road for one mile to Tall Timber.
>
> **Contact: Tall Timber Lodge**, 231 Beach Road, Pittsburg, NH 03592, 800/83-LODGE, website: www.talltimber.com.

Other Cabins and Cottages Nearby
- Timberland Lodge, First Connecticut Lake, Pittsburg, NH 03592, 603/538-6613 or 800/545-6613, website: www.timberlandlodge.com.

2. RAMBLEWOOD CABINS
on First Connecticut Lake

Luxury rating: ★★☆☆☆   **Recreation rating:** ★★★★★

Rank: Top 10 for Hiking, Top 10 for Backcountry Winter Adventures

Located on sparkling First Connecticut Lake, these unassuming cottages have a front-row seat for boating, fishing, swimming, snowmobiling, cross-country skiing, and hiking trails—including access to the newest portion of the long-anticipated Cohos Trail.

These are modern heated cottages. Some are situated right on the lakefront, some share lake and mountain views, and some are log cabins. Cottage 9 has a private location with a fieldstone fireplace. Cottage 5 has a fireplace, boat docks, and a sandy beach. Cottage 7 is a two-bedroom home on the lake; it has a kitchen with a dishwasher, a wood-burning stove, a CD

© RAMBLEWOOD CABINS

player, and a sundeck. West Bay Camp 8 is a timber log home with 200 feet of shorefront. All have televisions and phones.

In summer, there are paddleboats and rowboats on the beach, and canoes and motorboats can be rented. There are more than 180 acres of private nature trails, and there is a connection to New Hampshire's new Cohos Trail. This trail is stretching north on its way to becoming the longest foot-trail system in the state. With the newest maps, you should be able to follow some of it right from Ramblewood.

In winter, Ramblewood has private cross-country ski trails, great backcountry snowshoeing, and free use of a heated workshop for snowmobile repairs. Ice fishing is popular on the lake.

Keep your eye out for moose while you're driving up this way. If you're looking for these large creatures, locals call Route 3 (from First Connecticut Lake up to the Canadian border) "Moose Alley." Moose can be unpredictable, so it's usually a good idea to remain in your car while viewing them.

Facilities: Ramblewood's nine two- and four-bedroom cottages accommodate up to 11 people. There are restaurants within a mile of the cabins.

Bedding: Bedding is provided.

Reservations and rates: Regular rates range $90–240 per night. Additional adults over the pricing maximums are $40; kids 6–15 years old are $20, and children under five stay for free. Group rates may be arranged. Call ahead to inquire about the pet policy.

Directions: From Boston, take I-93 north past Franconia Notch, New Hampshire, to Exit 35. Then drive on Route 3 to Colebrook, and continue north to Pittsburg. The trip is approximately 219 miles.

Contact: Ramblewood Cabins & Campground, First Connecticut Lake, Pittsburg, NH 03592, 603/538-6948 or 877/RAMBLEWOOD, website: www.ramblewoodcabins.com.

3. LOPSTICK LODGE AND CABINS

near First Connecticut Lake

Luxury rating: ★★☆☆☆   **Recreation rating:** ★★★★★

Rank: Best for Skiing and Snowmobiling

© LOPSTICK LODGE AND CABINS

These housekeeping cabins, with views of First Connecticut Lake, are said to be Pittsburg's oldest-operating sporting camp. According to the owners, "lopstick" means a fir tree that has been stripped of its lower branches, and its top branches cut to point the way in several directions. (Maybe the term lost its popularity when no one wanted to leave the area.)

Pittsburgh is popular for fishing, hunting, snowmobiling, and moose watching. The Lopstick Cabins were known in the 1920s as the Currier Camps. They went through a number of owners, including Nicky and Ron Clermonth, of the local Nicky's Country Kitchen. Later owners changed the name to Lopstick and greatly improved the property before winning the Tri-State Megabucks lottery and moving on.

However, the cabins live humbly on. And these days you can get a guide for fly-fishing or hunting, you can buy tackle, rent a snowmobile, or relax in a hot tub—all on the property. All of the cabins are different, but all have televisions and either porches with views of the lake and mountains or remote woodsy surroundings.

Cabins 1–6 are the oldest cabins and the most rustic. Cabins 7 and 8 have two bedrooms that can sleep groups of eight comfortably. Cabins 9 and 10 have gas fireplaces and hot tubs. Eastwind is a smaller cabin that looks over two trout ponds. Lakeview is a small three-bedroom cottage on the lake. Woodside is a three-bedroom cabin just off Camp Otter Road. The Kiley Cabin is also a three-bedroom cabin. Another log cabin is being built on the banks of Perry Stream.

The Connecticut Lakes are deep cold-water lakes that offer well-known fishing opportunities. Fishing in nearby rivers for trout and landlocked salmon, and for brook, rainbow, and brown trout, are big area draws. Canoes and kayaks are available to rent. There are also many good opportunities for hiking to lakes, falls, and mountains.

Facilities: There are 16 cabins with one, two, or three bedrooms. All have fully equipped kitchens.

Bedding: Linens and towels are provided.

Reservations and rates: The cabins range in price $82–235 per night per couple. Open year-round. Well-behaved dogs and cats are allowed in certain cabins under certain rules. There is a $10 charge, except for crated hunting dogs staying in October and November.

Directions: Lopstick Lodge is about a five-hour drive from Boston. Drive north on I-93 past Franconia Notch. Take Exit 35 to Route 3 north to Pittsburg. Continue driving for eight miles on Route 3 north. There are several signs along Route 3; the one at Stewart Young Road is where you must turn. Watch for the sign on the left, about one mile past the First Connecticut Lake Dam. Lopstick is 350 yards off Route 3 on Stewart Young Road.

Contact: Lopstick Lodge and Cabins, First Connecticut Lake, Pittsburg, NH 03592, 800/538-6659, website: www.lopstick.com.

4. THE GLEN

on First Connecticut Lake

Luxury rating: ★ ★ ☆ ☆ ☆　　　　**Recreation rating:** ★ ★ ★ ★ ★

Rank: Top 10 for Value

Betty Falton has been running The Glen for more than 40 years, and that, plus the large number of repeat guests, creates a welcoming atmosphere. Whether you choose a cabin on First Connecticut Lake or on the hillside, you'll be happy with your view by day, and you'll go to sleep listening to the calling loons at night.

Here in this oasis, situated a mile down a private road set in 180 acres of woodlands, you're truly getting away from it all. In the cedar lodge, with its stick furniture and fieldstone, you will enjoy three meals a day served in the dining room. The cabins do have kitchenettes, despite the American Plan meals, so you can enjoy a cup of tea or a snack while sitting on the porch, admiring the view and congratulating yourself on your good fortune.

The cabins vary in size and are made of knotty pine, featuring braided rugs and covered porches. The lakeshore log cabins can hold families of up to seven people. Both of the hillside cabins have good lake views. One has a fireplace, and the other has a screened porch. All of the cabins have heating and daily housekeeping.

First Connecticut Lake is known for its great fishing, especially for trout and landlocked salmon. You can rent boats and motors at The Glen. The cove also makes for a safe swimming area. If you stroll through the woods or take a drive along "Moose Alley," you may meet one of the four-legged locals.

Facilities: There are 10 cabins. One is a four-bedroom, two are three-bedrooms, and five are one-bedrooms. All meals are provided in the dining room.

Bedding: Bring your own bedding.

Reservations and rates: Rates range $85–104 per day per person and include a complete American Plan. Closed mid-October–mid-May. Pets are allowed.

Directions: From Boston, take I-93 north through Franconia Notch. Take Exit 35 to Route 3 north and drive through Pittsburg to the shores of First Connecticut Lake. Follow the signs to The Glen.

Contact: The Glen, 77 The Glen Road, First Connecticut Lake, Pittsburg, NH 03592, 603/538-6500 or 800/445-GLEN (800/445-4536), website: www.theglen.org.

5. PARTRIDGE CABINS

on First Connecticut Lake

Luxury rating: ★★☆☆☆   **Recreation rating:** ★★★★★

Partridge Cabins has seven rustic, knotty-pine housekeeping cabins with screened porches, as well as two brand-new cottages. They are well spread out on a gentle slope under evergreens. Partridge Cabins has 600 feet of frontage on First Connecticut Lake.

Pittsburg is an area with infinite activities during all seasons. Whether you come to fish for landlocked salmon or trout (in the sun or through the ice) on any of the local lakes, or to hike alongside moose, or to snowmobile on groomed trails for miles, this area by the Canadian border is perfect for you.

There is a private beach at Partridge Cabins, a volleyball net, and horseshoes. There are 14-foot deep-hull boats with six-horsepower engines available to rent, and there is dock space for your own boat. Partridge will provide the bait for free.

If you're feeling lazy, get yourself some delicious hard ice cream at the adjacent Moose Alley Cones stand, and head up Route 3 a couple of miles to what is called "Moose Alley," a prime area for moose viewing. (The ice cream is for humans, not moose.) Then drive just a mile into Canada on Route 3 to the bottom of the hill. Drive another half mile and turn around so that you are by the sign (in French) that has instructions "1, 2, 3." Put the car in neutral, and you will be pulled backwards up Magnetic Hill.

The cabins are furnished in a simple, comfortable style, and you'll likely hear the loons calling on the lake or the peepers singing as you fall asleep, dreaming of riding moose, grilling legendary fish, and relaxing next to loaded blueberry bushes.

Facilities: There are seven older cabins, plus two new ones: Moose and Loon. The cabins accommodate 4–8 people. Boat rental with motor is $50 daily or $250 weekly. Canoes are $20 per day.

Bedding: Bedding is provided.

Reservations and rates: Cabins range $92–160 per night for double occupancy. Additional adults are $45; kids aged 2–12 are $28. Weekly rates are possible. Dogs are accepted in summer only, for a $10-per-day fee.

Directions: From Boston, take I-93 north and drive through Franconia Notch. Take Exit 35 to Route 3 north and drive through Pittsburg to the shores of First Connecticut Lake. Follow the signs to Partridge Cabins by Moose Alley Cones.

Contact: Jerry and Cathy Boutin, **Partridge Cabins**, R.R. #1, Box 57, Pittsburg, NH 03592, 603/538-6380, website: www.partridgecabins.com.

6. PHILLIPS BROOK BACKCOUNTRY RECREATION AREA

near Stark

Luxury rating: ★☆☆☆☆   **Recreation rating:** ★★★★★

Rank: Top 10 for Biking, Top 10 for Backcountry Winter Adventures

From the exhilaration of mountain biking through the spectacular fall foliage, to seeing a moose ramble past your outhouse, to skiing by moonlight in the wilderness, there's nothing quite like Phillips Brook Backcountry Recreation Area. Not only do you not have to pack in a tent, but you have a woodstove waiting for you.

Timberland Trails has been experimenting for some years now with leasing land from paper companies and the like as part of the sustainability of the forest and to provide low-cost backcountry recreation opportunities. Here in the Phillips Brook area, there is a base-camp lodge with yurts spread out throughout the hills. They range from car-accessible locations to four-mile uphill treks to backcountry skiing areas.

© BETHANY ERICSON

Located north of the White Mountains, the lodge overlooks Phillips Pond, where you can canoe, swim, or fish. The lodge offers a number of rooms, or you can use this as your launching pad to set off skiing, hiking, or biking to one of the remote yurts. A yurt near Dixville Notch has some accessibility by chairlift. You can also visit or spend the night in the Whitcomb Mountain Firetower. Dogsled races take place in the Phillips Brook area, and you may see teams periodically mushing past your yurt.

Phillips Brook is also the only hut-to-hut mountain biking and backcountry skiing system on the East Coast. Yurts, by the way, are Mongolian-style canvas-walled platform tents. Here they include woodstoves, Coleman-style stove tops, some pots and pans, and firewood. The trail system is made up of currently inactive logging roads, and the boundaries and exact locations of some yurts may change as land-leasing arrangements change.

Facilities: The yurts each sleep six in three bunk beds. The fire tower sleeps two people. Guides for mushing, mountain biking, and more are recommended on the Phillips Brook website.

Bedding: Bring your own bedding.

Reservations and rates: Exclusive use of a yurt is $145 per night, or $32 for the firetower.

Directions: From Boston, take I-93 north to Exit 35 (Twin Mount), and continue driving on Route 3 to Route 110 (Groveton, NH). Follow Route 110 and drive for about 11 miles to Paris Road. Turn left on Paris Road. Drive for about 3.2 miles to the office. Register here, and pick up maps and arrival packets.

Contact: The Paris Office is at 736 Paris Road, Dummer, NH; to contact **Phillips Brook Backcountry Recreation Area**: c/o Timberland Trails, Inc., P.O. Box 1076, Conway, NH 03818, 603/449-9900 or 800/TRAILS-8, website: www.phillipsbrook.org.

7. JOSSELYN'S GETAWAYS

off Route 2 in Jefferson

Luxury rating: ★ ★ ★ ☆ ☆   **Recreation rating:** ★ ★ ★ ★ ☆

Rank: Top 10 for Hiking, Best for Skiing and Snowmobiling, Top 10 Most Unusual

---

These are absolutely cozy, handcrafted log cabins built with style and whimsy. The Josselyns build log cabins as a business, and we're fortunate that they also rent eight different roomy, private cabins in the woods—right in the heart of hiking and snowmobiling activity in the White Mountains.

The log cabins also are full of unique, handcrafted wood furniture, from hat racks to thick wood-slab counters to unique uses of burls and sticks. The bathrooms have shower stalls and are clean. There are braided rugs on the floors. Some units have queen beds. Many of the cabins have decks or balconies.

Each cabin has a separate theme, from fishing to logging to a festive (but not overly cute) Christmas cabin (Jackson is also home to Santa's Village). The Workshop cabin is especially spacious. All have fireplaces, televisions with VCRs, radios, and telephones. There are kitchens and kitchenettes, and all have cookware, microwave, coffeemakers, and gas grills.

There are an astounding number of trails to hike on in the White Mountains, and Jackson is close to the Presidential Range. Corridor 5 is the main trail to connect to by snowmobile. You can rent your own sleds in Twin Mountain. There are lakes nearby and state parks for swimming. There is plenty of fishing and boating in the Connecticut and Israel Rivers.

It's very quiet here, just off of Route 2. The cabins are spread far apart from each other; many are hidden back in the woods. The logs these cabins were built from, mainly red spruce and white cedar, were all harvested in the area.

© BETHANY ERICSON

Facilities: There are eight cabins accommodating 2–10 people. Firewood is provided. You can use the wide variety of videos at the office for free.

Bedding: Bedding is provided.

Reservations and rates: Rates range $65–195 a night, and $390–1,170 weekly. Children under 18 with an adult stay for free. Josselyn's sees many repeat visitors; call up to a year ahead for reservations. Open year-round. Credit cards are not accepted. Pets are permitted.

Directions: Take I-93 north to Route 3 north to Twin Mountain. Turn right on Route 115 at a blinking light. Bear left onto Route 115A, turn left again on Route 2, and turn right onto North Road. (If you pass Santa's Village on the left, you've gone too far.) Josselyn's will be .5 mile down on the left on North Road.

Contact: Keith and Helene Josselyn, Josselyn's Sawmill, Inc. Log Homes and Lumber **(Josselyn's Getaways)**, 306 North Road Jefferson, NH 03583, 800/586-4507, website: www.josselyns.com.

8. MIRROR LAKE MOTEL AND COTTAGES

on Mirror Lake

Luxury rating: ★★☆☆☆   **Recreation rating:** ★★★★★

The three cabins at Mirror Lake Motel are favorites with anglers. The newest of the three is a knotty-pine cabin built in 1990; it's also popular with couples due to its whirlpool tub and fireplace. The other two cabins were built in the 1940s or 1950s and are more rustic, fishing cabins.

All of the cabins have kitchenettes with stovetops (but not ovens), small refrigerators, and basic pots and pans. There is also a restaurant located next door. All have cable television and older furniture. The two older units have bathrooms with shower stalls. There are picnic tables outside.

There is a beach for swimming in the 49-acre lake, and there are row-

boats and a dock. The fishing here is mainly for trout: brook, rainbow, and brown. There are also largemouth bass, pickerel, and horned pout in the lake. Call regarding the current regulations for ice fishing. There's a swing set and shuffleboard on-site and golf and tennis in the area.

Whitefield is a picturesque

© BETHANY ERICSON

New England town with great mountain views of the Presidential Range to the east, Lafayete and Cannon Mountains to the south, the Green Mountains of Vermont to the west, and the Kilkenny Range to the north.

Facilities: There are three cottages, each accommodating 2–4 people.

Bedding: Bedding is provided.

Reservations and rates: Rates range $45–110. Call two to three weeks ahead of your stay or three months ahead for Valentine's Day (there aren't a lot of whirlpool tubs in the area). The older units are rented long term in the winter. Open year-round. Pets are permitted.

Directions: Mirror Lake Motel and Cottages are located right on Route 3 in Whitefield.

Contact: Mirror Lake Motel and Cottages, Route 3, Whitefield NH 03598, 603/837-2544.

9. BAKER BROOK MOTEL & COTTAGES

on Route 302 in Bethlehem

Luxury rating: ★ ★ ☆ ☆ ☆   **Recreation rating:** ★ ★ ★ ★ ★

© BETHANY ERICSON

This unassuming colony is made up of somewhat rustic cabins spread out over 188 acres by Baker Brook Lake. Though generally basic accommodations, the cabins are kept clean, and most have stone fireplaces. Some have full kitchens; others have microwaves and coffeemakers. They are suitable for hunters or no-frills travelers, yet if these cabins could talk, you'd hear an interesting history of the area.

In the late 1800s, Bethlehem was a booming tourist town full of hotels, with frequent trains from Boston and New York. Then came the era of cars, which meant that those destinations previously reached by train now attracted fewer tourists. Bethlehem became a draw for Jewish families from New York, as it was considered a hay fever–free destination. By the 1920s, the Jewish community had grown and kept the hotels full.

In the mid-1900s, cottage colonies like Baker Brook became popular resorts, with nightly entertainment, restaurants, and efficient systems for survival. In the off season, the owner here would drain the lake and plant potatoes, or fill the lake and block ice to sell to motels. There were two pools and a tramway to ski at Aggasiz.

Today, cottages and hotels and kosher restaurants in the area are still filled with a community of traditionally dressed Hasidic Jews every July and August. And the Baker Brook cabins, having been in a bit of a decline, are slowly returning to their former glory with some tender loving care from the current managers.

The lake offers fishing for pickerel and horned pout, and one of two swimming pools is operational and is heated. There is also a communal lodge with a fireplace in winter and a five-person hot tub. In summer, this is a place to connect with the Jewish community and to hike. In winter, this is a skiing and snowmobiling destination, with trails right from the property.

Facilities: There are 25 cabins, 12 of them winterized. They hold 2–11 people.

Bedding: Bedding and towels are provided.

Reservations and rates: Rates range $49–110 per night. If you pay for six nights, the seventh night is free. Kids under 15 are free (call for youth-group rates). Reservations are taken for the summer beginning in January. July and August are the busiest months. Dogs are permitted in certain cabins.

Directions: Baker Brook is located 15 minutes north of Cannon Mountain and Franconia Notch. Drive on I-93 to Exit 40, and head east to Bethlehem on Route 302 (Main Street). Drive for about one mile, and the cabins will be on your left.

Contact: Don and Peggy Butler, **Barker Brook**, 1108 Main Street (Route 302), Bethlehem, NH 03574, 603/444-2147, website: www.bakerbrookcabins.com.

10. BOULDER MOTOR COURT

near Bretton Woods

Luxury rating: ★★☆☆☆   **Recreation rating:** ★★★★★

Snowy winters bring the majority of visitors to Boulder Motor Court. The big draws here are skiing at Bretton Woods, snowmobiling, and hiking—particularly during the spectacular fall foliage. There is so much to do in the White Mountains that your cottage will likely be more of a place to crash at night than a destination in itself.

The interiors of the cottages are kept clean. These are fairly basic lodgings with older, mismatched furniture. Some have wood paneling, while others are wallpapered. They all have fully equipped kitchens. Some have good mountain views, porches, or grills. Five of the cottages have fireplaces. All of

© BETHANY ERICSON

the units are heated, with shower-stall bathrooms and cable television.

Directly from its door, Mount Washington Snowmobile Tours runs trips in conjunction with Boulder for all levels of riders. The tours take you for rides of 20 miles or more on two-seater sleds over trails through the woods with great mountain views. Five miles down Route 302, Bretton Woods is a great family-oriented ski area. Ask about discounts at the Boulder office. Cannon Mountain has some advanced skiing terrain just 10 miles away.

In the summer and fall, the White Mountains attract hikers to a wide range of trails. Boulder Motor Court is located between gorgeous hiking areas in Franconia Notch and Crawford Notch. There is also a great deal of trout fishing in the area and any number of scenic drives. Motorcyclists in the area for the Laconia Bike Week rally will receive a discount.

Facilities: There are 10 cottages with one and two bedrooms that accommodate 2–6 people. No pets are permitted.

Bedding: Bedding is provided.

Reservations and rates: Spring and summer rates range $40–120 per night and $220–375 per week. Summer and winter rates range $65–135 per night, $325–650 per week. Monthly rentals in the summer range $850–875, and four-month winter season rentals run about $3,400. Maximum occupancy rates apply, depending on the size of the cottage.

Directions: From the south, take I-93 north to Route 3 to Twin Mountain. Drive on Route 302 East. Boulder Motor Court will be on your left, just past the intersection.

Contact: Boulder Motor Court, Route 302, East of Junction Route 3, Twin Mountain, NH 03595, 866/846-5437 or 603/846-5437, website: www.bouldermotorcourt.com.

11. CARROLL MOTEL AND COTTAGES

Twin Mountain

Luxury rating: ★★☆☆☆   Recreation rating: ★★★★☆

Rank: Best for Skiing and Snowmobiling

Twin Mountain is a popular spot to stay while hiking in the White Mountain National Forest. In winter, it's a popular spot for snowmobiling and skiing. Carroll Motel and Cottages has very large cottages for the area, and many of them are winterized. They are clean, cozy, and have character.

The cottages have heating but do not have fireplaces. They are charmingly decorated, with paneling, folk art, and whimsical New England–themed borders on the walls. The beds have nice quilts with outdoor motifs. The furniture is circa 1940s, but it is in great condition. Some of the cottages have screened porches, and many have picnic tables.

In the summer there is volleyball, horseshoe pits, a playground, and a heated pool with a slide, as well as weekend campfires. People tend to gather around and mingle. There are hikers, anglers, couples, and city apartment–renters looking to have their own separate house for once. In winter, there tend to be fewer families and more couples.

Close by, there is skiing at Cannon and Bretton Woods. There is access to local and state snowmobile trails right from your door, and snowmobile tours can be arranged. There are also numerous snowmobiling and winter hiking options.

Facilities: There are 12 cottages that have undergone extensive renovations in recent years. They can accommodate 2–5 people. Restaurants are a short drive away, general stores are within walking distance, and there is a gas station across the street.

Bedding: Bedding and towels are provided.

Reservations and rates: Rates range $47–140 per night for four people. There is a two-night minimum. Call three to four weeks in advance for reservations.

12. TARRY HO CAMPGROUND AND COTTAGES

on Ammonoosuc River

Luxury rating: ★ ★ ☆ ☆ ☆   **Recreation rating:** ★ ★ ★ ★ ★

This campground in Twin Mountain gets its friendly atmosphere partly from its welcoming owners, Josephine and Robert Dean. It has five spacious, winterized, housekeeping cottages and three more basic summer cottages.

The five winterized cottages are exceptionally clean, with older furniture and decor that results in an almost kitschy, retro 1940s or 1950s effect. Imagine pastel blue-and-white kitchens and nubbly-cushioned wooden furniture.

Cottage 8 is the most spacious, although there can be noise from the road. Cottage 5 has a fabulous view of Mount Washington from the deck. All of the cottages have cable television and porches; most have kitchens. They have bathrooms with shower stalls.

The cottages are near the entrance to the campsite, around two sides of a central lawn sports, playground, and swimming pool area. There is access to the rocky Ammonoosuc River, and Tarry Ho provides free inner tubes (the less you weigh, the more fun tubing is here). The river is stocked, and guests often fish right from the campsite shores.

In winter, this is a popular spot for snowmobiling and downhill and cross-country skiing. You can snowmobile right from your cottage. Bretton Woods is only five minutes away for skiing; be sure to inquire at the office about discount tickets. Sometimes there is also an outdoor ice rink at the campground. In summer, there is all the great hiking of the White Mountain National Forest nearby.

Facilities: There are eight cottages; five are winterized. The cottages have 1–3 bedrooms and accommodate 2–6 people. The camp store sells snacks, ice, firewood, and basic necessities. There are nearby restaurants, as well as a larger variety in Littleton, 20 minutes away.

Bedding: Bedding and towels are provided.

Reservations and rates: The cottage rates range $44–87. Call early for holiday reservations. Open year-round. Dogs are permitted with no fee but must be leashed and picked up after.

Directions: From Boston, take I-93 north to Exit 35 (Route 3 north). Drive nine miles on Route 3 north to Route 302. Turn left (west) at the light, drive .7 mile, and the campground will be on the left.

Contact: Tarry Ho Campground and Cottages, P.O. Box 369, Route 302 West, Twin Mountain, NH 03595, 603/846-5577, website: www.tarryho.com.

13. TWIN RIVER CAMPGROUND

at the junction of Routes 302 and 112

Luxury rating: ★★☆☆☆   **Recreation rating:** ★★★★★

On the Ammonoosuc and Wild Ammonoosuc Rivers, the Twin River Campground is convenient both to locations in Vermont and to the White Mountains in New Hampshire. Best of all, the cottage rentals are on a recreational trail for horseback riding, cycling, four-wheeling, and snowmobiling. There is a heated pool, and in the summer you can go

© BETHANY ERICSON

tubing and swimming in the rivers or canoeing in the nearby Connecticut River.

Kids love the fun of panning for gold in the Wild Ammonoosuc River. Prospecting supplies are sold in the campground store. One result of an ancient history of volcanic activity in this area is that there's enough gold in the streams and floodplains that you just might still find a flake or nugget.

The area has its share of charm. The Bath General Store is said to be the oldest-operating general store in the country. Next door, the gift shop was once where Morrison's English Liniment and Lady Poor's Ointment were made. Meanwhile, the Bath Covered Bridge is the longest covered bridge in the state, and the Bath/Haverhill Covered Bridge is said to be the oldest covered bridge in the country. There even is a third picturesque covered bridge, and there's more near-extinct fun—like a drive-in movie theater.

The housekeeping cottages are small and white, with fireplaces and little porches. They have one or two double beds and a living room. Cottage 5 has a glass door that goes onto a patio. Cottage 4 has a larger porch with a table and chairs. They all have picnic tables, televisions and VCRs, microwaves, coffeemakers, and small refrigerators. Those with kitchens have some pots, pans, and dishes. The Riverside Rustic Cabins have one room with a double bed and set of bunk beds, and a porch with chairs overlooking the Wild Ammonoosuc River.

The campground is within a short drive of the great hiking opportunities in the White Mountains National Forest. There is also plenty of good trout fishing and golf in the area. On-site, there are many planned kids' activities, like ice-cream socials or ceramics. There are horseshoes, a basketball court, and a recreation room with video games, a pool table, and air hockey.

Facilities: Only match-light logs are allowed in the fireplaces, and they are sold at the camp store. Children aged 13 and under must be accompanied by an adult to be in the pool.

Bedding: Bedding and towels are provided in the cottages, but not in the Riverside Rustic Cabins. All guests should bring their own pool towels.

Reservations and rates: Riverside Rustic Cabins are $45 per night. Cottages are $60–80 per night. Weekly, monthly, and seasonal rates are available. There is a visitor fee of $3 per day (all visitors must check in). All Rates are based on four people per night, except Cottage 3, which is for two people. Rates are lower prior to Memorial Day and after Labor Day. There is a AAA discount. Open year-round. There is a maximum of two dogs per site, and certain breeds are banned from the campground. All dogs must be leashed and accompanied at all times, and there is a small fee. Ask when making reservations.

Directions: From NH, take I-93 to Exit 32, Lincoln, then drive for 21 miles on Route 112 east.

Contact: Twin River Campground & Cottages, P.O. Box 212, Route 302 & 112, Bath, NH 03740, 603/747-3640 or 800/811-1040, website: www.ucampnh .com/twinriver.

14. COZY CABINS
brookside in Lincoln

Luxury rating: ★ ★ ☆ ☆ ☆   **Recreation rating:** ★ ★ ★ ★ ☆

Cozy Cabins is fairly rustic, affordable lodging for non-camping outdoors people. Those who come to enjoy hiking and mountain biking in Franconia Notch and grilling on an outdoor fireplace, but prefer a private bath and potentially money-saving cooking options will like this place. These cabins are by a  brook on Route 3, near the famous Clark's Trading Post, with its trained black bears.

It's a very short drive from here to the great trails of the White Mountains. You can challenge yourself on Mount Lafayette or Mount Lincoln, or drive over to climb Mount Washington. You're in the center of the original tourist destinations created in Franconia Notch too. There are guided walks through The Flume and plenty of motor rides through the scenic areas.

The Kancamagus Highway is a stunning route for a scenic drive, and trailheads for many fantastic hikes dot the edges of the road. Even on a short hike to a waterfall or a drive around the area, be sure to bring your camera. Deer, moose, and bear are not uncommon neighbors here.

The White Mountains are very accessible to people of all ages and abilities. A tramway brings visitors up to the top of Cannon Mountain, a cog railway chugs to the top of Mount Washington, and there are charming railroad rides through the scenery (dinner included). Kids are particularly fond of Story Land in Glen, and the Whale's Tale Amusement Park.

The cabins here are basic. There are two sizes of two-bedroom cabins, as well as one-bedroom units with kitchens. There are also units with two double beds and no kitchen, and one bedroom and no kitchen. They have paneling and cheap comforters, cable television, screened porches, and a very convenient location.

Facilities: There are nine rustic cabins with one and two bedrooms. One vehicle is allowed per unit.

Bedding: Linens are provided.

Reservations and rates: Rates range $49–92 per day. Holidays and special events have a three-day minimum, and the fourth night is free in May and June. Weekly discount rates are available, and seventh-night free deals may be found on the website. Open May–October. No visitors or pets are permitted.

Directions: From I-93 in Lincoln, take Exit 33, and drive south for .5 mile on Route 3 to Cozy Cabins.

Contact: Cozy Cabins, U.S. Route 3, Lincoln, NH 03251, 603/745-8713, website: www.cozycabins.com.

15. DRUMMER BOY MOTOR INN

on Route 3 in Lincoln

Luxury rating: ★★★☆☆   **Recreation rating:** ★★★★★

© BETHANY ERICSON

Drummer Boy Motor Inn is an above-average motel with all the amenities. The two-bedroom cottages and four-bedroom house that are offered are very clean and pleasant places to stay in the White Mountains. Best of all, the motel offers a heated pool, a hot tub, and a sauna room for post-activity relaxing.

The motel is just minutes from Attitash Bear Peak. In the summer, Attitash offers water and alpine slides, and chairlift rides for mountain bikers. There are horseback rides and a driving range. In the winter it is a fabulous family-oriented ski resort.

You are also minutes from fantastic hiking and biking in the White Mountain National Park. If you're unfamiliar with the area, Drummer Boy will arrange hiking tours, like a trip up Cannon by tramway with a hike to Lonesome Lake and down again to the Lafayette Campground. Nearby, there is a bike path by Echo Lake, and the motel can arrange mountain biking tours and rentals.

Drummer Boy arranges kayaking, rock- and ice-climbing, snowshoeing, and ski touring trips (all with a local outfitter), and offers golf, spa, dinner, romance and seasonal packages. They have an exercise room, a game room, a play and picnic area, and free breakfast.

Facilities: There are two two-bedroom cottages accommodating 2–4 people and one four-bedroom house accommodating eight. Laundry facilities are on-site.

Bedding: Bedding is provided.

Reservations and rates: The rates for the two-bedroom cottages range $99–129, and the rates for the four-bedroom house range $199–249. Open year-round. Pets are not permitted.

Directions: From I-93 in Lincoln, drive east on Route 3. The Drummer Boy will be on your left after just a block or two.

Contact: Drummer Boy Motor Inn, Route 3, Lincoln, NH 03251, 603/745-3661 or 800/762-7275, website: www.drummerboymotorinn.com.

16. MT. LIBERTY MOTEL AND CABINS

on Pemigewasset River in Lincoln

Luxury rating: ★★☆☆☆   **Recreation rating:** ★★★★☆

Mt. Liberty Motel and Cabins is located directly on Pemigewasset River. Pemigewasset is said to come from the Abenaki tribe's word for "swift water," *Pamijowasik*. Nearby Mount Pemigewasset is said to be named after an Abenaki leader of that name, and bears a silhouette in its cliffs known as the Indian Head, which prompts the odd signs for "Indian Head Viewing" in Franconia Notch State Park.

The river is a scenic treasure in New Hampshire, with its headwaters not far from the cabins at Profile Lake in Franconia Notch. You can swim and fish for trout near the cabins. Atlantic salmon are being restored to the river as well. The only public-access spots for boating are a bit south of Lincoln, in Plymouth and Bristol, but there are canoe and kayak outfitters in the area.

The cabins have great views toward the mountains, and some are named after Appalachian Mountain Club huts, which may inspire you to tie up your hiking boots. Franconia Notch is a phenomenal area for hiking and backpacking. There are also numerous areas for mountain biking, and a number of easy walks.

There is an outdoor, heated pool. The cabins themselves are in the shade and are about a car-space apart from each other. They have cable television and heat, but no air-conditioning. The kitchenettes are small, with a toaster, a two-burner cooktop, and a small refrigerator. There is a gas grill for guest use, and you are welcome to bring your own. Most of the units have screened porches.

Facilities: There are eight cabins accommodating 1–5 people.

Bedding: Linens are provided.

Reservations and rates: Rates range $50-95 per night. There are two night minimums on weekends, holidays, special events, and during foliage season. Weekly rates are the price of six nights. Open May–October. No pets are permitted.

Directions: Take Exit 32 off I-93. Drive west on Route 112 to Route 3. Turn south on Route 3. The cabins will be on your left.

Contact: Mt. Liberty Motel and Cabins, Liberty Road, P.O. Box 422, Lincoln, NH 03251, 603/745-3600 or 888/247-5212, website: www.musar.com/mtlibertymotel.

17. COUNTRY BUMPKINS FAMILY CAMPGROUND & CABINS

on Route 3 in Lincoln

Luxury rating: ★ ★ ☆ ☆ ☆   **Recreation rating:** ★ ★ ★ ★ ☆

This campground is just half a mile south of Clark's Trading Post, with its locally famous trained bears. Country Bumpkins has six cabins, three of which are located on Bog Brook. Ask for one off the road. The campground is also situated along the Pemigewasset River and has a duck pond with a deck. Wading and fishing are encouraged.

© BETHANY ERICSON

Most of the cabins have a sitting area with cable television, a bathroom with a shower stall, heating, a fully equipped kitchen (with oven) or kitchenette (burners only), a picnic table and campfire ring, and access to the river. Most have a screened-in porch.

Cabin 2 has a deck with a table overlooking the brook, a small refrigerator, and a microwave, but no other cooking facilities. Cabin 3 is closest to the playground. Cabin 4 has two floors. The campground has a camp store, ice, and firewood. There is a playground with swings and a sandbox, an arcade, and free morning coffee and muffins on weekends and holidays. There are numerous activities on-site, most notably pumpkin carving in the fall.

Lincoln is near Franconia Notch State Park, a beautiful part of the White Mountains National Forest. There are endless trails to hike and mountain bike in this area. There are also lots of guided walks through places like The Flume. Nearby, the tramway will take you to the top of Cannon Mountain.

There is trout fishing in the Pemi (and the campground duck pond, for that matter), as well as in streams and ponds across the White Mountains. White-water kayaking, canoeing, and biking on the paved bike path are also popular.

Facilities: There are six cabins, three on the brook. They all accommodate two adults, and some have additional room for one or two children.

Bedding: Bedding and linens provided.

Reservations and rates: Rates range $55–95 per night and $330–570 per week. Call in January for reservations. Open early April–November. One small (less than 30 lbs) dog is permitted (except Cabin 2, where no pets are allowed).

Directions: From I-93 north, take Exit 33. Turn left off the exit onto Route 3 south. Drive .5 mile, and the campground is on your left.

Contact: Country Bumpkins Family Campground & Cabins, Route 3, Box 83, Lincoln, NH 03251, 603/745-8837, website: www.countrybumpkins.com.

18. WHITE MOUNTAIN MOTEL AND COTTAGES

next to Clark's Trading Post

Luxury rating: ★★★☆☆   **Recreation rating:** ★★★★☆

This is a fun place to stay with the kids. The Hughes family has been running this motel and four cottages for more than 25 years. The cottages are above the banks of the pretty Pemigewasset River. The property is also directly next to Clark's Trading Post, a long-time favorite tourist stop.

At Clark's, you and your kids may get a kick out of the trained bear shows. Also popular at Clark's is a 30-minute train ride on one of only three wood-burning steam Climax Locomotives still running. The

© BETHANY ERICSON

tracks wend through the woods and cross the Pemigewasset on a historic covered bridge.

Cottage 1 has the best view. From under the quilt on your queen bed, you look across toward the only standing Howe-Truss covered bridge still in use today. It was transported to this location from East Montpelier in the 1960s. The kitchenette in Cottage 1 also has a picture window. The only other cottage with cooking facilities is Cottage 4, which has a microwave and refrigerator. Cottage 3 has a screened porch where you can hear, but not see, the river.

In Lincoln, you are of course near Franconia Notch, a wonderful place to hike and ski in the White Mountain National Forest. There are also mountain biking trails and a 10-mile paved bike path. There is fishing in the area for trout, as well as kayak and canoe outfitters. Loon Mountain is a family ski area just three miles away, and Cannon, with some slightly more technical trails, is seven miles away. And when you return to your cottage, you'll have a heated pool to enjoy at your leisure.

Facilities: There are four cottages accommodating 2–4 people.

Bedding: Linens are provided.

Reservations and rates: Cottages range $50–85 per night.

Directions: Take I-93 to Exit 33. Turn left at the exit onto Route 3, toward Clark's Trading Post. Drive .8 mile, and the cottages will be on the left.

Contact: White Mountain Motel and Cottages, Daniel Webster Highway, Lincoln, NH 03251, 603/745-8924, website: www.whitemountainmotel.com.

19. WILDERNESS INN AND CAFÉ

on Lost River in North Woodstock

Luxury rating: ★ ★ ★ ★ ☆   **Recreation rating:** ★ ★ ★ ★ ☆

Rank: Top 10 for Hiking, Best for Skiing and Snowmobiling

© BETHANY ERICSON

The green-shingled Wilderness Inn in North Woodstock has a very cute little green honeymoon cottage behind it, with a lovely deck over Lost River. Despite its wonderful New England setting, it's called the Caribbean Cottage because of the photos that decorate the walls. The cabin feels airy due to the white walls and white queen sleigh bed. The walls are stenciled, and the cottage has a wood floor with throw rugs. There is cable television, air-conditioning, a gas fireplace, a refrigerator, and a whirlpool tub.

Skiing at Loon Mountain (three miles away) and Cannon Mountain (eight miles away) are popular activities for guests here. Waterville Valley and Bretton Woods are also not too far of a drive. There is cross-country skiing, tubing, skating, snowshoeing, and more.

Swimming, canoeing, and white-water kayaking are all possible in this area. The inn and cottage are located near Franconia Notch, which is part of the grand White Mountains National Forest. This area offers endless trails for hiking and mountain biking.

You'll want to make sure you're active all day after a breakfast at the Wilderness Inn. Sitting by the fireplace or on the enclosed sun porch, you'll have your choice of at least 11 flavors of pancakes, crepes, or French toast with a variety of fruit syrups. There are eggs, omelets, home-baked muffins, and more.

Facilities: There is one cottage meant for a couple. Restaurants in town are within walking distance.
Bedding: Linens are provided.

Reservations and rates: The rates range $105–155. Pets and smoking are not permitted.

Directions: Take Exit 32 off I-93. Drive west on Route 112 to Route 3. Turn south on Route 3. The Wilderness Inn is one block south on the right.

Contact: Rosanna and Michael Yarnell, **Wilderness Inn and Café**, Route 3, North Woodstock, NH 03262, 603/745-3890, 800/200-9453, or 888/777-7813, web-site: www.thewildernessinn.com.

20. THREE RIVERS HOUSE

Woodstock

Luxury rating: ★ ★ ★ ☆ ☆   **Recreation rating:** ★ ★ ★ ★ ☆

© BETHANY ERICSO

Three Rivers House is an impressive inn and dates from the late 19th century.

Today, the inn is as lovely as ever, and tucked back behind this reminder of bygone days is an excellent hideaway cottage overlooking Lost River.

The cottage has an airy feel, with a beamed cathedral ceiling in the living room and sliding glass doors to the deck right over the river. There is a fireplace and cable television. There are two bedrooms, one with a king-sized bed (rarely found in cottages) and one with a double bed. There is a kitchen, and a full breakfast is provided in the inn.

The inn is located at the entrance to the Kancamagus Highway, which is beautiful to drive along. Nearby are numerous trailheads to the mountaintops.

The innkeeper, Brian Crete, likes to send people to the Sabbaday Brook Trail, an easy hike with a big payoff. (Bring a picnic to eat by refreshing Sabbaday Falls).

The cottage is located close to Loon Mountain and Cannon Mountain ski resorts. Loon offers a family atmosphere and tubing, as well as skiing and many summer activities. Cannon runs its tramway in the summer, affording a very easy route to the views at the summit.

Lost River is stocked, and it's possible to fish right from the property at the inn. You can swim in the area, and there are canoe rentals and white-water kayaking outfitters.

Facilities: There is one cottage that accommodates four people. There are laundry facilities within half a mile. There are numerous restaurants in Woodstock.

Bedding: Bedding is provided.

Reservations and rates: Rates range $155–175 per night and $900 per week for double occupancy. Rates for extra adults range $25–35. The charge for bringing extra children is $15. Rates include a full breakfast. No pets are permitted.

Directions: From I-93 north or south, take Exit 32. Turn right onto Route 112. Turn left at the traffic lights onto Route 3. Drive .2 mile, and Three Rivers House is on the right.

Contact: Three Rivers House, R.R. 1, Route 3, P.O. Box 72, North Woodstock, NH 03262, 603/745-2711 or 800/241-2711, website: www.threerivershouse.com.

Other Cabins and Cottages Nearby

- Lost River Valley Campground, 951 Lost River Road, North Woodstock, NH 03262, 603/745-8321, website: www.lostriver.com.

21. CHRISTMAS FARM INN

in Jackson

Luxury rating: ★ ★ ★ ★ ☆   **Recreation rating:** ★ ★ ★ ★ ★

Rank: Top 10 for Hiking, Best for Skiing and Snowmobiling, and Top 10 for Weddings

Christmas Farm Inn is an upscale collection of buildings, including the Main Inn, the Salt Box House, a barn for functions and some suites, a handful of cottages, a sugarhouse unit, and a log cabin made with logs from the property and with a remote-control fireplace. Most of the cottages have gas fireplaces and full baths.

It's a festive atmosphere, and even in the winter the Christmas theme is not completely overwhelming. Even the North Pole cabin is tasteful in its holiday decor. It is done in forest green and deep red, and there is an elegant reindeer border on the wallpaper. What you notice most is not the occasional Santa here, it's the gorgeous, sunny mountain views through the icicles on your window.

The inn has been part farm-house, part jail, and part church at various points in its history. Weddings are commonplace in the barn, which boasts huge hand-hewn beams and original mortise-and-peg joints. All in all, it's both a romantic spot and a fun spot for families.

© BETHANY ERICSON

The inn is associated with the Jackson Cross Country Ski Touring trails, and there are numerous alpine skiing options. The hiking in the area is phenomenal. You can also bike, boat, or fly fish for trout. You can swim in the Ellis River, Jackson Falls, or the on-site pool. There is also a hot tub next to the barn.

The cottages do not have cooking facilities, but breakfast and potentially dinner are included in your stay. There is a dining room and a pub. Bag lunches can be requested for an extra fee.

Facilities: There is a log cabin with two rooms, a sugarhouse that is best for couples, and five two-bedroom cottages accommodating 2–6 people. There is a fitness room for adults over 18. Laundry facilities are available.

Bedding: Bedding and towels are provided

Reservations and rates: Daily rates range $139–321 with breakfast, and $238–451 including dinner, for two people. The cottages are often booked a year ahead, particularly for Christmas. There are lots of packages available, with all kinds of extras. Open year-round. Pets are not permitted.

Directions: From Boston, take I-95 north to New Hampshire and exit to the left onto Route 16 north/Spaulding Turnpike in Portsmouth. Take Route 16 north and drive through North Conway. Stay on Route 16 in Glen, when it takes a sharp right turn north at the intersection with Route 302. When you see the Jackson Covered Bridge on your right, drive across it, and into Jackson Village on Route 16A. Where the road forks at the Jackson Grammar School, bear right onto Route 16B.

Contact: Christmas Farm Inn, P.O. Box CC, Route 16B, Jackson, NH 03846, 603/383-4313 or 800/HI-ELVES, website: www.christmasfarminn.com.

22. ELLIS RIVER HOUSE

overlooking Ellis River on Route 16

Luxury rating: ★★★★☆   **Recreation rating:** ★★★★★

Rank: Top 10 for Romance

Walk into the lobby of the Ellis River House and you'll get the idea: the plush red tones, the loveseat by the fire, the "Do Not Disturb, Romance in Progress" doorknob signs for sale. Monica and Jim Lee are the very warm and welcoming duo who run this romantic getaway (for couples only) in the middle of the mountains.

The inn has one separate cottage that was once the ice house. Wedged between the buildings that make up the inn, it is tall and narrow, and yet very private. Downstairs, there is a sitting room with a two-person whirlpool tub with mirrored edging and candles, and a view up to the forest hillsides behind the inn. There is a spiral staircase upstairs to the queen bed and fireplace.

The cottage has a refrigerator and microwave, and a grill on the patio in the summer. Breakfast is included in your stay, and it's worth venturing out of the cottage into the dining room, where you'll eat on quaint old sewing-machine tables. In the afternoons, be sure to check in the inn for cookies and cider, chili, or soup.

The infamous Jackson Cross Country Touring Foundation is within walking distance, and the most popular trail goes right behind the inn. The Ellis River Trail is also a popular hiking trail in the summer. The river is stocked with trout.

Attitash Bear Peak, Cranmore, Wildcat, and Black Mountain are nearby for alpine skiing, and hiking trails nearby travel all the way to New England's highest peak, Mount Washington. Scenic trails, like the one to Arethrusa Falls, are a short drive away. Canoeing and kayaking are popular in the Saco River. At the inn there is an outdoor heated pool open May–October and a whirlpool for six, should you tire of your two-person bath in the cottage.

Facilities: There is one cottage for two adults. Inquire about extras like flowers, fruit baskets, robes, and massages.

Bedding: Bedding and towels are provided.

Reservations and rates: Rates range $190–245. Call several months in advance for foliage season, summer, and early winter.

Directions: From Boston, take I-95 north to New Hampshire and exit by turning left onto Route 16 north/Spaulding Turnpike in Portsmouth. Follow Route 16 north and drive through North Conway. Stay on Route 16 in Glen as it takes a sharp right turn north at the intersection with Route 302. Drive for about 2.5 miles, and you'll pass the Jackson Covered Bridge on the right. At this point, look for the Ellis River House sign that will be on your left. (Ask when you call for short-cut directions to bypass the traffic in North Conway.)

Contact: Ellis River House, Route 16, P.O. Box 656, Jackson, NH 03846, 603/383-9339 or 800/233-8309, website: www.erhinn.com.

23. THE WHITNEY INN AT JACKSON

at Black Mountain

Luxury rating: ★★★☆☆   **Recreation rating:** ★★★★★

Rank: Best for Skiing and Snowmobiling

This is a dream spot for families that love to ski. These cottages are located at the base of Black Mountain, a family-oriented ski slope, and are also connected to the popular Jackson Ski Touring Trails. Come inside anytime you are tired or cold, and relax by your fireplace while still enjoying the view of the slopes.

© BETHANY ERICSON

Black Mountain has been in operation for 67 years. It has been kept small on purpose to retain a relaxed atmosphere with no big lift lines. Carter Notch protects it from the wind, and its southern exposure keeps the trails 5–8 degrees warmer than other nearby slopes.

The Whitney Inn is located at the base of the mountain, with the cottages off to the side. The cottages are basic two-bedroom units with a living room. They have a television, VCR, and serviceable couch. The cabins do not have phones. There are microwaves, coffeemakers, and minirefrigerators, but no cooking facilities. There is a full-service cafeteria at the base of Black Mountain, and The Grill Room restaurant is in the inn.

There is canoeing and kayaking in the Saco River nearby, and the inn has an outdoor pool and a hot tub. The White Mountain National Forest offers a dazzling array of mountains to climb, and there are mountain biking trails, fly-fishing, and golfing areas nearby.

Facilities: There are two cottages, each accommodating two adults and two children.

Bedding: Bedding is provided.

Reservations and rates: Rates range $155–255 per night.

Directions: From Boston, take I-95 north to New Hampshire and turn left at the exit onto Route 16 north/Spaulding Turnpike in Portsmouth. Follow Route 16 north and drive through North Conway. Stay on Route 16 in Glen when it takes a sharp right turn north at the intersection with Route 302. When you see the Jackson Covered Bridge on your right, drive across it, and join Route 16A, which takes you into Jackson Village. Where the road forks at the Jackson Grammar School, bear right onto Route 16B. Follow the road up the hill until you see the inn, at the base of Black Mountain.

Contact: The Whitney Inn, 5 Mile Circuit Road, Route 16B, Jackson, NH 03846, 800/677-5737, website: www.thewhitneyinn.com.

24. THE BARTLETT INN

Jackson

Luxury rating: ★★★☆☆   **Recreation rating:** ★★★★★

The Bartlett Inn is close enough to all of the activities in the Mount Washington valley, and yet far enough away from the crowds to be truly relaxing. Miriam Habert and Nick Jaques took over the inn early in 2003. They have continued a tradition of fine breakfasts and relaxed atmosphere. "There's no pressure to behave," laughs Nick, "no requirement to remove your shoes upon entering."

The inn is located right on the 37 miles of groomed Bear Notch Touring Center cross-country ski trails, and it is two miles from Attitash Bear Peak, New Hampshire's largest alpine ski area. Fabulous hiking is 10 minutes away in Crawford Notch State Park, and you can walk right from your door into the national forest and along the Saco River.

There is a strip of units here that are referred to as cottages, but they are more like cottage townhouses. They are connected multiroom units that have fireplaces and kitchenettes. There is a duplex cottage where extended families or friends traveling together can rent both halves. The studio is a standalone one-room unit closer to the road, with a double bed and a sofa bed, a deck, and a kitchenette.

The Bartlett Inn is 12 miles from North Conway. It's close enough to easily get to the family destinations like Story Land, dining options, and outlet shopping, but far enough away to feel more like a mountain getaway. It's the kind of place where the kettle is always on, and guests may start jamming on musical instruments together in the sitting room after a day of skiing, hiking, or rock climbing.

Facilities: Alongside the inn there is one separate studio cottage, an easily shared duplex cottage, and a strip of seven rooms set up like cottages with gas or log fireplaces that can sleep 2–5 people. All of the units have air conditioning, but none have telephones.

Bedding: Linens and towels are provided.

Reservations and rates: Rates range $89–155 per night. Book a year ahead for major holidays and school vacation weeks. Open year-round. Pets are welcome, but smoking is not.

Directions: In the summer, take I-93 north to Exit 32. Drive for 25 miles along the Kancamagus Highway east (Route 112). Turn left onto Bear Notch Road (closed in winter). Drive for nine miles on Bear Notch Road to Bartlett. Turn left at the blinking light onto Route 302 west. The Bartlett Inn is located one mile from the blinking light on the left (south) side of Route 302.

In the winter, follow I-93 north to Exit 35. Take Route 3 north to the junction of Route 302 (traffic light). Turn right at the light onto Route 302 east. Drive for 25 miles along Route 302. The inn is on the right. If you come to the blinking light in Bartlett Village, you've gone too far. Turn back one mile.

Contact: The Bartlett Inn, Route 302, P.O. Box 327, Bartlett, NH 03812, 603/374-2547 or 800/292-2353, website: www.bartlettinn.com.

25. SKY VALLEY MOTEL & COTTAGES

on Saco River by Attitash Bear Peak

Luxury rating: ★ ★ ☆ ☆ ☆   **Recreation rating:** ★ ★ ★ ★ ★

Rank: Best for Skiing and Snowmobiling

Sky Valley was started as a 1950s-style motor lodge with cottages that once stood out because it offered radios and electric blankets. Today, it has a unique location, with a beach on the Saco River and the Attitash Bear Peak Resort across the street.

© BETHANY ERICSON

This setting means that in summer there are alpine and water slides across the street, and in winter you can rent a cottage for the whole season and keep your winter gear and your food just steps from 70 trails of skiing and riding on the two connected mountains.

The cottages are simple fare: clean, functional, two- and three-bedroom units offering fully equipped kitchens, fans, heat, telephones, and televisions. They are wood-sided hideaways scattered throughout the 35 acres of wooded property far back from the noise of the highway. Loud parties are not tolerated.

Chalet 3 has two floors with excellent views of Bear Mountain, Mount Tremont, and Mount Carrigain. It has a fireplace, a washer and dryer, and a carport. Cottage 5 has two bedrooms and two baths. Cottage 6 has a screened porch and is closest to the river. Chalet 26 is an especially spacious two-bedroom (one with a king bed), two-bath unit with a fireplace.

At Sky Valley there is a large, semicircular pool with a fountain that shoots across it. The pool is open mid-June–mid-September and is surrounded by lounge chairs and umbrellas. The swimming beach on the Saco River is 500 feet from most of the cottages. A little wandering up- or downstream may find you a brown trout. Canoe trips can be arranged from near First Bridge in North Conway, where the river is deeper.

Facilities: There are five cottages accommodating 4–8 people. Pets are not permitted. Snowmobiles are not permitted on the grounds or driveways.

Bedding: Bedding and towels are provided, though you may want to bring beach towels. Sheets are changed every three days of your stay; towels are changed daily.

Reservations and rates: Summer rates typically range $159–179 per night per four people. If you stay six nights, the seventh night is free (in the same unit). Additional persons are $10 per night (with maximum occupancy limitations). Your first two children under age six are free. Fall-foliage rates run slightly higher. In the winter, the cottages are rented for the season for $4,400–$5,900 plus utilities. Cable television, trash-receptacle services, and plowing are included.

Directions: Take I-93 north to Exit 32 (Route 112, North Woodstock/Lincoln). Turn left onto Route 112 and drive east for 23 miles. Turn left onto Bear Notch Road (closed in winter) for about 10 miles. At the blinking light (Route 302), turn right. You will see Sky Valley in about one mile.

Note: In the winter, Bear Notch Road is closed. Instead, drive on Route 93 to Twin Mountain, and take Route 302 east to Sky Valley.

Contact: Sky Valley Motel & Cottages, Route 302, P.O. Box 397, Bartlett, NH 03812, 603/374-2322, cell 603/387-0128 or 800/675-4683, website: www.skyvalley4u.com.

26. A BETTER LIFE CABINS & CAMPGROUND

on Route 302 in Bartlett

Luxury rating: ★★☆☆☆   **Recreation rating:** ★★★★★

A Better Life is what Rick and Lynn Wilczek were in search of when they left New Jersey for a change of lifestyle, and took over these charmingly traditional white cottages in Bartlett in the early 1990s. The cottages weren't always charming. For 10 years they had been abandoned. Neighbors cheered when the Wilczeks rolled in and rolled up their sleeves.

© BETHANY ERICSON

The cottages are favorites with families in summer, and couples enjoy the foliage in the fall. Rick and Lynn call it a campground atmosphere for those who would normally stay in a motel. Basically, the cottages have a New England character and are affordable with some updated amenities to keep things comfortable.

Cottages 3 to 8 are pieces of history; they're the original (refurbished) units built in the 1930s. The others were added in the 1970s. The campground is a newer addition. They are all winterized and have cable television, microwaves, refrigerators, and coffeemakers. Some have cooking facilities. None of the cottages have telephones or air-conditioning. If it is hot, there are ceiling fans, and you can swim in the Saco River or just sit in the brook behind the cabins in a lawn chair.

Rick is an amateur astronomer. On a clear night you should urge him to bring out his telescope. Rick and Lynn are also happy to provide literature on nature topics and to share their recommendations for hikes in the area, from the awe-inspiring Presidential Range to easier walks to Diana's Baths.

You can cross-country ski right from the property, and opportunities to snowmobile and mountain bike are nearby. Alpine skiing is minutes away, at a variety of mountainsides. In the summer, there is a community fire-ring at night at a Better Life, where people tend to meet and share their experiences in the area.

Facilities: There are 10 cabins accommodating 2–6 people. Some email facilities are offered, particularly for Appalachian Trail hikers cutting through.

Bedding: All bedding is provided.

Reservations and rates: Rates range $35–125 per night, depending on the cabin size and season. Appalachian Trail through-hikers get special rates (lower than a hostel). Weekly rates range $350–700. In winter, the cabins are also rented for the whole season (six months) and rates range $2,395–4,595. Pets are not permitted.

Directions: Take I-93 north to Exit 32 (Route 112, North Woodstock/Lincoln). Turn left onto Route 112 and drive east for 23 miles. Turn left onto Bear Notch Road (closed in winter) for about 10 miles. At the blinking light (Route 302), turn right. Drive for .5 mile, and A Better Life will be on your right. (During winter months stay on I-93 to Exit 35 (Route 3). Proceed on Route 3 to Route 302. Turn right (east) on Route 302.

Contact: A Better Life Cabins & Campground, Rick and Lynn Wilczek, P.O. Box 478, Route 302, Bartlett Village, Bartlett, NH 03812, 603/374-6333, website: www.abetterlifecabinsandcampground.com.

27. NEW ENGLAND INN & RESORT

Route 16A (at the Intervale)

Luxury rating: ★★★★☆   Recreation rating: ★★★★☆

Rank: Top 10 for Hiking, Top 10 for Romance, Best for Skiing and Snow-mobiling, Top 10 Most Luxurious

The New England Inn & Resort is an upscale inn and lodge surrounded by ponds, lakes, and woods, as well as some fabulous cottages and log cabins with maid service, fireplaces, and whirlpool tubs for two. The log cabins are large, with king beds, and the cottages are smaller and with queen beds. The decor is casual country, but the effect is romance.

© BETHANY ERICSON

Imagine a stone chimney with a television out into it, and a flickering fire at the end of your quilt-covered four-poster bed. Perhaps you'll turn on the high-end stereo and invite your companion along for a soak in the whirlpool tub after a long day of hiking or skiing. Fluffy towels wait on wrought-iron racks.

The cabins and cottages have small refrigerators, but there are no cooking facilities. The tavern at the inn is known for its 25 beers on tap and 50 bottled beers, and it has a pub menu. The dining room offers New England specialties like Shaker cranberry pot roast and roasted turkey.

This is prime hiking and skiing territory, just minutes from the many trails and ski resorts in the White Mountain National Forest area. Also nearby are the popular cross-country skiing trails in Jackson, and skating at quaint Nestlenook Farms. The inn can arrange for tours and equipment rentals.

Canoeing and kayaking are popular on the Saco River, and there are fly-fishing guide services available for other rivers. Mountain biking, rock-and ice-climbing, and gentle forest walks are all possible within just a few miles. Back at the inn, there are a swimming pool, children's wading pool, and three championship clay tennis courts.

Facilities: There are three cottages and six log cabins meant for couples.

Bedding: Bedding and towels are provided.

Reservations and rates: Rates for cottages range $135–185; log-cabin rates range $175–250. Rates are based on double occupancy and include breakfast. There is also a MAP plan. Thanksgiving, New Year's, and Romantic packages are available. Pets are not permitted.

Directions: From Boston, take I-95 north to the Route 16/Spaulding Turnpike in Portsmouth. Drive north for about 85 miles on Route 16 and go through North Conway. After 1.5 miles past the center of town, turn right at the Scenic Vista Rest Area onto Route 16A, the Intervale Resort Loop. Drive another 1.5 miles and look for the New England Inn on your right.

Contact: New England Inn, Route 16A, P.O. Box 100, Intervale, NH 03845, 603/356-5541 or 800/82-NE-INN, website: www.newenglandinn.com.

28. MERRILL FARMS

in downtown North Conway

Luxury rating: ★ ★ ☆ ☆ ☆   **Recreation rating:** ★ ★ ★ ★ ☆

Merrill Farms is located off the stretch of outlet stores in North Conway. Back behind the inn are a series of old-fashioned knotty-pine cottages with daily maid service. This location, with its proximity to skiing and hiking trails, makes it a good place to stay if any of your family or friends are staying inside for the day.

© BETHANY ERICSON

The cottages are all different. Some have kitchenettes; all have decent furniture with country charm. There are glass-front woodstoves (wood provided), full baths, breakfast nooks, and nice views from the porches of the river and mountains. Request one of the cottages that faces out onto the Saco River.

Merrill Farms was once indeed a working farm, but it has been hosting guests for more than a century. These days, it is in the center of North Conway's popular outlet shopping centers and just a few minutes from multiple major ski areas—from Cranmore to Attitash Bear Peak to Wildcat to Black Mountain. Jackson's popular ski touring trails are a short drive away, as is the New Hampshire Snowmobile Trails System.

The resort offers free use of its canoes on the Saco River, and you can swim in the river and fish for trout nearby. There's also a pool at Merrill Farms. And of course, there are an incredible number of hiking trails in the White Mountains that are convenient to this location.

There is usually skating, with a lovely backdrop of snowcapped mountains, on the picturesque rink by North Conway's vintage railroad station. Overlooking the downtown area, the Mount Cranmore Ski Resort offers tubing in addition to skiing and snowboarding.

Facilities: There are 11 cottages. They are mostly built for couples, though a number of them have additional beds or sofa beds in the living area. They accommodate 2–6 people.

Bedding: Bedding is provided.

Reservations and rates: Call early for fall-foliage and school-vacation times. Discounts are given for AAA, AARP, Quest Card, and Encore Card, and there are some ski-and-stay packages and Internet specials. Rates range $69–120 per night. Open year-round.

Directions: From Boston, take I-95 north to New Hampshire. In Portsmouth at Exit 4, bear left onto Route 16, which is the Spaulding Turnpike. Continue driving on Route 16 until you reach North Conway. Merrill Farms will be on your left before the center of town.

Contact: Merrill Farms, 428 White Mountain Highway (Route 16), North Conway, NH 03860, 603/447-3000 or 000/446-1017, website: www.merrillfarm.com.

Other Cabins and Cottages Nearby

- Dick and Terry Potochniak, The Old Red Inn and Cottages, P.O. Box 467, North Conway, NH 03860, 603/356-2642 or 800/338-1356, website: www.oldredinn.com.
- Tanglewood Motel and Cottages, Route 16, Conway, NH 03818, 603/447-5932, 866-TANGLEWOOD, website: www.tanglewoodmotel.com.

29. SUNNY BROOK COTTAGES

on Swift Brook in Conway

Luxury rating: ★★☆☆☆   **Recreation rating:** ★★★★★

© BETHANY ERICSON

This sunny, compelling colony of white housekeeping cottages sits on three acres by the Swift Brook, just off Route 16, south of the bustle and traffic snarls of North Conway. It offers easy, affordable access to the hiking trails of the White Mountain National Forest and the plethora of nearby skiing resorts.

These cottages were first opened in 1932 and have undergone lots of renovations without losing their character. They have pine paneling and shutters with pine-tree cutouts, but each unit is slightly unique. Most of the cottages overlook the brook. All but one has a fireplace; that one has a cast-iron gas stove.

All have cable television and outside barbecue grills. Most have fully equipped kitchens, bathrooms with shower stalls, and covered porches with Adirondack chairs or patio furniture. There are throw rugs and quilts. Cottage 3 is the biggest unit and has a glassed-in sun porch.

You can hear the traffic on Route 16 here, but the grounds are pleasantly wooded with birch and pine, and there is a sandy beach and a waterfront deck with hammocks. The brook is shallow, and it's safe for kids to swim and tube in it. You can also fish here for brook and rainbow trout.

Facilities: There are 10 cottages that hold 2–7 people. Motorcyclists are welcome during Laconia's Bike Week rally.

Bedding: Bedding and towels are provided.

Reservations and rates: Cottage rates range $41–119. Call a couple of months ahead. If you want a specific cottage, call up to a year ahead. There are weekend and midweek rates. Your seventh night is free. Memorial Day, Columbus Day, Christmas, and the first weekend in October (the weekend of the Fryeburg Fair, in Maine) are all booked up quickly. Smoking is permitted. Pets are permitted with a small fee.

30. BRASS HEART INN

at the base of Mount Chocorua

Luxury rating: ★★☆☆☆   **Recreation rating:** ★★★★☆

Rank: Top 10 for Hiking, Top 10 for Weddings

Franklin D. Roosevelt, Shirley Temple, and Paul Newman are just some of the names on the old registers of the Brass Heart Inn. Built in the late 1800s, it has an incredibly pastoral setting—off the highway, across a river, and beneath a mountain. Yet in just 15 minutes you can be in crowds in Conway.

© BETHANY ERICSON

This land is on 300–400 acres that were given (along with a musket and a horse) to a Mr. Hayford in 1787 for his service in the Revolutionary War. The inn was known as Hayford House for years, then Stafford's in the Field. It's now named after the Hartes's collection of antique horse brass; they collect all heart shapes.

The inn has three cottages currently being rented; the others are in transition. Veery has a garden theme, with open white beams and white wicker. Locust has a yellow-and-blue French countryside flare, and Whipporwill has more of a rustic Adirondack or moose-lodge theme and includes a sleeping porch.

Hiking Mount Chocorua is a popular pastime here. This is a well-photographed mountain due to its horn-shaped profile and has some relatively easy hikes to the summit. The summit has a sharp drop-off, and the edge is a popular picnicking spot, as is the location where Chief

Chocorua either jumped or was shot. Friendly owner Don Harte will happily regale you with the tales of Chocorua's life and his famed curse.

There are any number of other mountains within a short drive. It is lovely countryside for biking, and you can swim in the nearby lake, fish for brook trout, go bird-watching, or simply sit in your rocking chair and enjoy a summer thunderstorm from the porch. Spring is a lovely season for hiking the mountain, and the grounds here will be filled with lilacs and bluebirds.

The 19th-century barn on the property has a great horseshoe balcony and seats 200 people. It's popular for dances, weddings, and even theatrical events.

Facilities: There are six cottages on the property, three of which are actively being rented. There are galley kitchens and a few full-size kitchens in the cottages, and there is an upscale dining room in the inn. The cottages sleep 2–8 people.

Bedding: Bedding is provided.

Reservations and rates: Rates for the cottages range $180–240 per night. Breakfast is included. Stays of longer than five days get a 20 percent discount. Call at least two months in advance. The inn is open year-round; the cottages are open in the summer only.

Directions: From Boston, take I-95 north to Route 16/Spaulding Turnpike. Follow Route 16 north to the blinking light in Chocoroa Village (at the intersection of Routes 16 and 113). Turn left onto Route 113. Drive .75 mile, and turn right onto Philbrick Neighborhood Road.

Contact: The Brass Heart Inn, 88 Philbrick Neighborhood Road, P.O. Box 370, Chocorua, NH 03817, 603/323-7766 or 800/833-9509, website: www.thebrassheartinn.com.

© BETHANY ERICSON

Chapter 4

Southern New Hampshire

CHAPTER 4—SOUTHERN NEW HAMPSHIRE

Waterlogged laughter echoing across the sparkling water, sunbathing on the deck of a boat, going into town for ice cream, fishing at dusk, and listening to the lonely cries of loons pierce the night . . . these are just a few of the reasons New Englanders have always loved New Hampshire's lakes. Newfound, Squam, Winnisquam, Wentworth, and the grand Winnipesaukee are some of the country's oldest summer vacation destinations.

Meanwhile, what seems like a tiny geographic slice of seashore (18 miles) has evolved from the state's coastal defense system into the parking lot–lined shores of Hampton Beach and the scenic, winding road to the salt marshes and sands of Rye north to burgeoning Portsmouth. Along with the lakes, this stretch of beaches and tiny state parks is one of the most popular places to be in summer.

This section of New Hampshire is known best for its many lakes. The essence of annual family trips to lakeside cottages was captured in the 1981 movie, *On Golden Pond*. Since that time, similar settings nationwide have compared their locations to Golden Pond, but true fans can visit the real scenery here, since the movie was filmed on Squam Lake.

Lake Winnipesaukee is the impressive centerpiece of the Lakes Region. The outlets from this 72-square-mile glacial puddle are the source of much of the area's history, once providing indigenous people with good places to trap migrating fish, then becoming shipping paths south to the bustle of Portsmouth, and finally turning into energy-producing sites for mills.

Evidence of this history abounds. The Winnepeseogee tribe once occupied a trade center called Aquadoctan, which we know today as the boulevard and bustle of The Weirs (named after the fish traps set at the mouth of the channel). Here, you can also see a later piece of history at the channel entrance: the initials of Governor Endicott, marking a contentious northern boundary of the Mass Bay Colony.

Once the lakes were surrounded by every kind of mill and filled with logging and shipping. Shipbuilding evolved with the industry, and eventually the majestic steam wheeler, the *Mount Washington*, was transporting passengers to opposite shores. Today, the diesel-powered *Mt. Washington II* competes only with the loon as the icon of the region.

With the introduction of train service, the Lakes Region became an increasingly popular pastoral escape from industrialism and war. Farm lodgings, Grand Hotels, mansions, summer camps, and cottages all popped up next. Henry David Thoreau even wrote about boarding a Concord coach to see the big lake. Today, the Grand Hotels have mostly been lost to fire, the military outposts on the seashore have been abandoned, and cottages encircle the lakes and dot the seashore.

All this history poses some challenges to travelers. Multiple generations of the same families are often booked at certain cottages for the same week of every year. Add to that the crowds during the Winni Derby (fishing) in spring, Bike Week (motorcycle) in summer, and the Winston Cup auto races, and you'd better be ready to reserve extremely early and be flexible with your dates.

The key is to become one of those regulars, because you'll definitely want to return.

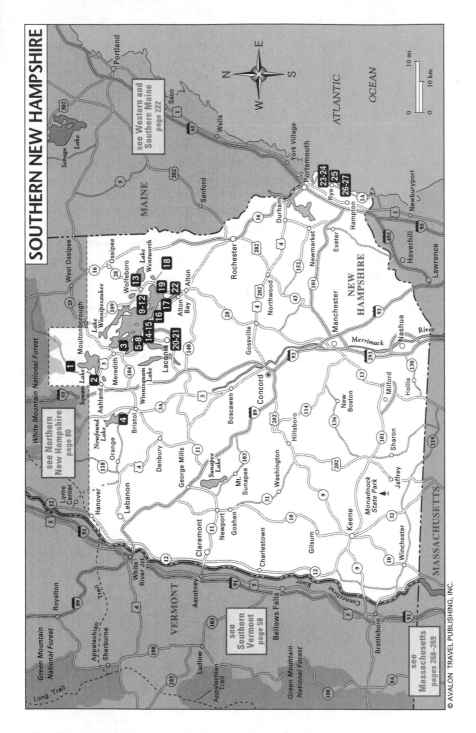

see Western and Southern Maine
page 222

see Northern New Hampshire
page 80

see Southern Vermont
page 58

see Massachusetts
pages 268–269

© AVALON TRAVEL PUBLISHING, INC.

CHAPTER 4
SOUTHERN NEW HAMPSHIRE

1. ROCKYWOLD–DEEPHAVEN CAMPS

on Squam Lake

Luxury rating: ★ ★ ★ ☆ ☆   **Recreation rating:** ★ ★ ★ ★ ★

Rank: Top 10 for Family Activities

This place is a truly joyous, old-style family vacation camp on Squam Lake. As you travel along the road, you may see at different stops kids of various ages pedaling into the woods with lunch in their backpacks, or a woman playing tennis with her grandson, or a friendly staff member leading an ecology walk or stringing lights

© BETHANY ERICSON

for a talent show. Or you may see the two-stage Japanese-derived bell tower, which beckons guests at mealtimes.

Explore further and you'll begin to see the 60 cottages of various sizes and shapes nestled in the trees and rocks with Arts and Crafts–style shed dormers, fireplaces, screened porches, and private docks. The cottages have antique iceboxes with ice harvested from Squam Lake delivered daily—a century-old tradition.

Rockywold–Deephaven Camps (RDC) has been a family camp since 1897, when two educators from the Hampton Institute in Virginia (one of the first colleges for blacks and Native Americans) started adjoining camps on Flagstaff Point and the north shore of Bennett Cove. There are still two separate dining halls, but what were (good-natured) rival activities of the past have been shared since the Rockywold and Deephaven camps merged.

There are eight tennis courts, a ball field, a basketball court, toddler playrooms, swimming floats, sporting tournaments, organized games and sports, picnics, boat and bicycle tours, hiking, swimming, sailing events, and more. Squam Lake has a healthy crayfish population that attracts both children and smallmouth bass. If all this isn't not enough activity, the camps are located on the northern edge of the Lakes Region and are just south of the incredible hiking opportunities of the White Mountain National Forest.

The camps passed through several generations of one family's owner-ship until 1978, when the stock was transferred beyond the family. The approximately 370 stockowners today are proud repeat guests and owners of this camp, where the community spirit combines with a back-to-nature atmosphere and results in bubbling laughter; "Champagne in a tin cup," is how Megan Thorn, author of *Roots & Recollections: a Century of RDC*, defined the atmosphere.

Facilities: There are 62 cottages that can sleep 2–16 people on 1.5 miles of shore-front. The cottages have twin beds, fireplaces, porches, and docks. There are no televisions or telephones. There are two "Ma Bell" buildings for making calls. Housekeeping and daily wood and ice delivery are provided. All meals are served buffet-style, with each family having their own table. Box lunch-es are provided to hikers and picnickers. Canoes, small sailboats, rowboats, kayaks, and bicycle rentals are available.

Bedding: Linens are provided.

Reservations and rates: Reservations are recommended; requests should be submitted before March 1 for the best chance of securing a spot. Guests are booked on a seniority basis. Cottages are rented weekly June–September and include full board. Rates range $2,120–6,360 a week, less in the spring and fall. There are also two lodges with rooms available for rent by night. New visitors may have the best luck in reserving for early June or late August, or may stand by on a waiting list. Open May–October. Pets are not allowed. Smoking is strongly discouraged and is not allowed in public areas.

Directions: From Concord, New Hampshire, follow I-93 north to Exit 24 Ashland. Drive 4.2 miles on Route 3/25 east to Holderness. Drive northeast for five miles on Route 113 to the Rockywold–Deephaven Camps sign on the right. Turn right on Pinehurst Road to the entrance.

Contact: Rockywold–Deephaven Camps, P.O. Box B, Holderness, NH 03245, 603/968-3313, website: www.rdcsquam.com.

2. LITTLE HOLLAND COURT

on Little Squam Lake

Luxury rating: ★ ★ ☆ ☆ ☆   **Recreation rating:** ★ ★ ★ ★ ★

These cheery, blue lakefront cabins with jaunty windmills on their red roofs have been a well-photographed landmark in Ashland since 1935. Most of the cabins front Little Squam Lake, where the boat livery in the channel and adjacent Squam Lake may also seem familiar, as they served as the setting for the movie *On Golden Pond*.

Most of the cabins are set around a front lawn, where kids meet and play horseshoes, volleyball, badminton, and more. Cabins on the lakefront look out on a sandy beach, whereas others back up to a stream that borders the property.

These are fairly basic, but clean, cabins. Some have tiny screen porches on both sides. Each has a picnic table and outdoor grill, and there is also a community bonfire pit.

On the waterfront there are two large docks where you can rent space for your own boat. Little Holland also rents rowboats, canoes, a 25-horsepower outboard motorboat for fishing, and a small electric motorboat for trolling. Ashland is easily accessible to the rest of the Lakes District and White Mountains National Forest.

Be sure to visit the wildlife or sign up for a Golden Pond Tour at the Squam Lakes Natural Science Center in Ashland.

Facilities: There are 16 housekeeping cottages that can accommodate 2–8 people. Kitchens come fully equipped and have refrigerators, though some have electric burners while others have ovens. Little Holland rents dock space and boats, and Ashland offers markets and restaurant dining.

Bedding: Linens are provided; towels are changed twice a week.

Reservations and rates: Reservations are accepted year-round with a non-refundable deposit. Rates range $450–850 per week. Open May–October. Credit cards are not accepted. Pets are allowed, except mid-June–mid-August.

Directions: From Boston, take I-93 north to Exit 24 Ashland. Drive for a few miles on Route 3/25 east. You can't miss the blue cabins on your right.

Contact: Linda and Tom Miller, **Little Holland Court**, R.R. 1, Route 3, Box 45, Ashland, NH 03217, 603/968-4434, website: www.littlehollandcourt.com.

3. OLIVER LODGE

on Lake Winnipesaukee

Luxury rating: ★ ★ ★ ☆ ☆   **Recreation rating:** ★ ★ ★ ★ ★

The Oliver Estate was built in 1906 on five acres of Meredith Neck, an area that still has retained its country charm. Today, the main buildings of the estate make up the room-filled lodge, while the Court House, Ice House, and island A-Frame (120 feet from the mainland) comprise the free-standing options available to guests.

The two-bedroom A-Frame cottage elicits childlike glee with its tiny separate island. Whether boating across in summer or pulling your bags and kids over to A-Frame cottage on a sled before curling up by the woodstove, the setting is enchanting. The Ice House and Court House are equally charming, though more *houses* than cottages. The post-and-beam Ice House (the original, 1906 icehouse of the estate) has four bedrooms and a huge deck overlooking the lake, while the Court House holds 14 people and looms judiciously over a tennis court.

Open year-round, Oliver Lodge offers endless outdoor fun. There's swimming at the three sandy beaches, as well as waterskiing and great lake fishing, and in winter you can go skiing, snowmobiling, and snowshoeing nearby. The lodge also has a clay tennis court and boat docks.

On the lake there is also a large boathouse with a dock that has an upper deck with lounge chairs and a sauna. The lodge provides free use of two canoes, two aqua bikes, a 14-foot rowboat with an optional motor, a small sailboat, a sea kayak, and a windsurfer. Additionally, the Olivers will direct you to local marinas to rent personal watercraft, pontoon boats, and ski boats.

Facilities: The A-Frame has two bedrooms plus a full-size futon. The Ice House and the Court House can hold 8–14 family members or friends. All have fully equipped kitchens (including dishwasher and microwave).
Bedding: Linens and towels are provided. Bring your own beach towel.

4. BUNGALO VILLAGE

on Newfound Lake

Luxury rating: ★ ★ ☆ ☆ ☆   **Recreation rating:** ★ ★ ★ ★ ★

Relax in a peaceful blue rocker on your porch overlooking the fall foliage on Newfound Lake, and one of the pet rabbits of the cottage community may hop by and join you for tea.

In summer, these rows of small, white cottages on the grassy hill overlooking the lake provide access to 200 feet of sandy beach just across reasonably safe West Shore Road. The cottages are very basic and simple accommodations for having some lakeside fun. There are docks, mooring spaces, Adirondack chairs, canoes, rowboats, and, as the locals know, a convenient sandbar (The Shallows) to park a boat on and picnic.

Newfound Lake is known for its clean waters, and it's a good place to fish for salmon, lake trout, smallmouth bass, catfish, and perch. The lake

is also ringed by a 17-mile road, which makes it a great place to walk, run, and bicycle.

Various recreational programs are offered in July and August, including campfires with a guitarist. There is a recreation hall with a game room, satellite television, books, ice, table tennis, a pool table, and toys.

Facilities: There are 20 small one- and two-bedroom cottages. They include televisions, shower baths, fully equipped kitchens, and heat. Markets and restaurants are nearby.

Bedding: Blankets are provided. Bring your own linens, towels, soap, and paper goods, or rent linens from Bungalo Village. Laundry is on the premises.

Reservations and rates: Reservations are accepted before April with a 50 percent deposit. (Be sure to reserve a mooring if you need it as well.) Rates range $525–775 per week. Two-night, seasonal, and package rates are offered. Open May 15–October 15. Credit cards are not accepted. Pets are not allowed (although yes, there really are pet rabbits on the premises).

Directions: From Boston, take I-93 north to Exit 23, and follow Route 104 west to Bristol. Drive north for two miles on Route 3A to the stone chapel at West Shore Road and Newfound Lake. Turn left here. Bungalo Village is .75 mile down the road.

Contact: Madeleine and Doug Thompson, **Bungalo Village Cottages**, P.O. Box 131, Bristol, NH 03222, 603/744-2220, website: www.bungalo.com.

Other Cabins and Cottages Nearby

- Timberloch Lodge & Cottages, 965 Mayhew Turnpike, Bristol, NH 03222, 603/744-5588.
- Sandybeach of Newfound, 95 Whittemore Point Road N, Bridgewater, NH 03222, 603/744-8473.
- Picture View Cottages, R.R. 1 Box 183, Bristol, NH 03222, 603/744-6158.

5. NASWA RESORT

Paugus Bay on Lake Winnipesaukee

Luxury rating: ★ ★ ★ ☆ ☆   **Recreation rating:** ★ ★ ★ ★ ★

Naswa Resort is well known on Lake Winnipesaukee for its unique, beachside, boat-in bar. With the summer breezes, festive bar music, and vivid pastel cottages lining the shore, just a few cocktails on the beach is all it will take to make you believe that you're in the Caribbean.

However, Naswa is undeniably New England. It's a third-generation business of the Makris family, with repeat customers who have been coming back for 25 years. Inside the bright cottages, with their jaunty weather vanes, you'll find New England–style knotty-pine walls and rustic furnishings. Modern touches include heat, air-conditioning, voicemail, and cable television.

On the 1,000-foot private sandy beach, you can relax on beach chairs and towels, swim, or rent a motorboat or personal watercraft. Canoes, kayaks, rowboats, and paddleboats are free for guests to use. Remember to stay sober on the boats!

The resort includes other lodgings, as well as a restaurant and gift shop. Although this is a party-fun kind of resort, it also offers some elegance. The grounds and buildings are well kept, and the lobby is exceptionally nice, with palm trees and fresh flowers and an always-courteous staff.

Lake Winnipesaukee is known for its salmon, trout, and bass fishing. In addition, Weirs Beach, golf, hiking, biking, boat cruises, water parks, and other attractions are nearby.

Facilities: There are 18 one-room (studio) and two-bedroom housekeeping cottages with shower baths, kitchenettes, and screened porches. The Naswa Restaurant and Bar serves breakfast and dinner; lunch and drinks are served at the World Famous Beach Bar and Grill. Free dock space and small watercraft are provided. Pets are not allowed. Smoking is not permitted in cottages.

Bedding: Bedding is provided, and there is daily towel service. Bring your own beach towels.

Reservations and rates: Call in January to make a reservation. Weekly rentals range $599–1,399, depending on the season; nightly and weekend rates are also available. Many special package deals are offered, and kids under 18 stay free. Open May–Columbus Day.

Directions: From Boston, take I-93 North to Exit 20. Turn left (north) on Route 3. Drive seven miles to Belknap Mall. Turn right on Route 3 and 11 North Bypass. Bear right at the end of the bypass and continue past the Wal-Mart Plaza. At the second set of traffic lights, bear right on Route 3. The Naswa Resort will be three miles north on your left.

Driving north on I-95, take the Spaulding Turnpike (Route 16) north to exit 15, and drive west for 27 miles on Route 11 to the junction of Routes 11 and 11B. Bear right and drive three miles. At the junction of 11B and Route 3, bear left. The Naswa Resort will be .5 mile down on the right.

Contact: The Naswa Resort, 1086 Weirs Boulevard, Laconia, NH 03246, 603/366-4341, website: www.naswa.com.

Other Cabins and Cottages Nearby

• Route 3, between Laconia and Weirs Beach, is lined with cabins and cottages.

6. CHANNEL COTTAGES

between Paugus Bay and Lake Winnipesaukee

Luxury rating: ★ ★ ☆ ☆ ☆   **Recreation rating:** ★ ★ ★ ☆

© BETHANY ERICSON

From the street, the Channel Cottages look like just another set of small, box-shaped cabins on the busy road, albeit with cheery window boxes of flowers. However, a closer look reveals a unique setting on the channel between Paugus Bay and Lake Winnipesaukee.

Guests sit on the large communal deck "island" in comfortable chairs by an outdoor fireplace reading newspapers, consuming drinks from the tiki bar, or simply allowing themselves to be entertained by the endless parade of boats moving through the channel. There are also gas grills with umbrella tables and chairs on the waterfront.

Boat slips are available with a reservation, and jet boat rentals are offered next door. There is a small sandy beach, but it is right on the Channel; Weirs Beach Boulevard and swimming is a one-minute walk from the cottages. The friendly host, Jose DeMatos, can direct you and will happily chat with you about local motor sports. The Channel Cottages are a fine place to stay during the Winston Cup or Bike Week activities.

Facilities: There are 12 one- and two-bedroom cottages in various setups. (Be sure to ask for a cottage on the channel.) Not all cottages include kitchenettes. Most include cable television, outgoing phones, fans, and shower baths. Weirs Beach offers many dining options, and a sub shop is directly across the street.

Bedding: Linens are provided, and towels can be exchanged daily.

Reservations and rates: Reservations are recommended. The cottages rates range $49–149 a night depending on the number of nights and time of year. Open May–October. Pets are allowed with permission, and owners must follow certain rules.

Directions: From Boston, take I-93 north to Exit 20. Drive for about four miles on Route 3 north to Weirs Beach.

Other Cabins and Cottages Nearby

- Route 3, between Laconia and Weirs Beach, is lined with cabins and cottages.

7. HALF MOON MOTEL & COTTAGES

center of Weirs Beach

Luxury rating: ★★☆☆☆   **Recreation rating:** ★★★★☆

Sometimes you just have to be in the middle of the party. Half Moon Motel & Cottages is located directly behind and above the restaurants, arcades, and tattoo parlors of the boulevard, the jetty, and sandy Weirs Beach. The famous boat *Mt. Washington* docks down the hill from the motel, and the scenic passen-

ger train departs from just across the boulevard. Also at the base of the hill, the jetty offers views of the social comings and goings of the waterfront in midsummer.

Several rows of typical Laconia-area, tiny, basic cabins with Adirondack chairs dot a hill that once was home to one of the Grand Hotels of New England, the New Weirs Hotel (it burned down in 1924). Today, the Ames family business also includes the Marketplace and Arcade down the street. In the center of the cottage complex is a 60-foot pool.

Sit on your porch or on the front lawn to enjoy frequent evening firework displays over Weirs Beach, or stroll around to hear bands playing, or attend Bike Week or the Winni Derby. Hiking, biking, boating, fishing, horseback riding, and golf are all within a short drive away. But why bother driving when you've parked yourself in the middle of the action? If you need to travel, boat and personal watercraft rentals are a short walk away.

Facilities: There are 19 cottages that can accommodate 2–6 people. They have wall-to-wall carpeting, small bathrooms with showers, air-conditioning, cable television, and heating. A pay phone is on the grounds. Only the larger cottages have kitchenettes.

Bedding: Linens and towels are provided.

Reservations and rates: Reservations are highly recommended. Nightly rates for two people range $82–100 in the high season. Special rates and minimum stays apply during certain event weekends. Stay for six nights, and the seventh night is free. Open May–October. Smoking is permitted in some cottages only.

Directions: Coming from the south or north on I-93, take Exit 20. Continue driving for about four miles on Route 3 north to Weirs Beach. Turn left on Tower Street and turn immediately right into the cottage complex.

Contact: Half Moon Motel & Cottages, P.O. Box 5183, Weirs Beach, NH 03247, 603/366-4494, website: www.weirsbeach.com/halfmoon/motel.html.

Other Cabins and Cottages Nearby

• Route 3, between Laconia and Weirs Beach, is lined with cabins and cottages.

8. THE ABAKEE COTTAGES

on Lake Winnipesaukee

Luxury rating: ★ ★ ☆ ☆ ☆   **Recreation rating:** ★ ★ ★ ★ ★

It's possible to escape the noise and bustle of Weirs Beach at the end of the day by driving less than a half mile away. Hidden down a private road, on the land once known as the Indian village Aquedoctan, a true old-fashioned camp experience still exists at The Abakee Cottages.

Spacious, sun-dappled, knotty-pine housekeeping cottages are situated on two acres of wooded hillside with plenty of space between them, all with porches and fabulous views of the lake. A sandy, gradual beach leads to the lake, and a floating swimming dock beckons.

Families love Abakee, and kids who spent their summers here return as

© BETHANY ERICSON

adults. It's also popular with groups, from running clubs to reunions. One couple even got married on the modest porch of the main house.

Besides on-site boating and swimming, there are boat cruises, seaplane rides, golf courses, and hiking trails all within easy driving distance. This is the kind of place where kids clamber the rocks of the shoreline and catch crayfish when they are done swimming at the beach.

Abakee Cottages has retained a very special rustic, summer-by-the-lake, New England flavor that is relaxing and idyllic. Owner Annette Poirier bought the place on a whim in the 1960s, and it's easy to see what she (and the 80 percent of customers who are repeats) found so attractive.

Facilities: There are 13 cottages that can accommodate 2–8 people. They include kitchens, shower baths, heat, a charcoal grill, and picnic table.

Bedding: Linens and towels are provided.

Reservations and rates: Join the Abakee mailing list on the website to get inside information on how early to reserve. Online reservations are possible. Cottage rates range $695–1,055 per week (Saturday–Saturday) in July and August. Daily rates are available in other months. Credit cards are not accepted.

Directions: Driving north or south on I-93, take Exit 23 onto Route 104. Drive for nine miles on Route 104 to Route 3 south. Follow Route 3 for four miles. Pass the Weirs Beach sign and drive over the stone bridge. Continue straight ahead for about 100 yards onto Route 11B. Turn left on Lucerne Avenue and drive to the parking lot. The office is in the big brown house.

Contact: The Abakee Cottages, P.O. Box 5144, Weirs Beach, NH 03247, 603/366-4405, website: www.abakeecottages.com.

9. POW-WOW LODGES

on Mirror Lake in Wolfeboro

Luxury rating: ★★★☆☆   **Recreation rating:** ★★★★★

In 1965, Charlie and Bev Fairbanks took over some run-down girls' camp cottages that had been moved to the isthmus between Lake Winnipesaukee and Mirror Lake. They completely revamped the structures and later added a four-unit motel. The result is Pow-Wow Lodges.

The breezy cottages are spacious by Lakes Region standards and are spread well apart in the evergreens. Each has a lovely screened porch facing the water and inviting day beds. The units are close enough to the road to hear traffic, but are focused on the lake, so road noise tends to fade in the distance.

Mirror Lake is a quiet, private lake with good fishing. The cottages with individual docks face Mount Shaw across the water. There is also a main dock, swimming dock, sandy beach, horseshoes, and badminton, volleyball, and basketball courts.

© BETHANY ERICSON

Wolfeboro offers access to numerous ponds and lakes, including all of the boating opportunities at Lake Winnipesaukee, plus local cruises, water-ski school, horseback riding, and hiking. Not far down Route 109, Abenaki Tower offers stunning views of Lake Winnipesaukee.

Facilities: There are four housekeeping cottages, each with two bedrooms, that can accommodate 2–6 people. There are televisions, shower baths, and fully equipped kitchens. All units have heat. Markets and dining are in nearby Wolfeboro. A rowboat, canoe, and small sailboat (for experienced sailors) can be rented for $15 a day.

Bedding: Linens are provided. Bring your own towels.

Reservations and rates: Reserve by winter for the following summer. Cottage rates range $995–1,050 weekly, less in spring and fall. There is a $400 deposit required per week. Open June–late October. Motorcycles are not permitted during Motorcycle Week except with permission, and then they must be on a trailer. Smoking is not permitted. Pets are not allowed.

Directions: From the center of Wolfeboro, drive for four miles west on Route 109 (Main Street). The sign for Pow-Wow Lodges will be on the right.

Contact: Charlie and Bev Fairbanks, **Pow-Wow Lodges**, North Main Street (Route 109), 19 GWH, Box 664, Wolfeboro, NH 03894, 603/569-2198.

10. MUSEUM LODGES

on Lake Winnipesaukee in Wolfeboro

🐾 🐟 🐷 🐂 🌊

Luxury rating: ★ ★ ☆ ☆ ☆   **Recreation rating:** ★ ★ ★ ★ ★

Built in 1944, Museum Lodges was once the next grouping of buildings on the map after the Libby Museum on what is now populated Route 109. The facility still retains its privacy and rustic charm.

As you drive down through the woods, past the irresistible cottages with their pillars of knobby tree trunks, red roofs, and dark wood, you'll pass a sign that reads "Slow: Grandparents at Play." In fact, everyone seems to be at play here on the shores of Winter Harbor. On a typical afternoon, various generations of families (some have been repeat guests for more than 22 years) can be seen swimming

and fishing from the docks and lunching outdoors in the shade of tall pines.

There is a canoe for guests, and a runabout with an outboard motor for rent. You can moor your own larger boat or launch a kayak here with ease. The sandy swimming area is kept separate from the motorboats for safety, and there are on-site trailer facilities. There is a communal outdoor barbecue area for relaxed sunset dinners, and a waterfront recreation hall (which was once a boathouse) with a library, lounge chairs, cable TV, table tennis, and pool.

Facilities: There are 10 rustic cottages with 1–2 bedrooms. All include sofa beds. The units are small but quaint, with the bed often located in an alcove off the living room, not in a separate room. There are ceiling fans, small kerosene heaters, and fireplaces. There are no telephones or televisions. Each has a fully equipped electric kitchen. Markets and restaurants are just a few miles away in Wolfeboro, and there is a collection of local menus at the lodge office. A public boat launch is less than a half-mile away. The lodge is 3.5 miles from the Wolfeboro Weigh Station during the annual May fishing tournament, the Winni Derby. Behind the Libby Museum, the Lang Pond Country Road is a pleasant place for a pastoral stroll.

Bedding: Bed linens, towels, and paper goods are provided. Bring your own beach towels.

Reservations and rates: Reservations are accepted up to a year in advance. (About 75 percent of its business is from repeat customers, so reserve as early as possible.) Cottage rates range $685–1,070 per week (Saturday–Saturday), less in the spring and fall. Credit cards are not accepted. Pets are allowed with permission in the off-season only.

Directions: From the center of Wolfeboro, drive on Route 109 (Main Street) west. After passing the Libby Museum on the right, drive another .5 mile to Museum Lodges (also on your left).

Contact: Leander and Rosalie Minnerly, **Museum Lodges**, P.O. Box 748, Wolfeboro, NH 03894, 603/569-1551, website: www.museumlodges.com.

11. CLEARWATER LODGES

Winter Harbor on Lake Winnipesaukee

Luxury rating: ★ ★ ☆ ☆ ☆   **Recreation rating:** ★ ★ ★ ★ ★

Rank: Top 10 for Fishing

Clearwater Lodges has the rustic feeling of a true old-fashioned New England cabin getaway. Just four miles north of Wolfeboro, the handcrafted pine cottages with original maple furniture form a line along a road through the woods to the waterfront.

© BETHANY ERICSON

One day, soap salesman Herb Vinnecombe turned to his wife, Anne, and said, "Hon, there must be something better. Let's go up to the lake." After a few summers searching, the Vinnecombes bought Clearwater Lodges on Lake Winnipesaukee and ran it for 45 years. Recently, they turned over the daily management to granddaughter Annie and her husband, Andre.

There is a diving board, a swimming dock, rental boats, and an outdoor fireplace on the shore. Just above the beach is a summer camp–style recreation hall with tables, a television, and games. Golf, horseback riding, hiking, and more water-sport activities are available nearby.

The cottages are popular with fishing enthusiasts in the spring, and lodgers can bring boats. Throughout the season, people from all over the world meet each other here and make lifetime friends. There is a great deal of repeat business here, with third and fourth generations of guests returning year after year.

Nevertheless, new guests can manage to get a reservation—as long as they can be flexible with their dates. There is also a waiting list, and putting yourself on one could get you a last-minute invitation. Guests often sign up for the following year as they leave; confirmations start in January.

Facilities: There are 14 cottages ranging in size from one to two bedrooms, all with kitchens, fireplaces, shower baths, and small porches. They do not have air-conditioning, radios, or televisions. Markets, restaurants, and bait are in Wolfeboro, four miles from Clearwater Lodges. Motorcycles are not allowed near the cottages. They may be left at the top of the hill or on a trailer.

Bedding: Bedding, linens, and towels are supplied.

Reservations and rates: Reservations are accepted a year in advance and are confirmed in January with a $175 deposit. Cottages are rented weekly (Saturday–Saturday) for $685–890. Daily rates $115–152 are available in the off-season. Open mid-May–mid-October. Smoking is permitted. Dogs are allowed only in the off-season and must be well behaved, leashed, and with the owner at all times.

Directions: From the center of Wolfeboro, drive four miles west on Route 109 (Main Street). Clearwater Lodges will be on your left.

Contact: Clearwater Lodges, 704 North Main Street, Wolfeboro, NH 03894, 603/569-2370, email: clearwaterlodges@conknet.com.

12. PIPING ROCK RESORT

on Lake Winnipesaukee

Luxury rating: ★ ★ ★ ☆ ☆   **Recreation rating:** ★ ★ ★ ★ ★

This motel and cottage colony offers 13 aqua-and-white housekeeping cottages with views of Lake Winnipesaukee. Piping Rock Resort sits on more than six acres of land, most of which is an open grassy hillside that leads down to a private sandy beach. The cottages are all architecturally different and elicit the feeling of a small, fun neighborhood.

Owned and built by Hans Bass, the motel and cottages at this resort were sold many times over the years and, like many lakeside lodgings, the cottages (and even individual motel rooms) were eventually sold at auction to different private owners. The fortunate twist here is that the condo association still rents all of these units out to the public.

In November, the owners reserve their own vacation dates. Then, the return requests that were submitted by guests from the previous summer are reserved; the rest of the public gets to fill in what's left. Confirmations are made in January.

Kids and adults alike rave about the fun to be had at Piping Rock Resort. Most guests tend to intermingle on the beach. There are sand toys, a floating swimming dock, a playground, volleyball court, and more. Canoes are provided for free. Those wanting to stay right on the water can book a small two-bedroom cottage space on the second floor of the boathouse. Lake Winnipesaukee offers endless amounts of water sports in the summer, and in winter, the area is a Mecca for ice fishing, skiing, and snowmobiling.

Facilities: There are 13 cottages, ranging in size from two to four bedrooms, with fully equipped kitchens, telephones, cable television, and knotty-pine interiors. Some have fireplaces. All units, except the boathouse, have terraces or screened-in porches and a charcoal grill. Boat slips and moorings are available for rent. Personal watercraft are not allowed.

Bedding: Linens are provided.

Reservations and rates: Reservations are accepted up to a year in advance and are confirmed in January. Cottages range $900–1,290 weekly. There is a two-night minimum in the spring and fall. Twelve of the cottages are seasonal (April–October); one three-bedroom cottage sleeps seven people and is open year-round. Pets are not permitted.

Directions: From Boston, take I-93 north to Exit 9N (Route 28). Drive for about an hour on Route 28 north to Wolfeboro. Route 28 takes a hard left at a blinking light. Stay on Route 28 and drive through town until the intersection with Route 109. By continuing straight, you will be driving on Route 109 (Main Street). Piping Rock Resort is about three miles north of the center of Wolfeboro.

Contact: Piping Rock Resort, 680 North Main Street, Wolfeboro, NH 03894, 603/569-1915 or 800/317-3864, website: www.pipingrockresort.com.

13. RAVEN COVE COTTAGES

on Lake Wentworth in Wolfeboro

Luxury rating: ★ ★ ☆ ☆ ☆   **Recreation rating:** ★ ★ ★ ★ ★

These cozy, yellow, basic housekeeping cottages are spread out along a rolling lawn edged with woods and the shore of Lake Wentworth. Though you can swim, row, and fish at Raven Cove Cottages, something about the friendly, relaxed, and unusually quiet atmosphere and the sun-dappled lawn may just convince you to relax and take that nap you've been meaning to take for the last few years.

Raven Cove has a great sandy beach with a swimming dock 100 feet off the shore of Lake Wentworth, which is a clean and welcome oasis on a hot summer day. It's a large lake with less boat traffic than Lake Winnipesaukee and provides decent fishing for small-

© BETHANY ERICSON

mouthed bass. Stroll down to the small dock and borrow a rowboat or canoe, or bring or rent a kayak. The Nature Conservancy preserves Stamp Act Island, the largest island in the lake. Although it is mostly off-limits to the public, a circumnavigation can provide good wildlife viewing. You may find beaver and turtles, as well as fish, in the marshy nooks and crannies of the lake, or you may see a pair of loons. Downtown Wolfeboro also offers access to Lake Winnipesaukee, and boat rentals and tours are just a few minutes away.

If you choose to float in the protected cove by the cottages, be sure to also take a walk through the woods or out on the isthmus. There is an indoor recreation room for rainy days and early evenings, and a handful of museums and shops are a short drive away.

Facilities: The two-bedroom cottages come with shower baths and fully equipped kitchens. Some have screen porches. Grills and picnic tables are provided at each unit, along with panoramic lake views.

Bedding: Blankets, pillows, and kitchen towels are provided. Bed and bath linens can be rented for an additional cost.

Reservations and rates: Make reservations early in the year. Cottages are rented weekly for $300–400. Open Memorial Day–Columbus Day.

Directions: Driving from Wolfeboro, at the intersection of Route 109 (Center Street) and Route 28, follow Route 109 east. Just as you've driven through Wolfeboro Falls, the cottages will be on your right. If you're coming from the intersection of Routes 16 and 109, drive along Route 109 toward Wolfeboro; the cottages will be on your left.

Contact: Raven Cove Cottages, 291 Center Street, Wolfeboro, NH 03894, 603/569-1914.

Other Cabins and Cottages Nearby

- King's Pine Lodges, Whitten Neck Road, Wolfeboro, NH 03894, 603/569-3556.

14. HOLIDAY BAY

Paugus Bay on Lake Winnipesaukee

Luxury rating: ★ ★ ☆ ☆ ☆   **Recreation rating:** ★ ★ ★ ★ ☆

Holiday Bay doesn't have the biggest beach on the block, and the beach is across a small private road. However, it is one of the few cottage colonies on Route 3 with a pool. In fact, the heated pool and the chaise lounges around it are a lively gathering spot.

© BETHANY ERICSON

At the beach there are rowboats and rental paddleboats for getting out on the lake. Docking is available for boats and personal watercraft if you're here for the expanse of water and the salmon, bass, and trout that Lake Winnipesaukee offers.

The cottages at Holiday Bay are close together, lining the road to the beach, but they are staggered to provide privacy. Families and couples have gotten to know each other here; some have been repeat customers for 50 years. This is a popular destination during Bike Week, when, according to soft-spoken owner Lillian Goulette, "We have some fun."

Cottage 15, up the hill near the pool, has big boulders flanking it that are popular with kids staying there. Near the pool there is a small game room for foul-weather days, and Fun Spot (the second-largest arcade in the country) at Weirs Beach is a short drive away.

Facilities: There are 13 efficiency cottages that can accommodate 2–10 people. Kitchenettes include full-size refrigerators, burners, and basic cookware. Most units have screened porches. Boat docking facilities are available.

Bedding: Linens are provided. Bring your own towels.

Reservations and rates: Reservations are accepted up to a year in advance. (Repeat customers are common here.) Cottage rates range $500–615 per week (Saturday–Saturday), less in the off-season. Walk-in nightly stays are occasionally available, especially in the off-season. Open April–October.

Directions: From Boston, take I-93 north. Take Exit 20 onto Route 3 north and drive for 14 miles to Holiday Bay. From all points north, take I-93 south to Exit 23 Bristol, then Route 104 to Route 3 south, and drive to Holiday Bay (about 15 miles from the I-93 exit).

Contact: Rich and Lillian Goulette, **Holiday Bay**, 690 Weirs Boulevard, Laconia, NH 03246, 603/366-4414, website: www.holiday-bay.com.

Other Cabins and Cottages Nearby

- Route 3, between Laconia and Weirs Beach, is lined with cabins and cottages.

15. LIGHTHOUSE COTTAGES

Paugus Bay on Lake Winnipesaukee

Luxury rating: ★★★★☆   **Recreation rating:** ★★★★★

These comfortably furnished deluxe cottages face the lake and have large windows. They are sunny, gray shingled, and spread out on a lovely landscaped property that includes a sandy beach and a swimming dock. Lighthouse Cottages exudes friendliness, but without any pressure to socialize. There are nightly bonfires with s'mores and cocktails, free paddleboats, tubes and rafts, and dock space for your boat. It's a true gem of an escape from the buzz of Weirs Beach.

© BETHANY ERICSON

Each cottage here is unique. The Lighthouse Cottage has been known to create the feeling of being on a boat, due to the stunning water views from inside. Guests in this cottage can also control the switch for the miniature lighthouse on the point out front.

The cottage popular with the young crowd is the top floor of the boathouse, right on the water. Three of the cottages are winterized and are five minutes from skiing at Gunstock Recreation Area. There aren't many places in this area where you can rent a cottage with a fireplace in winter. Bring your ice-fishing gear!

These cottages have to be seen to be believed. Linda Daly and her daughter have created a fun and cozy place to relax and play. They may even have you over for a game of poker.

Facilities: There are five very different cottages accommodating 2–10 people. They include full kitchens. There are many restaurants in the area, and kids get a kick out of motoring across the bay to a boat-in Burger King.

Bedding: Blankets and comforters are provided. Bring your own linens and towels or opt for the linen service.

Reservations and rates: Cottages cost $1,100–1,950 weekly (Saturday–Saturday) June–October. Call for rates during Bike Week and off-season. Credit cards are not accepted. Open year-round.

Directions: Driving north from Boston, or south from points north, take I-93 to Exit 20. Drive east on Route 3, toward Laconia. At the Jeep dealership (on the right), get into the right-hand lane to take the Route 11 bypass. Bear right on Route 11. Drive through two sets of lights, and bear right onto Route 3, toward Weirs Beach. At Christmas Island Steakhouse and Resort (about two miles from the turnoff), turn left onto Prescott Avenue (it bears to the right behind the restaurant). Follow the road about .5 mile to 90 Prescott Avenue (look for a large boulder).

Contact: Lighthouse Cottages, 90 Prescott Avenue, P.O. Box 5001, Weirs Beach, NH 03247, 603/366-4488, website: www.lighthousecottages.com.

Other Cabins and Cottages Nearby

• Route 3, between Laconia and Weirs Beach, is lined with cabins and cottages.

16. SILVER SANDS RESORT

Gilford on Lake Winnipesaukee

Luxury rating: ★ ★ ★ ☆ ☆   **Recreation rating:** ★ ★ ★ ★ ★

Rank: Top 10 for Boating

Silver Sands Motel and Cottages are adjacent to the Silver Sands Marina, with complete boat launching and docking facilities, boat sales, gas, and more. Together, they are known as Silver Sands Resort. If you want to bring your own boat, or arrive by boat—and you're spending your days fishing for salmon, bass, or trout—this is an unusually convenient place to come.

The cottages sit just steps from the lakeshore on a long, sandy beach. They are an unusual construction for the Lakes Region, built of large pink bricks with louvered windows, and standing right on a sandy beach. This solid construction and beach location somehow adds to the feeling of privacy on the open beach. And in the bright sun, it's easy to imagine that the hemlocks are palm trees.

Silver Sands has its own pool and provides beach chairs and pink-and-white striped umbrellas. Visitors swim, relax, water-ski, and visit Weirs Beach. The resort is sandwiched between yacht clubs and is not far from Ellacoya State Park.

Boating families reserve these cottages more than a year in advance. Other families reserve space in the apartment lodgings, waiting to get into the cottages. You'll definitely want to call early and be flexible with your dates if you're determined to have a cottage all to yourself.

Facilities: Two- and three-bedroom cottages hold 4–6 people. Basic kitchens, shower baths, and cable television are included. There is no air-conditioning. There are full marina services on-site; ask about details for bringing your own boat.

Bedding: Linens and towels are provided except in July and August, when linens are provided, but you should bring your own towels.

Reservations and rates: Reservations are recommended up to a year in advance. Cottage rates range $130–140 per night and $900–950 per week, less in the off-season. Children under 12 stay free. Open April–October. Pets are not allowed.

Directions: Coming north from Boston on I-93, take Exit 20. Turn left at the end of the ramp onto Route 3/11, to Laconia. Drive seven miles, turn right (east) onto Route 11, and drive to the intersection with 11B. Turn left onto Route 11 and drive for 1.75 miles. Then, at a light, turn left onto Route 11B; Silver Sands Resort is .5 mile on the right.

Via I-95 and Portsmouth, take Route 95 north, then take the Spaulding Turnpike (Route 16) to Exit 15, and drive west for 27 miles on Route 11. Be sure to stay on Route 11, especially when you come to the rotary circle in Alton. At the junction with Route 11B, turn right at the light; Silver Sands Resort is .5 mile farther on the right.

Contact: Silver Sands Resort, 103 Weirs Road, Saunders Bay (Route 11B), Gilford, NH 03249, 603/293-4481, website: www.ssmotel.com.

Other Cabins and Cottages Nearby

• Smithholm Cottages, R.R. 11, Laconia, NH 03246-9812, 603/366-4611.

17. AMES FARM INN

between Alton and Laconia on Lake Winnipesaukee

Luxury rating: ★★☆☆☆   **Recreation rating:** ★★★★★

If you're looking for a beach experience away from the noise of the Weirs but with a cabin right on a social sandy beach, Ames Farm is for you. The basic white lakeshore cabins are set far from the road and offer a decent amount of privacy with space between them.

James Noah Ames started the establishment in the late 1800s on lakeshore, field, and mountain woodland passed down through his family since his grandfather was a pioneer settler near Gilford.

Finding a cabin on a quarter mile of beach in this area is unusual, and Ames Farm offers great swimming and boating facilities. Docks and ramps are available for guests' boats, and a limited number of rental boats are available. If you purchase a fishing license, available in the office, you'll have your pick of salmon, trout, perch, and bass. There are volleyball, table tennis, and horseshoe facilities.

Mount Major is a short drive away, a strenuous short climb worthy of your hiking boots. There are also walking trails in Weeks Woods, several golf courses, Weirs Beach, and nearby Ellacoya State Beach. Boat trips on the lake are available in the area.

Facilities: The 17 one- or two-bedroom lakefront cabins come with showers, kitchenettes with dishes and utensils, living rooms, and screened porches facing the lake. There is also a small cabin and a three-bedroom cottage situated away from the lake but offering good views. All accommodations are heated. There are fishing-tournament facilities for up to 250 boats. There is a store on the lower floor of the main house with snacks, newspapers, fishing licenses, local crafts, and souvenirs, and the spacious Ames Farm Restaurant serves breakfast and lunch from Motorcycle Weekend to Labor Day.

Bedding: Linens and one blanket per bed are provided in cabins. Cribs and cots are available at an additional charge.

18. GREY SHINGLES

on Rust Pond in Wolfeboro

Luxury rating: ★★☆☆☆   **Recreation rating:** ★★★★★

Grey Shingles is an unassuming small row of affordable cabins off the beaten path on a 1.5-mile pond in Wolfeboro. Families often rent all five cabins for reunions or other gatherings. The cabins are quite basic, but very clean; they provide a refreshing escape.

Grey Shingles has been a Wolfeboro institution for years, owned by the Windhorst family and later the Clarkes. After years of being guests at the cabins, the hospitable Hunt family took over the business in 1997.

The cabins have been purposefully kept simple, with no televisions, telephones, or air-conditioning units. There is plenty of shady trees, and the units face a large lawn with a basketball hoop and badminton. There is a big barn on one end of the lawn, providing dry space on rainy days for playing the piano, reading by the electric fireplace, or playing board games.

Grey Shingles is located on six acres of land and includes a dirt path that takes you to the quiet and clean waters of Rust Pond in under three minutes. A tiny private beach, swimming raft, and space to launch a canoe or kayak will keep you entertained for hours. Just a few miles down the road, Wolfeboro also offers access to all that the Lakes Region has to offer—boating, swimming, fishing, parasailing, golf, horseback riding, kayaking, and hiking.

Facilities: There are five cottages that can accommodate 3–6 people. They are small, clean cabins with tiny, fully equipped kitchenettes and small bathrooms with showers. From the cabins you can take a short walk to fine dining at the Cider Press Restaurant and Tavern. Wolfeboro Center, with its markets and restaurants, is a short drive away.

Bedding: Linens are provided. Bring your own beach towels.

Reservations and rates: Reservations are accepted with a 50 percent deposit. Cabin rates range $65–75 per night, $400–500 per week, with no minimum stay. Open Memorial Day–Labor Day. Credit cards are not accepted. Pets are not allowed.

Directions: From Wolfeboro Center, take Route 28/109 and drive for about three miles to where the highway takes a sharp right turn at a blinking light. Continue driving straight onto Middleton Road, rather than following the highway to the right. Grey Shingles is .3 mile from the intersection, on your left.

Contact: The Hunts, **Grey Shingles**, 76 Middleton Road, Wolfeboro, NH 03894, 603/569-6536, email: greyshingles@aol.com.

19. BROOK AND BRIDLE SUMMER HOMES AND INN

off Roberts Cove Road in Wolfeboro

Luxury rating: ★ ★ ★ ★ ☆   **Recreation rating:** ★ ★ ★ ★ ★

Don't be shy at the wine-and-cheese "icebreaker" party at the beginning of your month-long stay at Brook and Bridle Summer Homes and Inn. It's arranged so that the other renters in the cottage homes won't be strangers to each other. Yet, with 10 architecturally different homes spread out over 30 acres, you'll have to consciously choose to run into the other guests. Two of the cottages even have their own private beaches.

Bonnie Dunbar took over the business of renting this unique neighborhood of cottages from her grandmother, who founded the business in the late 1920s. Bonnie and her husband, Glen McLean, really enjoy continuing a tradition of "gracious hospitality."

You can extend this hospitality to your own visitors as well—the Brook and Bridle Bed and Breakfast offers exclusive lodging and breakfast (on a separate rate schedule) only to friends of those renting the cottage homes May–August. While you'll have privacy and your own kitchen in your cottage, your guests will enjoy the use of a whirlpool tub and rave about (and possibly even pho-

tograph) Bonnie's outstanding breakfasts over in the main house.

On a typical day, guests of all ages can be seen playing at the beach and on the swimming dock, heading out to mountain bike, picking berries, and fishing in the Beaver Brook. There are canoes, paddleboats, small sailboats, and moorings available. Knights Pond Conservation Area offers an isolated pond shore walk nearby. On rainy days, the beach house has a stone fireplace, and the laundry room is a veritable book-and-toy swap.

Brook and Bridle is popular for reunions and honeymoons (and the 50th anniversaries of folk who once honeymooned there). Bonnie believes in matching the right cottage to your needs and also works with a wedding coordinator to host intimate weddings.

Facilities: Each of the 10 houses has 1–4 bedrooms with comfortable country furnishings, fully equipped kitchens, heat, and a wood-burning fireplace. Many have sun porches and sunset views. You'll find a VCR, cable television, and your own telephone with your own number and unlimited local calling. Brook and Bridle has built ramps for guests in the past, but no cottage has a wheelchair-accessible bathroom. Laundry facilities are available. Final cleaning is the responsibility of the renter; cleaning service can be arranged.

Bedding: Warm bedding and kitchen towels are provided. You can bring your own sheets and towels or rent them.

Reservations and rates: Reservations are accepted. Cabin rates range $4,950–7,850 in July and August, when only 30-day (five weekends) rentals are available. In spring and fall, weekly rentals range $1,340–2,250. Open May 1–October 20. Smoking is permitted in the cottages. Pets are not allowed.

Directions: From the center of Wolfeboro, drive four miles south on Route 28. Turn right on Roberts Cove Road. The Brook and Bridle Summer Homes and Inn will be on your right.

Contact: Brook and Bridle Summer Homes and Inn, On Lake Winnipesaukee, P.O. Box 270—Mailboat, Wolfeboro, NH 03894, 603/569-2707, website: www.brookbridle.com.

Other Cabins and Cottages Nearby

• Eye-Joy Cottages, Roberts Cove Road, Alton, NH 03809, 603/569-4973.

20. THE ANCHORAGE

on Lake Winnisquam

Luxury rating: ★ ★ ☆ ☆ ☆   **Recreation rating:** ★ ★ ★ ★ ★

The Anchorage is a 50-year-old family-oriented setting with a whole lot of beach. The Anchorage has a full mile of lake frontage on Lake Winnisquam and three private sandy beaches, each with rafts. Rowboats, paddleboats, and canoes are available, and you can dock your own boat here after a day of fishing for salmon, bass, and trout in the lake.

© BETHANY ERICSON

The basic knotty-pine cottages with linoleum floors are set well back from the road, mainly in the trees by the lake. The center of the property has a large lawn for ball games, picnics, and the happy buzz of children. There are also walking trails, an apple orchard, and raspberries and blackberries to pick.

The Anchorage organizes pony rides, community cookouts, and end-of-the-week campfires. Tennis, golf, and hiking are nearby. On rainy days (or when the kids are waterlogged), there is a game room. Weirs Beach, Mount Major, Weeks Woods, and the Canterbury Shaker Village are all a short drive away.

Facilities: The 30 cottages and two houses accommodate 2–18 people. The Farm House, with its five bedrooms, is next to a three-bedroom apartment and is often used for reunions. The Trapp House is on its own private point with a dock and has six bedrooms. Cottages come with kitchenettes, shower baths, screened porches, electric heating, and charcoal grills. Boat docking and rentals, life preservers, maid service, and childcare can be arranged.

Bedding: Linens and towels are provided. Bring your own beach towels and paper goods. Cribs and cots can be arranged.

Reservations and rates: Reservations are accepted. Call as early as you can to reserve—the Anchorage sees a high percentage of repeat guests. Cottages in the peak season range $530–1,345 per week (Saturday–Saturday). The

Farm House can be rented for $1,850 and the Trapp House is $3,015. Open May–October. Pets are not allowed.

Directions: From Boston, take I-93 to Exit 20, and drive to Route 3 north. The Anchorage is three miles north on the right.

Contact: Gary and Gail Archibald, **The Anchorage**, 725 Laconia Road, Tilton, NH 03276, 603/524-3248, website: www.anchorage-on-lake.com.

21. THE LORD HAMPSHIRE

on Lake Winnisquam

Luxury rating: ★★☆☆☆   **Recreation rating:** ★★★★★

These very clean cottages on the shore of Lake Winnisquam are popular with families and leaf-peepers, as well as motor-cyclists attending Bike Week.

© BETHANY ERICSON

While basic, the cottages are very nicely kept, with new curtains, quilts, bedspreads and carpets. Some have fireplaces. You'll find a radio and television, but visitors and telephones are not allowed here. Owner Dick Bernard believes people "don't want to hear from their brother-in-law when they're vacationing." You are here to truly escape.

Bring or rent a motorboat, swim from the dock, or dive from the tower on the floating raft. On the shore is a 30- by 35-foot deck over the water, a sandbox for children, and a barbecue. In the lake are salmon, bass, trout, and more.

The cottages are somewhat close together, although extended families that *do* want to hear from each other on vacation often take advantage of such arrangements.

Facilities: There are 12 cottages accommodating 4–7 people in full or queen beds. They have shower baths, heat, wall-to-wall carpeting, kitchenettes, and sundecks or screened porches; markets are nearby. Pontoon, pedal, and aluminum boats, as well as personal watercraft and canoes, are available for rental. Reserve boats in advance.

Bedding: Sheets, towels, and blankets are provided.

Reservations and rates: Reservations are accepted online. Cottages are offered weekly (Saturday–Saturday) in the summer for $580–1,195, less in the off-season. A 10 percent discount is available for AAA and AARP members. Pets are not allowed. Open April–late October.

Directions: From Boston, take I-93 to Exit 20, Route 3. Drive north for four miles on Route 3, and look for The Lord Hampshire on the right.

Contact: Dick and Pat Bernard, **The Lord Hampshire**, 885 Laconia Road, P.O. Box 455, Winnisquam, NH 03289, 603/524-4331, website: www.lordhampshire.com.

22. SANDY POINT BEACH RESORT

Alton Bay on Lake Winnipesaukee

Luxury rating: ★ ★ ★ ☆ ☆   **Recreation rating:** ★ ★ ★ ★ ★

Sandy Point is a family resort, run by the Ouellette family since 1905. It has 2,000 feet of waterfront on Lake Winnipesaukee, with a private beach, boat ramp, and docks.

While the lake is a fabulous place to cool your heels in the summer, this area of the lake is also known for spring salmon fishing, and the foliage in fall is spectacular. The resort has paddleboat and canoe rentals, as well as facilities for basketball and horseshoes. Nearby there is tennis, golf, and horseback riding, plus conservation land to hike, and Mount Major for a strenuous two-hour climb.

Sandy Point has been a local institution with repeat customers since 1950. You can usually find extended families staying here, and some seasonal renters have even decorated their cabins and have standing reservations every weekend at the long-established Sandy Point Restaurant. The restaurant is known on the lake for its lobster and prime rib, and it has a three-drink limit in order to preserve a friendly atmosphere.

Owner Bric Ouellette inherited the business from his father; his first job at the resort was to collect $.10 from visitors going to the beach. Bric's son is the current manager. It's

© BETHANY ERICSON

not unusual to see visitors return after 30 years with their children, hoping to introduce them to Bric.

Facilities: Most of the 36 cottages are seasonal rentals, claimed year after year by the same guests; they sleep 2–6 people. Typically, two cottages accommodating 2–5 people are offered as Saturday-to-Saturday rentals. There is also a beach apartment and motel.

Bedding: You can provide your own linens or can lease them seasonally.

Reservations and rates: Reservations are accepted up to a year in advance. Rates for seasonal cottages range $4,500–7,000. The weekly cottages run $450–550 a week. Lower rates apply off-season (prior to June and after Labor Day). A $100 deposit is required, with 50 percent of the total due 30 days prior to arrival. Give 30 days' notice to cancel for a refund (with a $20 service charge). The cottages are open May 1–October 15. Pets are not allowed.

Directions: From Portsmouth, drive north on I-95 to Route 16 (Spaulding Turnpike) to Exit 15. Take Route 11 west to the Alton Traffic Circle. Continue on Route 11 and drive to Alton Bay. From Boston, drive north on I-93 and take Exit 15E at Concord to Route 4/202 east. Drive on Route 4/202 to Route 28. Drive north on Route 28 and join Route 11 at the Alton Traffic Circle. Continue west on Route 11 to Alton Bay. Sandy Point will be on your right.

Contact: Sandy Point Beach Resort, Route 11, Box 6, Alton Bay, NH 03810, 603/875-6000.

Other Cabins and Cottages Nearby

- Horse & Buggy Cottages, Bay Hill Road, Alton Bay, NH 03810, 603/875-6771.

23. HOYT'S LODGES . . . COTTAGES BY THE SEA

near Wallis Sands State Park

Luxury rating: ★★★☆☆   **Recreation rating:** ★★★★☆

The cottages at Hoyt's Lodges, with their fresh white paint, table umbrellas, and bright day lilies, are an inviting place to relax after a sunny day seeing the coast.

A romantic stroll across the road offers gorgeous views of the rocky shore, and a nice place to read, fish, or sunbathe. Five to seven minutes of walking brings you to Wallis Sands State Park, with its sandy beaches and full amenities.

Hoyt's Lodges is popular with both families and couples seeking a romantic week away. The rugged shoreline offers a beautiful, yet blissfully short, drive north to the activity of Portsmouth and south to festive Hampton Beach.

Also just north of Hoyt's is Odiorne State Park, with 137 acres of protected coastline. There are hiking, biking, and walking trails; picnic areas; and a boat launch.

Repeat guests, as well as wedding guests from events at places like Odiorne State Park, often reserve at cottages along Route 1A; be sure to make your reservations early.

Facilities: The 10 one- and two-bedroom cottages have fully equipped kitchens, shower baths, cable television, and porches with tables and chairs.

Bedding: Linens are provided.

Reservations and rates: The rentals range in price $525–950 per week mid-June–Labor Day. Off season rates are lower; inquire about daily rates. Open April–October.

Directions: From Portsmouth, take I-95 to Exit 3. Turn right at the exit lights onto Route 33; drive through one set of traffic lights to a second set of lights. Turn right onto Peverly Hill Road and continue straight to the intersection with Route 1. Continue driving straight across Route 1 onto Elwyn Road, until you reach its intersection with Route 1A at Foyes Corner. Drive south on Route 1A. Hoyt's is on the right at 891 Ocean Boulevard.

Contact: Hoyt's Lodges, 891 Ocean Boulevard, Route 1A, Rye, NH 03870, 603/436-5350, website: www.hoytslodges.com.

24. WALLIS SANDS PLACE

Wallis Sands Beach

Luxury rating: ★★☆☆☆   **Recreation rating:** ★★★★☆

Rank: Top 10 for Ocean Beach Activities

Wallis Sands Place is a very friendly community of repeat customers and some new folk, attracting a mix of couples and honeymooners as well as families. It is just five miles south of the Portsmouth traffic circle, and across the street from Wallis Sands State Park.

© BETHANY ERICSON

These cottages are along the scenic stretch of Route 1A. Seven of them have been recently updated, some with spiral staircases. Another three of them remain retro, with exposed beams, older floors, and wood paneling. Some repeat customers actually prefer the older units. All cottages have screened porches, most have ocean views, and you can go to sleep listening to the sound of waves crashing.

Route 1A is known as the boulevard along the shore here and is a great place to walk or bike (use care when biking on Route 1A). Wallis Sands Beach has full services. The lobby at Wallis Sands Place has brochures to help you find boat tours, kayak rentals, whale-watching tours, fishing-boat rentals, and more.

On the cottage grounds there are shade trees, landscaped flowers, picnic tables, and charcoal grills.

Facilities: All cottages include cable television, fully equipped kitchens, and fans. They do not have telephones.

Bedding: Blankets or "puff" comforters, bedspreads, and pillows provided. Bring your own sheets and towels.

Reservations and rates: Rentals are weekly; some weekend and overnight reservations may be available. Rates are $475–688 weekly in season. Cash and travelers checks only. Open May–September. Pets are not allowed.

Directions: From Portsmouth take Route 95 to Exit 5. The exit ramp takes you onto the Portsmouth traffic circle, a large traffic rotary. Take the first exit you see, which will take you to Route 1 south. Drive two miles on Route 1 to Elwyn Road, where you'll see an intersection with traffic lights. You'll see signs that read "Route 1A and All Beaches." Turn left onto Elwyn Road, which is marked Route 1A. Drive for about two miles on Elwyn Road, turn right on Brackett Road and drive for another two miles, and you'll hit the shoreline. Turn right on Route 1A, and you'll see Wallis Sands Beach on the left and Wallis Sands Place on the right.

Contact: Wallis Sands Place, 1035 Ocean Boulevard, Rye, NH 03870, 603/436-5882, website: www.wallissands.com.

25. ATLANTIC FOUR WINDS EFFICIENCIES

Poolside in Rye

Luxury rating: ★ ★ ☆ ☆ ☆   **Recreation rating:** ★ ★ ★ ★ ☆

These cottages, located on Route 1A (the main scenic road in Rye), are a good deal for being so close to the beach. Be sure to bring a fun-loving attitude toward the din of splashing children, since the teal cottages with white trim form a horseshoe around the very popular pool. Kids scream and laugh their way down the pool slide and run around on the lawn.

© BETHANY ERICSON

Just across the busy road is a path allowing public access to the ocean beach of Wallis Sands State Park. The pool is a nice plus for those days when, despite the heat, you just can't get yourself to brave the chilly, New Hampshire seawater.

Atlantic Four Winds Efficiencies is run by Petey, the same person who runs Petey's Summertime Seafood & Bar, which is just down the street. Next door to the Four Winds's office you'll find pizza, subs, and ice cream.

Facilities: There are 11 standalone cottages, many with only one room, and a duplex cottage. The cottages sleep 2–4 people. All include kitchenettes, shower bath, cable television, and screened porches.

Bedding: Linens and towels are provided. Bring your own beach towels.

Reservations and rates: The cottage rates range $90–130 (daily) and $550–775 (weekly). There are lower rates in the off-season. Credit cards are required for reservations. Pets are not allowed.

Directions: From Portsmouth, take Route 95 to Exit 5. The exit ramp takes you onto the Portsmouth traffic circle, a large traffic rotary. Take the first exit you see, which will take you to Route 1 south. Drive for two miles on Route 1 to Elwyn Road, where you'll see an intersection with traffic lights. You'll see signs that read "Route 1A and All Beaches." Turn left onto Elwyn Road, which is marked Route 1A. Follow Elwyn Road for about two miles, turn right on Brackett Road, and drive for another two miles until you hit the shoreline at Wallis Sands State Park. Turn right onto Route 1A. Four Winds is located on Route 1A and is directly between Portsmouth and the intersection with Route 101.

Contact: Atlantic Four Winds Efficiencies, 1215 Ocean Blvd., Wallis Sands, Rye, NH 03870, 603/436-5140, website: www.atlanticfourwinds.com.

26. CROWN COLONY COTTAGES

on Ocean Boulevard in Rye

Luxury rating: ★ ★ ★ ☆ ☆   **Recreation rating:** ★ ★ ★ ★ ☆

On a grassy granite ledge overlooking scenic Route 1A, the Crown Colony Cottages have a commanding view of the ocean. The grassy grounds offer very little shade but are decorated with cheerful flowers. Fuchsia beach roses grow along the road near the pebble beach.

Just a 10-minute drive south of Portsmouth, the cottages are close to great swimming and sunbathing at Wallis Sands Beach, and nearby Rye Harbor provides boat docking and touring services. This stretch of Route 1A is a gorgeous, winding road along the ocean, bordered by beach roses and Queen Anne's lace.

The office has a multitude of brochures to help you plan your activities, whether you want to rent a kayak or go whale-watching. There are also boat trips to the nearby Isle of Shoals. Innkeeper Bill McCann knows the area and its history and can help direct you.

Facilities: There are 17 cottages that can accommodate 2–4 people. They have fully equipped kitchenettes, heat, and cable television. Seafood restaurants and Portsmouth are nearby.

Bedding: Fresh linens are provided, but you'll need to bring your own towels.

Reservations and rates: Reserve by January 1; repeat visitors are common. Cottage rates range $650–750 a week. There are lower rates and some nightly availability in the off-season. Open May–October. Credit cards are not accepted.

Directions: From Portsmouth, take Route 95 to Exit 5. The exit ramp takes you onto the Portsmouth traffic circle, a large traffic rotary. Take the first exit you see, which will take you to Route 1 south. Drive for two miles on Route 1 to Elwyn Road, where you'll see an intersection with traffic lights. You'll see signs that read "Route 1A and All Beaches." Turn left onto Elwyn Road, which is marked Route 1A. Drive for about two miles on Elwyn Road, turn right on Brackett Road, and drive for another two miles and you'll hit the shoreline near Wallis Sands State Park. Turn right on Route 1A, and continue to Rye, where you'll see Crown Colony Cottages on the right.

Contact: Crown Colony, 1381 Ocean Blvd., Rye, NH 03870, 603/436-8923.

27. RYE BEACH MOTEL AND COTTAGES

Straws Point in Rye

Luxury rating: ★★☆☆☆   **Recreation rating:** ★★★☆☆

© BETHANY ERICSON

A good way to beat the crowds and save some cash is to rent a cottage that's a short walk from the ocean, rather than right on the sand. Rye Beach Motel and Cottages is a pleasant .5-mile walk (or easy bike ride) through a flat residential neighborhood to a lovely sandy beach. Best of all, you won't have to deal with beach parking.

The white housekeeping cottages are very basic, with screened porches, gas grills, and those ubiquitous 1950s-style, round orange patio chairs. There are enough trees and umbrella tables to provide some shade, and the units are off the main road and very quiet.

The town of Rye takes up eight of New Hampshire's 18 miles of coast, and picnic areas, boat and fishing excursions, and nature trails abound.

Tennis and golf facilities are one mile away. The Seacoast Science Center, which has an aquarium and educational facilities, is also nearby.

For BMX riding, skateboards, or in-line skating, Rye Airfield, one of the "most advanced" extreme-sports parks in the country, is just a few miles away.

Facilities: There are eight cottages that can accommodate 2–6 people. The cottages have telephones, shower baths, cable televisions, and equipped kitchenettes including microwaves. Each also has a grill. General stores, supermarkets, and restaurants are all nearby.

Bedding: Linens and towels are provided.

Reservations and rates: Rentals are on a Saturday-to-Saturday basis and range $435–650 per week in high season. Reservations are taken year-round, but call early in the year, as there are many returning guests. Open mid-May–mid-October. Some well-behaved, small pets are occasionally allowed, but only with advance permission.

Directions: From Portsmouth, take Route 95 to Exit 5. The exit ramp takes you onto the Portsmouth traffic circle, a large traffic rotary. Take the first exit you see, which will take you to Route 1 south. Drive for two miles on Route 1 to Elwyn Road, where you'll see an intersection with traffic lights. You'll see signs that read "Route 1A and All Beaches." Turn left onto Elwyn Road, which is marked Route 1A. Follow Elwyn Road for about two miles, and turn right on Brackett Road. Drive for another two miles and you'll hit the shoreline near Wallis Sands State Park. Turn right on Route 1A and continue driving to Rye. You'll see Locke Road on your left; the cottages are at Locke and Old Beach Road.

Contact: Rye Beach Motel and Cottages, Old Beach and Locke Road, P.O. Box 371, Rye Beach, NH 03871, 603/964-5511 (in-season) or 978/458-3729 (off-season).

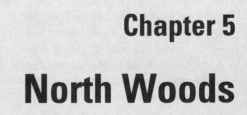

© BETHANY ERICSON

Chapter 5

North Woods

CHAPTER 5—NORTH WOODS

There is a tremendous amount of land in northern Maine to explore: the outlying areas of Bangor, the fabled Allagash, white-water rafting and snowmobiling territory, Baxter State Park, and the townships in Aroostook County. Maine's camps are evolving to offer a wide range of recreation beyond just fishing and hunting, and they are often an inexpensive alternative to other kinds of vacations. It's unlikely to become overcrowded anytime soon, but keep in mind as you travel here that the outdoors is the main focus of many people's visits. Most Maine camps are affordable and wild because they remain fairly rustic and spare; they're out in the woods, not hidden behind fake cell-phone tower trees. May it always be this way.

In the late 1970s, when log drives ceased, a few intrepid souls began riding the rapids down the Kennebec, Dead, and Penobscot Rivers just for fun. Thanks to them, and to the controlled dam releases by hydroelectric companies, white-water rafting began in Maine, and the popularity of the sport took off like Class V rapids. The Forks is also home to Moxie Falls, the highest falls in New England. Between Solon and Jackman Station (on Route 201) are a plethora of competing rafting outfitters, many with cabins and cottages to lodge their patrons. In winter, the area transforms into a major snowmobiling center. At all times of the year it is a common place to see moose.

The Penobscot River begins north of here, as does the Kennebec River. The latter finds its headwaters at 40-mile long Moosehead Lake. Greenville is the main town on the massive lake and is known as the largest seaplane base in New England. Once home to train stations and massive summer hotels that have long since disappeared, the great lake has retained a good number of Maine camps on its more than 400 miles of shoreline. Like Lake Winnipesaukee's *Mount Washington*, Moosehead Lake has a ghost that glides across the lake in the form of a steamboat, the *Katahdin*.

On the western shore, the area around Rockwood is home to The Birches, one of Maine's better-known camps. Rockwood faces one of the lake's most notable landmarks, the island peninsula of Mount Kineo. Its cliffs have produced the stone for many arrowheads in New England, and its slopes have been home to massive resort hotels. A relatively easy hike on Mount Kineo, which provides an incredibly rewarding view, is a must-do. In winter, there are miles of cross-country ski and snowmobile trails. Ice fishing is popular, as is skiing at Big Squaw Mountain.

The Appalachian Trail travels just south of the lake to Gulf Hagas, known as "the Grand Canyon of Maine." This gorge-ous place is known for its towering slate walls and enchanting waterfalls. Little Lyford Pond Camps are perfectly located for exploring the gorge. To see the majestic white "King's" pines that are the source of some esteemed wide floorboards in New England inns, visit the Hermitage here as well.

The Appalachian Trail eventually finds its terminus miles northwest of the gulf, atop Maine's highest peak, Mount Katahdin, in 250,000-acre Baxter State Park. Millinocket is the major access town to the park and nearby cabins. There is nothing quite like hiking the narrow Knife's Edge trail on Mount Katahdin, whose notoriety attracts crowds in summer and fall. The park also has a large number of ponds, lakes, streams, and waterfalls (don't forget your bug spray). Many visitors come just to see the moose, while others search out the variety of wood warblers, thrushes, and flycatchers.

Contrary to popular mythology, the area north of here is not all potato fields. Millions of acres of forest make up the northern woods, and it is here where you will find the isolated waters of the legendary Allagash Wilderness Waterway. This river corridor winds through working forest for 92 miles. A large percentage of visitors to the North Woods still arrive by canoe (the Allagash flows north to the Saint John River), yet the number of roads are multiplying, and remote cabins that once required visitors to arrive by water or air are now increasingly accessible.

Aroostook County is almost the size of Massachusetts and is the least populated part of Maine. It is mostly wooded; the potato fields, broccoli, and rotating grain crops are found in the rolling hills of central Aroostook. The culture of the land is a mix of Micmac, Maliseet, Acadian, and Swedish people, and those who farm, hunt, and fish. Over the centuries, the sounds of the many Native American place-names have been softened by French and then hardened by English, making them nearly impossible to accurately translate.

Just over the Saint John River is Canada. If you are exploring, or even just having dinner across the border, keep in mind that New Brunswick is on Atlantic time, while Maine is in the Eastern time zone.

When traveling north, be prepared for long drives, fewer services, and rougher roads. Pickup trucks and snowmobiles are the way to travel here; the road to the lake or mountain you seek may easily be down a muddy logging road that crosses a river—without a bridge. Check your spare tire, bring a flashlight, and make sure you're arriving when you're expected so that gates aren't locked on access roads. Stay alert for speeding logging trucks and moose, and enjoy.

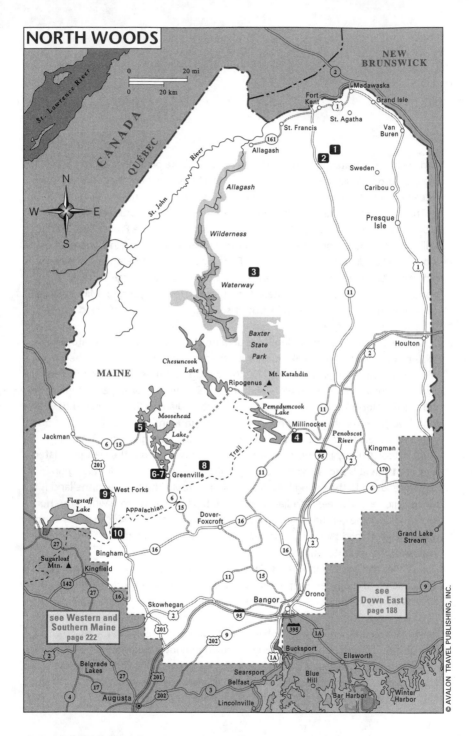

NEW BRUNSWICK

St. Lawrence River

Madawaska

Fort Kent

Grand Isle

St. Agatha

St. Francis

Van Buren

CANADA

QUÉBEC

Sweden

Allagash

Caribou

St. John River

Allagash

Presque Isle

St. John

Wilderness

Waterway

Houlton

Baxter State Park

Chesuncook Lake

Ripogenus

Mt. Katahdin

MAINE

Moosehead Lake

Pemadumcook Lake

Millinocket

Penobscot River

Kingman

Jackman

Greenville

West Forks

Flagstaff Lake

Appalachian

Trail

Dover-Foxcroft

Grand Lake Stream

Sugarloaf Mtn.

Bingham

Kingfield

Skowhegan

Bangor

Orono

see Down East page 188

see Western and Southern Maine page 222

Belgrade Lakes

Searsport

Belfast

Blue Hill

Bucksport

Ellsworth

Winter Harbor

Augusta

Lincolnville

Bar Harbor

© AVALON TRAVEL PUBLISHING, INC.

0   20 mi

0   20 km

CHAPTER 5
NORTH WOODS

1. EAGLE LAKE SPORTING CAMP

on Eagle Lake

Luxury rating: ★★☆☆☆   **Recreation rating:** ★★★★★

Rank: Top 10 for Fishing

Between beautiful Eagle Lake and Square Lake is a winding, shallow thoroughfare surrounded by Maine Public Lands. At the mouth of the Square Lake Thoroughfare, on a peninsula on Eagle Lake, the Eagle Lake Sporting Camp has resurrected some of the most beautiful old cabins that were once known as the Michaud Camps.

© EAGLE LAKE SPORTING CAMP

In the late 1800s, L. S. Titus, a New York sportsman, built these cabins with great skill as a place to hunt and fish with his friends. Later, they were taken over by the Michaud family and run as a camp. In the late 1930s, Eagle Lake Camps were accessible from the booming town by barges that ran twice a day. The trains arrived from the major cities regularly, and families would summer here while the fathers came up for weekends.

Today, some of those old trains sit in disrepair in the woods, and the town now has only a few stores and a hotel. For years, the Eagle Lake Camps have sat on this birch knoll over the lake like ghosts of another era. However, more and more people are beginning to return to the wilderness to relax, and the camps are being brought back to life as the Eagle Lake Sporting Camp.

The 13 birch bark–paneled log cabins all have been, or are being, renovated. They are accessible only by boat or by floatplane. All are heated and screened, with electric lights and bathrooms with running water. Each has a covered porch facing the lake and the peaks of the Three Brooks Mountain. The main lodge has a renovated version of the original stone fireplace; when it was built, it was said to be the largest fireplace in the state of Maine, using six-foot logs.

There is excellent fishing here for salmon and trout, and the cabins are all named after fishing flies. Moose are very frequently found grazing in the thoroughfare. Square Lake has an excellent fossil-laden point, and there are many places to hike and mountain bike in the area.

Facilities: The cabins can accommodate 1–10 people each, with a total capacity of 40 guests.

Bedding: Bedding is provided.

Reservations and rates: Be sure to reserve as early as possible, particularly while some of the cabins are undergoing renovations. Most cabins are rented on the American Plan. Adult prices range $75–95 nightly per person or $475–620 weekly (seven nights) per person. Discounts are available for children under 17. For families, there is a special rate of $1,450 for seven nights for two adults and two children. The Queen of the Water is the largest cabin and the only housekeeping cabin. The rate is $450 weekly (seven nights) for up to four guests, with a minimum stay of three nights. Additional guests are $20 per night or $100 per week. Ask about special rates for large groups and extended stays. No refunds are given for early departure. Gratuities for the staff are encouraged.

Directions: Directions are provided upon reservation; you can either take a boat or a canoe yourself across from Eagle Lake, or arrange with the camp to be picked up by boat.

Contact: Ed & Paula Clark, **Eagle Lake Sporting Camp**, P.O. Box 377, Eagle Lake, ME 04739, 207/752-0556, website: www.eaglelakesportingcamp.com.

2. FISH RIVER LODGE

on Eagle Lake

Luxury rating: ★ ★ ☆ ☆ ☆   **Recreation rating:** ★ ★ ★ ★ ★

Rank: Top 10 for Value

There are several Eagle Lakes in Maine; you'll know you're at this one if you've driven nearly as far north as it is possible in Aroostook County. This is a beautiful wilderness site, located just 1.5 miles from Route 11 (parts of which are a National Scenic Highway), but bordered by 26,000 acres of Maine Public Lands.

These camps have been in operation for more than 70 years and are basic accommodations frequented by anglers and hunters. More and more families and couples are using these camps to canoe, explore, and mountain bike on endless logging roads. If you have a camera, it's difficult to leave here without a picture of a moose.

The cabins are named after the local wildlife and include basic furnishings, gas heat, fully equipped kitchens, bathrooms with shower

© BETHANY ERICSON

stalls, and front porches facing the lake. A canoe is provided with your cabin.

Fishing is a huge draw in this area from early May until late September. This cold-water lake produces record levels of salmon and trout. Gas, fishing licenses, and some lures are available. Trolling with a fly rod is a popular way to fish here. If you bring your own boat, dock space is available. Boats with motors are also available for rent.

While anglers and hunters frequent this area, anyone with an interest in wildlife should consider visiting. Get up at dawn to canoe upstream from the Fish River Lodge, then turn and let the river bring you downstream. Moose, bear, deer, otter, and muskrat populate the area. There are easy and challenging mountains to hike, and you can take a boat to Limestone Point on Square Lake to hunt for fossils.

Guests are welcome to arrange for a guide for fishing or hunting expeditions ahead of time. At the end of the day you can relax in the lounge and watch television or videos, or simply join others on the spacious porch to listen to the loons and the splashes of all the ones that got away.

Facilities: There are eight cabins accommodating 2–8 people. There is an American Plan, individual meals on request, or you can shop for groceries 1.5 miles away. Boats are available for rent at $50 per day. Rental includes boat, motor, six-gallon tank of gas, paddles, and personal flotation device (PFD) for each occupant. During the summer months, canoes are included with the weekly rental of a cabin.

Bedding: Bedding is provided. You may want to bring your own beach towels.

Reservations and rates: Reservations are recommended. The daily rate is $80 per night, double occupancy, with a $30 fee for each extra adult, and $20 for each child 7 to 12 years old. The weekly rates range $400–500 per week, based on four-person occupancy, plus $120–140 for each extra adult, and $60 for a child 7 to 12 years old. Children under 7 are free. An American Plan is also available; inquire about rates. Open April–November. Credit cards are accepted, but $10 extra will be added to your rates. Quiet, leashed pets are welcome at no charge, and dog walking is available.

Directions: Fish River Lodge is about six hours north of Portland. Take I-95 to Exit 58. Drive north on Route 11 to the town of Eagle Lake. There are several stores that make up the village. Turn right by the general store and drive 1.5 miles on a paved road to the camps.

Other Cabins and Cottages Nearby

- Crooked Tree Lodge and Camps, P.O. Box 203, Portage, ME 04768, 207/435-6413, website: www.crookedtreelodge.com.

3. LIBBY CAMPS

Millinocket Lake and Beyond

Luxury rating: ★ ★ ☆ ☆ ☆   **Recreation rating:** ★ ★ ★ ★ ★

Rank: Top 10 for Fishing

The Libby family has been hosting fly-fishing fanatics for more than a century on Millinocket Lake, north of Baxter State Park. Owner Matt Libby is the fourth generation of his family to run the camps. These days, the family has something of an empire, with the main lodge and cabins, outpost camps scattered in the wilderness, and a lodge in Labrador. Unlike many Maine camps that are trying to diversify their activity options to attract a wider demographic, Libby Camps is an Orvis-endorsed facility that remains focused on fly-fishing for salmon and trout.

There are eight hand-hewn peeled-spruce and fir log cabins looking out over the lake. They are in the trees and are decently spaced apart. They have kerosene lamps and propane lights, and are heated by woodstoves. There are antique or handmade wooden beds. The cabins are rustic, but they do have flush toilets and showers and are cleaned daily. Canoes or 14-foot boats and motors are included with your cabin rental.

There are 10 varied cabins built in different spots in the wilderness. The Libbys will fly you in to these cabins, and they can also fly you to remote fishing spots. The cabins range from 40 to 60 miles from the nearest town, and most have trails to outlying ponds or mountains. Some are even winterized. If you love fly-fishing and dream of fishing where you aren't within earshot of another person, one of the Libby outpost cabins is for you.

The main lodge is a long building built on posts with a big back porch. Inside, you'll find a library full of fishing books to read in big Adirondack chairs while contemplating the lake. The dining room, where Matt's wife, Ellen, will provide your meals, is a great log room with chandeliers made from moose antlers, and with trophy fish decorating the walls. A cookbook of Ellen's recipes is available for purchase.

Come to Libby Camps for some good old-fashioned fishing on the headwaters of the Allagash, Aroostook, and Penobscot Rivers. Catch-and-release fishing is encouraged here, but if you reel in a real trophy, the camp will skin it for the taxidermist.

Facilities: There are eight cabins by the main lodge, accommodating up to five people, and 10 outpost cabins with at least four beds in each. Nonresident fishing licenses are available.

Bedding: Bedding is provided.

Reservations and rates: Cabin rates vary considerably depending on the package you take. Package rates for double occupancy range $135–265 per day per person. They include lodging, meals, maid service, boats, motors, and canoes. Some include seaplane flyouts or outpost cabin overnights, and some also include fishing licenses or full-guide service. You can even design your own package. Inquire about special rates for children under 15 or large groups. Outpost cabin rates range in price $100–1,045 per night, depending on the cabin and the number of people staying. Rates may be reduced for longer stays. Deposits of 30 percent are required and are nonrefundable.

Directions: Libby's home camps on Millinocket Lake are located in Township 8, Range 9 (between Baxter State Park and the Allagash Wilderness Waterway), 45 miles and nearly 1.5 hours of driving on private, gated, logging roads from Ashland to camp. You can drive in (directions given upon registration), or arrange to be picked up by seaplane (for a fee) from Presque Isle, Bangor, Millinocket, Old Town, Greenville, or Matagamon Lake (near Patten). Van transportation (for a fee) is also possible from Presque Isle or Bangor Airports and from Ashland or Oxbow (end of paved road).

Contact: Libby Camps, P.O. Box 810, Ashland, ME 04732, 207/435-8274, website: www.libbycamps.com.

Other Cabins and Cottages Nearby

- Umcolcus Sporting Camps, General Delivery, Oxbow, ME 04764, 207/435-8227, website: www.umcolcus.com.
- Bradford Camps, P.O. Box 729, Ashland, ME 04732, 207/746-7777 (May–November) or 207/439-6364 (December–April), website: www.bradfordcamps.com.

4. TWIN PINES CAMPS, NEW ENGLAND OUTDOOR CENTER

on Millinocket Lake

Luxury rating: ★ ★ ★ ☆ ☆   **Recreation rating:** ★ ★ ★ ★ ★

The New England Outdoor Center (NEOC) offers rafting, snowmobiling, and kayking adventures, as well as nearby lodging in two areas (here in Millinocket and at the Osprey Center Resort in Caratunk). The cabins located here at Twin Pines Camps are at NEOC's kayak-school location and have direct snowmobile access to Maine's Interconnected Trail System (ITS) 86 and NEOC's Wild Kingdom Trail. Just 14 miles away is NEOC's Rice Farm base lodge, where you can take on the technical challenge of rafting the Penobscot River. The cabins are also conveniently located for hiking in Baxter State Park, canoeing, fishing, and hunting.

© COURTESY/NEW ENGLAND OUTDOOR CENTER

There are small, medium, and large cabins, as well as a big lake house. The cabins vary in construction and age, but all include fully equipped kitchens. The small cabins tend to have a double bed and two twin bunk beds. Big Mud and Little Mud Cabins have great views of Millinocket Lake and Mount Katahdin. Grant Brook Cabin is on the cove and has a woodstove, and Wadleigh Brook Cabin is the most private location.

Medium-sized Bears and Hammond Ridge Cabins are right near the pool and whirlpool tub. Bears Cabin has only bunk beds, while Hammond Ridge has a cove view and a double bed, plus four bunks. Millinocket Stream Cabin is the largest log-cabin rental; it includes a fireplace and is near a small beach. Sandy Stream is a modern log cabin looking toward the mountain, and Guides Cabin has a cozy woodstove. Lookout Cabin is set further apart, which may come in handy for large groups of snowmobilers.

The Lake House Cabin has a big deck on the lake and good mountain views. It's half a mile away from the rest of the cabins, though guests have use of all Twin Pine Camps amenities. It has five bedrooms, a master bedroom with a deck, a whirlpool tub and a gas fireplace.

Lodging packages that include rafting trips are popular. Penobscot rafting trips begin with a calm section before dropping through the exhilarating Class V rapids of Ripogenus Gorge in the afternoon. Fall is a less-crowded and particularly beautiful time to raft, and the prices are often lower.

The kayak instruction begins in the lake before transitioning to the river. Snowmobilers will find that there are more than 130 groomed trails in the Katahdin region, and NEOC can set you up with a sled. The scenery is gorgeous here, whatever activity you choose.

Facilities: There are 11 cabins accommodating 6–13 people. There are also budget cabin tents available at the Rice Farm base lodge campground.

Bedding: Bedding is provided.

Reservations and rates: Adventure packages that include lodgings are offered. Cabin rates for accommodations only range $176–264 nightly and $985–1,478 weekly, plus $25 per person for each person over the designated occupancy. The large Lake House is $480 nightly and $2,688 weekly (based on eight people sharing). Pets are not permitted. Open year-round.

Directions: In Millinocket, drive along Route 157 through two sets of stop lights. At the second set of blinking lights, bear right just past a large white-and-brick school building (the Stearns Assisted Living Center). You will then see a sign to take your second left toward Twin Pine Camps and Baxter State Park. Take the second left. Twin Pine Camps is eight miles from town, on the right, at Millinocket Lake. You will see a sign for Twin Pine Camps and a 35 mph sign just before the gravel road. If you drive past North Woods Trading Post, you've gone too far. Turn right at the entrance road to Twin Pines, and follow Black Cat Mountain Road for one mile. The road will bear to the left and up a hill. The phone number at Twin Pines is 207/723-5523.

Contact: New England Outdoor Center, P.O. Box 669, Medway Road, Millinocket, ME 04462, 207/723-5438 or 800/766-7238, website: www.neoc.com.

Other Cabins and Cottages Nearby

- Pleasant Point Camps, P.O. Box 148, Millinocket, ME 04462, 207/460-5226, website: www.pleasantpointcamps.com.
- Katahdin Lake Wilderness Camps, Box 398, Millinocket, ME 04462, Camp Radio Telephone: 207/723-4050, Base Telephone (winter): 207/723-9867, website: www.katahdinlakecamps.com.
- White House Landing Camps, P.O. Box 749, Millinocket, ME 04462, 207/745-5116, website: www.mainerec.com/ware.shtml.
- Bowlin Camps, P.O. Box 251, Patten, ME 04765, 207/365-4500, website: www.bowlincamps.com.
- Buckhorn Camps, P.O. Box 639-SC, Millinocket, ME 04462, 207/745-5023, website: www.buckhorncamps.com.

5. THE BIRCHES RESORT

on Moosehead Lake

Luxury rating: ★ ★ ☆ ☆ ☆   **Recreation rating:** ★ ★ ★ ★ ★

Rank: Top 10 for Backcountry Winter Adventures

There are so many ways to enjoy a stay at The Birches that it's hard to decide what to do while you're there. This may be why visitors have been returning every year since the 1930s, staying in the bustling lodge, cabins, lakeside houses, yurts, and tent cabins on 11,000 private acres by Moosehead Lake.

© ROBERT MULLER/RESORT WEBMASTER

There are moose cruises twice a day, white-water rafting expeditions, ski and snowmobile trails, horseback riding, sailing lessons, kayaking, mountain biking, guided hikes, canoe trips, and a challenge course. Boats, skis, bikes, snowshoes, and more are available to rent. Guests are even allocated a boat-mooring space (be sure to reserve when you call), and guides are available for most activities.

The hand-hewn log cabins have numbers and names, most of them seemingly from a Henry Mancini album. They are all slightly different, but all are along the lake, with a woodstove or a fireplace and kitchens or kitchenettes. Cabin 2, Rambling Rose, has the only bathtub (the rest have showers) and a pier; Cabin 5, Catch a Rising Star, is near the beach; Cabin 7, Born Free, is near the beach and has snowmobile trail access; and Cabin 20, The Honeymoon Cabin, is nearest to the marina.

There are three year-round yurts on the cross-country (or mountain biking) trails. They are outfitted with double-burner propane stoves, gas lighting, a woodstove, pots and pans, five gallons of water, and an outhouse. Two of the yurts are within two miles of the lodge. Lookout/Overlook Yurt has a particularly nice view. Six miles away is the Poplar Hill Yurt on Brassua Lake. You can avoid skiing out with your pack, as The Birches will transport your gear and have your fire lit for you as you slog your way there unencumbered.

In the summer there are also affordable cabin tents available with plywood floors and elevated mattresses. They have electric lights (but not power outlets) and fire pits. Some are closer to the lake and some are in the trees. On the other end of the spectrum, there are a number of small houses rented by The Birches. Inquire for more information about what is available.

Back at the main lodge, with its canoe in the rafters and lake views, a full American meal plan is available in the summer. Trail guides and equipment rentals are based here, and you can curl up by the hearth. Behind the lodge are a hot tub and sauna open to all guests—a perfect way to end a very active day.

Facilities: There are 15 housekeeping log cabins, three yurts, 12 cabin tents, and about seven waterfront homes rented by the Birches. The cabins sleep up to six adults, and the yurts and tent cabins can accommodate four people.

Bedding: Bedding and linens are provided in the cabins. Sheets and linens are provided in the yurts and tent cabins; bring your own sleeping bag. Pet blankets may be requested, to help keep cabin furniture fur-free.

Reservations and rates: The cabin rates range $550–1,275 per week per cabin. Cabin tents are $140–150 per person per week or a $370 minimum. Yurts are $150–180 per person per week or a $245–270 minimum. Meal plans are also offered and are required for cabin dwellers in July and August. Shorter stay pricing is available. There is a $10 per night or $50 per week pet fee. Children under two are free, and those ages 3-12 years are half price. Wilderness Expeditions carry additional charges. Open year-round. Pets and smoking are allowed.

Directions: From the south, take I-95 to Exit 39. Drive north on Route 7 to Dexter, then take Route 23 to Guilford and Routes 6/15 to Greenville. Continue driving to Rockwood. After the Village Store, turn right across a bridge and then right again at the camp sign. The Birches driveway is several hundred yards farther on the right.

Contact: The Willard Family, **The Birches Resort**, P.O. Box 41, Rockwood, ME 04478, 800/825-WILD, website: www.birches.com.

Other Cabins and Cottages Nearby

- Gray Ghost Camps, P.O. Box 35, Rockwood, ME 04478, 207/534-7362, www.grayghostcamps.com.
- Maynard's in Maine, Maynards Road, Rockwood, ME 04478, 207/534-7703 or 888/518-2055, website: www.maynardsinmaine.com.

6. BEAVER COVE CAMPS

on Moosehead Lake

Luxury rating: ★ ★ ☆ ☆ ☆   **Recreation rating:** ★ ★ ★ ★ ★

Rank: Top 10 for Backcountry Winter Adventures

On the eastern shore of Moosehead Lake, these basic fishing and hunting cabins have been in operation since 1905. Ownership changed in the 21st century, and friendly hosts Marilyn and Dave Goodwin are continuing a legacy of affordable lodgings and outdoor activity. This is a quiet location, yet it is a very convenient eight-mile drive from Greenville, where equipment, outfitters, and restaurants abound.

© BEAVER COVE CAMPS LLC 2002

This is the kind of place where you can really have some fun. Imagine a May weekend trolling along Moosehead Lake or one of the many streams and ponds around. Or, even better, imagine some good, muddy mountain biking with your fishing gear and camp stove, then hooking a salmon on your Nymph and frying it up with some fiddleheads. Perhaps later in the summer you'll stroll through the woods to a hidden canoe and do some fly-fishing. Now that is Maine. Don't forget the bug dope.

The cabins have fully equipped kitchens, baths with showers, heat, porches, and picnic tables. All but one (the Honeymoon Cabin) have twin beds or bunk beds. Two of the cabins were built in the early 1900s, and one is a French Canadian vertical-log construction cabin.

Some of the cabins look out over the lake or at Burnt Jacket and Big Squaw Mountains. These are all rustic camp-type cabins with no frills. Some rooms have curtain dividers rather than doors, and there are no clocks, radios, televisions, or phones. What you get here is unlimited access to the outdoors.

Whether you are fishing in spring (ice-out is May 1 on Moosehead Lake), going on moose safaris or seaplane rides, white-water rafting, starting an Allagash expedition, hunting, skiing, or snowmobiling, you can't go wrong staying in this area.

Facilities: There are six housekeeping cabins, accommodating 2–10 people. Boat rentals and gas are available at a nearby marina.

Bedding: Linens and towels are provided.

Reservations and rates: Rates are $75 per night double occupancy with a two-night minimum. Additional guests are charged $17 each per night. Children under three stay for free. Reduced rates are available for clubs and large parties. Personal-watercraft riding is not permitted here. Open year-round. Pets are permitted with a small fee.

Directions: From the south, follow I-95 north to Exit 39 Newport, take Route 7 north to Dexter, drive on Route 23 north to Sangerville, and drive on Route 15 north to Greenville. Continue driving straight through the yellow flashing light in Greenville on Lily Bay Road. Drive 6.5 miles to Black Point Road (look for the sign on the left .5 mile past the marina). Turn left and stay on Black Point Road for 1.5 miles to the camps (you will veer left at two intersections: North Ridge Road and Cross Ridge Road. The camps are on the left, and there is a sign at the top of the access road.

Contact: Marilyn and Dave Goodwin, **Beaver Cove Camps**, LLC, P.O. Box 1233, 648 Black Point Road, Greenville, ME 04441, 207/695-3717 or 800/577-3717, website: www.beavercovecamps.com.

Other Cabins and Cottages Nearby

- Foster's Maine Bush Sporting Camps, P.O. Box 1230, Greenville, ME 04441, 207/695-2845.

7. MOOSEHEAD HILLS

on Moosehead Lake and Wilson Pond

Luxury rating: ★ ★ ★ ☆ ☆   **Recreation rating:** ★ ★ ★ ★ ★

Rank: Best for Skiing and Snowmobiling

You get the best of both modern and traditional camps when you find one with new log cabins. Moosehead Hills has beautiful cabins with creative woodworking touches. Even better, there is a choice of lakes. There are three cabins at the 50-acre home base on Moosehead Lake, and another cabin with a private dock on lovely Wilson Pond.

Only three miles from downtown Greenville, Moosehead Hills Cabins still manage to preserve a wilderness setting. The log cabins all have fully equipped kitchens, wood stoves or fireplaces, and charming stone chimneys. Some have whirlpool tubs. All have great decks with gas grills and views of the lake, the mountains, and the sunset.

Moosehead Lake offers a lot of room to explore. You can walk or drive from your cabin to the dock and moorings on the lake. Kayak rentals are available. Wilson Pond is smaller but less populated. The Sunrise Lodge cabin there has a dock, and you can rent a kayak, canoe, or 14-foot aluminum boat with a two-horsepower motor there. Both are favorite places to fish for salmon, as well as lake and brook trout.

Paddle yourself up the West Outlet to the Kennebec River, or explore the coves of the lake all day. You can fish, look for moose, and just relax here. Moosehead Hills can provide a van shuttle for your canoe or kayak trip and can also take you on a guided moose safari.

The home-base cabins are located in a wide expanse of land. Hike or snowshoe close to home and you may see moose, bubbling streams, fields of flowers, berry thickets, and a wide variety of birds. Your friendly hosts, Bill Foley and Sally Johnson, are well versed in local day hikes for all abilities; just ask.

You can also snowmobile from your cabin onto the Interconnecting Trail System. The Moosehead Trail circumnavigates the lake for 160 miles, and you can find gas and food along the way. You can also arrange to dogsled from your cabin, potentially even by moonlight. Cross-country skiing trails abound, and Big Squaw Mountain Ski Resort is nearby. And if all this activity is too much, just arrange ahead with your hosts, and they'll send a licensed massage therapist by your cabin.

Facilities: There are four cabins; three are on Moosehead Lake, and one is on Wilson Pond. They accommodate 5–8 people. Kayaks, canoes, rowboats, and a 14-foot aluminum boat are available for rental.

Bedding: Bedding is provided.

Reservations and rates: Rates for up to four people range $125–270 nightly, and $750–1,800 weekly. Additional guests are $30 per day or $180 per week. Children under 12 years are charged half price, and those under 6 stay free.

There is a two-night minimum stay, and a three-night minimum stay in July, August, and holidays at Moosehead Lake. Sunrise Lodge has a one-week minimum stay in July and August, and a three-night minimum stay on holiday weekends. Group rates are available. Open year-round. Pets are permitted in the Mooshead Lake cabins with a charge of $15 per pet per day.

Directions: From Massachusetts, take I-95 north to Exit 39 Newport, Maine (north of Waterville). Turn left at the end of the exit ramp. Follow Route 7 to Dexter, then Route 23 to Guilford, then Route 15 to Greenville. In Greenville, drive straight through the blinking yellow light and continue on the 418 Lily Bay Road (Kokadjo Road) for three miles. Moosehead Hills Cabins will be on your left.

Contact: Moosehead Hills Cabins, 418 Lily Bay Road, P.O. Box 936, Greenville, ME 04441, 207/695-2514, website: www.mooseheadhills.com.

Other Cabins and Cottages Nearby

- Wilson Pond Camps, P.O. Box 1354, Greenville, ME 04441, 207/695-2860.

8. LITTLE LYFORD POND LODGE

near Gulf Hagas

Luxury rating: ★ ★ ☆ ☆ ☆   **Recreation rating:** ★ ★ ★ ★ ★

Rank: Top 10 for Hiking, Top 10 for Backcountry Winter Adventures

Whether you arrive by car in the summer, or by skis or dogsled in the winter, Little Lyford is certain to charm you. These log cabins on the ridge by the west branch of Pleasant River were built in the 1890s. They remain in the wilderness, and they retain the atmosphere of a long-gone era. In order to preserve this piece of Maine heritage, the Appalachian Mountain Club (AMC) has just purchased the camps.

Located 20 miles east of Greenville, near Gulf Hagas, the cabins have gas lights and kerosene lamps, log-built furniture, cold water, wood-burning stoves, and outhouses. There are hot showers in summer and a cedar-camp sauna in winter. There is also a secluded housekeeping cottage, as well as a remote cabin you can backpack into. It is the only cabin on Mountain Spring Pond, and it has its own dock, canoe, and hand-pumped water.

Little Lyford is one of the best places to cross-country ski or dogsled in the winter. In winter, you need to arrive either of these ways or get picked up in Greenville. Equipment can be rented in Greenville. Fishing is another big draw, and previous owner and current camp manager Bob LeRoy has run workshops teaching fly-fishing to women and kids. The emphasis at Little Lyford is on catch-and-release fishing. Fishing rods may be rented on-site, but details of the AMC ownership are still being worked out.

Meals are served to the log-cabin dwellers in the main lodge. It's family style, and there is an emphasis on vegetarian dishes. Lunches are packed for trails or boats. Baked goods are cooked on the premises, organic vegetables and herbs are grown in the gardens, and eggs are from the hens kept here. Organic coffee roasted in Maine is served.

Nearby is the Appalachian Trail, which winds through Gulf Hagas (the Grand Canyon of Maine). This is a stunning area to hike, ski, and snowshoe—a four-mile-long gorge with enormous slate walls and spectacular rushing water and falls. Hikes to nearby Indian, Chairback, and White Cap Mountains also offer significant challenges. In the winter, dog sledding can be arranged, and in the summer there is complimentary use of rowboats and canoes on the ponds in the area.

Facilities: There are eight log cabins accommodating 1–4 people.

Bedding: Bedding and towels are provided.

Reservations and rates: Membership in the AMC is not required. Cabin rates are $120 per person per day, double occupancy. Special AMC member and children's rates apply. Transportation in winter is $20 per person for a round-trip gear shuttle, $35 per person to get a snowmobile ride and gear shuttle, and mushing can be arranged. Rates include breakfast, trail lunches, and dinner. There is a two-night minimum stay, and a three-night minimum stay during certain holidays. Open year-round. Credit cards are not accepted. Pets and smoking are not permitted.

Directions: From Greenville, turn east onto Pleasant Street (uphill) toward the airport, drive past Moosehead Farms and Rum Ridge, and follow the camp's blue-and-white signs for 12 miles to North Maine Woods Gate (fee). Drive another five miles to the Little Lyford Pond Camps driveway.

Contact: AMC Reservations Office, **(Little Lyford Pond Lodge)**, 603/466-2727 (Monday–Saturday 9 A.M.–5 P.M.).

9. THE MARSHALL HOTEL CABINS, MAGIC FALLS RAFTING COMPANY

West Forks

Luxury rating: ★★☆☆☆   **Recreation rating:** ★★★★★

Like most rafting outfitters in the Forks area, Magic Falls Rafting Company offers lodging, as well as white-water rafting trips, rock climbing, snowmobiling, and more. The Forks is known for its white water on the Kennebec and Dead Rivers. Lodging-and-rafting packages are common; be sure to inquire.

There is nothing quite like swooping into and over massive rapids to get your adrenaline flowing, and the post-raft atmosphere can be all about partying. Magic Falls took over the Marshall Hotel, a Forks landmark, as well as the hotel's associated cabins. The hotel features bands every Saturday night, as well as a large outdoor deck with a hot tub. The cabins, located across Route 201, give the option of more privacy and quiet.

The cabins come in three sizes, and are all winterized and heated. They have full baths, gas fireplaces, fully equipped kitchens, and back decks overlooking the Kennebec River. Eagles and osprey frequent the view.

The Kennebec River has a popular 12-mile run that is truly beautiful during the fall foliage. It has Class V rapids in spots, but most of the big action happens in the first part of the trip. If you're looking to have a gentler start to the day, the Dead River run starts in calmer waters but soon roils up to one of the longest white-water stretches (16 miles) in the region. Magic Falls Rafting Company also has some runs with sport boats, the smallest rafts legally viable on the rivers.

> **Facilities:** There are five cabins that accommodate 4–10 people. Additional lodging is available in the Marshall Hotel and the Trailside House Bed & Breakfast.
>
> **Bedding:** Bedding is provided, but you should bring your own towels.
>
> **Reservations and rates:** The rate for cabins is $120 per night for four people. Additional people are charged $30 per night. There is a two-night minimum on weekends.
>
> **Directions:** From Portland, take I-95 north. Get off at Exit 36 drive on Route 201 north for approximately 65 miles. The Marshall Inn will be on the right, with

the cabins located across the road. Check in at the Hotel.

Contact: Magic Falls Rafting Company, **(Marshall Hotel Cabins)**, P.O. Box 9, West Forks, ME 04985, 800/207-7238, website: www.magicfalls.com.

Other Cabins and Cottages Nearby

- Northern Outdoors, P.O. Box 100, The Forks, ME 04985, 800/765-RAFT, www.northernoutdoors.com.
- Cedar Ridge Outfitters, P.O. Box 744, Attean Rd., Jackman, ME 04945, 207/668-4169, website: www.cedarridgeoutfitters.com.

10. THE OSPREY CENTER RESORT, NEW ENGLAND OUTDOOR CENTER

on Wyman Lake in Caratunk

Luxury rating: ★★★★☆   **Recreation rating:** ★★★★★

New England Outdoor Center (NEOC) offers rafting, snow-mobiling, and kayaking adventures, as well as nearby lodging in two areas (here in Caratunk and at Twin Pines Camps, in Millinocket). The Osprey Center Resort has some new, very modern lakeside cabins and guest houses, as well as cabin tents. Caratunk is a rural set-

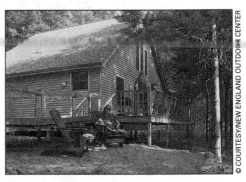

ting convenient for rafting on the Kennebec and Dead Rivers and for snowmobiling on Maine's Interconnected Trail System (ITS) 87, which leads to the Jackman, Moosehead, and Rangeley regions.

The Kennebec River has a popular 12-mile run that is known for its remote setting and roller-coaster waves ranging 2–12 feet high. The majority of the drama is in the first half of the run. The Dead River has the longest continuous white-water stretch (16 miles) in the region.

The Osprey Center Resort is also a good base in winter and is great for hunting, fishing, or moose-viewing. It has a 14-person outdoor hot tub, snowmobile rentals, volleyball nets, a swimming area, and free use of canoes and sit-on-top kayaks. The cabins come with housekeeping services and have full kitchens, picnic tables, gas grills, and fire pits.

The swanky Point House is a spacious lakeside house that sleeps up to 13 people and includes a black leather couch and a game room. The three Silver Cove Guest Houses overlook the lake. They have four queen beds in their knotty-pine interiors. The six Sterling Lakeside Guest Houses are also on Wyman Lake. They have cathedral ceilings, two downstairs bedrooms, and extra loft bedrooms with three double beds.

From April to October there is also a budget option. Canvas Cabin Tents have screened doors and windows, cots with bedding, gas lights, and a fire ring.

Facilities: There are nine guest houses, plus the Point House. Additionally, 13 cabin tents are available April–October.

Bedding: Bedding is provided.

Reservations and rates: Cabin rates range $258–318 per night and $1,444–1,780 weekly, plus $25 per person for each person over the designated occupancy. Canvas Cabin Tent Lodging is $22–25 per person. It's open year-round (except for Canvas Cabin Tents, which are open April–October). Pets are not permitted.

Directions: From Portland, follow I-95 to Exit 36 at the 133 mile marker. Drive on Route 201 north, through Skowhegan (watch for the right turn on Route 201, over the Kennebec River as you enter Skowhegan). Driving north, you will pass through the towns of Solon and Bingham. From Bingham, The Osprey Center Resort is 13 miles north on Route 201. The entrance to the base is on the left, across from the Sterling Inn.

Contact: New England Outdoor Center, **(The Osprey Center Resort)**, P.O. Box 669, Medway Road, Millinocket, ME 04462, 207/723-5438 or 800/766-7238, website: www.neoc.com.

Other Cabins and Cottages Nearby

• North Country Rivers, P.O. Box 633, Bingham, ME 04920, 800/348-8871, website: www.ncrivers.com.

© BETHANY ERICSON

Chapter 6

Down East

CHAPTER 6—DOWN EAST

I n this part of Maine, you'll find the largest whirlpool in the Western Hemisphere, the only fjord on the East Coast, and the stunning red-and-green rocks of Jasper Beach. Inland lakes and rivers offer world-renowned fishing. This area has a piece of the unpopulated, rugged, salty coast that early settlers might have found in other parts of the East Coast. It still calls for creative harvesting of natural resources for survival today. The coastline has a great deal of character with its many bays and islands, and the economy in many areas is still based on fishing, boatbuilding, and blueberries.

The Blue Hill peninsula is known for its high population of craftspeople and musicians. There are numerous galleries and a lending library just for sheet music. The area has long been a center for boatbuilding.

Near Stonington, at the tip of Deer Isle, lies Isle au Haut, which contains a portion of Acadia National Park. Meanwhile, downtown Castine is a quiet, pristine town that came back from a post-shipping era slump with the arrival of the Maine Maritime Academy. It is a very quiet and picturesque town, with an ancient post office, a smattering of stores, and fabulous baked goods. Four countries have owned Castine in its lifetime. It's said that it is named after a rich Frenchman who settled down here with a Penobscot Native American princess.

East of here, Mount Desert Island is made up of four very different towns and is the biggest part of Acadia National Park. Bar Harbor, on deep Frenchman Bay, is a busy tourist town in summer. It offers charter boats to see wildlife or fish, as well as the ferry to Nova Scotia, and is a port of call for cruise ships. The rich and famous once built mansions on this island, and in the late 1800s, hotel rooms had to be booked two years in advance. A great fire in 1947 demolished many of these old buildings. Fall is a very beautiful and less-crowded time of year to visit the island.

The other towns of the island are full of yachts and fishing boats. The split in the shape of the island is created by Somes Sound, a large, beautiful, natural fjord. Acadia National Park has a driving loop that includes Cadillac Mountain, where you can see the sun rise before anyone else in the country from the one of the highest spots on the Eastern Seaboard. Also, along the loop are beaches, cliffs, and crashing waves. All throughout the park are hiking trails and a network of carriage paths that make for fantastic biking. There are beautiful kayaking spots and lakes for swimming and canoeing. There are numerous cabins and cottages on Mount Desert Island; the ones profiled here are only a sample.

The majority of the Down East coast lies east of here, yet the majority of travelers never set foot east of Ellsworth. It is to their great loss. Take a look at this area on a map. To one side of the highway is the ocean, to the other, nary a road. Routes 1 and 186, where they loop around to the Schoodic Peninsula, are National Scenic Byways, and Route 186 takes you to the Schoodic Point section of Acadia National Park. Signs posted along Route 1 offer jobs for sea-urchin divers. Great kayaking and sailing harbors are visible behind towering piles of lobster traps.

Enormous Washington County's delicious-smelling balsam firs give way to blueberry barrens and Maine Public Reserve Lands out of sight to the north. There are still traditional Passamaquoddy basket makers on the reservation near Eastport, where stone-ground mustard is also still milled like it was years ago to pack sardines. Lubec, with its widely photographed striped lighthouse, is the access point to Roosevelt's beloved summering island of Campobello, which is part of Canada. It's not unusual to see whales from the shore.

Far Down East, the Gulf of Maine polishes an astounding beach of red-and-green jaspar and rhyolite, and the Grand Manan Channel sweeps past seals and puffins into Passamaquoddy Bay, where the Old Sow whirlpool can be seen from boats and even the shore. The tidal differences in this area can be as much as 24 feet; where the water rushes through a narrow channel into Cobscook Bay, it creates Reversing Falls. At low tide, you can search for fossils and soft-neck clams. Petroglyphs in the area show evidence that the Etchimins, a seafaring tribe, witnessed the arrival of European ships. More than 200 species of birds visit Moosehorn National Wildlife Refuge.

West of Calais (pronounced CAL-us) and Princeton, Grand Lake Stream attracts families and anglers. Once it was the home to one of the world's biggest tanneries. A great business arose from hosting and entertaining the customers waiting for their skins. Today, the area is filled with fishing camps, hiking trails, and excellent areas for mountain biking. The Atlantic salmon, once the big catch in the Narraguagus and Machias Rivers, are currently protected, but the landlocked salmon, trout, and smallmouth bass are plentiful here, as well as in Schoodic, Bog, Cathance, and other lakes.

From the souvenir stores in Bar Harbor to the Rogue Bluffs State Park, to the Bay of Fundy, to the vast inland wilderness, Down East is real Maine. Drive until you feel moved by the tide to stop, and then stay and explore for as much time as you can afford.

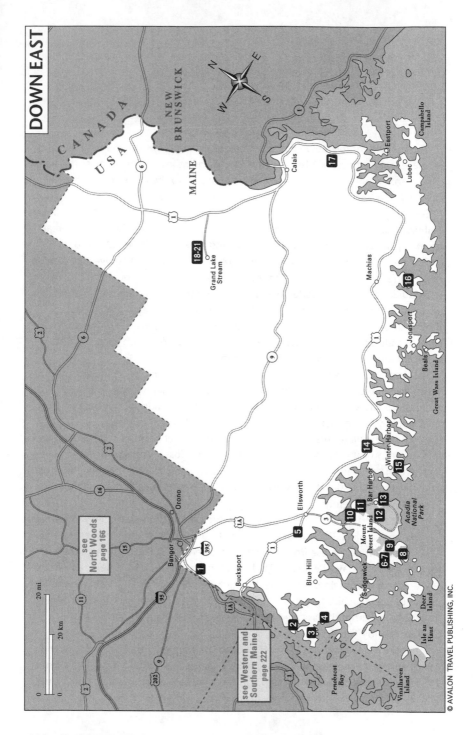

DOWN EAST

CANADA

USA

NEW BRUNSWICK

MAINE

Grand Lake Stream

18-21

Calais

17

Eastport

Campobello Island

Lubec

Machias

16

Jonesport

Beals

Great Wass Island

Winter Harbor

14

15

Ellsworth

Bar Harbor

11 **13**

10 **12**

Mount Desert Island

Acadia National Park

9

6-7 **8**

Sedgewick

Blue Hill

5

Bucksport

1

Bangor

Orono

see North Woods page 166

see Western and Southern Maine page 222

2

3

4

Penobscot Bay

Deer Island

Isle au Haut

Vinalhaven Island

20 mi

20 km

© AVALON TRAVEL PUBLISHING, INC.

CHAPTER 6
DOWN EAST

1. LOON HOLLOW

on Fields Pond in Orrington

Luxury rating: ★ ★ ★ ★ ☆   **Recreation rating:** ★ ★ ★ ★ ★

Rank: Top 10 Most Unusual

The owner is of a group of cottages can make all the difference in the world. In this case
that person is Linda, whom
you will quickly come to
adore. She believes in creative
enrichment; whether you
want to schedule an artistic
retreat or join her and the kids
in creating your own Loon
Hollow T-shirts, it's possible

here. The creative surroundings make this an ideal environment for
self-expression.

Loon Hollow is an unexpected magical escape located close to the city
of Bangor. Tucked away on a pond in Orrington, you will find privacy
and seclusion, as well as completely personalized warmth and care for
you and your soul.

There are three cottages here: Honeymoon Cottage, the Victorian, and
the enchanting little gingerbread house known as the Well House. You
will not find a television or phone in any of them. You *will* find personalized notes, surprise baked goods, fresh flowers, incredibly creative decor,
and even some artwork done by previous guests.

Fields Pond is a 180-acre rocky-bottom pond with otters, eagles, and
herons. Here you can fish for perch, pickerel, and smallmouth bass. Loon
Hollow offers kayaks and boats. Nearby is the Audubon Nature Center,
with 180 acres of trails along the lake. A short drive away is a gentle day
hike on Bald Mountain. Meanwhile, grand Mount Katahdin, Mount Battie, and Mount Blue are within a 40-minute drive. Linda is happy to help
design day trips for you and will perhaps send you with a bike and a picnic to an island via a mail boat, or on a horseback ride though fabulous
scenery. Down the street, the Curran Homestead is creating a living-history farm for the kids to explore.

Facilities: There are three cottages that can accommodate 1–9 people. These are housekeeping cottages, but if you are staying for a long period of time, Linda will help you clean.

Bedding: Linens are provided. The Victorian has a washer and dryer.

Reservations and rates: Rates range $595–1,495 per week, and there are lots of specials. The Well House and Honeymoon Cottage are rented Saturday–Saturday and the Victorian is rented Sunday–Sunday. Call as early as possible. By the end of the previous year, the Victorian and Honeymoon cottages are typically booked. Open year-round. No credit cards are accepted.

Directions: Directions will be provided upon reservation.

Contact: Loon Hollow, 22 Loon Hollow, Orrington, ME 04474, 207/825-3128, website: www.loonhollow.com.

2. CASTINE COTTAGES

East Penobscot Bay

Luxury rating: ★ ★ ☆ ☆ ☆   **Recreation rating:** ★ ★ ★ ★ ★

Rank: Top 10 for Value

Out on the peninsula town of Castine, set well back from the road on a great lawn, these six log housekeeping cottages offer wonderful water views. This is a peaceful spot to roam the 1,500 feet of beach on Hatch's Cove, gathering mussels or digging for clams to cook up in your own seaside cottage.

© BETHANY ERICSON

The entire town of Castine, with its quaint, elm-lined streets, is on the National Register of Historic Places. Nearly half of the town's population are college students attending Maine Maritime Academy. The Academy is host to the annual L.L. Bean Atlantic Coast Sea Kayak Symposium, a very popular event, with workshops and boat demonstrations.

Alan and Diane Snapps are the third generation of their family to run these cozy, clean cottages. It's a casual atmosphere, where you may check yourself in to relax on your screened porch, or get comfortable by the woodstove while contemplating the romantic view toward the Bagaduce

River, Blue Hill, and the Brooksville Hills. (Be a little careful in Cottage 1; one couple conceived both times they visited there!)

The cottages have small kitchens with apartment-size ovens, full sinks, and lobster pots. There is nice wood paneling and wood floors, as well as cassette radios. The bathrooms have shower stalls, and the living rooms have braided rugs and picture windows. These are older cottages but are well kept and comfortable. Down on the cove, you can easily launch a kayak, rowboat, or canoe.

Castine has tennis courts, a yacht club, and one of the oldest nine-hole golf courses in the country. There are walking and hiking trails nearby in Witherle Woods; the hearty can swim in the cold water off the rocky-sand beach at Wadsworth Cove (Back Shore); and you can fish off the rocks at Dyce's Head Lighthouse. And don't miss the pastries at Bah's Bakehouse, in town.

Facilities: There are six cottages that can accommodate 2–5 people. One is winterized.

Bedding: Blankets are provided; linens are not.

Reservations and rates: Rates range $430–500 a week, double occupancy. During the off-season period, the units are rented nightly for $75–150. Credit cards are not accepted. You may bring a small dog with Castine Camp's permission.

Directions: If you are driving north on Route 1, turn right (after passing through Bucksport) onto Route 175. After driving for approximately 12–13 miles, bear left at the fork in the road onto 166 (not 166A). The cottages are 3.6 miles from the point where you turned left. Look for the sign on your left.

Contact: Alan Snapp, **Castine Cottages**, 33 Snapp's Way, Castine, ME 04421, 207/326-8003, www.castinecottages.com.

3. HIRAM BLAKE CAMP

on Cape Rosier

Luxury rating: ★ ★ ☆ ☆ ☆   **Recreation rating:** ★ ★ ★ ★ ★

Rank: Top 10 for Boating

Cape Rosier still feels like old-school Down East Maine, and Hiram Blake Camp, on the southern end of the cape, is the perfect place to bask in an appropriate camp atmosphere. These weathered gray cottages are on the rocky shore of Penobscot Bay, a famous sailing area. In fact, a short drive away (in Brooklin) is the WoodenBoat School, where you can build your own sailboat.

The cottages are scattered across gardens and woods among the outbuildings of the camp, but all are within 200 feet of the shore. There are rowboats to explore in and a recreation room for kids. The dining hall is also an impressive library.

After a day of kayaking in the bay, you can relax in front of your stone fireplace or woodstove and eat fresh-caught fish on 1950s dishware. Hike the trails surrounding the camp and nearby Holbrook Island Sanctuary on a sunny day, and stroll through the apple trees by the garden on a starry night.

This is a family operation that has been run by generations of Captain Hiram Blake's family. Dinner and breakfast are served in the peak season here, family style. Thanks to the family fisherfolk, dinner typically involves fresh seafood. Lobster is always available.

The Good Life Center, well-known authors Helen and Scott Nearing's nonprofit organization dedicated to simple sustainable-living philosophies, is at nearby Forest Farm, and workshops are still run there.

Facilities: There is a one-room cottage and six one-bedroom cottages—five with two bedrooms, and one with three bedrooms. The Oaks Lodge is a duplex for six. Each has a wood-burning stove, and some have a fireplace as well.

Bedding: All linens are provided.

Reservations and rates: In season, the cottage rates range $450–2,225. Off-season, meals are not included, and rates range $200–700. Credit cards are not accepted. Restrained pets are allowed.

Directions: Heading east from Bucksport on Route 1, bear right onto Route 175 (Castine Road). After about eight miles, turn right onto Route 175/176. Follow Route 176 and turn right onto Cape Rosier Road. Drive along this road to the intersection with Weir Cove Road.

Contact: Hiram Blake Camp, Deborah Venno Ludlow, Manager, 220 Weir Cove Road, Harborside, ME 04642, 207/326-4951.

4. OAKLAND HOUSE SEASIDE RESORT

on Eggemoggin Reach

Luxury rating: ★ ★ ★ ☆ ☆   **Recreation rating:** ★ ★ ★ ★ ★

Rank: Top 10 for Weddings

Oakland House is one of the large Maine resorts that once dotted the shore at the beginning of the 20th century. Few of these coastal grand dames are left. This is a fabulous location for kayaking with the seals and loons in Eggemoggin Reach, while osprey and bald eagles soar overhead.

The resort was started by Emery H. Herrick in 1889. Four generations of innkeeping later, Jim Littlefield still carries on the family tradition. In addition to the inn, the resort now includes 15 cottages and the Oakland House restaurant.

The cottages are scattered across 50 wooded and shoreline acres. Some of them are log cabins built in the 1920s and have campy furnishings, others were built more recently, from timber on the property. One cabin overlooks the bay from atop a hill, one is a converted boathouse right on the water's edge, another has an office with a desk to pen your ocean-going memoirs. All are cheery with vintage charm, and the resort is oriented toward the setting sun and the lovely Pumpkin Island Lighthouse.

The resort has beaches, a wharf, guest moorings, and rowboats. It is also just a short walk to a sandy beach on Walker Pond for swimming in water a tad warmer than the northern Atlantic. In the area there are boat tours, whale-watching cruises, kayak rentals, and fishing charters. A short drive away is Acadia National Park, Holbrook Island Sanctuary, the WoodenBoat School, and Haystack Mountain School of Crafts.

Most of the cottages have cooking facilities. Some of the cottages have granite fireplaces made from stone quarried nearby, and some are true log cabins. Be sure to specify if you want to be in the woods or on the edge, with views of Eggemoggin Reach and Penobscot Bay, and don't miss the art classes, bike and boating tours, and other events offered through the resort.

Facilities: There are 15 cottages with 1–10 bedrooms.

Bedding: All linens are provided.

Reservations and rates: Rates range from $415 a week without meals in the off-season to $4,040 per week with meals for a family of four in high season. During high season, cottages are rented per person per cottage per week. During the off-season, they are rented without meals, maid service, or firewood. Inquire about discounts and special packages. Pets are not permitted.

Directions: Oakland House is 50 miles south of Bangor. From Blue Hill, drive along Route 15 south for 10 miles until you see the signs for Oakland House. It's close to the Deer Isle Bridge that crosses from the mainland to Deer Isle.

Contact: Oakland House Seaside Resort, 435 Herrick Road, Herricks Landing, Brooksville, ME 04617, 207/359-8521, website: www.oaklandhouse.com.

5. PATTEN POND CAMPING RESORT

on Patten Pond near Bar Harbor

Luxury rating: ★★☆☆☆   **Recreation rating:** ★★★★★

Cabins in campgrounds cover the full range of the meaning of "rustic." Here at Patten Pond, you'll find clean camping cabins in a well-run campground for a reasonable price. The hot property here is the Loon's Cry cottage, located right on the pond. But for a simple roof over your head at night and all the amenities of a camping resort, the Baby Bug cabins fit the bill.

The campground offers swimming and great fishing from its beach. They have a wide range of boat rentals available, from canoes and kayaks to sailboats and motorboats. The campground also has bike rentals, basketball and volleyball courts, horseshoes, a playground, a video game room, and a modem center.

The lakefront cottage has nice water views, and there is nothing like the sound of loons at night. It has knotty-pine paneling and fairly basic furniture, a full kitchen, a bathroom with shower stall, and one bedroom with a queen bed. There are two futons that pull out in the living room. It also has a porch, picnic table, and fire ring.

The four camping cabins are quite small, but clean, and very convenient to the impressively modern and clean bathhouse and laundry building. They are knotty pine with microwaves and a tiny table. There are two bunk beds with mattresses. One of the

© BETHANY ERICSON

lower bunks fits two people. The small covered porches look at the playground.

If you don't mind the cutesy ladybug theme prevalent throughout the campground, you may appreciate the high level of organization. On-site you'll also find an enclosed entertainment pavilion; a store with supplies, groceries and gifts; and a free shuttle connecting with the *Island Explorer*, the free shuttle traversing Acadia National Park and beyond.

Facilities: There are four Baby Bug cabins accommodating 1–5 people in the campground, and Loon's Cry, a lakeshore cottage that holds five people.

Bedding: Linens are available for rent.

Reservations and rates: The Baby Bug camping cabins are rented for $350–450 a week, while the Loon Cry lakefront cottage is rented for $600–990 per week. Rates are based on a family of four staying, meaning two adults and two children under 18. Inquire about AAA discounts. Open May 1–October 31.

Directions: From the south, take I-95 to Portland. Then drive on Coastal Route 1 toward Ellsworth. Continue driving for 11.5 miles past Bucksport, and you will see Patten Pond Camping Resort on the right.

Contact: Patten Pond Camping Resort, Routes 1 and 3, 1470 Bucksport Road, Ellsworth, ME 04605, 207/667-7600 or 877/667-7376, website: www.pattenpond.com.

6. PARSONS OCEANFRONT COTTAGES

overlooking Blue Hill Bay

Luxury rating: ★ ★ ☆ ☆ ☆   **Recreation rating:** ★ ★ ★ ★ ★

For a great private sunset view while staying on Mount Desert Island, head to the southwest coast of the "quiet side." Looking out over the great expanse of Blue Hill Bay, Parsons Oceanfront Cottages has a spectacular view and a casual and cheery atmosphere.

There are three homey cottages at Parsons. The very cute little First Mates Cabin is the closest to the waterfront. It's tiny, with a sofa bed, but it is clean and fun, and is a cheap way to stay on the island with a loved one.

The Captain's Cottage is nearby, with two bedrooms and a great wrap-around deck for grilling some fresh fish while enjoying the view. The Guest House is the largest unit. It's set over the gardens and also looks at the water for inspiration. The kitchen in the Guest House is spacious, and the dining table has a sliding glass door next to it.

All the clean and cozy cottages are heated, have cable television, outdoor decks or cooking spaces, and offer kitchen facilities. There is a pebble beach at Parsons, but the water is fairly cold for swimming.

© BETHANY ERICSON

The southwestern portion of Mount Desert Island is easily accessible to Acadia National Park, with nearby hiking, cycling, and freshwater ponds—as well as all the sailing, kayaking, and fishing your heart could desire.

Facilities: There are three cottages that hold 2–7 people.

Bedding: Bring your own linens and towels.

Reservations and rates: Rates range $450–775 per week. The cottages are rented weekly Saturday–Saturday. Open May–October. Pets are permitted with advance permission.

Directions: From Ellsworth, drive on Route 3 to Mount Desert Island. At the intersection with Route 102, take Route 102 through Southwest Harbor to West Tremont. Turn left onto Richtown Road and follow the signs.

Contact: Parsons Oceanfront Cottages, West Tremont, ME 04612, 207/244-5673 or 941/426-9612 (January–April), website: www.acadiainfo.com/parsons.htm

Other Cabins and Cottages Nearby

- Sunset Cottages, P.O. Box 223, Bernard, ME 04612, 207/244-3760 or 800/276-7084, website: www.sunsetcottagesacadia.com.

7. SEASIDE COTTAGES

on Blue Hill Bay

Luxury rating: ★ ★ ★ ☆ ☆   **Recreation rating:** ★ ★ ★ ★ ☆

Your privacy is well guarded at Seaside Cottages, on the "quiet side" of Mount Desert Island. Caring owner Kathy Shields won't let nonguests wander the grounds or allow anything to invade your space while you're spending time here. And especially if you've come here from a city, you'll definitely feel you've escaped the minute you see the amazing view across Blue Hill Bay.

Like many of the residents and business owners of this quieter side of the island, Kathy aims to keep things relaxed and quiet. The cottages are well maintained, she doesn't allow reunions or large parties, there are no televisions in the cottages (though you are welcome to bring a portable set), and she's on-site most of the time in case you need anything. She has no plans to add more cottages.

Seaside is on seven acres and has 500 feet of frontage on a stone beach looking southwest. There are two cottages with woodstoves and with decks looking out over the bay. These two, Pinelodge and Cedarlodge, sleep four people, while the third cottage, Paul's Cottage, is a three-bedroom place. Paul's Cottage has a cathedral ceiling in the living room, a giant granite fireplace, a kitchen with a dishwasher, and a 400-square-foot deck overlooking the bay.

This is the less commercial side of the island, with plenty of hiking and beach activities on the western side of Acadia National Park. You can bring and launch a kayak here at Oceanside, though arriving by a larger boat would be more difficult.

Facilities: There are three different cottages accommodating four people in each.

Bedding: Pillows and blankets are provided. Bring your own bed, bath, and kitchen linens.

Reservations and rates: Rates range $600–2,100 per week, and cottages are rented Saturday–Saturday. Reservations are taken year-round. Open May–October. Credit cards are not accepted.

Directions: Directions will be given when you reserve.

Contact: Seaside Cottages, HC33 Box 172, West Tremont, ME 04612, 207/244-7746, website: www.seasidecottages.com; off-season: P.O. Box 100, 80 Mill Street, Orono, ME 04473, 207/866-3546.

8. BASS HARBOR COTTAGES

quiet side of Mount Desert Island

Luxury rating: ★ ★ ★ ☆ ☆   **Recreation rating:** ★ ★ ★ ★ ☆

At Bass Harbor Cottages, they're trying to keep the "quiet side" of Acadia quiet. And tidy. Located on the southern end of the southwestern half of Mount Desert Island, these lovely cottages have wonderful water views of Bass Harbor and Blue Hill Bay. If you are most comfortable where you know it will not be a party scene at night, where no one will be picnicking or cooking outdoors, and where no one will leave kayaks on the grounds, then this place is for you.

Folks on the "quiet side" like to say that you can hear the birds sing and the waves crash rather than the tourists merrymaking. Many visitors to the park never even visit this side of the island during their stay. Bass Harbor is predominantly a fishing village. It's a great place to take a stroll by lobster boats and sailboats on the rocky shoreline. And it's a quiet alternative for lodging when exploring all that Acadia National Park offers.

For easy hikes in the area, there are the Wonderland Trail and the Ship Harbor Nature Trail. Slightly more strenuous is Seal Cove, and Flying Mountain is good for families. Bring water shoes for wading; a staircase leads to the water's edge, and the tides range 9–13 feet. You cannot launch a kayak from here.

Pines shade the cottages, and all face the water. They differ in size. The Carriage House cottage holds up to six people in three bedrooms, but be sure to get dibs on the cozy master bedroom, which has a balcony, skylights, and a sauna. The Pine Cottage is smaller and more basic but has nice touches, like skylights and a fireplace. The Boat House Cottage is a duplex unit that looks out toward the harbor. It has a nice second-floor queen suite with a deck and a modern kitchen. The cottages have cable television and no phones.

Facilities: There are three cottages accommodating 1–6 people. In the high season, the units are rented by the week, and in the off-season, there are minimum stay requirements. Call to be matched to your expectations. This is a small, quiet place that does not invite reunions or large parties. Well-behaved, supervised kids are welcome. Kayaks must be kept on vehicles. Quiet hours are 9 P.M.–9 A.M. A convenience store is .5 mile away, and the grocery store is three miles away.

Bedding: Linens are not supplied for weekly rentals.

Reservations and rates: Rates range $600–1,600 weekly. The inn is open year-round, but not all of the cottages are. Pets are not permitted.

Directions: The cottages are on Route 102A in Bass Harbor on Mount Desert Island. From Ellsworth, follow the signs to the Swans Island Ferry from Route 3 to Route 102, then to the second intersection of Routes 102 and 102A. Turn left before the Texaco Station. Drive .6 mile down Route 102A, and the cottages are on the right.

Contact: Bass Harbor Cottages, P.O. Box 40, Route 102A, Bass Harbor, ME 04653, 207/244-3460, website: www.bassharborcottages.com.

9. THE CLAREMONT HOTEL

near the mouth of Somes Sound

Luxury rating: ★★★★☆   **Recreation rating:** ★★★★★

The Claremont Hotel is a lovely resort on the "quiet side" of Mount Desert Island, and it is known for its Croquet Classic (nine-wicket tournament) the first week in August. It was built in the late 1800s, and it survived the 1947 fire that destroyed most of the Grand Hotels in the area.

Beside the hotel there are connected waterside cottages and standalone log cabins. From the large back porch, you can see across the attractive lawn, with its line of Adirondack chairs and the American flag waving proudly to a

© BETHANY ERICSON

long dock. It's common to arrive at the Claremont Hotel by boat, and there are 12 moorings that can be rented. Many hikers who are exploring Acadia National Park stay here, and it is possible to launch a kayak from the beach. The inn also provides free rowboats.

About half of the cottages are studios meant for couples,

while the log cabins have 2–3 bedrooms. All have wood or gas fireplaces. Cottage W-4 has spectacular water views and a deck over the water. There is also the large Rowse House, a four-bedroom house by the water with a woodstove and a wraparound deck.

Breakfast and dinner are served in the dining room overlooking the sound. Lunch is also served at the boathouse in July and August. The Claremont is a popular spot for weddings and reunions. Storytelling and guest lectures on geography, music, and politics are not uncommon. The main inn building has a living room with a television, VCR, and lots of couches.

There are also bikes available, as well as a clay tennis court. Nearby you have all of Acadia National Park, including warmer freshwater swimming.

Facilities: There are numerous cottages of various sizes and connected in various ways. The woodland log cabins are standalone units, as is the large Rowse House.

Bedding: Linens are provided.

Reservations and rates: MAP rates range $140–190 per night. Add $20 in high season (June 20–September 14). The Rowse House is rented weekly. The cottages are open May–October. Credit cards are not accepted.

Directions: Take the Maine Turnpike to Augusta. Exit Route 3 Acadia. Drive along Route 3 into Ellsworth, to the Trenton Bridge and Mount Desert Island. Take Route 102 to Southwest Harbor and follow the signs to the Claremont.

Contact: The Claremont Hotel, PO Box 137, Southwest Harbor, ME 04679, 800/244-5036, website: www.acadia.net/claremont.

10. WOODLAND PARK

on Frenchman Bay in Bar Harbor

Luxury rating: ★★☆☆☆   **Recreation rating:** ★★★★★

Woodland Park is a short drive or pedal down the street from the entrance to Acadia National Park, downtown Bar Harbor, and the "Cat" (high-speed catamaran) line to Nova Scotia. Hidden in tall pines, there are eight basic housekeeping cottages scattered about the property, with porches looking north across the narrows toward Lamoine Beach.

The cottages come in a variety of sizes and shapes, but tend to be larger than many of the older coastal cottages. They have clean, fully equipped kitchens with vintage camp dishware. All have private baths

© BETHANY ERICSON

with showers; some have tubs. They are sunny, pleasant spaces where the point is to get away from phones and televisions. You can hear the road from the cabins, but that also means you are within walking distance of the shuttle bus that traverses the island, taking you to the activities in town and to hiking trails.

Owners Paul and Julie Mun couldn't be nicer. They'll help orient you and share some of their favorite places to visit, whether it's the private Rockefeller Gardens (the one week a year they are open), a good lake to swim in, or a spot to pick blueberries. Paul's parents bought the property more than 30 years ago, and he took over in the early 1990s. Many guests have been joining them here every year since then.

Woodland Park has a dock with rowboats and kayaks. One guest routinely fishes for all of his meals during his entire stay. Shellfish regulations change, but for some time this northern side has been the one area of the island where it is safe to clam—and you can send the kids out to harvest mussels. There are picnic tables and barbeque grills.

Facilities: Eight heated housekeeping cottages accommodate 1–5 people.

Bedding: Linens are provided; towels can be exchanged during the week.

Reservations and rates: Rates range $475–925 for one-week stays. Be sure to book by at least January or February for the summer months. Credit cards are not accepted. Open mid-May–mid-October.

Directions: Take I-95 north to Exit 45A. Drive on I-395E toward Bangor/Brewer. Take Exit 6A to Route 1A to Bar Harbor/Ellsworth. Drive about six miles to a traffic light and the intersection with Route 46. Drive along Route 1A. After about 18 miles, there is a stoplight where Route 1A ends and joins Routes 1 and 3. Drive straight past the Dunkin Donuts onto Routes 3 and 1. Continue on Route 3. Turn at the left fork, and continue driving on Route 3 after crossing the bridge to Mount Desert Island. Woodland Park is four miles from the light.

Contact: Paul and Julie Mun, **Woodland Park**, 3 Woodland Loop, Bar Harbor, ME 04609, 207/288-4016, website: www.woodlandparkcottages.com.

11. EMERY'S COTTAGES ON THE SHORE

Sand Point in Bar Harbor

Luxury rating: ★ ★ ★ ☆ ☆   **Recreation rating:** ★ ★ ★ ★ ☆

Emery's Cottages are a picture-perfect colony of white cabins on a green lawn overlooking Sand Point. From the point, you have a panoramic view of Frenchman Bay and can even spot Schoodic Head, a hill in the often-forgotten northern portion of Acadia National Park. You'll want to sit here on the lush grass under an apple tree and watch the sun set.

© BETHANY ERICSON

The cottages have a motel-room feel to them. They are very clean and are located .5 mile from Route 3 and five miles from downtown Bar Harbor—a convenient launching point for all of your Mount Desert Island explorations. All cottages have electric heat and cable television; only some of them have kitchens (the three closest to the water do not). They all have comfortable furniture and rocking chairs.

Morning coffee is provided to all in a common laundry area, and there is also a common kitchen that can be used and is especially encouraged for lobster boils, so that the cottages don't take on a permanent lobster odor.

Acadia National Park is down the street, as well as whale-watching trips and kayak and bicycle rentals. In fact, a hike-bike-kayak outfitter will bring your equipment right to Emery's, where you can keep it for the week. You can swim here, and walk along the shoreline. At low tide, you can walk for 10 minutes up the shore to the Ovens (cavelike arches carved by the ocean). Bird-watchers may spot bald eagles, osprey, piliated woodpeckers, kingfishers, and more.

Facilities: There are 21 cottages. Be sure to specify if you need a kitchen.
Bedding: All linens are included.
Reservations and rates: Rates range $330–875 per week. There are daily rates

in the off-season period. You can make reservations from January 2, and you'll want to call immediately, as Emery's sees a 70 percent return rate. Open May–late October.

Directions: From Ellsworth, Maine, drive for about 15 miles along Route 3 toward Bar Harbor. Drive across the Trenton Bridge. Stay on Route 3 as it bears to the left. Drive 5.4 miles from the gas station (watch for an Emery's sign on the right side of Route 3), and turn left onto the Sand Point Road at the top of the hill.

Contact: Emery's Cottages on the Shore, Box 172, Bar Harbor, ME 04609, 207/288-3432 or 888/240-3432, website: www.emeryscottages.com.

12. STONE HAVEN

Mountainside in Acadia

Luxury rating: ★★★☆☆   **Recreation rating:** ★★★★★

Hidden away in the middle of Mount Desert Island, on a 20-acre mountain-top area at the edge of Acadia National Park, Stone Haven is an unusually secluded group of little cottages. At the same time, it is only four miles from downtown Bar Harbor, and the island's free shuttle bus stops at the end of the road.

You can walk from your door and explore, pick blueberries, or hook up with the trails and carriage roads in the park. Just a half mile walk from your Stone Haven house is the picturesque (and shallow) Aunt Betty's Pond.

At the end of a rocky road among the birches and pines, the small houses that make up Stone Haven are well constructed and winterized. They offer cathedral ceilings and fieldstone fireplaces. Fully equipped

© BETHANY ERICSON

kitchenettes also include lobster pots. They have microwaves and stove-top burners, but no ovens. You can choose between the sound of cable television or the wind in the trees. All of the houses have private decks with fabulous views and outdoor fire pits.

13. MANOR HOUSE INN

Downtown Bar Harbor

Luxury rating: ★ ★ ★ ☆ ☆   **Recreation rating:** ★ ★ ★ ★ ☆

Sometimes when you're traveling as a couple, you want to be near outdoor recreation facilities and to be able to shop in town. You want someone to feed you breakfast, but you also want the privacy of a cottage. You can have it all at this landmark inn in the middle of Bar Harbor.

© BETHANY ERICSON

Manor House Inn is a mansion that was built in 1887 and is now on the National Register of Historic Places. Hidden behind it, on 1.5 acres of lovely landscaping, are two additional buildings with suites and the two incredibly cute Shaker-style Garden Cottages.

Here you'll have a gas fireplace, a queen bed, a private porch, a television, and no phone. You'll be mere blocks away from downtown Bar Harbor's shops and restaurants, kayaking, whale-watching, sailboat trips, and lobster- and fishing-boat charters. You're also just one mile from Acadia National Park. A full-course breakfast is served buffet-style daily in the butler's pantry of the mansion, and you'll find lemonade, tea, or hot cider in the evenings.

Lest this great variety of opportunities overwhelm you, the staff at the Manor House Inn is very familiar with the area and will help you plan your days exploring the ocean activities and town, as well as navigating the miles of hiking and carriage trails throughout the park.

Facilities: There are two cottages meant for couples. Children under 12 are not permitted.

Bedding: All linens are provided.

Reservations and rates: The cottage rates range $125–195 per night. Open April–November. Pets are not permitted.

Directions: From Ellsworth, drive along Route 3 to Bar Harbor. As you approach Bar Harbor, you will drive past the main entrance to Acadia National Park on the right, in Hulls Cove. Just as you enter the town, turn left on the first cross street, West Street. The Manor House Inn will be on your right.

Contact: Manor House Inn, 106 West Street, Bar Harbor, ME 04609, 207/288-3759 or 800/437-0088, website: www.barharbormanorhouse.com.

14. SULLIVAN HARBOR FARM SMOKEHOUSE & COTTAGE RENTALS

on Sullivan Harbor

Luxury rating: ★ ★ ★ ★ ☆   **Recreation rating:** ★ ★ ★ ★ ★

Rank: Top 10 for Boating

Close your eyes and imagine staying in a comfortable, casual cottage on a fantastic sea-kayaking harbor, beyond major tourism but near state parks, and backed by forested Maine Public Lands, where hidden canoes can take you on wilderness adventures. In fact, imagine your host has spent years as a Maine Guide, but also runs a smokehouse where the seafood is ranked No. 1 by *Cooks Illustrated* and is sold to high-end restaurants. This is Sullivan Harbor Farm.

There are three cottages here alongside Joel and Leslie's house and smoked-salmon business. Guzzle is a whole house, Cupcake is a moderate-sized cottage, and Milo is a smaller cottage. They're located just off of Route 1, but here, north of Acadia, Route 1 is a more rural experience. Despite being mere feet from the highway, it's safe to go clamming.

Even the air seems much cleaner here.

Guzzle has lovely modern furnishings, two big bathrooms, laundry machines, a gorgeous wood floor, a beautiful view to the water from the living room, and a mahogany deck outfitted with a stainless-steel boat railing. The kitchen is modern, with stone-tile flooring and matte-chrome under-the-counter refrigerators. Cupcake is more of a cottage, but it's a spacious two-bedroom with a fireplace, television, phone, and laundry machines. Milo is more of a camp cottage; a small, cute unit that feels private on the lawn and does not have a phone.

Just across the road is Sullivan Harbor, and the property's right-of-way to the sea dates from the 1800s. You're in good company here if you enjoy rowing, kayaking, canoeing, or generally messing about in boats. The kayaks and canoes are free to use, and there are two sailboats that can be used with supervision. This is quiet water with a stiff current. Your hosts can also guide you to the best trails, to-die-for backcountry swimming, hiking, hidden canoes, and more. They also are familiar with restaurants all over the Down East area.

Facilities: There are three cottages that can accommodate 2–6 people.

Bedding: All linens are provided.

Reservations and rates: Rates range $700–1,450 per week. Call as early as you can to make a reservation. Call to inquire about the pet policy.

Directions: From Ellsworth, drive 12 miles east on Route 1.

Contact: Sullivan Harbor Farm Smokehouse & Cottage Rentals, U.S. Route 1, P.O. Box 96, Sullivan Harbor, ME 04664, 207/422-3735 or 800/422-4014, website: www.sullivanharborfarm.com.

Other Cabins and Cottages Nearby

- Edgewater Cabins, P.O. Box 226, Sullivan Harbor, ME, 207/422-6414 (June 15–September 15), 603/472-8644 (off-season), website: www.acadia.net/edgecab.

15. THE PINES

Gateway to Schoodic Point

Luxury rating: ★★☆☆☆   **Recreation rating:** ★★★★★

There is another portion of Acadia National Park that few tourists visiting Mount Desert Island ever see. It's north of the island, on Schoodic Point. The Pines is conveniently located right by the entrance to the park. "I have one of the best backyards in the world," says owner Marshall Rust.

The cabins here are tiny, but clean. The quilted bed in a cabin takes up most of the space. All cabins have televisions, narrow showers, and no kitchens. There are also two log cabins. A cemetery on one side flanks the log cabins, but piled lobster traps obscure the view from the lawn, and no windows face that direction.

The log cabins are rather cute, with logs that have been decorated with shells by many seasons of guests. There is a futon couch, plus a loft with twin beds. The log cabins have a two-burner stovetop, sink, small refrigerator, coffeemaker, toaster, television, and heater. There is also a four-bedroom log home for rent, with a large deck off the master bedroom. Marshall has plans for a restaurant on the property as well.

This is one of the nicest peninsulas between Hancock and Calais. The mix of locals and summer residents here, and the fewer tourists, give the area a nice, nonyuppy feel when compared with Deer Isle or Mount Desert Island. And you can't get any closer to this portion of Acadia National Park.

Marshall is happy to direct you to both the known and unmarked special places in the park, whether you're looking to picnic by crashing waves or to kayak in them. There are kayak and bicycle rental companies nearby. Schoodic Head is the small mountain here and could be compared to Cadillac Mountain, on Mount Desert Island.

Facilities: There are two log cabins fit for two people, four cottages for 2–4 people, and a 2,300-square-foot log home with four bedrooms.

Bedding: All linens are provided.

Reservations and rates: Cottages are rented nightly for $45 double occupancy. The log cabins are $60 per night. Call to inquire about weekly rentals of the log home. August is the busiest month here, so be sure to reserve by April or May. Open year-round.

Directions: Take Route 1 east from Ellsworth, through Sullivan, to West Gouldboro. Drive on Route 186 and follow the signs for Schoodic Point.

Contact: The Pines, Main Street, Route 186, Winter Harbor, ME 04693, 207/963-2296, website: www.ayuh.net.

16. MICMAC FARM GUEST HOUSES

on Machias River

Luxury rating: ★★☆☆☆   **Recreation rating:** ★★★★★

All the way Down East, Micmac Farm Guest Houses are sweet, simple cabins on the tidal portion of the Machias River, which connects to the five Machias Lakes. If you are interested in a varied and technical white-water canoeing experience, local outfitters like Sunrise County Canoe and Kayak run several spectacular day trips on the Machias.

© BETHANY ERICSON

The river runs through some of Washington County's blueberry barrens and into the ocean near the absolutely stunning Jasper Beach, down the street from the cabins. This beach is a delight for geology buffs and beachcombers alike, covered in beautiful sea-polished jasper and rhyolite.

There is no lack of things to do Down East. You can launch a kayak or canoe from the backyard of your cabin, fish for stripers, explore ancient petroglyph sites, visit West Quoddy State Park or the Moosehorn Wildlife Refuge, see the puffins on Machias Seal Island, and more. And since Washington County in Maine provides 85 percent of the world's wild blueberries, if you are staying in the Machias area during August, you might want to visit the Wild Blueberry Festival. The cabins are even named after the Micmac Native Americans, who migrate annually from Canada to pick and harvest blueberries here.

Each cabin has two double beds with wicker-scrollwork headboards and festive-striped bedspreads, kitchenettes, electric heating, and sliding glass doors facing the river. Inside, they have knotty-pine walls and floors, and outside, the cabins have Adirondack chairs waiting for you under the birch trees, overlooking the river's shoreline nature trail.

The Gardner House, an 18th-century farmhouse, also has rooms for rent. The office for the three cabins is here, and you might find a casual note from the owner, Bonnie Dunn, welcoming you and allowing you to check yourself into your cabin.

Facilities: There are three cottages that can accommodate 2–4 people.

Bedding: Linens are provided.

Reservations and rates: In June, September, and October, the cabins are rented for $55 per night and $350 per week. In July and August, cabins are rented for $70 per night and $425 per week.

Directions: From Machias, drive south for two miles on Route 92. The Gardner House and Micmac Farm Guest Houses will be on your left.

Contact: Micmac Farm Guest Houses, Route 92, Machiasport, ME 04655, 207/255-3008, website: www.micmacfarm.com.

Other Cabins and Cottages Nearby
• Sharon and Peter Stackpole, Bluebird Motel, Route 1, Box 45, Machias, ME, 04654, 207/255-3332 or 207/255-3662.

17. ROBINSONS COTTAGES
on Denny's River

Luxury rating: ★ ★ ☆ ☆ ☆   **Recreation rating:** ★ ★ ★ ★ ★

Rank: Top 10 for Fishing, Top 10 for Value

Robinsons Cottages are a fabulous deal. Gladys and Jim Robinson offer huge, secluded cottages with fieldstone fireplaces—in the woods along the river or on their private pond—for half the cost of many smaller places in other areas of the state. Jim's grandfather started these cottages as hunting and fishing lodges, but now the place gets a range of family vacationers as well.

The spring that provides water to the cottages is the same spring Jim's grandfather used to start the Atlantic Salmon Hatchery in the late 1800s. Recent restrictions on salmon fishing have cut down the numbers of visiting fishing enthusiasts, but you can still fish for trout and bass in Denny's River, and Cathance Lake has landlocked salmon, bass, and perch. You can even fish and swim right in the pond on the property. Jim's grandfather also dug the pond, so there's no license necessary.

© BETHANY ERICSON

There are paddleboats and canoes to use for free. The Robinsons are happy to direct you to better kayaking areas. There is great hiking in the area, and plenty to do, such as visiting West Quoddy Head, Campobellow Island, the Reversing Falls in Pembroke, the town of Eastport, and the Machias Blueberry Festival in August.

Family reunions are popular here, and the warm weather of July and August sees the highest number of guests. The cottages have a variety of bed configurations and usually contain one full bed and varying numbers of twin beds. They have screened porches and bathrooms with shower stalls. Some are two-story cottages, and all but one are log cottages.

Facilities: There are seven cottages that can accommodate 4–8 people. There is a store with lunch counters in town, as well as nearby restaurants.

Bedding: Linens are provided.

Reservations and rates: Rates range $350–375 per week. Call a year ahead for reservations. Open mid-April–mid-November. Smoking is permitted. Call to inquire about the pet policy.

Directions: Drive on Route 1 to Route 86 in Dennysville, and follow the signs to the office.

Contact: Robinsons Cottages, Route 86, Dennysville, ME 04628, 207/726-3901, website: robinsonscottages.com.

18. WEATHERBY'S

Grand Lake

Luxury rating: ★ ★ ★ ☆ ☆   **Recreation rating:** ★ ★ ★ ★ ★

Rank: Top 10 for Fishing

Jeff McEvoy and Beth Rankin were recently passed the torch by longtime Weatherby's owners, Charlene and Ken Sassi. Jeff has been a guide for 20 years, fishing on East Grand and canoeing on the Machias and Saint Croix Rivers. After five years of working to conserve the North Woods, he felt comfortable having his business and family here. Beth Rankin has taken on the cooking, and together they are living their dream in the woods.

The remote Grand Lake area has more registered Maine Guides than any other area in the state, and Weatherby's typically employs 25–30 of them, so you can always find your way—and your fish. The camp was started in the mid-1800s to provide housing and recreation for customers waiting 4–6 months for the world's largest tannery to work their hides. Now it is a high-end fishing camp, complete with Internet access, daily maid service, and a "cabin boy," who supplies your ice and fills your wood box.

The cottages are roomy and spread out. They cater to those who are looking for a nature-based experience, but who do not want accommodations that are too rustic. The cabins all have electricity, gas heat, either an open-brick or Franklin fireplace, a screened porch, and indoor plumbing.

Guests gather in the clean, cozy lodge dining room for breakfast and dinner. The room sports a tin ceiling and a variety of mounted game fish. For an additional fee, Beth can prepare you a picnic lunch, or your guide can provide you with a memorable hot cookout. There are also special fishing programs, including one just for women.

While fishing is the main theme here, it's also a wonderful place to swim, go bird-watching, and explore. There is a basketball and tennis court adjacent to the camp, as well as areas for croquet and horseshoes.

In the lodge, there's a collection of books, a television, a piano, and a large fireplace. There are plenty of opportunities for privacy, or to meet others and swap fishing tales.

Facilities: There are 15 cottages that can each accommodate 2–6 people. Breakfast and dinner are provided. Lunch is provided for a fee. A village store is within walking distance. Guide service is provided for $150 per day. Boat and motor rentals, as well as rod-and-reel rentals, are available. Fishing licenses are sold at the camp. The L.L. Bean Fly Fishing School offers courses through Weatherby's.

Bedding: Bedding is provided, and there is daily maid service. Towels are laundered upon request.

Reservations and rates: Reservations are recommended. Rates for adults are $108–140 per person. Children and family rates are available. A $150 per person deposit must be received within seven days of making a reservation. Open May–October. Personal checks are accepted. Visa and Mastercard can be used, but add 4 percent to your rates. Pets are not permitted.

Directions: Take I-95 to exit 55 in Lincoln. From there, drive on Route 6 east to Topsfield. Turn right on Route 1 South and drive for about 15 miles. Turn right onto Grand Lake Stream Road, and drive about 10 miles to Grand Lake Stream. The camps will be on your right.

Contact: Jeff McEvoy and Beth Rankin, **Weatherby's**, P.O. Box 69, Grand Lake Stream, ME 04637, 207/796-5558, website: www.weatherbys.com.

Other Cabins and Cottages Nearby
- Shoreline Camps, P.O. Box 127, Grand Lake Stream, ME 04637, 207/796-5539, website: www.shorelinecamps.com.

19. INDIAN ROCK CAMPS

by Grand Lake Stream

Luxury rating: ★★☆☆☆   **Recreation rating:** ★★★★★

Rank: Top 10 for Backcountry Winter Adventures

While Grand Lake Stream is known for its fabulous fishing, it's also a prime area for hiking, bird-watching, mountain biking, and photography. Indian Rock Camps will help you get out of the city and into this gorgeous setting so you can get ready to do whatever will make you happy, even if that means doing nothing. Unlike most camps in the area, these are open year-round; you can come up to the wilderness and come back to a fire after skiing or ice fishing.

Grand Lake Stream is known to anglers all around the world for its landlocked salmon fishing. Ice-out is typically May 1. From then until early June, the salmon and lake trout glide just below the surface. Note that the exciting fall fishing in early October is catch-and-release only. Big Lake is also known for smallmouth bass fishing.

Indian Rock Camps is the third-oldest camp in the area; it was started in the late 1800s. The little brown housekeeping cabins have fully equipped kitchens, woodstoves or furnaces, and screened porches. They do not have phones or clocks. Guests and the public are welcome to use the restaurant.

Families come to Indian Rock to fish, swim, canoe, pick blueberries, and relax. Grand Lake has a folk-art festival every summer that is growing in popularity, and the early-August Blueberry Festival in Machias is always a draw. Micmac and Passamaquoddy heritage and artifacts are a particular interest as well. Indian Rock Camps also offers many workshops on topics from fishing to soap-making. If you love to fish, you'll be ecstatic, and if you're simply a nature enthusiast, you'll also be right at home here.

Facilities: There are five two-bedroom log cabins. Boat rentals are $35 (plus gas), and canoe rentals are $15 per day. Guides are available for approximately $135 per day (lunch may be extra). There is no dinner bell, and dinner is BYOB.

Bedding: Bedding is provided.

Reservations and rates: The American Plan rate is $62 per night. There is a special package for five days, double occupancy with the American Plan for $299, and a summer week rate for $350. Under the Housekeeping Plan, rates for double occupancy are $27 per night. Children under 12 are half price. One night's deposit is forfeited in the event of an early departure. Open year-round. Pets are welcome.

Directions: From the south, take I-95 to Exit 55, then drive on Route 6 and turn right onto Lake Road (it's marked). Drive for 10 miles to Grand Lake Stream village. Look for the sign; the camp's driveway is by a church.

Contact: JoAnne and Ken Cannell, **Indian Rock Camps**, PO Box 117, Grand Lake Stream, ME 04637, 207/796-2822, website: www.indianrockcamps.com.

Other Cabins and Cottages Nearby

- Grand Lake Stream Camps, P.O. Box 17, Grand Lake Stream, ME 04637, 207/796-5562.

20. COLONIAL SPORTSMEN'S LODGE

Grand Lake

Luxury rating: ★☆☆☆☆   **Recreation rating:** ★★★★★

After a long history of sustaining the Passamoquoddy tribe, Grand Lake Stream became known as the world's biggest tannery. Today, it's known for its excellent fishing. In fact, some of the cabins at Colonial Sportsmen's Lodge and at Weatherby's were part of the first commercial sporting camps in the area.

© BETHANY ERICSON

Fishing enthusiasts flock to Grand Lake Stream to try their hand at fly-fishing for landlocked salmon in early spring, catch smallmouth bass in the lake in midsummer, and catch spawning salmon in the stream in the fall. There is excellent trolling along Grand Lake's 100 miles of shoreline. Besides salmon, there are brook trout and togue (lake trout), white perch, and pickerel. According to locals, you can catch a 20-pound togue here, but you're a bit more likely to find a four- to six-pound fighter on your line. Colonial Sportsmen's Lodge employs some fantastic guides, who will also cook you a hot lunch.

The lodge operates cottages on both a housekeeping plan, with no meals, and an American Plan, with all three meals. Meals are hearty, aimed at folks spending their days on the water. For the non-fishermen staying at the lodge, there is a sandy beach on the lake here, as well as plenty of hiking, mountain biking, and more in the area.

These are basic cabin accommodations. The kitchens have pots and pans, and there is linen service, but remember that this is a fishing camp. Go for the outdoor experience, not for the indoor luxury.

Facilities: The lodge has five cabins that can accommodate four people in each.
Bedding: Linens are provided.

21. LEEN'S LODGE

West Grand Lake

Luxury rating: ★ ★ ☆ ☆   **Recreation rating:** ★ ★ ★ ★ ★

Rank: Top 10 for Fishing, Top 10 for Value

Leen's is a fabulous find; the cabins are absolutely beautiful, and the setting is the happy wilderness of Grand Lake Stream. This area is quite famous for its fishing. That said, Leen's is also a fantastic destination for family vacations and a great place to canoe, kayak, hike, mountain bike, and more.

May and June are the best time to be at Leen's, trolling a fly line to snag landlocked salmon and lake trout. Early in the season is best for fly-fishing in the stream. Don your waders, and get your coffee and fish tales at the general store in the middle of town. Then ignore everything they've been telling you and head out with a Maine Guide, arranged at Leen's. You'll have much better luck.

Birding, boating, and hiking are other favorite activities in Washington

© BETHANY ERICSON

County. Moosehorn National Wildlife Refuge, Petit Manan National Wildlife Refuge, and West Quoddy Head State Park are great places to hike and go bird-watching, and Machias Seal Island is a special spot for seeing puffins. Midsummer is the best season for birding in this area, and you can catch the Grand Lake Stream Folk

Festival in late July, or the Blueberry Festival in Machias in early August.

Back at Leen's you'll return to find delicious lobster, steak, and chowder meals served in the dining lodge, with its great deck looking out toward the sunset, and afterdinner chats in the Tannery Room. Then you can retire to sit by the fireside in your rustic, yet charming, private cabin by the lake.

Facilities: There are 10 basic cabins with 1–8 bedrooms. Most have twin beds, with a few double and king size beds. Daily maid service is provided.

Bedding: Linens are provided.

Reservations and rates: Cabins are rented by the day with a Modified American Plan at $100 per day for double occupancy, or $125 per day for single occupancy. Children under 12 are half price. Children under five stay for free. Late in the season (October), as heating costs rise, expect a $10 increase. Open May–October, with grouse-hunting guests welcome until December 31. Leashed pets are welcome.

Directions: Leen's is located 110 miles from Bangor, Maine. There are two scenic ways to travel there: You can take I-95 from Bangor to Lincoln, from there drive on Route 6 East to Topsfield, and then take Route 1 South to Grand Lake Stream. Or, you can take Route 9 from Bangor to Baring, and drive on Route 1 north to Grand Lake Stream. Detailed directions up the dirt road are provided when reservations are made.

Contact: Charles Driza, **Leen's Lodge**, P.O. Box 40, Grand Lake Stream, ME 04637, 207/796-2929 or 800/99-LEENS, website: www.leenslodge.com.

Chapter 7

Western and Southern Maine

CHAPTER 7—WESTERN AND SOUTHERN MAINE

To the east of New Hampshire's Connecticut Lakes, western Maine is a fabulous land of mountains and hundreds of lakes, often ignored by tourists. (Maybe it's because so many of the lakes are hard to pronounce: Mooselookmeguntic, Parmanchenee, Cupsuptic. . . .) While Rangeley Lake has a decent amount of development on its shores, you can pull over on Route 27, at the Height O'Land viewpoint, and from here you really get a good sense of the thousands of acres of preserved land and pristine lakes that remain unspoiled.

These waters are home to some legendary fish tales. In fact, it is said to be the birthplace of modern fly-fishing. The Appalachian Mountain Trail runs through this area, and it travels by Maine's huge Sugarbush ski resort and Saddleback, its quieter neighbor. In winter, this is where to find one of the most extensive and well-maintained networks of snowmobile trails in the state—as well as some fairly reliable snow. This also makes for good cross-country and backcountry skiing.

These aren't the only gems in this area. South of here, in Oxford County, the land is incredibly rich in minerals and has yielded amethysts, tourmaline, garnet, and topaz. The trees and waters are filled with more than a hundred species of birds. Outward Bound's Hurricane Island School, the lakeside beach at Mount Blue, and Sunday River (another immensely popular ski resort) are tucked away in these woods.

Many Portland residents spend their summers lakeside at nearby Sebago Lake, as Augusta residents escape to the Belgrade Lakes. Both of these places have a rustic, summer camp feel. Meanwhile, the southern coast of Maine, with its sandy beaches and boardwalks, completely transforms to accommodate the throngs of tourists that arrive to play in the waves in the hot months.

The Maine coast south of Portland is widely known for its wide, sandy beaches, lighthouses, and lobster shacks. The towns differ in personality. Once the vacation spots of Boston Brahmins, York is better known for saltwater taffy and Wild Kingdom, while Old Orchard Beach is boardwalk-central with its roller coasters, carousels, and water slides nearby in Saco. York also has little Mount Agamenticus, which has become a popular place to go mountain biking.

Ogunquit is known more for its artistic leanings. It's a good place to gallery hop. It has a several-mile-long beach, and is known for its pleasant cliff walk, called Marginal Way. Wells has a seven-mile beach, and is known for its National Estuarine Research Reservation, at Laudhom Farm. Here and at Biddeford you will find various great birding spots. Nearby South Berkwick was home to writer Sarah Orne Jewett, who captured the essence of the Maine shore in works like *The Country of the Pointed Firs*.

Kennebunkport is probably the most well known of these towns, as it's the summer residence of former President George Bush. Although area residents are full of Bush-encounter stories ("He flicked a bug off my shoulder once!"), don't expect to be able to visit. The compound is highly secured.

Portland is Maine's largest city, and it is a great restaurant town. From Portland, there are regular ferries and a mail boat that travel to the Casco Bay Islands, and you can easily kayak to some, like Peaks Island. Great Chebeague is a pleasant place to bicycle around, and Eagle Island has the summerhouse of Admiral Peary, the North Pole explorer. His house has a hearth designed with local stones and Arctic quartz crystals.

North of Portland, Freeport is known for its outlet shopping and the headquarters of L.L. Bean. The coast here changes dramatically, and juts out from Brunswick, Bath, Wiscasset, and Damariscotta with octopus-like arms. In these craggy cliffs and coves lies an impressive history of fishing and shipbuilding. Seafaring is still the major focus. These are good places to kayak; sail; take wildlife-viewing tours to visit seals, puffins, and whales; tour working lobster and fishing boats; and eat as much fresh seafood as you can manage.

Boothbay Harbor is a major tourist center and an easy place to base your explorations of the area from. New Harbor is a bit quieter, yet with all the outfitters and scenery you could desire. Offshore, the Maine Island Trail is a popular sea kayak–touring route. Some of the islands in this area, like Southport, Westport, Orrs, and Bailey, are connected to the land by bridges. Covered in beach roses and surrounded by crashing waves, on land these are places you don't really mind when it's stormy. It's too thrilling.

North of here, the towns from Rockland to Searsport are well populated year round and filled with antiques and art galleries. There's the famous Windjammer Days, in Camden, and frequent ferries cross to Vinalhaven, Monhegan Island, and other islands from Rockland. You can hike Mount Battie in Camden, mountain bike through Camden Hills, sea kayak from Linconville, swim in Damariscotta or Megunticook Lakes, or just relax and listen to the constant sound of the waves and know you're in exactly the right spot.

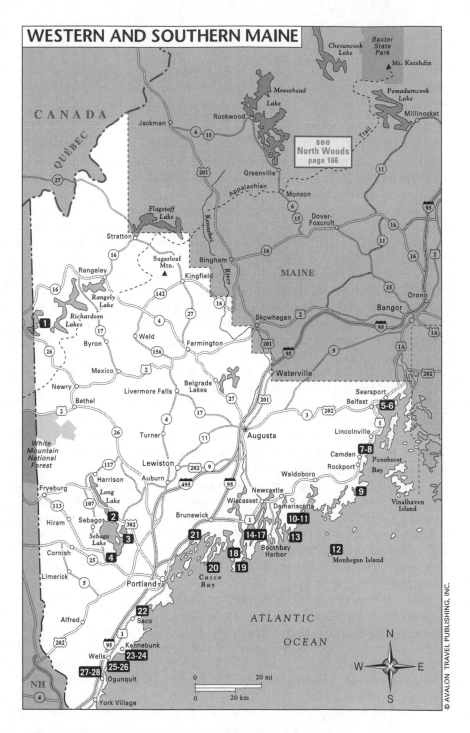

WESTERN AND SOUTHERN MAINE

CANADA

QUÉBEC

Chesuncook Lake

Baxter State Park

Mt. Katahdin

Moosehead Lake

Pemadumcook Lake

Millinocket

Jackman

Rockwood

6   15

see North Woods page 166

Trail

201

Greenville

Appalachian

Monson

95

Flagstaff Lake

Kennebec

6

15

Dover-Foxcroft

16

Stratton

16

Sugarloaf Mtn.

Bingham

11

Rangeley

16

Kingfield

142

MAINE

16

15

Orono

Richardson Lakes

Rangely Lake

27

16

Bangor

1

4

17

Skowhegan

2

95

26

Byron

Weld

Farmington

201

1A

Newry

156

Mexico

2

95

Waterville

1A

202

Bethel

Livermore Falls

Belgrade Lakes

27

Searsport

2

4

17

201

3

202

Belfast

5-6

White Mountain National Forest

Turner

11

Augusta

Lincolnville

1

Fryeburg

117

Lewiston

202

9

Camden

7-8

Harrison

Auburn

495

95

Rockport

Penobscot Bay

113

Long Lake

107

Waldoboro

9

Hiram

Sebago

302

Newcastle

Vinalhaven Island

Cornish

Sebago Lake

2

Wiscasset

Damariscotta

10-11

25

3

Brunswick

21

1

4

14-17

13

Limerick

5

18

Boothbay Harbor

12

Monhegan Island

Portland

20

19

Alfred

Casco Bay

202

22

Saco

ATLANTIC

95

Kennebunk

OCEAN

N

Wells

23-24

W   E

27-28

25-26

Ogunquit

S

NH

4

York Village

0   20 mi

0   20 km

© AVALON TRAVEL PUBLISHING, INC.

CHAPTER 7
WESTERN AND SOUTHERN MAINE

1. BOSEBUCK MOUNTAIN CAMPS

on Azischohos Lake

Luxury rating: ★★☆☆☆   **Recreation rating:** ★★★★★

Rank: Top 10 for Fishing

Bosebuck Mountain Camps were built in the wilderness in 1909, and today remain miles from the nearest paved road. Owners Diane and Bob Schyberg enjoyed the camps as guests for years before they took over the place in 1997. The cabins are surrounded by wilderness and look out across Azischohos Lake, near the con-

fluence of the Big and Little Magalloway Rivers. A dam, built in the early 1900s for the logging industry, deepened this lake, and it supports a large population of brook trout and landlocked salmon.

While hunting and fishing are popular activities here, there is also a great deal of backcountry to explore on foot or with a mountain bike. You can relax here in the comforting isolation of the woods, listening to loons, taking a dip in the lake, writing the next great outdoor guidebook, or gliding about in a canoe.

Most of the somewhat small cabins at Bosebuck are located on the lakefront. They vary in size, and the only two not by the lake still have good views. The cabins are relatively basic, but charming, with horizontal knotty-pine paneling, woodstoves, and gas lights when the generator is turned off at night. Although they may be rustic, they have daily maid service.

In the fall, when the water is low, archaeologists and history-minded enthusiasts sometimes search the lake for Paleo-Indian tools and other artifacts. The dwelling and hunting area here was discovered in the 1980s and is estimated to be 10,500–11,000 years old. Guests are not permitted to dig.

Bosebuck caters to reunions and family vacations, as well as to those looking to fly-fish or hunt. There is a dockhand to help you with the boats and "keepers," and the chef is happy to cook up your catch, should you decide not to throw it back. All meals (and snacks if you so desire) are served in the dining room, a cozy spot with white chairs and a woodstove.

Facilities: There are eight cabins, each accommodating 2–4 people. Boats and motors can be rented for $40 per day. Access to fishing in private Parmachenee Wilderness Area is $40. Guides can be arranged.

Bedding: Bedding is provided.

Reservations and rates: There is a two-night minimum stay required on weekends. Family rates and packages are offered in the summer. Rates are full American Plan, and include use of canoes and kayaks. Adults are $110 per person per night; children under 16 are $60, and children under six are free. Open May –November. Pets are accepted. Smoking is permitted.

Directions: From Boston, take I-93 north to Exit 41 at Littleton, New Hampshire. Follow Route 116 east to Route 2. Drive east on Route 2 until you are just outside Gorham, New Hampshire, then take Route 16 northeast to the Wilsons, Maine, area. Drive for about 20 miles and go past Errol, New Hampshire. Turn left at the Bosebuck Sign (Parmachenee Road). Drive about 3.5 miles to the fork in the road, bear right, and drive another 10 miles. The driveway and sign will be on the right.

Contact: Bob and Diane Schyberg, **Bosebuck Mountain Camps**, P.O. Box 1213, Route 16, Wilsons Mills, ME 04970, 207/243-2945 in summer, 207/486-3238 in winter, website: www.bosebuck.com.

Other Cabins and Cottages Nearby

- Bald Mountain Camps, P.O. Box 332, Oquossoc, ME 04964, 207/864-3671 or 888/392-0072, website: www.baldmountaincamps.com.
- The Kawanhee Inn, Route 42, Lake Webb, Weld, ME 04285, 207/585-2000; Winter address: 7 High Street, Farmington, ME 04938, website: www.lakeinn.com.

2. MIGIS LODGE

on Sebago Lake

Luxury rating: ★ ★ ★ ★ ☆   **Recreation rating:** ★ ★ ★ ★ ★

Rank: Top 10 for Weddings

Gorgeous Migis (pronounced MY-giss) Lodge was built in 1916, in the pines, on 3,500 feet of shoreline on Sebago Lake. From May 1 to June 15 the lodge is the site for many group gatherings and weddings. For the rest of the summer and fall it is a very popular old-school summer resort, with

© MIGIS LODGE

a great variety of activities, all meals provided, and jackets required for the gentlemen (and the rest of the men) in the evening.

The numerous beautiful pine cabins at Migis Lodge have fieldstone fireplaces and look out on the lake and distant mountains. (The only cabin that does not face the lake is particularly spacious, with a cathedral ceiling.) They are well spaced for privacy and rustic in charm but elegant and modern in amenities, with a bathroom to go with each bedroom. There is maid service, ice and firewood delivery, cable television, a wet bar, and even high-speed wireless Internet access.

This is a fun place to swim, sail, water-ski (instructions are even provided), canoe, and fish. Several other lakes are connected to Sebago, and there are 32 miles of waterway to boat. The lodge offers cruises around the lake, including special moonlight dessert cruises.

Also on-site are walking trails, three tennis courts, a boccie court, two shuffleboard courts, and a fitness center. For kids there are llamas to visit, a playground, special supervised programs, and dinner menus. Indoors, there are table tennis, a pool table, and more.

The owners have invested millions in upgrading the resort since the 1990s, and you can see the results. And after a full day of activity, a massage, and great homemade food by the lake, you can wrap a quilt from the bed around you, sit in the rocker on the porch over the lake, and count all of your lucky stars.

Facilities: There are 29 cottages with 1–4 bedrooms. Some are duplex units. Two are wheelchair-accessible. All boating is free, except for the rental charge for boats with motors ($25 for a day and $15 for half day). There is also a larger motorboat that can be rented for $250 per day and $175 for a half day.

Bedding: Bedding is provided.

Reservations and rates: Call as early as possible. No credit cards accepted. Rates range $215–300 per person, double occupancy, including all three meals and use of the facilities. Preference is given to weekly stays, but there are always shorter openings available. Children are welcome; ask about discounted rates. Open mid-June–mid-Oct. Smoking is not permitted in the dining room. Pets are not permitted, but the lodge can recommend and arrange for local kennel accommodations.

Directions: From Boston or Portland, take the Maine Turnpike (I-95) to Exit 8; turn right at the end of the ramp. Drive straight through two sets of stoplights. At the third set of lights, turn left onto Route 302 (West). Follow Route 302 for

19.4 miles until you see the Migis Lodge sign on the left (immediately after the Cry of the Loon Gift Shop). Turn left onto the lodge road.

Contact: Tim and Joan Porta, **Migis Lodge**, P.O. Box 40, South Casco, ME 04077, 207/655-4524, website: www.migis.com.

3. SEBAGO LAKE LODGE & COTTAGES

on Sebago Lake

Luxury rating: ★ ★ ★ ☆ ☆   **Recreation rating:** ★ ★ ★ ★ ★

Rank: Top 10 for Boating, Top 10 for Fishing

Sebago Lake is known for its clean water, ideal for swimming, boating, and fishing for landlocked salmon, smallmouth and largemouth bass, and lake trout. In the fall, the foliage colors are spectacular. Sebago Lake Lodge & Cottages are in a quiet location with 700 feet of lake frontage and fabulous boat and guide services.

The cottages are clean and well maintained, with nice details like linoleum kitchen floors and cozy oriental rugs. They are set on a hill looking out over the lake. The newer Deluxe cottages are pretty, two-level structures with lofts and beautiful windows on the lake. The cottages have phones and televisions.

A basic continental breakfast is provided in the lodge, and picnic tables and a charcoal grill are located by the shore. Also lakeside is a small swimming area, and free use of canoes, kayaks, and rowboats. There is a fitness room available for adults.

If you are more than 21 years of age, you can rent ski boats, fishing boats, personal watercraft, and towing equipment for waterskiing. If you're bringing your own boat, you can launch it next door at the marina. Dockage is available for boats less than 40 feet long, and moorings are also available. The lodge has nonresident fishing licenses for sale and offers Registered Maine Guide services for help in finding the fish.

The lake is said to be one of the 20 cleanest lakes in the country, but if you get tired of its pristine waters, the coast of Maine and the White Mountains of New Hampshire are both less than an hour's drive away.

Facilities: There are nine housekeeping cottages rented weekly (Saturday–Saturday) and three waterfront resort cottages rented Sunday–Sunday. Reserve boats ahead of your arrival. One of the waterfront cottages is wheelchair-accessible.

Bedding: No linens are provided, except to foreign travelers and people with similar special circumstances.

Reservations and rates: Rates range $500–1,195. Call to reserve at least six months in advance. Pets are allowed with permission and a fee, and are not to be left unattended.

Directions: From the south, take I-95 north to Portland. Take Exit 8 (Portland/Westbrook), turn right onto Riverside Street, and turn left onto Forest Ave., Route 302. Take Route 302 to North Windham, turn left on Route 35, and then turn right onto Whites Bridge Road.

Contact: Debra and Chip Lougee, **Sebago Lake Lodge & Cottages**, P.O. Box 110, Whites Bridge Road, North Windham, ME 04062, 207/892-2698, website: www.sebagolakecottage.com.

4. SEBAGO LAKE FAMILY CAMPGROUND

on Sebago Lake

Luxury rating: ★★★☆☆   **Recreation rating:** ★★★★★

Sebago Lake Family Campground is a family-oriented campground with great swimming and boating opportunities from a 600-foot private beach on Sebago Lake, the second-largest lake in Maine. There are seven cot-

tages under the pines, across the road from the lake. They are rustic, but more than basic camping cabins.

The pine cottages have bathroom and kitchen facilities, screened porches, fireplaces or woodstoves, and color televisions. Some have tubs and showers, others just showers. There is a variety of bed sizes and sleeping arrangements. Two of the cottages have double beds in a bedroom, whereas many of the units have twins with larger sofa beds.

The cottages have fairly comfortable casual furniture, dining tables, and painted wooden floors. There are decent-sized kitchen facilities, picnic tables, and barbecue grills. There is also a snack bar across the street, and snacks and ice are sold in the campground office. From inside your cottage you will be able to hear the waves and calling loons of the lake, as well as any passing cars on the road.

The beach is raked sand. There are paddleboats and rowboats, as well as boat mooring rentals. Three miles up the road at Nathan's Beach is a boat launch. Nearby Douglas Mountain offers good views of Sebago and Long Lake. Two cottages are open year-round, and there is snowmobiling and ice fishing in the area.

Facilities: There are eight cottages accommodating 4–6 people. Two are open year-round. They have 21 moorings that are rented for $425 a season, $10 per night or $50 per week. Laundry facilities are on-site.

Bedding: No linens provided. (If you just drop in, they will help you out.)

Reservations and rates: Rates range $440–625 weekly (Saturday–Saturday) and $68–100 daily with some minimum stay requirements. There is a great deal of repeat business here; be sure to call to reserve as early as possible for holiday weekends. Open year-round. Pets are not permitted.

Directions: Sebago Lake Family Campground is just 25 miles north of South Portland and nine miles south of Naples, on Route 114. Drive on the Maine Turnpike to Exit 6, then follow the signs to Route 114. Drive north on Route 114, through Gorham to Lake Sebago. Sebago Lake Family Campground is located on the left, directly on Route 114.

Contact: Sebago Lake Family Campground, 1550 Richville Road, Route 114, Standish, ME 04084, 207/787-3671, website: www.sebagolakecamping.com.

5. HOMEPORT INN

on Penobscot Bay

Luxury rating: ★ ★ ★ ★ ☆   **Recreation rating:** ★ ★ ★ ★ ★

The Homeport Inn is a grand captain's mansion, with a drive-up loop decorated with statuary, located directly on Route 1 in Searsport. Venture behind this splendid inn and walk down a path under pear trees and evergreens, past chicken coops, peacock coops, and a grape arbor. Across the lawn you will discover three cheerful Victorian cottages available for weekly rental.

The brown, gray, and blue cottages are all different, but all have two bedrooms, full kitchens, and share a beautiful ocean view. The brown cottage looks at the water and has a porch that looks at the garden. The gray cottage is a bit more modern and has a loveable porthole window in a play nook. The blue cottage is the newest. It is open-plan with arch-shaped windows, knotty-pine walls, a cathedral ceiling and a sunny porch.

© BETHANY ERICSON

The furnishings are casual, with nice touches like antiques or oriental rugs. All have televisions, but not phones. The two-bedrooms have one full bed and two twins. The cottages are all heated, but only two are winterized. The inn is listed on the National Historic Register, and "Doc" and Mrs. George Johnson have captured the rich decor of the late 1800s. The lawn between the inn and the cottages is a common site for weddings.

Searsport is a good place to take scenic sailing cruises or steam rides on the historic Boston Maine Line Railroad, to cycle or walk along the shore, or to cross-country ski. You can moor boats half a mile away at Searsport Landing and launch kayaks from the shore at the inn. You can also play badminton and croquet on the lawn.

Facilities: Each of the three cottages can accommodate four people

Bedding: All linens are provided.

Reservations and rates: Rates range $700–850 per week. Call a year ahead for July and August reservations. Open year-round. The brown and gray cottages are generally rented by the season in winter, while the blue cottage is usually rented only in summer.

Directions: The inn is on Route 1 (Main Street) in Searsport. From the south, drive on I-95 to Augusta and take Route 3 (Acadia Trail) to Belfast. Homeport is just five miles north of Belfast.

Contact: Homeport Inn, Box 647, Route 1, East Main Street, Searsport, ME 04974, 207/548-2259 or 800/742-5814, website: www.bnbcity.com/inns/20015.

Other Cabins and Cottages Nearby
- Wonderview Cottages at Belfast, Route 1, RFD 1 Box 5339, Belfast, ME 04915, 207/338-1455.
- Seascape Motel & Cottages, U.S. Route 1 Belfast, ME 04915, 207/338-2130, www.seascapemotel.com.

6. SEARSPORT SHORES CAMPING RESORT

between Camden and Bar Harbor on Penobscot Bay

Luxury rating: ★ ☆ ☆ ☆ ☆   **Recreation rating:** ★ ★ ★ ★

Astrig and Steven Tanguay, along with her parents Rosalie and Zaven Koltookian, took over this 40-acre campground as a way to stay together as the family ages. The creative, family-friendly atmosphere of Searsport Shores is the result. Searsport Shores is a well-organized camping resort with a covered picnic area and out-

© BETHANY ERICSON

door fireplace, a great playground, Saturday lobster bakes, table tennis, online access, comfy couches, ice-cream socials, a piano, art classes for the public, a store with snacks and sun hats, and even its own ATM. It has a water garden and benches by the beach. It's also a fabulous kayak campground.

There is one cute 22-by-12-foot camping cabin with pine tree shutters placed between the RV area and the group camping area; the tenting area is separated from the rest of the campground by a small creek. More cabins may be in the works. Adding extra guests in a tent next to the cabin is acceptable here.

The cabin has one room with two bunk beds (one with a double-bottom bunk), and it also has a day bed. There is a refrigerator and a table, a covered porch with a loveseat, and an outdoor picnic table and fire ring. The campground bathrooms have hot showers and are clean.

Kayaking is popular here in the land of seal and porpoise, and rentals can be arranged with ease. There is a free launch for larger boats just a mile away in town. (Keep in mind that there is an enormous tidal difference in this area.) You can walk on the beach from the campground to the trails of Moose Point State Park, and nearby Sears Island offers an afternoon of walking around its perimeter.

Facilities: There is one camping cabin that can accommodate 2–6 people. Laundry facilities are on-site.

Bedding: Bring your own bedding.

Reservations and rates: Rates range $65–75 per night. Call to reserve by January. Weeklong cabin reservations are encouraged and will help guarantee your dates. Open mid-May–mid-October. You may bring one small pet with Searsport Shores's permission.

Directions: The campground is in Searsport, directly on Routes 3 and 1. Driving from the south, look for the signs on the right.

Contact: Searsport Shores Camping Resorts, U.S. Routes 3 and 1, Searsport, ME 04974, 207/548-6059, www.campocean.com.

7. CEDARHOLM GARDEN BAY

Camden on West Penobscot Bay

Luxury rating: ★ ★ ★ ★ ★   **Recreation rating:** ★ ★ ★ ☆ ☆

Rank: Top 10 for Romance, Top 10 Most Luxurious

Travel just a few miles north of hectic downtown Camden, on Route 1, and you will find yourself uniquely situated. To the west is Camden Hills State Park, and on the other side of that is Lake Megunticook. To the east is West Penobscot Bay, looking toward Isleboro. With all the biking, hiking, swimming, boating, and winter sports possible in the area, a series of beautifully designed cedar cottages on the shore seems almost too much to ask for.

Barry and Joyce Jobson took over this property in the 1990s and worked some serious magic. Their daughters, Erika and Kristin, also play pivotal roles where the decor and gardening are concerned. The cedar cottages are, for the most part, fairly new, with fabulous Maine birch and maple woodwork. You'll admire the detail that has been put into the cottages: a blue-tiled whirlpool tub here, a stone fireplace there, a dramatic sleeping loft, decks looking at the ocean, and views of the Owls Head light in Rockland.

Not surprisingly, these cottages are particularly popular with couples. The cottages are privately spaced (nearly 100 feet apart) with plenty of trees and foliage between them. Four are on the waterfront down a private road into the woods, and two sit higher on the property overlooking the water. You'll meet other cottage dwellers while munching some of Joyce's fresh-baked muffins (made with berries picked on the property). Guests are invited to sit together at one long table in a cozy dining room, surrounded by Scandinavian folk art, for an expanded continental breakfast.

It's just three miles to Mount Battie, with its lovely view over Camden Harbor and beyond, and as you walk up the road from the cottages to the dining area, you can marvel at the beautiful gardens or the sight of Bald Rock Mountain in Camden Hills State Park. The park has over 30 miles of trails. If you're lucky enough to have snow before the cottages close in December, you can ski or snowmobile here as well.

Just north on Route 1 is a kayak outfitter, where you can take trips on the coast or out to Isleboro, and you can launch your own boat from Lincolnville Beach. Camden has a renowned windjammer festival and popular lobster festivals. Be sure to book early for summer weekends.

Facilities: There are six cottages on 16 acres. Four are on the oceanfront, and two of those are considered deluxe cottages, with amenities like whirlpool baths. The cottages are one and two bedroom lodgings.

Bedding: All bedding and linens provided.

Reservations and rates: Rates range $159–325 per night. Open May 1–December. No pets permitted.

Directions: Drive four miles north of Camden on Route 1; look for the sign on the right.

Contact: Cedarholm, LLC, RR3 Box 3294, Atlantic Highway, Lincolnville Beach, ME 04849, 207/236-3886, website: www.cedarholm.com.

Other Cabins and Cottages Nearby
- The Lodge at Camden Hills, P.O. Box 794, Camden, ME 04843, 207/236-8478 or 800/832-7058, website: www.thelodge atcamdenhills.com.

8. THE INN AT SUNRISE POINT

on Penobscot Bay in Camden

Luxury rating: ★★★★★   **Recreation rating:** ★★★★☆

Rank: Top 10 for Romance, Top 10 Most Luxurious

If you wander off Route 1, down a well-maintained dirt fire road fringed with wildflowers and through a peaceful birch grove, you may find yourself at a sophisticated fairytale inn with some of the closest cottages to the water on the East Coast. Despite the closeness of Camden Hills State Park, and the kayak outfitter at the head of the road, you may even begin hoping it rains so that you have a good excuse to stay in your cottage all day.

This is especially true in the romantic Fitz Hugh Lane cottage. After a full gourmet breakfast in the inn's glass conservatory, you may already be looking ahead to an evening listening to the moonlit waves of Penobscot Bay lapping against the rocks beneath your windows while curled up in bed by the fireplace. Or perhaps you are thinking about taking a luxurious bath in your double whirlpool tub.

But don't miss the day. You can swim in the cold Maine waters from the private popple-stone beach if you're feeling hardy, or you can drive to a nearby lake to swim and fish. Lincolnville Beach is also quite close and is a convenient place to launch a kayak. The mountains of Camden Hills are excellent picnic destinations. You can also read by the roaring fire in the cozy library, play croquet by the rose garden, or simply work hard at doing nothing.

Owners Stephen and Deanna Tallon left fast-paced lives in New York not so long ago to take over the inn. They intend to add more cottages to their fleet over time, and are planning a very private sanctuary tucked back behind the inn. An additional cottage on the shore, dedicated to the former owners of the inn, is their newest addition. Stephen is Irish, and claims to make a killer soda bread; be sure to let him know what you think if you find it on your breakfast menu.

All of the cottages face West Penobscot Bay. This is a great destination for unwinding to the sounds of the ocean. If you time it right (and reserve very early), you might sit on your deck and spend the afternoon watching the famous windjammer fleet as it cruises by your cottage.

Facilities: There are five cottages, and more in the works. They are high-end lodgings, with phones, mini-refrigerators, and private baths with robes. One cottage is wheelchair-accessible.

Bedding: All bedding and linens are provided.

Reservations and rates: Rates range $350–415 a night. All cottages are for two adults only and include breakfast. Open May–October. Pets are not permitted.

Directions: The inn is four miles north of Camden harbor on Route 1. Traveling north on Route 1, turn right at the Fire Road 9 sign (FR-9) and drive down to the water. Traveling from the north, you'll see Fire Road 9 one mile past Lincolnville Beach.

Contact: Stephen and Deanna Tallon, **The Inn at Sunrise Point**, P.O. Box 1344, Camden, ME 04843, 207/236-7716, website: www.sunrisepoint.com.

9. LOBSTER BUOY CAMPSITES

on Mussel Ridge Channel

Luxury rating: ★ ☆ ☆ ☆ ☆   **Recreation rating:** ★ ★ ★ ★ ★

The main draw at Lobster Buoy Campsites is the ocean. The sites and the cabins are set directly on the shore. This is a very good place to base your kayak or sea-canoe explorations of the Mussel Ridge Archipelago, a series of little islands named for their blue mussels, located about three miles from the campground. The islands in this chain are separated by reefs and narrow channels, and thus lack significant large boat traffic. They are beautiful places for viewing scenery, sea birds, and seals. Sea ducks and gulls fish off the shore in front of the cabins, and kids play in the frigid water.

© BETHANY ERICSON

The campground was started in the late 1960s, and the owners have retained its happy, salty atmosphere as they've developed it. You may wake in the middle of the night wondering if you've drifted out to sea, due to the crashing waves or the early morning lobster-boat motors. June and September are quiet times to camp here. July and August are a bit more hectic, with tourism and mackerel fishing at a high point.

You swim and boat at your own risk at the campground, but you are welcome to leave a float plan at the office if you're going boating for the day. The area is prone to strong crosswinds and currents. Plan your channel crossing carefully, and remember that those gorgeous schooners that frequent the area are a bit harder to paddle around than to photograph from shore.

At night, you'll return to homemade pie and baked goods at the campsite. These camping cabins are fairly simple and rustic, but surprisingly pleasant. Quiet hours are 10 P.M.–8 A.M.. It's a short drive to restaurants and ferries in Rockland.

Facilities: There are two cabins that can accommodate up to four people.

Bedding: Linens are not provided.

Reservations and rates: Cottages are $475 per week in the high season for four people with one vehicle and are rented Saturday–Saturday. In the off-season they rent for $90 per day. Call very early to book for July or August rentals. Open May 15–October 15. One quiet, leashed dog is allowed per unit. Be prepared to clean up after your dog.

Directions: From the junction of Route 1 and Highway 73 in Rockland, drive seven miles south on Highway 73 to the campground.

Contact: Lobster Buoy Campsites, 280 Waterman Beach Road, So. Thomaston, ME 04858, 207/594-7546.

10. THE GOSNOLD ARMS
on New Harbor

Luxury rating: ★★☆☆☆   **Recreation rating:** ★★★★★

New Harbor is a quaint and relatively quiet working fishing village. The Gosnold Arms is located directly on the wharf, a rambling white farmhouse at the bend in the road with a delightful breakfast porch. This is the main inn building, which houses a sunroom and a library with antique furnishings and a stone fireplace.

This was once the Danforth farm, renovated into summer lodgings in the early 20th century, when visitors began arriving in the area by steamship. The inn's namesake, Bartholomew Gosnold, was a British explorer in the early 1600s. The cottages are all very different but are mainly simple, pine-paneled quarters either  scattered amongst shady trees and lawn behind the inn, or dockside across the street. One unit on the wharf has a fireplace.

You can arrange to arrive at the Gosnold Arms by boat, as there are three moorings for guests. There are also rental companies and a town landing nearby. And the much-loved Hardy Boat trips leave from Shaw's Fish and Lobster Wharf just steps away. These boat trips will take you to Monhegan Island, or to see seals and puffins. Reserve early for a cottage and a space on the boat to watch fireworks in the summer.

Nearby, the Rachel Carson Salt Pond Preserve, on the edge of Muscongus Bay, is worth a visit with your binoculars. The Pemaquid Lighthouse and its museum are a favorite destination, and they are a popular place with visitors to paint, photograph, and say "I do." The soft sand of Pemaquid Beach is also just minutes away.

Facilities: There are 10 cottages. One, the Wharf House, contains three double units. Well-behaved children are welcome.

Bedding: Bedding and linens are provided.

Reservations and rates: The rates for cottages are based on double occupancy and range $89–200 per night. A breakfast buffet is included. Off-season rates with breakfast are discounted by 15 percent. There are minimum stay requirements in certain cottages. Open mid-May–mid-October. No pets are permitted.

Directions: From the Maine Turnpike, take Exit 9 and follow Route 95 to Exit 22 Brunswick, and then drive on Route 1 to Damariscotta. From Damariscotta, take Route 130 to New Harbor, and then drive for one mile on Route 32 to the inn.

Contact: The Gosnold Arms, 146 State Route 32, New Harbor, ME 04554, 207/677-3727 (summer), 561/575-9549 (winter), website: www.gosnold.com.

11. THE THOMPSON HOUSE AND COTTAGES

New Harbor

Luxury rating: ★★☆☆☆   **Recreation rating:** ★★★★★

The Thompson Cottages are in four places. The two Harbor Cottages are on high land overlooking New Harbor and the ocean. The three Back Cove Cottages face a footbridge and lobster pound adjacent to Back Cove. Ten Front Ocean Cottages and four Back Ocean Cottages face the Gulf of Maine. Almost all of the cottages have cozy fieldstone fireplaces.

© BETHANY ERICSON

The Harbor Cottages sleep four people in two bedrooms, with a queen in one and two twin beds in the other. They have lovely decks. The Back Cove Cottages sleep five in two bedrooms, with a double bed and a single bed in one bedroom and two twins in the other. These have screened porches with views. The Ocean Cottages hold five people in two bedrooms and have decks and large picture windows. There is also a cottage called the Rec Room, which is built on pilings over New Harbor. It sleeps five and has five picture windows and a deck on the harbor. It is the only unit without a fireplace, but it does have a woodstove.

There is a lovely trail to the ocean and a sandy beach across a little bridge. Kids ride by on bikes here and fish for crabs. Adults play badminton and croquet. Guests are often seen writing and painting on easels set along the various scenic spots on the property. In Back Cove, there is a boathouse, wharf, and float with rowing skiffs. You can launch a kayak here, and kayak guide services can be arranged. This harbor is home to the Hardy Boat that takes passengers to see puffins.

Owner Merle Thompson's parents started the cottages in the 1920s. They are good, basic, casual New England cottages. There are no televisions and no phones ("It's a service we offer," says Merle). Merle's wife and co-owner, Karen, started visiting the cottages as a guest when she was a small child. Was it the great location or was it Merle that brought her back to stay?

Facilities: There are 21 cottages, 14 on the ocean. They can accommodate 1–5 people. Family reunions are encouraged.

Bedding: Bedding and linens provided.

Reservations and rates: Rates range $850–1,500. Open May 1–November 1. Pets are permitted.

Directions: Take Route 95 through Portland. After about 20 minutes, you will see signs for Bath and the coastal area; take Exit 22 into Brunswick. Stay on Route 1 through Brunswick. After 10 to 15 minutes you will arrive in Bath, where traffic may be held up at the bridge. In another 15 minutes or so, you will come to Wiscasset; you may be held up again at this bridge. The Newcastle-Damariscotta exit is 10 or 15 minutes after Wiscasset. Turn right down the ramp into Newcastle. On your right, coming down the ramp, is the view of the two towns; a bridge connects them. Drive across the bridge (this is Main Street), and as you start up the hill you will see the First National Bank of Damariscotta on the right. Turn right, directly after the bank, onto Route 130, and drive for approximately 12 miles. Route 130 will narrow as you come into the little village of New Harbor. You will see the puffin sign on the roof of Harbor Ice Cream in a fork in the road; bear left here. Almost immediately you will come to South Side Road—turn left again here (Reilly's Market will be on your right). Drive down the big hill (New Harbor is to the left at the bottom of the hill) to a white, three-story house on the right, the Thompson House; the office is at the head of the driveway.

Contact: Merle and Karen Thompson, Thompson House and Cottages, 95 South Side Road, New Harbor, ME 04554, 207/677-2317.

12. HITCHCOCK HOUSE

Monhegan Island

🌲 🏠 🐟 🛶 🌊

Luxury rating: ★★☆☆☆   **Recreation rating:** ★★★★★

Fairies are said to live on Monhegan Island, and evidence of their little bark-and-leaf homes are often visible in Cathedral Forest if you look carefully. You can't stay in any of these homes unless you are quite tiny, though you may want to add your own. (You never know when a fairy might find themselves homeless on this island of artists and fishermen.)

Humans looking for cottages on Monhegan Island can find a rental through Shining Sails Real Estate, or can stay in the studio behind the

Hitchcock House. The island is 10 miles out to sea from Boothbay Harbor and Port Clyde. It's predominantly a land trust and is thus mostly wild, webbed with walking trails through the evergreens, over rocky bluffs, and across meadows. It is not unusual to see seals or whales from the shore.

© BETHANY ERICSON

Hitchcock House overlooks Monhegan village from the top of Horn Hill. You can walk from the ferry landing, by the swimming and fishing beaches in the small village of art galleries and markets (and owner Barbara Hitchcock's Black Duck gift shop), to anywhere you want to go on Monhegan Island. To get to Hitchcock House, take a short, uphill walk to a hidden path and then down to a platform deck complete with hammock and grill. It is like a hidden treehouse here, surrounded with vines and berry bushes and a panoramic view from the highest spot on the island. Bring good shoes and a flashlight for your stay.

The studio is set apart from the four-room inn, just above the deck. It has a high ceiling in the main living and bedroom area, a double bed, a kitchen, and a bathroom with a shower stall. It's good for couples. Don't worry if you're arriving off the ferry with luggage. A motor service meets each ferry to help you haul your belongings for a fee.

The 17 miles of hiking trails on the island are maintained by the land trust, and bicycles are not allowed on the trails. The island is 1.7 miles long and about .7 mile wide. Beware of the surf on the eastern side. The island is on the Atlantic Flyway, and spring and fall are good times to bring your binoculars. There are also boat trips offered throughout the summer to see puffins and seals. No smoking is permitted beyond the village.

Facilities: There is one cottage at Hitchcock House.

Bedding: Bedding and linens are provided.

Reservations and rates: Rates range $75–105. Weekly rates are also available; call to inquire. Open April–October. Pets are not permitted.

Directions: There are ferries from Port Clyde, Boothbay Harbor, and New Harbor. Go up the hill from the dock. Turn right at the Spa and walk straight to the Monhegan House on the left. Turn left and climb up the dirt road to the top of the hill. The road forks at two twin houses and a sign for Burnt Head. Our road is on your left. Come down the road until it ends. Walk right on the faint path down the hill, through the hedge and to the main house (you'll know it by the deck).

Contact: Barabara Hitchcock, **Hitchcock House**, Monhegan Island, ME 04852, 207/594-8137, website: www.midcoast.com/~hhouse.

Other Cabins and Cottages Nearby

- Shining Sails, P.O. Box 346, Monhegan Island, ME 04852, 207/596-0041, website: www.shiningsails.com/rentals.html.

13. THE BRADLEY INN

Pemaquid Point

Luxury rating: ★ ★ ★ ★ ☆   **Recreation rating:** ★ ★ ★ ★ ☆

Rank: Top 10 for Weddings

The Bradley Inn is a wonderfully landscaped mansion in the mist, with a gazebo set out front among the shrubs and flowers and a romantic Garden Cottage. The inn itself was a romantic gift from a ship captain to his wife in the late 1800s, and is set a short walk down the rocks from the Pemaquid Lighthouse.

The lovely Garden Cottage is carpeted and very tastefully decorated with antiques, Audubon bird prints, and an optional television residing under a lace cover. A chimney and fireplace are in the center of the open-plan cottage, separating the queen bed from the sitting area. There is a sink and a small refrigerator, as well as a pleasant screened porch.

While the gray-shingled cottage is located right on the front lawn of the inn, it is ingeniously sequestered behind the landscaping in such a way that you have complete privacy, and yet there's plenty of light inside the cottage. Next to the cottage, a similarly romantic gazebo offers a lovely space to sit for two.

The inn has a knowledgeable staff to help guide you to hiking trails, bike paths, good picnic spots, and where to get the ferry to Monhegan Island. Fishing and lobstering harbors, with a wide range of boat and fishing charters, surround the Pemaquid Peninsula. There are also a number of good lakes and ponds for paddling and swimming. Pemaquid Beach is just a few miles away.

The Bradley Inn is a popular spot for weddings, with numerous wedding parties taking photos in front of the lighthouse. It also has a fine-dining restaurant offering local oysters and house-smoked salmon and boasting a large selection of wines.

Facilities: There is one cottage that can accommodate two people.

Bedding: Bedding and linens are provided.

Reservations and rates: The cottage is rented for $195–250 per night, depending on the season. There is a 10 percent AARP discount, and a 10 percent AAA discount in the off-season. Open year-round.

Directions: The Bradley Inn is centrally located between Boothbay Harbor and Camden. Take the Maine Turnpike to Exit 6A and drive on Route 295 to Route 95 (Falmouth). Drive for 21 miles on Route 95 to Route 1 (Brunswick). Continue driving north for 27 miles on Route 1 to Routes 129/130 (Damariscotta). Follow Route 130 to Pemiquid Point, and the Bradley Inn will be on your right.

Contact: The Bradley Inn, 3063 Bristol Road, Pemaquid Point, New Harbor, ME 04554, 207/677-2105 or 800/942-5560, website: www.bradleyinn.com.

14. HARBORFIELDS ON THE SHORE

West Boothbay Harbor

Luxury rating: ★ ★ ☆ ☆ ☆   **Recreation rating:** ★ ★ ★ ★ ★

Rank: Top 10 for Boating

Harborfields is a casual and friendly vacation spot on a half mile of saltwater shoreline on West Boothbay Harbor. Harborfields is convenient for town, and it has a secluded, salty, cheerful atmosphere. It's a place to escape the crowds with a cup of coffee on your porch by the sea, and a place to happily mess about in boats—wooden boats, in particular.

Harborfields is also home to Rick Prose's Finest Kind Wooden Boats company. Rick was a master builder at Buck Meadow Boats, in Denmark, Maine, and attended the famed Landing School of Boatbuilding Design. He builds, repairs, and rents skiffs, as well as some original wooden boats called Boothbay Harbor One Designs, which were raced out of the nearby yacht club in the 1930s and 1940s. Harborfields has a dock, floats, and moorings, and is a mile across the water from busy Boothbay Harbor village. There is a dock fee, and it is also a convenient location to bring boats and launch kayaks.

The fully equipped house-keeping cottages (and two rental houses) are scattered across 10 acres of woods and fields, most of which overlook the activity in the harbor. You may even find overnight accommodations are available on a 32-foot sailboat. The home and office of the managers (the wonderful Prose

© BETHANY ERICSON

Family) is an 1870 farmhouse in a field above the harbor.

The cottages see a large amount of repeat business. They do not offer televisions or phones, and are very private. They are mainly one-bedroom units that also have the possibility of a bed in the living room. One cottage has two floors. Each has a picture window facing the water and a fireplace or woodstove.

When you aren't out boating, you can swim here in the cove, or fish off the dock for stripers and mackerel. There is hiking in the Porter Preserve, and the Boothbay Region Land Trust offers planned hikes. You can play volleyball, shuffleboard, and horseshoes on-site, or tennis nearby. The aquarium is down the street, and all the restaurants and activity of Boothbay Harbor are two miles away by land.

Facilities: There are seven cottages and two rental houses. The cottages can accommodate 2–6 people. One rental house, the 1750 House, is connected to the 1870 Main House and holds up to four people. The other is a Cape that sleeps up to 10 people. The Galaxy (the 32-foot sailboat) holds four people in two cabins.

Bedding: Bedding and linens are provided.

Reservations and rates: Rates for the cottages and houses range $675–1,000 per week (Saturday–Saturday in season). The boat is rented for $50 nightly. There is a 20 percent off-season rate reduction before June 21 and after Labor Day. Reduced rates may be offered for longer-term stays. Home-schooling families traveling off-season are offered an additional 5 percent discount. Repeat guests begin calling in December, new guest reservations are accepted beginning January 2. The cottages are typically reserved for midsummer by the end of January. Open mid-May–mid-October. Credit cards are not accepted. One or two pets may be permitted with a security deposit.

Directions: From Route 1, north or south, drive on Route 27 through Boothbay Harbor, and follow the signs to Southport. After you have passed St. Andrews Hospital and BBH Yacht Club, drive across the causeway, and turn left on McKown Point Road. Harborfields is 100 years ahead, on your left.

Contact: Harborfields on the Shore, PO Box 524, West Boothbay Harbor, ME 04575, 207/633-5082, website: www.harborfields.com.

15. OCEAN POINT INN

East Boothbay Harbor

Luxury rating: ★★★☆☆   **Recreation rating:** ★★★★☆

Secluded Ocean Point Inn, in East Boothbay, has a very separate identity from Boothbay Harbor or West Boothbay. Here, grand resorts were built during the era of steamboat travel. The Ocean Point Inn is more than a century old, though the cottages have all been updated. While unwinding in the cozy main living room and library,

© BETHANY ERICSON

be sure to find the inn's copy of its own history, written by a guest.

The atmosphere here is more like that of a hotel than a summer camp, with casual and formal dining rooms, a pristine clapboard cottage and inn, and lodge units spread across the lawn. Most of the cottages do not offer much in the way of cooking facilities. Instead, the bar and dining areas in the main resort building are the center of activity. The breakfast room looks at the harbor and is a delightful place to plan out your day's activities.

Many guests are here to play golf and tennis, or to swim in the area's largest heated outdoor pool. There is boating in Grimes Cove, and tours and boat rentals are offered up the street at the East Boothbay Kayak Company. The wharf is a stone's throw away and is a decent place to fish. The nearby Linekin Preserve offers a couple of miles of hiking trails along the Damariscotta River, and East Boothbay is a common place to see visitors walking, biking, and jogging.

The cottages are very clean, wallpapered units with comfortable furniture and daily cleaning services. More than half of the cottages are duplex units that can either be rented separately or together with other members of your family or party. All have televisions, phones, and mini-refrigerators; some have kitchenettes.

Even drizzling foggy Maine days seem cheerful at Ocean Point. The colors of the flowers pop out, and the waves sound comforting. Guests stroll hand in hand down the road in bright yellow slickers or curl up by the fire in the living room to read.

Facilities: There are seven cottages that can accommodate 2–5 people. Four of these are duplex cottages. Of the three standalone cottages, Glimpse is a single room cottage with a queen bed, Seaward is a large two-bedroom with a queen and two twins, and Sea Chest is a single suite cottage with one queen bed.

Bedding: Bedding and linens are provided.

Reservations and rates: Rates range $69–85 per night for Glimpse or Sea Crest and $737–1,145 weekly for Seward. Call by February or March for summer reservations. Open late May–mid-October. Pets are not permitted. Call ahead to inquire about wheelchair accessibility.

Directions: Drive north on I-95 from Boston. In Maine, I-95 becomes the Maine Turnpike. Just beyond Portland, take Exit 9 (you leave the turnpike, but you're still on I-95). Continue driving north on I-95 to Brunswick, and take Exit 22 onto Coastal Route 1. Follow Route 1 and drive through Brunswick, Bath, and Wiscasset. After crossing the bridge just beyond Wiscasset, turn right onto Route 27 and head toward Boothbay Harbor. Continue driving for about 12 miles and, just before entering the business district, turn left at the traffic light onto Route 96 (East Boothbay/Ocean Point). Drive on Route 96 for about 6.5 miles to Ocean Point, and then turn right onto Middle Road. At the bottom of Middle Road, turn right onto Shore Road to the inn.

Contact: Ocean Point Inn, Shore Road, P.O. Box 409, East Boothbay, ME 04544, 207/633-4200 or 800/552-5554, website: www.oceanpointinn.com.

16. GRAY HOMESTEAD CAMPGROUND

Southport Island on Boothbay Harbor

Luxury rating: ★★☆☆☆   **Recreation rating:** ★★★★★

From Boothbay Harbor, cross the Townsend Gut on a scenic bridge to Southport Island. Here, on the rocky shore under vast evergreens, you'll find that the only oceanfront campground in the Boothbay region not only has two lovely rustic cabins, but it also offers lobster delivery to your door.

Friendly second-generation owner Stephen Gray goes out on his lobster boat daily, just for the campground. You can cook 'em up in your cabin's small kitchen, or have them delivered cooked. When asked if they also bring melted butter, Stephen replied, "We're a full-service operation; we'll even eat them for you!"

The Hillside Cottage is set in the pines up above the water, looking out toward Squirrel Island. Adirondack chairs on the rocky point offer a fantastic place to contemplate the view. The cottages are rustic, with pine walls, simple furnishings, and clean, cotton table coverings. Hillside has a covered porch and two bedrooms, and a

new second cottage with three bedrooms has been built on what was previously site 17D. Both have an evocative New England atmosphere, with the waves crashing outside and homey window-filled interiors with warming fireplaces.

Gray's is a great spot for launching a kayak; there is a safe beach with sand and small stones that is reasonably gentle on boats. The campground rents both single and double Old Town Loon boats. You can trailer boats down to the beach. You can also moor boats up to 30 feet here.

On the campground property you can play volleyball, basketball, and horseshoes. In the area you can go whale-watching, indulge yourself in a true Maine clambake, go fishing from the rocks or charter boats, golf, play tennis, and visit numerous lighthouses. Keep an eye on Gray's. Stephen has plans for adding a number of new cabins.

Facilities: There are two cabins—one sleeps six and the other sleeps four. They are located in a campground with 30 sites for tents and RVs and a handful of apartment units.

Bedding: Bring your own sheets and towels.

Reservations and rates: Hillside Cottage is $700 per week. The newer cottage is $800 per week. Open May 1–October 10. No credit cards are accepted. No pets are permitted.

Directions: From the south, take I-95 north to Maine and the Maine Turnpike. Drive past Portland, and take Exit 9 (off the Maine Turnpike, but still I-95) to Route 1, Coastal Exit 22 for Brunswick and Bath. Follow Route 1 and drive through Bath and Wiscasset to Route 27 South. Follow Route 27 to Boothbay Harbor (takes approximately 10 minutes), then continue driving on Route 27 to Southport (for about 10 more minutes). At the second bridge, turn left onto Route 238 and drive for about two miles. The campground will be on your left.

Contact: Suzanne and Stephen Gray, **Gray Homestead Campground**, 21 Homestead Road, Southport, ME 04576, 207/633-4612, website: www.graysocean-camping.com.

17. THE SPRUCE POINT INN

Boothbay Harbor

Luxury rating: ★ ★ ★ ☆ ☆   **Recreation rating:** ★ ★ ★ ★ ★

Well off the beaten track, on 15 acres of a point overlooking the entrance to Boothbay Harbor, this large destination resort has a wide variety of lodgings. The lodgings include some large, updated guest cottages that are like small houses. With pine walls and floors, and braided rugs, they retain New England cabin charm while offering modern amenities.

Most of the cottages have two bedrooms and stone fireplaces. Some have full kitchens and others are efficiency-style. There are private decks and large televisions. Wicker and other cottage-style furniture are well cared-for and comfortable.

The saltwater pool and whirlpool set above the waves are popular spots on warm sunny days. There is also a freshwater pool if you're feeling that less salt is better. Championship tennis courts, an adult gym, croquet, table tennis, and pool tables are also on-site. There is also a playground and special programs for kids. The Boothbay Harbor golf course is nearby, and there is a complimentary shuttle into town.

The inn offers a gourmet restaurant serving a wide range of food, including fusion inventions like lobster spring rolls with a ginger-sesame sauce and Japanese-themed salmon with *ponzu* sauce. Codfish cakes and lobster Benedict grace the breakfast menu, and a bistro menu is available at the Whistling Whale Pub, where there is often evening entertainment.

Weddings are popular at Spruce Point, and people often make use of the outdoor dining pavilion. But even if you aren't celebrating or honeymooning, there's no reason you can't act like it here. After a day of activities, enjoy an on-site massage, dine on gourmet food, watch the copper sunset, and disappear into your private cottage.

Facilities: There are two oceanside cottages and five partial view cottages holding 2–6 people.

Bedding: Bedding and linens are provided.

Reservations and rates: Rates range $250–550 per night (based on four guests sharing), depending on the season and whether the cottage has a full or partial view of the ocean. Minimum stay requirements may apply. Frequently there are special packages available that include meals and activities. Open mid-May–October. Pets may be permitted in one cottage; call to inquire.

Directions: From Boston, take I-95 north to Maine and the Maine Turnpike, drive past Portland, and take Exit 9 (off Maine Turnpike, but still I-95) to Route 1 (Coastal Exit 22 for Brunswick and Bath). Follow Route 1 and drive through Bath and Wiscasset to Route 27 South. Drive on Route 27 for approximately 10 miles. Go through the intersection with the traffic light. At the First National Bank of Damariscotta (with the time-and-temperature sign), bear right onto Oak Street. Drive one block and turn left at the first left-hand turn (Union Street). Follow Union Street past the Gulf Station to Atlantic Avenue. Turn right onto Atlantic Avenue and drive approximately 1.5 miles to the inn.

Contact: Spruce Point Inn, Box 237, Boothbay Harbor, ME 04538, 207/633-4152 or 800/553-0289, website: www.sprucepointinn.com.

18. SEBASCO HARBOR RESORT

on Casco Bay

Luxury rating: ★★★☆☆   **Recreation rating:** ★★★★★

Rank: Top 10 for Weddings, Top 10 for Family Activities

Whatever you're looking for, there's a good chance it's here. Sebasco Harbor Resort is a resort destination on 600 acres of the southwestern edge of the Phippsburg peninsula, by the ocean. It offers a staggering array of activities and 23 cottages in a wide variety of sizes and shapes.

Some of these cottages are tucked in the woods together as a convenient family compound, others overlook a flower garden with a dazzling spectrum of colors, not far from the water. Some dot the golf course; still others are on the coast next to the resort's wedding cake–tiered lighthouse rooms, looking across Sebasco Harbor toward Harbor Island, a basking grounds for hundreds of seals.

The resort has docking and mooring space on the harbor, and its own tour boat, the *Ruth*. There is a saltwater pool, sailing lessons, sea-kayak rentals and lessons, and a freshwater lake where you can use canoes for free. Sebasco has its own golf course and pro shop, as well as all-weather tennis courts. Guided nature and bird walks on Phippsburg Land Trust areas or on Mount Merritt are offered, and it is a short drive from sandy Popham Beach. Saltwater fishing and tours of working lobster boats can be arranged. Mountain bikes are available to rent.

© BETHANY ERICSON

Basketball, shuffleboard, horseshoes, and softball are all on-site, as is an organized children's activity program. Raining? Enjoy bingo, movie screenings and rentals, video game machines, a health club with salon and spa services, or the tiny ice cream shop. Or you can drive to the outlets in Freeport.

Wedding parties are often seen at Sebasco, with lobster bakes, ceremonies by the gazebo on the lawn, and dancing in the lovely old dining room, with its wooden floor and enormous ceiling fans. The resort's nearby candlepin bowling lanes await for more casual fun.

The cottages themselves run the range from small modern spaces with whirlpool tubs to rambling, comfortable, shorefront units with large stone fireplaces and nostalgic camp furnishings. There is even a 10-bedroom, 10-bathroom unit used for reunions. Kitchen facilities vary; inquire as to your needs. There is a fabulous dining room overlooking the harbor, and handy binoculars hung by its large windows.

At the end of all this activity, relax in a rocking chair on an absolutely enormous screened porch that looks out across the rocks uncovered by the tide, while gulls float overhead and sailboat halyards clang on masts like Maine wind chimes.

Facilities: There are 23 cottages (1–10 bedrooms) spread throughout the property alongside the larger inn buildings and the lighthouse. Several of the cottages have wheelchair-accessible ramps, and Shore Ledges has the biggest bathroom. Call ahead to inquire if you have specific concerns.

Bedding: All bedding and linens are provided.

Reservations and rates: Cottages range $249–1,450 daily. There is a 10 percent discount for stays of seven days or more. There is a Modified American Plan (MAP) option (breakfast and dinner) for an extra $35 per day. Children aged 10 and under eat from the children's menu at no charge when accompanied by an adult. Open June 19–September 1.

Directions: Take Maine Turnpike Exit 9 (Falmouth) to I-95 heading north. Then take Exit 22 off I-95 to Coastal Route 1 and head for Brunswick and Bath.

Follow the signs to Bath, then in Bath, bear right onto Route 209. Drive on Route 209 for 11 miles to Route 217. Then drive for 1.3 miles on Route 217 to Sebasco Harbor Resort.

Contact: Sebasco Harbor Resort, Sebasco Estates, ME 04565, 207/389-1161 or 800/225-3819, website: www.sebasco.com.

19. OCEAN VIEW PARK CAMPGROUND

on Popham Beach

Luxury rating: ★ ★ ☆ ☆ ☆   **Recreation rating:** ★ ★ ★ ★ ★

Rank: Top 10 for Ocean Beach Activities, Top 10 for Family Activities

Popham Beach is a repeat destination for many New Englanders. It's not just a longtime
summer colony; it's the location of the first (unsuccessful)
colony settlement in the country. It's pure Maine, with a long
sandy beach, rocky outcrop-
pings, seal and osprey sight-
ings, two lighthouses (that you
can see from the beach), and a

© BETHANY ERICSON

quaint fishing village nearby for post-beach pig-outs. Beach scenes for the
Kevin Costner movie *Message in a Bottle* were shot here.

Ocean View Park Campground offers camping and cottages just steps
from the sand. The cottages are small and basic, but all you need is a
place to sleep after a day playing at the shore. The campground also
offers a store with essentials and ice, and the beach has a lifeguard. It's
a very convenient base from which you can spend your days sunbathing, shell collecting, and swimming. The beach is so large that it
doesn't normally feel too crowded. It also has its own picnic area and
bathhouses.

At low tide you can walk to Fox Island (watch the tides for your
return). There are hiking trails through Morse Mountain and a hilly
nature trail and bird sanctuary managed by Bates College near the beach.
Two miles down Route 209, at the end of the Kennebec River, is Fort
Popham, an unfinished project started during the Civil War. Nearby on

Sabino Hill is Fort Baldwin, a WWI submarine lookout tower with a good view of the nearby islands.

The Kennebec and Morse Rivers act as bookends for the beach and are a great area for kayaking and fishing. The Kennebec is a spawning ground for striped bass, and the area is also good for bluefish and mackerel. There are numerous boat-cruise companies in the area for fishing and seeing the lighthouses. All cruises run by the Maine Maritime Museum include a two-day museum pass.

> **Facilities:** There are 13 cottages accommodating 4–6 people.
>
> **Bedding:** Bedding is provided.
>
> **Reservations and rates:** Cottages range $600–900 weekly for four people. Book a year ahead for summer. Open mid-May–mid-October.
>
> **Directions:** Drive on Maine's Route 209 for 14 miles from Bath to Phippsburg—follow signs to the park.
>
> **Contact:** Charlie and Bernadette Konzelman, **Ocean View Park Campground, Inc.**, P.O. Box 129, Route 209, Popham Beach, Phippsburg, ME 04562, 207/389-2564 (summer) or 207/443-1000 (winter).

Other Cabins and Cottages Nearby

- Hidden Mountain Cottages & Gift Shop, 1659 Main Road, Phippsburg, ME 04562, 207/389-1457, website: www.hiddenmtn.com.

20. THE DRIFTWOOD INN

Bailey Island

Luxury rating: ★ ★ ☆ ☆ ☆   **Recreation rating:** ★ ★ ★ ★ ★

Rank: Top 10 for Value

If you're looking for a rustic cabin by crashing waves, without a long drive Down East, come to the Driftwood Inn, located on three acres between the Giant Staircase and Pinnacle Rock. It's the oldest inn on Bailey Island, and the inn has been in the same family for more than 75 years.

The cabins are a bit weather beaten, and the showers and some of the furniture show signs of their age, but it somehow feels appropriate. On a good gray Maine day, as the waves crash high on the Driftwood Inn shores, doing anything to show up the spectacle of Mother Nature seems blasphemous. The cabins, the pine dining room, and the porches all look out over the sea, helping to make this a favorite spot for artists and writers, as well as for groups on work retreats.

Kayaking is popular here, and you can launch by the lodge. Be wary of the tides in this area. There is an outfitter in nearby Orrs Island. Boats big and small can be launched in Mackerel Cove. The Androscoggin River Bicycle Path offers miles of pedaling between Brunswick and Cooks Corner. There are beaches within a short drive, and the inn has a saltwater swimming pool.

The cabins are all quite different from each other. Some have decks or covered porches, picnic tables, and small charcoal grills; one is a log cabin. There are basic kitchenettes in most of them. They aren't fancy, but they are clean.

Bailey Island is just 20 minutes from Brunswick. The island is thought to have been named after Deacon Timothy Bailey, who is rumored to have made more than a few native enemies in his day. It's said he named the island after himself after buying it from a trader for a pound of tobacco and a gallon of rum.

Facilities: There are six housekeeping cabins that accommodate up to four people.

Bedding: Bedding is provided.

Reservations and rates: The inn sees a tremendous number of repeat customers, and the summer is often book a year in advance. Call in January and be flexible with your dates. Cottages rent for $600–635 per week, breakfast and dinner are included in July and August. Open May 20–October 12. Credit cards are not accepted. Pets are permitted.

Directions: From Boston, take I-95 to Exit 24. Turn right and continue on the Coastal Connector. The Coastal Connector takes you to Route 1. Follow the signs to Brunswick. Continue driving for approximately two minutes on Route 1 and exit at Cook's Corner. Drive straight through the traffic light at the intersection and drive south for 13 miles on Route 24. Cross the Cribstone Bridge onto Bailey Island, turn left on Ocean Street, and then turn right on Washington Ave.

Contact: The Driftwood Inn, P.O. Box 16 Washington Ave., Bailey Island, ME 04003, 207/833-5461 or 508/947-1066 (off-season).

Other Cabins and Cottages Nearby

• Sea Escape Cottages, Sea Escape Ln., Bailey Island, ME 04003, 207/833-5531, website: www.seaescapecottages.com/.

21. WOLFE'S NECK FARM RECOMPENCE SHORE CAMPSITES

on Casco Bay in Freeport

Luxury rating: ★☆☆☆☆   **Recreation rating:** ★★★★★

Rank: Top 10 for Boating

Past the outlet shopping and L.L. Bean in Freeport, there is a fabulous shoreline that many visitors pass by in their shopping frenzy. Recompence (which means to give back) Shore Campsites is operated by a foundation belonging to its neighbor, Wolfe's Neck Farm. This is an all-natural farm that raises chemical-free beef, which is sold at the campground store. The farm offers educational programs for kids, and you can visit the sheep, pigs, and cows. There are also miles of walking and cross-country ski trails.

There are four basic camping cabins. They're rustic kinds of places—in the woods by the ocean—places that you might decorate with odd shells and feathers after hanging your hat and binoculars on the hooks after a day of fishing or kayaking, perhaps as a participant in one of the L.L. Bean workshops. Three are small one-bedroom cabins with a living room, kitchen, and sliding glass door to an open porch. They have outhouses. The cabin called Cove has a loft, though it isn't for the arachnophobic. There is also a large two-bedroom cabin that holds six people. The cabins have woodstoves and can be rented in the winter.

The campground has easy walking trails dotted with raspberries and blackberries in the summer. At the Salt Marsh Classroom you may see a great blue heron or a snowy egret. You can go tidal swimming, try catching mackerel from the shore, or ride a mountain bike on the dirt roads. There are volleyball and softball areas too.

Nearby is Wolfe's Neck Woods State Park, Mast Landing Bird Sanctuary (this area is good in the spring and fall for migration), Bradbury Mountain

State Park, and Crescent Beach State Park. This is also an excellent camping spot for families or friends who are split between doing outdoor activities and shopping.

Facilities: There are four camping cabins, three with one bedroom and one with two.

Bedding: Bedding is not provided.

Reservations and rates: Cabin rates range $50–60 per night. Call to reserve between January and April for popular summer weekends and holidays. Open May–mid-October. Inquire about the pet policy.

Directions: Drive on I-95 or U.S. Route 1 to Freeport. Across from L.L. Bean, turn onto Bow Street, which becomes Flying Point Road. Drive for approximately 3.5 miles and bear right onto Wolfe's Neck Road.

Contact: Recompence Shore Campsites, 134 Burnett Road, Freeport, ME 04032, 207/865-9307, website: www.freeportcamping.com.

22. ACORN VILLAGE

Old Orchard Beach

Luxury rating: ★★☆☆☆   **Recreation rating:** ★★★★☆

Old Orchard Beach is a very busy place in the summer, with crowds heading to the beaches and amusement-park atmosphere of Town Square. The Amtrak train stops right in the center of the action. If you're looking to stay somewhere a little quieter, but don't want to have to walk far for fun, Acorn Village is a good destination. It's a .25-mile

© BETHANY ERICSON

walk to the town and beach, and it's even a stop on the town trolley.

These are very clean and orderly white cottages, with aqua trim in neat rows under shade trees. Some have kitchens, and some have kitchenettes. The bathrooms have shower stalls. All have dining areas and a picnic table by the door. Back behind the cottages spreads a campground with 75 sites for tents and recreational vehicles, plus an outdoor pool and playground.

Old Orchard Beach is popular with New Englanders and French Canadians for its seven miles of white sandy beach, as well as the festive atmosphere of the pier and amusement-park area. The area is also host to endless events in the summertime, from fishing tournaments to sandcastle contests to powwows. From late June through Labor Day, there are often free concerts, and every Thursday there are fireworks.

Also in the area is Scarborough Marsh Nature Center, the largest salt marsh in the state. There are canoe rentals for exploring the area, and it's an excellent place for birding. Other good nature hikes in the area are at Gilsland Farm, Audubon Sanctuary in Falmouth, and the Rachel Carson Wildlife Preserve and Laudholm Farm in Wells.

Facilities: There are 20 one- and two-bedroom cabins in three sizes. They hold two adults in the one-bedroom cabins, two adults and two children in the medium two-bedroom cottages, and four adults and two children in the largest cottages. Laundry facilities are on-site.

Bedding: Linens are provided.

Reservations and rates: The cottages range $395–720 per week, and $70–115 per day. No pets are permitted.

Directions: Directions provided with reservations. Located just .25 mile from Route 9, in the center of Old Orchard Beach.

Contact: Lionel and Cynthia Bisson, **Acorn Village**, 42 Walnut Street, Old Orchard Beach, ME 04064, 207/934-4154 website: www.campmaine.com/acornvillage.

Other Cabins and Cottages Nearby
- The Edgewater, White Lamb and Pine Scrub Cottages, 57 West Grand Avenue, Old Orchard Beach, ME 04064, 207/934-2221 or 800/203-2034, website: www.janelle.com.

23. BUFFLEHEAD COVE
on Kennebunk River

Luxury rating: ★ ★ ★ ★ ★   **Recreation rating:** ★ ★ ★ ★ ★

Rank: Top 10 Most Luxurious

Once upon a time, retired lobsterman Jim Gott and his wife, Harriet, bought a large house, raised kids, and then started a bed-and-breakfast as a hobby. Today, Bufflehead Cove is a serious business with one of the most remarkable romantic honeymoon cabins in New England.

The lovely, airy River Cottage is like a small house, and it's located more than 200 yards from the main inn on the Tidal Kennebunk River. It boasts fabulous furniture, including a king sleigh bed in the upstairs master bedroom. The large bathroom includes a dressing room, a two-person whirlpool tub, and a glassed-in shower.

Downstairs, there is satellite television, a comfortable couch, a wood-burning fireplace, and an impressive radio and CD player. The large windows and private deck have fantastic views of the river and wildlife. There is a modern kitchen with a ceramic pike swimming in the tiles, and an iron heron flies the skies of the cathedral ceiling.

The Gotts believe in personal attention and will be sure to help you plan your day's activities or make your dinner reservations. You can launch your own kayak from the cottage's dock on the river, walk in the woods, or walk less than a mile to downtown Kennebunkport.

Bufflehead Cove has some beach permits for guest use. Local beaches include Kennebunk Beach, Parson's Beach, and Goose Rocks Beach. In town, you can fish off the docks, and there are schooner, lobster, and fishing-boat charters, as well as kayak rentals. Bird-watchers may want to visit the Rachel Carson National Wildlife Refuge.

Facilities: There is one luxury honeymoon cottage for adults only. Maid service is provided.

Bedding: Bedding is provided.

Reservations and rates: The cottage rates range from $350 nightly to $2,275 weekly. There is a strict two-night minimum. Open year-round. Small pets are sometimes accommodated in the cottage. It is a smoke-free inn.

Directions: From the south, take the Maine Turnpike (I-95) north to the Wells-Sanford Exit (Exit 2). After exiting, turn left onto Route 9 east. Drive for 1.5 miles to the light and turn left, continuing on Route 9 east and Route 1 north. After 1.8 miles, follow Route 9 east as it forks to the right. At the second traffic light, turn left onto Route 35 north. Watch for the sign for Bufflehead Cove, .5 mile from the light on the right.

Contact: Bufflehead Cove, P.O. Box 499, Kennebunkport, ME 04046, 207/967-3879, website: www.buffleheadcove.com.

24. THE SEASIDE MOTOR INN AND COTTAGES

Gooch's Beach in Kennebunkport

Luxury rating: ★ ★ ★ ☆ ☆   **Recreation rating:** ★ ★ ★ ★ ★

Rank: Top 10 for Ocean Beach Activities

© BETH-ANY ERICSON

John Gooch settled in Wells in the mid-1600s, and was asked by an agent of the King to set up a ferry at the mouth of the Kennebunk River. There was a Native American summer campground on the other side of the river, and when hostilities were running high, travelers would get stuck on his shore. So he started an inn. Later, in 1667, he left the inn and tavern to his son. This area was part of Massachusetts then.

Fast-forward to the early 21st century, and you'll find folks strolling down to the beach in sunglasses they bought while vacationing here in the 1950s, and the 12th generation of the Gooch-Severance family might just introduce you to the 13th. This is now Maine, through and through.

It's no surprise why so many family members would want to stay and run the business over the years; it's incredibly pleasant here. Guests are of a wide range of ages, and many of them know each other from years of vacationing side-by-side in the cottages. The cottages are spread widely apart on 20 acres, with shade trees, a great lawn, and bursts of beach roses. They all have a view of either the ocean or the Kennebunk River, which offers excellent striper fishing.

Down on the private sandy beach, couples walk hand in hand, stopping to examine sand dollars and shells as sanderlings and toddlers chase the waves. The property goes right to the beach, rather than being separated by a road. Kayaks can be launched here.

The cottages themselves are large, immaculate, and rather like small homes. They're made to be more relaxed than kitschy, and have forgone the wicker for more comfortable furniture. They are either painted or wallpapered, with wall-to-wall carpeting. There is a fully equipped kitchen, and dining and living rooms. Hostilities across the river are no longer a concern, but if John Gooch could see how happy the guests on his property are today, he'd certainly know he built for the future.

Facilities: There are 11 housekeeping cottages, accommodating 2–7 people in each. Laundry facilities are on-site.

Bedding: Linens are provided and can be exchanged if you're staying more than a week. Bring your own beach towels and paper goods.

Reservations and rates: Rates range $770–1,545 per week, and $2,750–7,345 per month. There are limits on the numbers of guests. Cottages are rented monthly only in July and August. Watch the website for special packages. Call by January 1 to put your name on a wish list; it is not a guaranteed waiting list, and with the high percentage of loyal repeat guests here, you are wise to be flexible with your dates. Open May 1–October 31. One or two well-behaved pets are accepted in eight of the units, with permission and a deposit.

Directions: From either north or south, take the Maine Turnpike (I-95) to Exit 3, Kennebunk. After leaving the turnpike, turn left on Route 35 south to Kennebunk. Drive on Route 35 south for approximately six miles. Drive through the junction at Route 9. The Seaside is .7 miles on your left where the road meets the ocean.

Contact: The Seaside Motor Inn and Cottages, Gooch's Beach, P.O. Box 631, Kennebunkport, ME 04046, 207/967-4461 or 866/300-6750 (out-of-state toll-free), website: www.kennebunkbeach.com.

25. OCEAN VIEW COTTAGES AND CAMPGROUND

Wells

Luxury rating: ★★☆☆☆   **Recreation rating:** ★★★☆☆

Sometimes campgrounds with a high proportion of seasonal RVs and off the beaten track from the main beach areas have less-than-stellar cabins, but this isn't the case here. These are really pleasant cottages with outstanding views across the salt marshes. By staying just two miles from the beach crowd, you can have a decent cabin at a great price.

The cabins are older units but are very clean. The views and chirping birds, and kids playing in the pool, provide a welcome happy atmosphere after the busy confusion of the Route 1 area. Each two-bedroom cottage has an eat-in kitchen separated from the living area by a breakfast bar.

The bedrooms each have one double bed and two twins, and the bathrooms have shower stalls. The single bedroom units run a bit smaller and older but have the same stunning view. One of the larger cabins is next to the pool.

© BETHANY ERICSON

Besides the pool (no lifeguard), there are tennis courts, shuffleboard, a basketball court, and a playground. There is also a recreation hall and game room. There is fishing just .5 mile away, and the miles of ocean beaches are just two miles from your door—you can get there on a short ride on the town trolley (which stops at the campground), on a rented moped, or on your bike.

There are lifeguards on duty all along Wells Beach and at Drakes Island Beach, which is a slightly less busy beach within walking distance of the nature trail that goes through the Rachel Carson National Wildlife Refuge (a good birding spot). Another interesting destination in the area is Crescent Beach, which is just .5 mile south of busy Wells Beach. Starfish and crabs populate numerous tidepools, and with a good scope you may be able to spot seals hauled out on the rocks.

Facilities: There are 12 cottages accommodating 2–6 people. Laundry facilities are on-site.

Bedding: Linens and blankets are provided. Bring beach towels.

Reservations and rates: Cottages range $340–666 per week and are rented Saturday–Saturday. Discounts are available in the off season (before June 21 and after Labor Day). Open May–October. You may bring a dog with permission, but your pet must be accompanied at all times; note that mid-June–mid-September, dogs are not allowed on beaches in Wells.

Directions: Take I-95, the Maine Turnpike (toll road), north to Exit 2 (Wells, Sanford). Turn left off the ramp onto Route 9/109 toward Route 1. At the end of Route 109, turn right onto Route 1, then turn immediately right onto Harbor Road (near the fire station). Drive .1 mile and look for the campground on your left.

Contact: Ocean View Cottages and Campground, 84 Harbor Road, P.O. Box 153, Wells, ME 04090.

26. COTTAGE IN THE LANE MOTOR LODGE

Bordering Rachel Carson Preserve

Luxury rating: ★★☆☆☆   **Recreation rating:** ★★★★☆

Drakes Island Beach is the second largest of the sandy beaches in Wells, and Cottage in the Lane is within walking distance. The cottages are on a large lawn near a quiet residential road, on property that borders the Rachel Carson Wildlife Refuge and the Wells National Estuarine Research Reserve at Laudholm Farm.

The cottages here are roomy and are well spaced from each other, with four or five rooms each, and double beds in the master bedrooms. There are picnic tables under shady pine trees, with vintage round orange chairs. It's a pretty area, and the quiet road is a ladder of speed bumps, which keeps it safe for kids.

On-site there is a large heated swimming pool with a deck area, and a playground. Next door, the Rachel Carson Wildlife Refuge has a mile-long nature trail through the woods and marshland that was once harvested for hay. It's an excellent birding area and sees a wide variety of birds during spring and fall migrations. The Laudholm Farm and Rachel Carson Wildlife Refuge are highly populated with deer, and Laudholm Farm's beach area is a piping-plover nesting area.

The nearby beach has lifeguards, restrooms, and occasional visits from ice-cream trucks. More beaches are in the area, as well as boating and fishing outfitters, golf, and tennis. The leaves turn color in this area in early October.

Facilities: There are 11 housekeeping cottages accommodating up to five people.

Bedding: Linens, blankets, and towels are provided.

Reservations and rates: Rates range $410–795 per week (Saturday–Saturday) and $65–85 per day. Rates are for three people in a one-bedroom cottage or five people in a two-bedroom cottage. Cottages are rented weekly only in July and August. Pets are not permitted.

Directions: Take the Maine Turnpike (I-95) to Exit 2 (Wells, Sanford). After the toll-booth, turn left onto Route 109 and follow the road to a traffic light at Route 1. Turn left, and drive approximately .75 mile before turning right onto Drakes Island Road. Drive down a hill, and look for the sign on your left.

Contact: Cottage in the Lane Motor Lodge, 84 Drakes Island Road, Wells, ME 04090, 207/646-7903, website: www.cottageinthelane.com.

27. THE DUNES ON THE WATERFRONT

Ogunquit

Luxury rating: ★★★☆☆   **Recreation rating:** ★★★★★

Rank: Top 10 for Ocean Beach Activities

The Dunes cottages are on 12 acres bought as pasture land in 1936, north of Ogunquit Village on the Ogunquit tidal river. At low tide you can wade across the river to the protected Ogunquit Beach peninsula; at high tide, the Dunes provides rowboats. Either means puts you right in the middle of the peninsula, in the least-crowded section of the wide, white-sand beach.

The cottages are on the local trolley line and are also within walking distance of restaurants and the Marginal Way footpath. There is a pool, shuffleboard, and croquet. Canoeing and kayaking in the Ogunquit Tidal River are popular. Nearby is easy hiking at Mount Agamenticus, in York, and there is lots of coastal cycling.

The grounds are beautifully landscaped, with a gorgeous array of color in the butterfly-filled center flower garden. The white cottages are spaced pleasantly, with shade trees and paths between them. The atmosphere is friendly, and the cottages are clean. Although the cottages are fairly simple, they have nice wood floors and immaculate kitchens. It feels like a treat to be in one of these comfortable cottages, which have crescent moons on the shutters.

© BETHANY ERICSON

Owners Cindy and Aaron Perkins are the third generation to run the cottages. They grew up with tales of the guests arriving with trunks in the 1930s. Today the cottages have full kitchens, and one or two bedrooms. Some have fireplaces and screened porches. Some are considered "cottage suites," which means they are really adjoining units in a larger cottage building.

Facilities: There are 19 cottages, each accommodating 2–6 people. Some are suites.

Bedding: Bedding is provided.

Reservations and rates: Rates range $110–270 per night. Bookings begin in December, and preference is given to repeat guests. Start by trying to get a reservation in a guest room and work up to a cottage, and then to a cottage by the water. Open late April–late October.

Directions: From Boston, take I-95 north to Exit 4 (York, Ogunquit), and turn left on Route 1. Drive for seven miles to the center of Ogunquit. Continue driving north for .5 mile. The Dunes is on the right.

Contact: The Dunes on the Waterfront, 518 Main Street, P.O. Box 917, Ogunquit, ME 03907, 207/646-2612, website: www.dunesmotel.com.

Other Cabins and Cottages Nearby

- Echo Motel and Oceanfront Cottages, 8 Traynor Street, Old Orchard Beach, ME 04064, 207/284-5413.
- Moontide Motel, Apartments and Cabins, 10 Traynor Street, Old Orchard Beach, ME 04064, 207/934-2759, website: www.moontidemotel.com.

28. HOLIDAY HOUSE

near Ogunquit Center

Luxury rating: ★ ★ ☆ ☆ ☆   **Recreation rating:** ★ ★ ★ ★ ☆

This cute colony of white cottages is set back from the road, with the cottages spaced nicely apart from each other. They make up a nicely landscaped neighborhood loop, with flower-filled window boxes on the houses. They are right on Route 1, and the local trolley will stop here to take you to the beaches.

There are miles of soft, white-sand beaches in Ogunquit, with Ogunquit Beach and Footbridge accessible from the trolley, and Moody Beach just a 10-minute walk away. Also nearby is Perkins Cove, a picturesque fishing village, and Marginal Way, a fabulous walk along the crashing

© BETHANY ERICSON

waves and beach roses.

The cottages have one or two bedrooms, a living room, and fully equipped kitchens. Some have screened porches, and some have decks. All have picnic tables. There is a playground and a kidney-shaped pool with a large deck and covered patio.

Ogunquit is a liberal, artistic town near the boardwalk bustle of Old Orchard Beach and the long sandy beaches and nature walks of Wells. There are fishing and sightseeing charters, golf, and tennis in the area, as well as many novelty amusement-park attractions. Rainy days often find visitors at the many outlet stores in Kittery.

Facilities: Cottages can be rented with or without daily cleaning services.

Bedding: Linens are provided.

Reservations and rates: For housekeeping cottages, the rates range $725–865 per week. For full-service cottages, the rates range $840–1,050 per week. Weekly rentals run Saturday–Saturday. Open May–October. No pets are permitted.

Directions: From I-95, take Exit 4 to Route 1 and turn left onto Route 1. Holiday House is located 1.5 miles north of the center of Ogunquit on Route 1.

Contact: Holiday House Motel and Cottages, P.O. Box 714, Ogunquit, ME 03907, 207/646-5020 or 888/254-7893, website: www.holidayhousemotelwells-maine.com.

© BETHANY ERICSON

Chapter 8

Massachusetts

CHAPTER 8—MASSACHUSETTS

Massachusetts is the most populated state in New England, and has a long and storied history of academics, immigration, industry, and politics. From the indigenous peoples that lived here, to the landing of the Pilgrims, to its rise as the intellectual capital of the country and key early industrial center, it has always been a significant state.

Despite its large population, the state has hundreds of forests, hills, rivers, lakes, and beaches. In fact, some of the oldest conservation organizations in the country protect a large amount of its land.

Boston is the biggest city in New England and is one of the hardest cities to navigate by car in the country. Take the subway (the "T") or walk. The city is known for its more than 100 colleges, and it is one of the nation's top scientific and medical hubs. While here, walk the old neighborhoods such as Beacon Hill, ride a swan boat in the Public Garden, see the Red Sox play, take a boat to the harbor islands, and visit neighboring Cambridge.

North of Boston you'll find historical, maritime, and art museums in Salem and Gloucester. This is also the land of fishing harbors and salt marshes, and great federal mansions built by sea captains. Once upon a time this was Boston vacationers' Gold Coast, filled with Great Hotels and sailing regattas. Today, it has a lower-key identity and is a prime spot for a beach vacation that includes eating fried clams, fishing, kayaking, and whale-watching.

To the northwest, in Lowell and Lawrence, there are tours of the old textile mills that sparked the industrial revolution, of a tribute park to Beat author Jack Kerouac, and of the birthplace of Robert Frost. Slightly farther south, Lexington Green witnessed the first shots of the Revolutionary War. In Concord, Henry David Thoreau stayed by Walden Pond, and nearby are the houses of Louisa May Alcott, Nathaniel Hawthorne, and Ralph Waldo Emerson.

South of Boston, Plimouth Plantation brings the Pilgrims to life in the large town of Plymouth. This area is home to beaches, the state's famed cranberry bogs, and Myles Standish, the first state forest in Massachusetts. Woods Hole and New Bedford are filled with marine explorations and whaling history, as well as ferries out to the Elizabeth Islands. Dartmouth's quaint sailing villages are also great for biking, birding, and kayaking.

East of here is the wildly popular summer destination of Cape Cod. The goal of most visitors to the cape is to play on the beach. The area also offers secluded dune walks on Race Point, artists colonies, fishing ports, and a convenient bike path—the Cape Cod Rail Trail. Most of the beaches of the cape are either on Cape Cod Bay or Nantucket Sound; the Great Beach of the National Seashore runs from Chatham to Provincetown on the Atlantic side. Ferries leave Hyannis to Nantucket and Martha's Vineyard.

In central Massachusetts, you can visit a number of small art museums, pick apples near the birthplace of Johnny Appleseed, visit the Fruitlands Museum (a Utopian community founded by Louisa May Alcott's father in the early 1800s), and hike or ski Mount Wachusett. Many a Massachusetts child has taken a field trip to the living-history museum at Old Sturbridge Village.

Strangely, few Bostonians are aware that their drinking water comes from a massive reservoir that takes up what were once four towns in the Smith River valley of central Massachusetts. The Quabbin Reservoir is a beautiful state park; note that there are occasionally security restrictions here.

Traveling west of here—past college towns, farmland, maple sugaring operations, the thriving cultural and arts scene of Northampton, and white-water rafting and kayaking opportunities—you can drive right to the summit of Mount Greylock (the tallest mountain in Massachusetts) and get a good look west at the Berkshires.

In the late 1800s, extremely wealthy families built summer estates around Lenox, and the area took on a Newport-like atmosphere. Many of the country inns with cottages tucked back behind them are the renovated summer "cottages" of the friends and neighbors of the Carnegies and Westinghouses. Tanglewood (summer home to the Boston Symphony Orchestra), ski resorts and touring trails, MASS MoCA (the Museum of Contemporary Art), and the intense colors of autumn foliage are the biggest draws to this area.

While the Bay State has some serious cultural credentials, what comes to mind for many vacationers who return year after year are the great beaches, foliage, major-league sports, seafood, and the outdoor fun.

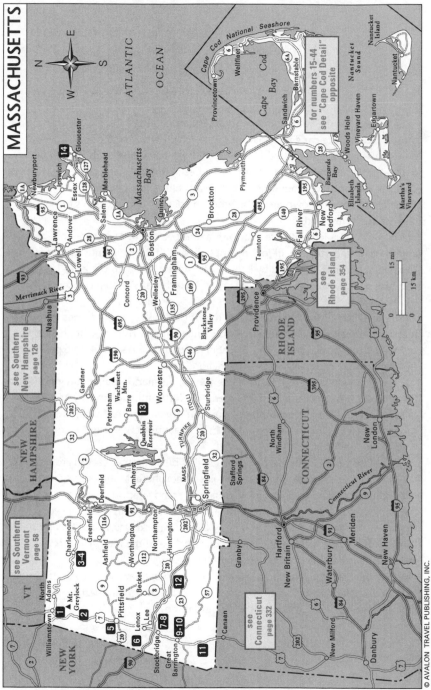

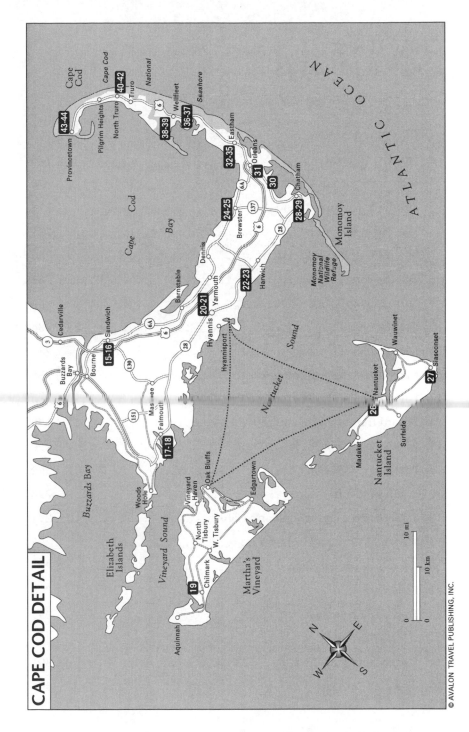

CAPE COD DETAIL

Cape Cod
Cape Cod
National
Seashore

40-42 Truro
North Truro
Pilgrim Heights
43-44 Provincetown

38-39
36-37 Wellfleet
6
32-35 Eastham
31 Orleans
30 Chatham

Cape Cod Bay

Cedarville
Sandwich
15-16 Bourne
3
Buzzards Bay
130
Mashpee
17-18 Falmouth
151
Woods Hole

6A
6
Barnstable
20-21 Yarmouth
22-23 Harwich
Dennis
Hyannis
Hyannisport
28

24-25 Brewster
137
6A
6
Chatham
28-29
6
28
137

Monomov Island
Monomov National Wildlife Refuge

Nantucket Sound

Wauwinet
Nantucket
26 Madaket
Surfside
27 Siasconset
Nantucket Island

Buzzards Bay

Elizabeth Islands

Vineyard Sound

19 Aquinnah
Chilmark
North Tisbury
W. Tisbury
Vineyard Haven
Oak Bluffs
Edgartown
Martha's Vineyard

ATLANTIC OCEAN

N
W   E
S

10 mi
0
10 km
0

© AVALON TRAVEL PUBLISHING, INC.

CHAPTER 8
MASSACHUSETTS

1. JERICHO VALLEY INN

on the Williamstown–Hancock Border

Luxury rating: ★★★☆☆   **Recreation rating:** ★★★★☆

Rank: Top 10 for Viewing Fall Foliage

A few miles south of Williamstown, the Jericho Valley Inn is a favorite of skiers, as it is located on the way to Brodie Mountain and Jiminy Peak Ski Area. And back behind its main, motel-like quarters in the woods are a number of cozy and brightly colored cottages with fireplaces.

While skiing is a big draw, fall is an exceptionally beautiful time to visit this corner of the Berkshires. The colors are especially nice on Route 2 (the Mohawk Trail) and from the top of Massachusetts's tallest mountain, Mount Greylock—whether you drive, hike, or bike to the summit. There are a number of mountains surrounding Greylock, most of which have been named after past presidents of Williams College; the Green Mountains of Vermont are a short drive away.

You can canoe and kayak both white water and lakes here. There are plenty of good fishing spots, and hiking trails galore. Some pleasant, short, scenic walks in the area include the Cobbles and Waconah Falls State Park in neighboring Dalton. There are two golf courses (Taconic and Waubeeka) in town. The inn offers golf, ski, and hunting packages.

You'd even be happy relaxing at the inn. The Jericho Valley Inn has 350 acres of property and a heated swimming pool. The cottages have been fairly recently renovated and redecorated. They have televisions, heating and air-conditioning, telephones, and decently sized kitchens. There are sofa beds for adding extra guests. After a crisp fall day or a snowy day of skiing, a cottage with a fireplace is heavenly.

You're also well located if the weather doesn't cooperate. Williamstown is a culturally rich college town. There are more than 30 Renoir paintings at the Sterling and Francine Clark Art Institute. MASS MoCA, in neighboring North Adams, is a 27-building mill complex transformed into what may be the world's largest museum of contemporary art.

Facilities: There are four cottages that can accommodate 2–8 people. There is one three-bedroom cottage, two two-bedroom cottages, and two one-bedroom cottages. They have double and queen beds. There is complimentary coffee, juice, and muffins in the morning in the main inn.

Bedding: Bedding is provided.

2. OLD STONE SCHOOL

Lanesboro near Mount Greylock

Luxury rating: ★ ★ ★ ☆ ☆   **Recreation rating:** ★ ★ ★ ★ ☆

Rank: Top 10 for Viewing Fall Foliage

Ephraim Bradley was forced to house British soldiers during the Revolutionary War. While they slept, their gold was stolen. A few years later, Bradley donated a lot of money for the building of a one-room schoolhouse. It successfully operated as a school from 1832 until 1950.

© CHERYL SACKS

Bob and Prudy Barton renovated the old school for a decade. Today, it is a two-story unit with a beautiful mountain view. During the day the first floor is a small, quiet art gallery that retains the old blackboards and tall windows. Here you will see the work of Cheryl Renée Sacks, an outdoor photographer who specializes in the Berkshires.

On the second floor of the school is a cottage apartment. It's fairly cozy, with exposed stone walls and wood beams, and skylights in the sloping ceiling above the king bed. It has a lovely antique floor, a fully equipped kitchen, and a dining area, and there is a sofa bed, as well as extra mattresses.

On the grounds of the school there is an English garden to stroll in and five acres of pasture. There are apple trees, and horses to feed the apples to. There are miles of surrounding roads good for running or biking. Hikers and mountain bikers love the proximity to Mount Greylock, the highest mountain in the state.

Mount Greylock was Massachusetts's first state park. It has more than 60 miles of trails, including part of the Applachian Trail. There is an auto road to the summit in the summer and fall, and on the top there are camping and backpacker shelters, and Bascom Lodge. This makes for good people-watching, as you can see Appalachian Trail through-hikers and coiffed urban tourists intermingling. Some say that the Mahican tribe did not climb Mount Greylock because they considered it sacred, but if your spirituality allows you to, it's got a really nice view.

Facilities: There is one schoolhouse cottage that accommodates 2–5 people.

Bedding: Bedding is provided.

Reservations and rates: Rates range $125–145 for three people; weekly and months rates are available. Extra people are $10 per person per night. Continental breakfast is included. Call a couple of months in advance for popular summer weekends. Open year-round. No smoking or pets permitted.

Directions: From Boston on the Mass Pike, take Exit 2 (Lee), which is at mile marker 11. After paying the toll, turn right onto Route 20 west. Route 20 eventually becomes Route 7 north. Drive on this road for about 19 miles, until you arrive at North Main Street. You will pass through the towns of Lee, Lenox, and Pittsfield before arriving in Lanesboro.

Contact: Old Stone School B&B, 732 North Main Street, P.O. Box 1689, Lanesboro, MA 01237, 413/442-0996 or 888/442-0996, website: www.oldstoneschool.com.

Other Cabins and Cottages Nearby

- Breckenridge on the Lake, 636 South Main Street, Lanesborough, MA 01237, 413/443-3530, website: lakeview636.tripod.com.

3. BLUE HERON FARM

two miles from Charlemont

Luxury rating: ★★☆☆☆   **Recreation rating:** ★★★★★

Rank: Top 10 for Family Activities, Top 10 Most Unusual, Top 10 for Viewing Fall Foliage

---

There are surprisingly few cabins and cottages on working farms in this region. Blue Heron Farm is a 140-acre sustainable organic farm that's been going strong for more than two centuries. Unplug the kids from the computer games and see what happens when they milk Nubian and French-Alpine dairy goats, pick blueberries for their own pancakes (that they can eat with maple syrup tapped from nearby trees), and drink water from your cottage's private well.

© BLUE HERON FARM

Pitching in with the farm work is certainly not obligatory, but a lot of it is fun (especially when you don't have to do it fast or every day). Friendly Bill and Norma Coli have run this farm for more than 25 years, and are a wealth of information. Besides raising dairy goats, cultivating high-bush blueberries, and producing syrup, they also raise big, sweet-tempered Norwegian Fjord horses.

There are four very pleasant cottages here: the Sugarhouse, the Cottage, the Log Cabin, and the Maples. All are winterized and have kitchens, televisions, VCRs, telephones, and grills. Some have washers and dryers, and some have dishwashers.

The Sugarhouse has two floors connected by a circular staircase, 1.5 baths, a washer and dryer, and a dishwasher. The Log Cabin is also winterized and has a small washer and dryer. The Cottage has two bedrooms and three floors, a dishwasher, and a sun porch and large deck. The Maples is like a small house; it has two large bedrooms, a fireplace, and a deck. It was built for Bill's dad originally, and it's fully wheelchair-accessible.

The nearby Deerfield River has Class III and IV white water for paddling or rafting, and there are several outfitters in the area. There are also great stretches for swimming, tubing, and trout fishing. There are old-growth state forests with hiking trails nearby, and downhill and cross-country skiing. Imagine your kids feeding milk to baby goats and apples to the horses, or exclaiming over a ghostly green luna moth fluttering against the screen at night. It's a great place to get in touch with the land.

Facilities: There are four cottages that can accommodate 2–6 people.

Bedding: Bedding is provided.

Reservations and rates: Rates range $90–250 per night, and $375–900 per week. Call a few months in advance. Open year-round. Credit cards are not accepted. Pets and smoking are not permitted.

Directions: From Boston, take Route 2 west to Charlemont (18 miles west of the intersection with I-91). In the village, turn right onto Route 8A north. Drive across a small bridge, and continue for about two miles to Warner Hill Road 2, which is the third left off of 8A and is marked with a sign. Drive up Warner Hill for about .75 of a mile to a three-way fork, and take the left-most fork, marked Warner Hill Road 1. The farm is at the end of this road.

Contact: Blue Heron Farm, 8 Warner Hill Road 1, Charlemont, MA 01339, 413/339-4045, website: www.blueheronfarm.com.

Other Cabins and Cottages Nearby

- Holiday Farm, Holiday Cottage Road, Dalton, MA 01226, 413/684-0444, website: www.holidayfarm.com.

4. MOHAWK TRAIL STATE FOREST

off Route 2 in Charlemont

Luxury rating: ★☆☆☆☆   **Recreation rating:** ★★★★★

Rank: Top 10 for Viewing Fall Foliage, Top 10 for Backcountry Winter Adventures

Hidden away at the base of Todd Mountain, in the Mohawk Trail State Forest, is a gem of a campground with six log cabins, a nature trail, and a swimming area. This forest includes pine trees more than 100 feet tall, miles of rivers and streams with good trout fishing, and hiking trails—including a beautiful section of ridges on the old Indian path known as the Mahican-Mohawk Trail, which is thought to have connected the Atlantic Ocean with the Hudson River.

The log cabins are fairly nice for totally basic camping cabins, some of which were hand-hewn in the 1930s by the Civilian Conservation Corps. Woodstoves provide enough heat for cozy, rustic winter visits. Some cabins are divided into a food preparation area, sitting/sleeping area, and extra bunkroom. There is no water in the cabins; a heated restroom with hot showers is nearby. The quiet campground is situated in the trees alongside the Cold River.

This forested area, flanking Scenic Byway Route 2 in Florida and Charlemont, includes Monroe State Forest to the north and Savoy Mountain State Forest and Mohawk Trail State Forest to the south. It's some of the most picturesque woodland in the state, with enormous pine forests saved from logging by rough slopes.

A short interpretive nature trail leads from the campground to the Mahican-Mohawk Trail, which winds up to Todd Mountain and beyond to Clark Mountain. Mohawk Trail State Forest and neighboring Savoy Mountain State Forest have double- and single-track mountain biking paths, as well as cross-country ski trails. Savoy Mountain State Forest has a lovely waterfall called Tannery Falls.

Facilities: There are six log cabins that accommodate 3–5 people. Small Cabin 5 and large Cabins 6 and 7 are wheelchair-accessible. Bring food in critter-safe containers or keep it in the car. No cooking utensils are provided. Firewood and maps are available at the campground.

Bedding: No bedding is provided.

Reservations and rates: Rates range $30–35 per night. There is an $8 reservation fee. The cabins are available by reservation up to six months in advance. They are rented Sunday–Sunday only mid-June–early September. A two-night minimum is required in winter. The phone number for reservations is different than the number for Mohawk Trail State Forest information; call 877/422-6762 Monday–Friday. Leashed, attended pets are permitted; be prepared to clean up after your pet.

Directions: From Charlemont, drive four miles west on Route 2 and follow the signs down a steep grade to the campground.

Contact: Mohawk Trail State Forest, P.O. Box 7, Route 2, Charlemont, MA 01339, 413/339-5504, website: www.state.ma.us/dem.

Other Cabins and Cottages Nearby

- Savoy Mountain State Forest, R.F.D. 2, North Adams, MA 02147, 413/663-8469; state campground reservation line: 877/422-6762.

5. BONNIE BRAE CAMPGROUND

near Pontoosuc Lake in Pittsfield

Luxury rating: ★☆☆☆☆   **Recreation rating:** ★★★★☆

Bonnie Brae Campground is a tent and RV campground with a separate lane of small, simple brown cottages near Pontoosuc Lake, convenient to many local attractions and just down the street from the lake. The cottages are a pleasant place to experience pink sunsets or reflections of the fall foliage. Be sure to keep an eye out for the lake's legendary spirits: two Native American lovers paddling in a white canoe.

The cabins are in a row on their own road of the campground, on a lawn with ample shade trees. They are fairly rustic, with double beds, mini-refrigerators, and hot plates. There is no water in the smaller cabins, and the larger cabins have cold water only. Restrooms and showers are in a separate building.

The campground has a swimming pool for registered guests, and there is swimming, boat rentals, tennis, and golf nearby. This is a basic, quiet place to sleep at night while enjoying the sites of the Berkshire Hills, and it is a popular camping spot for those attending the Falcon Crest Folk Festival.

Pittsfield State Forest is a good place to visit in June, when the 65 acres of pink, wild azaleas are in bloom. There's a swimming beach there, and a good fishing spot at Berry Pond. Berry Mountain is also a good place to watch the sun set. While in the park, make sure the kids see if they can topple the 165-ton Balance Rock off its base.

Facilities: There are seven cabins. One is a two-bedroom, and the rest are one-bedrooms. All bedrooms have double beds. Firewood and laundry facilities are available on-site. Daytime visitors must register and pay $3, and no visitors are permitted after 9 P.M.

Bedding: Linens are provided; bring your own towels.

Reservations and rates: Rages range $55–75 per night for two people. Additional people are $4. The charge for children under 13 is $1. Open May 1–October 15. Pets are allowed only in the one-bedroom cabins.

Directions: From Pittsfield Business Center, take Route 7 north and drive for three miles. Turn right onto Broadway at Pontoosuc Lake.

Contact: Bonnie Brae Campground, 108 Broadway, Pittsfield, MA 01201, 413/442-3754, website: bonniebraecampground.tripod.com.

6. THE INN AT RICHMOND

on Route 41 in Richmond

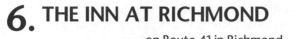

Luxury rating: ★ ★ ★ ★ ★   **Recreation rating:** ★ ★ ★ ★ ★

Rank: Top 10 for Romance, Top 10 Most Luxurious

© THE INN AT RICHMOND

The Inn at Richmond is an elegant country inn on 27 acres near the New York border. It is minutes from Tanglewood and is convenient for Jiminy Peak, Butternut Basin, and Brodie Mountain ski areas. Some guests come for the adjacent equestrian center, or to cross-country ski right on the property.

There are three recently renovated, upscale cottages here, resplendent with antique furnishings and luxurious bedding. They all have one queen or king bed, an extra sofa bed, and a fully equipped kitchen. Each cottage has a telephone, cable television, a VCR, heating, and air-conditioning.

The Carriage House is a two-floor cottage. The sitting room and bedroom are on the second floor, taking advantage of the great views. The bathroom has a shower and tub, and the living room couch opens up into a double bed. Cherry and hand-painted country furnishings populate the bedroom.

The sunny Cottage is almost entirely decorated in blue and white. There is a wood-burning fireplace in the living room. The bedroom furniture, including the four-poster queen bed, is white. There is a sofa bed. Antique china and quilts decorate the Cottage, also known as The Honeymoon Cottage.

The Kenilworth is the most luxurious of the three, with a whirlpool tub, two cast-iron gas stoves, and a kitchen with a dishwasher. It has a classic Wedgewood Blue and yellow theme throughout. The romantic bedroom has a king four-poster bed and a forest green stove. There is a private deck with excellent views.

Breakfast at the Inn at Richmond is delightful, with offerings like homemade lemon poppy-seed bread, lime marmalade, and a smoked-salmon frittata with asparagus and Vidalia onions. Whether you spend

the day snowshoeing on the property; llama trekking, hiking, or biking in
the nearby hills; canoeing, trout fishing, or swimming in nearby lakes; or
golfing, it is a lavish treat to return to this pastoral setting.

Facilities: There are three cottages that accommodate 2–4 people.

Bedding: Bedding is provided.

Reservations and rates: Rates for two people range $195–325 per night, and
$850–1,500 per week. Extra guests are $25 per person. Weekly rental of cottages includes midweek housekeeping, but not breakfast. Kids 10 years old
and older are permitted in the cottages all year; younger children are only permitted November–May. Monthly rentals can be arranged. Open year-round.
Pets and smoking are not permitted.

Directions: From Route 7 in Great Barrington, bear left onto Route 41. Follow
Route 41 and drive through West Stockbridge into Richmond. Drive through
Richmond and past Route 295. Continue for one mile on Route 41.

Contact: Jerri and Dan Buehler, **The Inn at Richmond**, 802 State Road (Route
41), Richmond, MA 01254, 413/698-2566, website: www.innatrichmond.com.

7. THE BLUE WILLOW BED AND BREAKFAST

on Housatonic River in Stockbridge

Luxury rating: ★★★★☆   **Recreation rating:** ★★★★★

Blue Willow is a traditional early 19th-century house that has been renovated to accommodate guests. It is a small, elegant bed-and-breakfast with
separate lodging in the carriage house. The inn sits close to Stockbridge
center, and its backyard meets the shore of the Housatonic River.

Just across the river is Beartown State Forest. A footbridge over the river
leads to the Ice Glen, a great place to explore in hot weather. The boulder-
strewn hemlock gorge retains cool air and ice in its crevices and small
caves for much of the summer. You can also walk up the short, steep hill
to Laura's Tower for some nice views of the surrounding mountain ranges.

Monument Mountain is another particularly nice nearby hike. This
quartzite monolith is made of some of the oldest rock in the Berkshires. There is a sad legend of a Housatonic woman who jumped to
her death here when she was kept from marrying a man from another
tribe. This summit is also said to be where Nathaniel Hawthorne first
met Herman Melville.

There is skiing nearby at Butternut Basin and Catamount, and lots of walking, biking, and hiking in Beartown State Forest and October Mountain State Forest (the largest state forest in Massachusetts). Nearby lakes offer swimming and fishing opportunities, and there are canoe rentals in the area. Do not consume fish caught in this section of the Housatonic River. Stockbridge is also convenient for Tanglewood and the Norman Rockwell Museum.

The carriage house has a cozy country feel with exposed beams and antique furnishings, like white-painted iron beds. It has a small refrigerator and microwave, but no real cooking facilities.

Facilities: There is one cottage that accommodates 2–3 people. There are restaurants nearby in Stockbridge.

Bedding: Bedding is provided.

Reservations and rates: Rates range $90–180, including breakfast. Book a couple of months in advance for summer weekends or October foliage. There is a three-night minimum in July and August. Open year-round. Kids, smoking, and pets are not permitted.

Directions: From Stockbridge Center (Red Lion Inn), follow Route 102 (Main Street) east and drive .5 mile. Look for Lincoln Lane on the right. It is a small gravel road. Blue Willow is the last house on the right; gray with a white picket fence.

Contact: The Blue Willow Bed and Breakfast, 2 Lincoln Lane, P.O. Box 843, Stockbridge, MA 01262, 413/298-3018, website: www.bluewillowbb.com.

8. THE RED LION INN
Stockbridge

Luxury rating: ★ ★ ★ ★ ★   **Recreation rating:** ★ ★ ★ ★ ☆

The Red Lion Inn, with its large front porch, is a well-known landmark in the center of Stockbridge. Built in the 1700s, it has been a town tavern, a stagecoach stop, and the site of revolutionary protests, and it was captured for longevity in Norman Rockwell's painting *Stockbridge Main Street at Christmas*.

The inn has a number of buildings associated with it, including two individual units. The Firehouse, which was also pictured in a Rockwell painting, is one of them, and, three miles away, the former studio of Daniel Chester French is the other. French was the sculptor of Abe Lincoln at the Lincoln Memorial and the artist of *The Minute Man* in Concord, Massachusetts.

The Meadowlark was French's summer studio. Red Lion Inn guests can stay there, on the grounds of the Chesterwood Estate, thanks to a deal with the inn and the National Trust for Historic Preservation, the owners of Chesterwood. The estate, with its formal gardens and wide lawns, is very popular for weddings.

Inside the spacious cottage, there are two bedrooms (one upstairs and one down) with queen beds, an extra sofa bed in the living room, a small kitchen, and a dining room. The spacious living room retains an open-studio feel, with French doors opening out onto a large deck that has excellent river and mountain views.

The Firehouse is the fanciest of the Red Lion suites. It has a four-poster king bed, a whirlpool tub for two, and a sitting area upstairs, where the village volunteer fire department once gathered. Downstairs is a living room large enough that it once held fire trucks, a second bathroom, a back porch, and a dining or meeting room with a table that can seat a dozen people.

Stockbridge is centrally located for all of the cultural offerings of the Berkshires, and it is near numerous state parks and forests with fishing, boating, hiking, and swimming opportunities. There is a heated pool on-site, and golf, alpine and cross-country skiing, and more are just a short drive away.

Facilities: There are two cottages associated with the Red Lion Inn, Meadowlark and the Firehouse. They accommodate 2–6 people.

Bedding: Bedding is provided.

Reservations and rates: Rates for the Firehouse range $300–425 per night. It is open year-round. Rates for Meadowlark range $300–385 per night. Extra guests are $20 per night. There is a two-night minimum stay on summer and fall weekends, in December, and on holidays. Open May–October.

Directions: The inn is located on Main Street in Stockbridge at the corner of Routes 7 and 102.

Contact: The Red Lion Inn, 30 Main Street, Stockbridge, MA 01262, 413/298-5545, website: www.redlioninn.com.

Other Cabins and Cottages Nearby

- Devonfield (Queen Wilhelmina Cottage), 85 Stockbridge Road, Lee, MA 01238, 413/243-3298 or 800/664-0880, website: www.devonfield.com.

9. TURNING POINT INN

Great Barrington

Luxury rating: ★ ★ ★ ★ ☆   **Recreation rating:** ★ ★ ★ ★ ★

Rank: Top 10 for Weddings

© COTTAGE AT TURNING POINT INN

Who doesn't want to stay in a chef-owned bed-and-breakfast? Imagine a gourmet breakfast before hiking on the Applachian Trail, savoring the food at a Turning Point wedding, or enjoying a picnic packed by the Inn while at Tanglewood. Or how about a minivacation to view fall foliage or to ski, with a special Saturday night dinner at the inn?

No matter when you book the converted barn cottage behind this 200-year-old Federal-style converted tavern, you'll eat well; breakfast is included with your stay. If you're there on a Saturday, be sure to reserve a space for dinner. In the main inn, you'll get to admire the character and charm of this antique building. Some of the details retained include the pine plank floors, original fireplaces, and a brick oven.

The converted barn cottage has two bedrooms and a large living room. There is a fully equipped kitchen and a heated sun porch with a day bed. It has simple and comfortable furnishings. Guests can also relax by the fireplace in the sitting room of the main inn.

Just three miles from the center of Great Barrington, Turning Point is right next to Butternut Basin Ski Resort. The Appalachian Trail is nearby, as it traverses East Mountain State Forest and Beartown State Forest. There are cross-country skiing areas nearby, and lots of hiking, swimming, fly-fishing, and mountain biking.

The fall foliage is spectacular here. Keep an eye on the website for special packages, and for cooking classes offered at the inn. Of course, everything may taste better in the Berkshires than when you recreate it at home. That's the beauty of the place.

Facilities: There is one cottage with two bedrooms that can accommodate five people comfortably.

Bedding: Bedding is provided.

Reservations and rates: Rates range $229–255 per night. Additional cots are $10, and additional people for breakfast are $10. There are two-night minimum stays on weekends during summer and fall seasons, and a three-night-minimum stay on holidays. Credit cards are not accepted. Courteous smokers are accepted in the cottage. Pets are accepted (no charge).

Directions: From Boston, take the Massachusetts Turnpike (I-90) west to Exit 2 in Lee, MA. From the exit, drive on Route 102 west to Route 7 south to Route 23 east. Turn right on Lake Buel Road; the inn is at the corner of Lake Buel Road and Route 23.

Contact: Turning Point Inn, 3 Lake Buel Road, Great Barrington, MA 01230, 413/528-4777, website: www.turningptinn.com.

10. ANNABELLE LEE'S

Great Barrington

Luxury rating: ★★★☆☆   **Recreation rating:** ★★★★☆

Annabelle Lee's offers several guest rooms in a Victorian house and two cottages a mile from downtown Great Barrington, not far from Simons Rock College of Bard. If you're looking for your own private little house while skiing at Butternut Basin Ski Resort or attending a concert at Tanglewood, this is a convenient location.

Cottage 1 has a hayloft door hidden in the attic that suggests it may have had a previous life as a barn in the early 1900s. Long since renovated, it now offers two bedrooms, a fully equipped kitchen, a living room with a sofa bed, and a deck on the south side. One bedroom has a queen brass bed, and the other is a garret-style room up a flight of stairs from the first bedroom. It has a double bed under the sloping ceiling.

Cottage 2 has one bedroom with a queen bed under a sloping ceiling, and a sofa bed in the living room. The eat-in kitchen is fully equipped and sports wainscoting. Both cottages have cable television, and telephone service can be arranged for long-term stays. The furnishings are simple.

Paths lead a half mile down to Lake Mansfield, where there is a town beach. There is also good swimming in Benedict Pond in Beartown State Forest, along with fishing, mountain biking, and hiking—part of the Appalachian Trail runs through here. There are many places to fish and boat in the area, including Lake Buel, Lake Garfield, and the Konkapot and Green Rivers. The pastoral roads in Great Barrington are very pleasant for road biking.

Facilities: There are two cottages. Cottage 1 can accommodate 3–5 people, and Cottage 2 can accommodate three people.

Bedding: Linens and towels are provided for stays of one week or less.

Reservations and rates: Rates range $340–600 per week and $1,120–2,000 per month. Shorter-term rentals may be available. There is a minimum two-night stay. October through May the cottages are rented monthly for $765–865 per month plus utilities. No smoking is allowed on the premises. Pets may be allowed with permission. Call first.

Directions: From the center of Great Barrington, drive on Route 41 north and bear left on Christian Hill Road.

Contact: Annabelle Lee's, 45 Christian Hill Road, Great Barrington, MA 02130, 413/528-8410, www.annabellelees.com.

11. RACE BROOK LODGE
on Race Brook in Sheffield

Luxury rating: ★ ★ ★ ☆ ☆   **Recreation rating:** ★ ★ ★ ★ ★

Located at the base of the Taconic Mountains, this 1790s timber-peg country barn, along with its various outbuildings, is a wonderfully updated yet charmingly rustic base for exploring the Berkshires.

All of the rooms in the lodge, as well as the cottages with guest suites and the standalone Brook House cottage, are informal and cozy. They have exposed hand-hewn beams, quilts, and tasteful stenciling. There are no telephones or televisions, though there are business facilities on-site.

The Race Brook and Sage Cottages are multiunit buildings with regular lodge-type rooms. The Brook House is a separate bungalow cottage near the brook that is ideal for families, with its queen bed and two twin beds, full kitchen, and front porch.

The path along the brook leads to Race Brook Falls and the summit of Mount Everett, the highest point in this part of the Berkshires. The summit, with its observation tower, is a particularly good location for viewing hawk migration September–early October. From here the path also connects with the Appalachian Trail.

There are two downhill ski resorts in the area—Catamount and Butternut Basin—and plenty of cross-country skiing trails. The impressive waterfall at Bash Bish Falls State Park, and the 500-million-year-old marble and quartzite hills of Bartholomews Cobble, are short drives. You can also canoe the Housatonic and enjoy fly-fishing in nearby rivers.

Race Brook Lodge is also known for its meeting space. There is a very pleasant big barn with 2,000 square feet of open space, plus additional rooms and a kitchen for all kinds of activities. The skylights and beams in the barn really make a lovely atmosphere.

Facilities: There are 20 rooms, and one cottage that accommodates 4–6 people. It has both heating and air-conditioning. The Stagecoach Restaurant on the premises is open for dinner, and there are other restaurants in the area.

Bedding: Linens are provided.

Reservations and rates: Rates range $150–255 per night. Reserve at least two months in advance. There is a two-night minimum stay (three nights on in-season weekends). A homemade continental breakfast is included in the rates. Open year-round. Smoking is not permitted. Small pets are welcome.

Directions: Race Brook Lodge is located just 15 minutes south of Great Barrington, right on Route 41.

Contact: David Rothstein & Allegra Graham, **Race Brook Lodge**, 864 Under Mountain Road, Sheffield, MA 01257, 413/229-2916 or 888/725-6343, website: www.rblodge.com.

12. LAKESIDE ESTATES BED & BREAKFAST

on Otis Reservoir

Luxury rating: ★ ★ ★ ☆ ☆   **Recreation rating:** ★ ★ ★ ★ ★

Sometimes all it takes to make you happy is a really comfortable front porch, and Lakeside Estates has one of the best. Located on eight acres near Tolland State Forest, this is the only bed-and-breakfast right on Otis Reservoir. The bed-and-breakfast itself has several rooms, plus a separate cottage, called the Bunk House, for extra privacy. The simple but cozy Bunk House can be configured to your needs. It has one room that can have either a king bed or two twin beds, and a separate room with a sofa bed. It has a table, chairs, a refrigerator, and a coffeemaker, but no real cooking facilities.

Otis Reservoir covers 1,050 acres and may be the largest recreational body of water in the state. There is a sandy beach and a public boat launch at Lakeside Estates. The Farmington River releases come down out of the Otis Resevoir, and there is Class III to Class IV white water between the Tolland State Bridge and New Boston Route 8 Bridge. In the winter, the B&B has special packages to picnic on the ice and learn about ice fishing.

There are hiking trails from Lakeside Estates to Tolland State Forest. There are a number of trails here, including a 3.3-mile loop. If you're mountain biking, you can even continue south to Granville State Forest to find even more trails. Wear orange during hunting seasons; the forest has hunting for all types of game, including turkey, bear, and deer.

In the winter, cross-country skiing and snowmobiling are popular in the State Forest. There are about 15 miles of off-road vehicle trails and old logging roads by the reservoir. Butternut Basin Ski Resort, in Great Barrington, is a short drive away, and the B&B offers special stay-and-ski packages in the winter.

If that's not enough, there is fishing, a pool table, table tennis, horseshoes, and boccie. If it's too cool for the porch, there is also a screened porch.

Facilities: The B&B has three bedrooms, a two-bedroom suite, and the Bunkhouse, which sleeps 2–6 people.

Bedding: Bedding is provided.

Reservations and rates: Rates for two people range $130–150. Additional guests are $25 each. Book six weeks in advance for popular summer weekends. There is a two-night minimum in the summer, and a three-night minimum on holiday weekends. Open year-round. Credit cards are accepted except for deposits. Pets and smoking are not permitted.

Directions: From the intersection of Routes 8 and 23, in the center of Otis, drive for three miles on Route 23 East. Turn right onto West Shore Road. There will be a sign there for Lakeside Estates Bed & Breakfast (on the right). Drive .7 mile to next sign for Lakeside Estates (on the left). Turn left onto Tolland Road. Drive .8 mile to the next sign for Lakeside Estates (on the left). Turn left onto Kibbe Road. Lakeside Estates is the first and second driveway on the left.

Contact: Lakeside Estates Bed & Breakfast, 99 Kibbe Road, P.O. Box 830, East Otis, MA 01029, 413/269-9900, website: www.lakesideestatesbnb.com.

13. PINE ACRES FAMILY CAMPING AREA

on Lake Dean in Oakham

Luxury rating: ★★☆☆☆   **Recreation rating:** ★★★★★

© BETHANY ERICSON

Pine Acres is a destination campground for many vacationers, but it is also a centrally located spot to stay while skiing at Mount Wachusett, picking apples, strolling through the Brimfield Antiques fairs, or catching a show at the Worcester Centrum. The campground has eight cabins right on the shore of Lake Dean.

Four of these are full-service cabins, which are set on-site and have private docks and gas grills. These cabins have covered porches with Adirondack chairs. The full-service cabins have fully equipped kitchens, tub and shower baths, a bedroom, and a sleeping loft (accessible by a wooden ladder from the kitchen). They also have furnaces, which you'll need if you're spending a winter's weekend skiing or ice fishing.

The other four cabins are considered rustic cabins. These are pleasant, two-room log cabins with covered porches. The rustic cabins do not have water; heated restrooms are nearby. They have mini-refrigerators and a small table. Outside by the lake there is a fireplace and gas grill.

Lake Dean is a popular boating, swimming, bass-fishing, and water-skiing spot. The campground has a marina with a bait shop and small boat rentals. There are a wide variety of planned activities on the calendar at Pine Acres all year. There are themed weekends and many free activities, although some special events require tickets. There are three beaches, a boat launching area and boat slips, a snack bar, a video arcade and recreation hall, a large playground, miniature golf, and tennis courts.

Facilities: There are eight cabins. Four are rustic cabins, and four are luxury cabins. Laundry facilities, ice, and firewood are available on-site.

Bedding: Linens and towels are not provided, but can be rented; reserve in advance.

Reservations and rates: Cabin rates range $65–95 per night and $375–595 per week. Rates are based on two adults and three children or four adults. Cabins are rented Friday–Friday in July and August. There is a two-night minimum stay, and holiday weekends may have three-night minimum-stay requirements. Payment in full is required at time of booking, personal checks are not accepted, and a security deposit may be requested. No pets are permitted in the cabins.

Directions: From Boston, take the Massachusetts Turnpike (I-90) west to Exit 10 (Auburn), then drive on Route 20 west. Turn right onto Route 56 north (drive through Leicester), then turn left onto Route 122 north, and turn left again onto Route 148 south. Watch for campground signs on Route 148.

Contact: Pine Acres Family Camping Area, 203 Bechan Road, Oakham, MA 01068, 508/882-9509, website: www.pineacresresort.com.

14. SEWARD INN

Rockport on Cape Ann

Luxury rating: ★★★☆☆   **Recreation rating:** ★★★★☆

Rockport, once home to the quarries that supplied many of the granite blocks that built Boston, has an imposing rocky shore with some big waves. Out on the granite ledge over Sandy Bay, the Seaward Inn has been hosting guests since the 1940s. Recently, the youngest daughter of founders Anne and Roger Cameron took over the business.

© BETHANY ERICSON

From the Seward Inn you can walk down to the rocky beach and contemplate the waves, birds, and twin lighthouses of Thatcher Island. You can take a stroll into town to the many shops and fish restaurants, or you can ride your bike around Cape Ann. Bikes are available at the inn. Rockport, and neighboring Gloucester, are excellent places to sea kayak, and a trip here is not complete without a whale-watching excursion.

There are just a handful of cottages on the immaculately landscaped lawn of the inn. There are flowering gardens, stone terraces, and a very special hammock under its own roof. Some of the cottages have fireplaces and kitchenettes. They have a beachy, casual atmosphere on the inside, and all of them contain writing tables.

The inn has a glass-walled sun room and a pine-walled dining room. The Sea Garden Restaurant is known in the area for its fine dining. Note that Rockport is a dry town, so BYOB. There are fishing charters in the area, and good surf-casting locations, as well as blueberry bushes through-out the cape, should you want to forage for yourself.

Facilities: There are four cottages on the grounds next to the inn and the carriage house.

Bedding: Bedding is provided.

Reservations and rates: The rates range $169–259 per night, depending on size and season. Rates include daily maid service and breakfast. Pets are not per-mitted.

Directions: From the Boston area, take Route 128 north, and drive toward Glouces-ter. After crossing the Annisquam Bridge, continue straight through two rotaries, following the Rockport signs. Continue driving for about .5 mile to the traffic light and turn left on Route 127. Drive about four miles (you are now in Rockport) to a five-street intersection. Bear right, following the signs to Rockport Center Route 127-A. Follow the road to the end, which is about .25 mile. Turn right (still on 127-A) and drive .5 mile to the Seaward Inn sign (it will be on your left), directing you down Marmion Way to the inn.

Contact: The Cameron Family, **Seward Inn**, Marmion Way, Rockport, MA 01966, 978/546-3471 or 877/473-2927, website: www.seawardinn.com.

Other Cabins and Cottages Nearby

- Rocky Shores Inn and Cottages, Renate and Gunter Kostka, 65 Eden Road, 978/546-2823 or 800/348-4003, website: www.rockportusa.com /RockyShores.

15. PETER'S POND PARK

Lakeside in Sandwich

Luxury rating: ★☆☆☆☆   **Recreation rating:** ★★★★★

Far away from the Cape Cod crowds, this campground is at the center of the landmass that makes up the base of the cape. It is an enormous, man-aged community of 450 campsites behind a security gate. Besides the campsites, there are cabins clustered together on the top of a rise overlook-ing the lake, and a couple of tepees for a fun, alternative accommodation.

The cottages have one or two bedrooms, kitchens, and great views over rocky beaches. There are also sandy beaches on the property. The tepees are large, 17 feet in diameter, and on platforms with no bathrooms or cooking facilities, but with electricity. They are located near public restrooms.

There are endless planned activities here, two recreation buildings, a recreation hall with video machines, rowboats, a five-acre playing field, softball, horseshoes, boccie, badminton, a boat ramp, fishing, and even a 20-acre conservation area.

The enormity of this facility makes for an interesting atmosphere. Rallies are welcome, but there are strict rules. Accommodations are restricted to families that consist of "husband, wife, and unmarried children." There is a neighboring airbase that may add fighter planes to your scenery.

Facilities: There are five cabins with two bedrooms, two efficiency (one-room) cabins and two tepees.

Bedding: Linens are not provided.

Reservations and rates: Two bedroom cottages are $700 per week, efficiency cabins are $350 per week, and tepees are $250 per week. Nightly rates are available in the off-season. Specials are advertised on their website. Open April–Columbus Day.

Directions: From the Boston Area, take Route 93 south to Route 3 and drive to the Sagamore Bridge. Cross the Cape Cod Canal onto Route 6 (the Mid-Cape Highway). Proceed on Route 6 to Exit 2 (Route 130). Turn right. From the bottom of the ramp, drive three miles to Quaker Meeting House Road. Turn left. Drive .8 mile to Cotuit Road. Turn right. Continue .7 mile to Peters Pond Park, which will be on the right.

Contact: Peter's Pond Park, 185 Cotuit Road, P.O. Box 999, Sandwich, MA 02563, 508/477-1775, website: www.campcapecod.com.

16. PINE GROVE COTTAGES

on 6A in East Sandwich

Luxury rating: ★ ★ ☆ ☆ ☆   **Recreation rating:** ★ ★ ★ ★ ☆

© BETHANY ERICSON

These comfortable cabins are up on a hill on busy Route 6A, just 1.5 miles from two town beaches. They are a classic old Cape Cod colony with charming renovated cabins that are between 45 and 70 years old. Although not directly on the beach, they offer a great value.

The cabins are soundly cared for, and they have homey finishing touches like window boxes, paint stenciling, and pretty bedspreads. Some of them are set further off the road than others; be sure to inquire when making a reservation.

The units vary in size and set-up, but they tend to have paneled walls, fully equipped kitchens with apartment-sized ovens, and casual cottage-style furnishings. The entire village of cabins holds 42 people and can be rented out for family reunions.

Families that know Pine Grove tend to return. Its convenient location, octagonal in-ground pool, cleanliness, and low prices are welcome in a land of poorer-quality roadside lodgings. Sandwich is a pleasant town to visit, and there is light walking at the Greenbrier Nature Center and Heritage Plantation, biking on the paved path that hugs the Cape Cod Canal, and easy access to ocean and freshwater beaches and fishing.

> **Facilities::** There are 10 units, five two-bedrooms and five one-bedrooms of varying sizes and styles.
>
> **Bedding:** All linens are included. Bring your own beach towels.
>
> **Reservations and rates:** Rates range $50–135 nightly, and $310–775 weekly. Book early, Pine Grove sees a lot of repeat guests, especially in July and August. Open May 1–November 1. No pets permitted.
>
> **Directions:** From the Boston area, take Route 93 south to Route 3 and drive to the Sagamore Bridge. Cross the Cape Cod Canal onto Route 6 (the Mid-Cape

Highway). Continue driving on Route 6 to Sagamore Bridge and to Exit 3, Quaker Meetinghouse Road. Turn left at the end of the exit ramp and drive one mile on 6A. Turn right on 6A and continue for .25 mile. Pine Grove will be on your right.

Contact: Victor Babiarz, **Pine Grove Cottages**, P.O. Box 74, 358 Route. 6A, East Sandwich, MA 02537, 508/888-8179, website: www.pinegrovecottages.com.

17. BEACH ROSE INN

off Route 28A in West Falmouth

Luxury rating: ★ ★ ☆ ☆ ☆   **Recreation rating:** ★ ★ ★ ★ ☆

The Beach Rose Inn has a little housekeeping cottage with a spacious front yard on its own plot of land. It is set off from the quiet road. In 2002, it underwent some cosmetic surgery. It's a unique and comfortable place to call home while exploring the cape, islands, or Woods Hole, especially if you are traveling with a dog.

© BETHANY ERICSON

The cottage has two bedrooms; one is a narrow room with a bunk bed. There is a fully equipped kitchen, bath with shower, larger sitting area, and very pleasant large deck. The rooms run on the small side, and the ceilings are slightly low. The inn itself is on the National Register of Historic Places, and rooms are rented in the main inn as well as the Carriage House. Breakfasts at the inn are not included with the cottage rental.

This part of the cape is particularly convenient for city dwellers who want to get to the cape without driving very far. The ocean is just a mile away from the Beach Rose, and there are freshwater swimming areas nearby. The entire myriad of cape activities is easily accessible from West Falmouth, from boating to kayaking to fishing to tennis to golf. On a rainy day, take a trip to the National Marine Fisheries Aquarium in Wood's Hole.

Facilities: There is one housekeeping cottage that sleeps five people.
Bedding: Linens provided, including beach towels.

Reservations and rates: The cottage is rented weekly; rates range $750–850. See the website for specials. Open May–November. Well-behaved dogs are welcome with approval and a small fee.

Directions: From the Greater Boston area, take Route 24 to I-495 to Route 25, or take Route 3 and follow the signs at the end of the road to "Falmouth and the Islands," to the Bourne Bridge. From the bridge, drive south on Route 28 until you reach the Thomas Landers Road exit. Turn right at the bottom of the ramp. Turn left on Route 28A. Drive .5 mile to Chase Road, which will be on the right.

Contact: David and Donna McIlrath, Innkeepers, **The Beach Rose Inn Bed and Breakfast**, 17 Chase Road, West Falmouth, MA 02540, 508/540-5706 or 800/498-5706, website: www.sjoholminn.com.

18. SIPPEWISSETT CAMPGROUND AND CABINS
close to Vineyard Ferry in Falmouth

Luxury rating: ★★☆☆☆   **Recreation rating:** ★★★★☆

Sippewissett is the closest campground to the Martha's Vineyard ferries and is a good place to base any number of cape explorations. The information display at the campground is a good place to research your outdoor fun, and the campground is an authorized ticket-seller for many ferries, beaches, and local attractions.

The cabins are clustered in a courtyard setting on a hill and differ greatly in size and setup. Cabins 1, 2, and 6 are the largest units, with two bedrooms, a combination kitchen, and living rooms. Cabin 12 is a one-room studio with a little kitchenette, like many of the others, but it also has a large outside deck. The cabins with kitchens are housekeeping units and have cooking utensils and dishes.

Cabins 13–15 are simple camping cabins. All of the cabins, including the camping cabins, have private baths. The camping cabins do not have showers, but guests can use the nonmetered hot shower facilities of the campground. All of the units have picnic tables and barbecue grills.

Falmouth boasts seven beaches, all on the warm-water side of the cape. It also has two public windsurfing beaches. The rest of the cape, with fishing, boating, biking, golfing, and more, is just a short drive away. On a rainy day, visit the Oceanographic Institute and National Marine Fisheries Aquarium at Wood's Hole.

Facilities: There are 11 cabins in a variety of sizes that can accommodate 2–8 people. There are laundry facilities on the premises.

Bedding: Linens provided in housekeeping units.

Reservations and rates: Rates range $235–650 weekly.

Directions: From the Greater Boston area, take Route 24 to I-495 to Route 25, or take Route 3 and follow the signs at the end of the road to "Falmouth and the Islands," to the Bourne Bridge. From the bridge, drive south on Route 28 to the Route 28A/Sippewissett exit. Turn immediately left at the blinking light. Drive .5 mile and the campground will be on your right.

Contact: Sippewissett Campground & Cabins, 836 Palmer Avenue, Falmouth, MA 02542, 508/548-2542 or 800/957-CAMP, website: www.sippewissett.com.

19. MENEMSHA INN AND COTTAGES

on Menemsha Bite in Martha's Vineyard

Luxury rating: ★ ★ ★ ☆ ☆   **Recreation rating:** ★ ★ ★ ★ ★

Rank: Top 10 for Ocean Beach Activities

This is the part of Martha's Vineyard known to locals as Up-Island, a less crowded area of breathtaking ocean views and a 300-year old fishing wharf that seems to have become quite dear to Anne Rivers Siddon's readers. Things are less hectic here, and spacious. The Menemsha Inn and Cottages is on more than 10 acres of land, with woodland and garden landscaping, a path that leads across the salt marsh to Menemsha beach and the docks, and access to private Lucy Vincent Beach.

The weathered, gray cottages have fireplaces in the living rooms (with complimentary wood), decks, and screened porches facing the sunset. They have fully equipped kitchens, comfortable furnishings, VCRs, outside showers for washing off the sand, and grills.

Martha's Vineyard is the perfect place to ride a bike, as there are paths across the island. The inn can provide you with wheels, or you can bring your own. Menemsha Pond is a good place to launch a kayak, and rentals are available in the area. The island has miles of conservation land for hiking and bird-watching. At the inn there are tennis courts, a fitness center, horseshoes, and table tennis. Golf courses are nearby.

Menemsha is also a hot spot for surf casting. If you want to avoid the summer crowds and try your hand at reeling in a monster, book a cottage at the very end of the season, in October. The beach between Dogfish Bar and the Brickyard is a paradise of stripers, bluefish, and bonito. All year there are guides and charter fishing trips. If you happen to win a daily pin at the Martha's Vineyard Striped Bass & Bluefish Derby in the fall, you can stay that night for free. If you win the Derby, your whole stay is free.

Facilities: There are 10 one-bedroom cottages and one two-bedroom cottage alongside the inn. Daily maid service and breakfast can be provided for an additional fee. Two of the cabins are wheelchair accessible. Markets are in the area, there are special food deliveries from the local market, and the West Tisbury Farmers Market is a short drive away.

Bedding: Bedding is provided.

Reservations and rates: Rates range $1,100–2,625 per week in cottages, or $180–250 per night. August is the busiest month, and many cabins are already reserved the summer before. August usually fills up in January, and reservations for the rest of the season start in earnest in January as well, especially for weekends (they do a lot of weddings), and especially for the one two-bedroom cottage, which sometimes is booked solid the previous year. Cottages are rented weekly in summer, and there is a two-day minimum the rest of the time. A deposit of 50 percent is required for all advance reservations. For reservations of three nights or less, the entire amount is requested. Payment in full is due upon arrival. Open mid-April–October. Smoking is not permitted. Credit cards are not accepted. Pets are accepted off-season in the cottages.

Directions: Turn left with the traffic as you leave the ferry. After one block, turn right at the stop sign. Continue up a slight hill, bearing slightly to the left after one block, and stay on the main road that goes out of town (South Main Street, then becomes State Road). After about 2.5 miles, bear right at the fork. After another 2.5 miles, watch for a right turn toward Menemsha on North Road. Continue driving on North Road for about 5.6 miles, and Menemsha Inn & Cottages will be on your right. Watch for the sign; it's right after the left turn for Menemsha Cross Road.

Contact: Kristin and Jim Travers, **Menemsha Inn and Cottages**, P.O. Box 38B, Menemsha, MA 02552, 508-645-2521, www.menemshainn.com.

20. CAPTAIN GOSNOLD VILLAGE

Residential Hyannis

Luxury rating: ★★★☆☆   **Recreation rating:** ★★★★☆

This gray-shingled, pink-shuttered cottage colony set in a residential neighborhood, resembles an old Cape Cod village. There are a variety of sizes of weathered cottages, set at angles for privacy. Each of the cottages is privately owned and thus individually decorated. Many of them are duplex units. All of them have wall-to-wall

© BETHANY ERICSON

carpeting, are kept clean, and have nice homey touches. The office handles the rentals.

The grounds and gardens at Captain Gosnold are impeccably kept, and there is a pool with a lifeguard. It's very conveniently located near beaches and town without being right in the middle of the hustle and bustle. Three different beaches are within walking distance. The closest is only a quarter of a mile away.

If hustle and bustle is more your speed, you're only a 10-minute walk or short pedal through residential streets to the shops and restaurants on Main Street in Hyannis. Hyannis Harbor is always buzzing with boats coming and going. Here you can pick up fishing charters or hop on an island ferry to Nantucket or Martha's Vineyard with your bike.

The cottages all have fully equipped kitchens, including lobster pots. Another nice touch is that each bedroom has its own bathroom. And daily maid service gives a nice touch of luxury. On the grounds are a playground, basketball hoop and shuffleboard court. There are public tennis courts in the area and nearby golf.

Facilities: There are one-, two-, and three-bedroom cottages with daily maid service. Only the three-bedroom cottages are standalone units.
Bedding: Linens provided; bring your own beach towels.

21. BREAKWATERS

on Nantucket Sound in Hyannis

Luxury rating: ★★★☆☆   **Recreation rating:** ★★★★☆

This well-kept little village of gray-shingled cottages is at the end of a quiet street that dead-ends at the sand of Nantucket Sound. You can sit and enjoy the boats passing in the harbor, or swim in the heated pool.

© BETHANY ERICSON

Many of these cottages contain multiple units, but there are some standalone lodgings. Some are larger units and are closer to the beach; these are popular with families, as they have more room around them and are farther off the road.

The sunny interiors of the cottages are comfortable and houselike. The antique and country furnishings and white-painted panels with wallpaper give it a colonial feeling. All of the units are heated, and cozy quilts await you on the beds.

This is a convenient location for lounging and swimming at the Sea Street Beach, with its 70°F waters, and for visiting Hyannis Center and other local attractions by bike or foot. In Hyannis, you can rent a boat, catch the island ferries to Nantucket or Martha's Vineyard with your bike, or arrange for charter fishing trips.

Facilities: There are one-, two-, and three-bedroom units, mostly in duplex form. All have daily maid service.

Bedding: All linens provided.

Reservations and rates: The rates range $1,000–2,000 per week during the high season. Weekly rentals are Saturday–Saturday. Open May–mid-September. No credit cards accepted. No pets permitted.

Directions: From the Boston area, take Route 93 south to Route 3 to the Sagamore Bridge. Drive across the Cape Cod Canal onto Route 6 (the Mid-Cape Highway). Continue along Route 6 east to Route 132 (Hyannis Exit). Turn right on Route 132 and right again at the Cape Codder Hotel, onto Bearse's Way. Continue driving until you reach Main Street and turn right. At the first light, Sea Street, turn left, and follow the road for one mile.

Contact: The Breakwaters, Sea Street Beach, P.O. Box 118 Hyannis, MA 02601, 508/775-6831, website: www.capecodtravel.com/breakwaters.

22. TOM THUMB COTTAGE

on Grand Cove in West Dennis

Luxury rating: ★ ★ ☆ ☆ ☆   **Recreation rating:** ★ ★ ★ ★ ☆

Tom Thumb is one of four cottages at the end of the road. As its name indicates, it is a wee cottage. One of the big draws to this area is watching the incredible sunsets reflect off the molten-copper waves from the cottage's west-facing location on Grand Cove, across the Bass River.

© BETHANY ERICSON

Enjoy dinner outside on the bistro setting patio; the yard is separated from the water by only a white picket fence. After the post-dinner sunset show, you can retire indoors to light a fire in your living room, where the pine paneled interior glows in honey hues.

The cottage is cozy but at last visit was badly in need of an exterior paint job. It's a nice, private getaway, however, where you can bring a bike and ride to the Cape Cod Rail Trail in South Dennis, or swim in the 70°F waters at the one-mile-long West Dennis Beach. Boating and kayaking are also available in the area.

The cottage is set up best for a small family or for two couples. It has one bathroom. The walls are all knotty pine, and the kitchen has a paneled breakfast nook–style dining area that looks at the water.

Facilities: There is one cottage that accommodates up to four people.

Bedding: Linens provided; towels available for a fee.

Reservations and rates: The cottage is rented weekly for $500, except in July and August, when the rate is $950. Open May–October. No credit cards are accepted.

Directions: From the Boston area, take Route 93 south, to Route 3, to the Sagamore Bridge. Drive across the Cape Cod Canal onto Route 6 (the Mid-Cape Highway). Proceed along Route 6 east to Exit 9-A; this will take you to Route 134. Drive for approximately two miles along Route 134 to the intersection of Route 28. Turn right onto Route 28, drive about .4 mile, and turn right onto Old Main Street. Drive just a short distance to 20 Old Main Street, and the driveway will be on your left. Tom Thumb cottage will be directly ahead.

Contact: The Tom Thumb Cottage, 20 Old Main Street, West Dennis, MA 02670, 508/398-5400 or 617/484-1769, website: www.capecodtravel.com/tomthumb.

23. DENNIS SEASHORES

on Nantucket Sound in Dennisport

Luxury rating: ★★★☆☆   **Recreation rating:** ★★★★☆

Rank: Top 10 for Ocean Beach Activities

Dennis Seashores is an older cottage colony with a private beach. It once had an owner but was later sold as individual units. Today, a business manager in the windmill-shaped office handles the rentals of all of the cottages, whether you choose one of the seven well-spaced cabins directly on the water or a private escape

© BETHANY ERICSON

tucked away in the woods just across from the beach.

The sandy beach brings a sense of community to the area and ties together the wide range of lodgings. The atmosphere is social and appealing, with a strong spirit of camaraderie. Friendships develop here and the people schedule their return visits to coincide.

All but one of the cottages has a fireplace and cable television in the living room. They are nicely furnished in a simple country style and decorated with a lot of natural wood. There are wonderful wide-board pine floors and braided rugs. They have two, three, or four bedrooms, one or two baths, fully equipped kitchens and dining areas. The cottages all have picnic tables and chairs and charcoal grills.

The primary focus here is the beach, used for swimming and boating. The beaches on Cape Cod Bay are just nine miles away. There are a number of nearby golf courses, tennis courts, biking paths, ferries to the islands, and fishing charters.

Facilities: There are 33 two-, three- and four-bedroom cottages. Laundry facilities are nearby in Dennisport.

Bedding: All linens are provided.

Reservations and rates: Rates range with the season and size of the cottage $465–3,995 per week. Cottages are rented weekly June–mid-September; there is a three-night minimum at other times. Open May 1–October 31. No pets are permitted.

Directions: From the Boston area, take Route 93 South, to Route 3, to the Sagamore Bridge. Drive across the Cape Cod Canal onto Route 6 (the Mid-Cape Highway). Drive on Route 6 east to Exit 9-A (Route 134). Turn right on Route 134 south. Drive through four traffic lights to the end of the road. Turn left on Lower County Road to the four-way blinker light. The Wee Packet Restaurant is on the right. Turn right on Depot Street and go to the very end. The road will bear to your left, which is Chase Avenue. Look for the windmill office on the left.

Contact: Dennis Seashores, Chase Avenue, P.O. Box 98, Dennisport, MA 02639, 508/398-8512, website: www.dennisseashores.com.

24. LINGER LONGER BY THE SEA

near the beach in Brewster

Luxury rating: ★ ★ ★ ☆ ☆   **Recreation rating:** ★ ★ ★ ★ ★

Linger Longer is a campus of small, gray-shingled cape cottages and Garrison colonials scattered among the trees and grass. These casual beach rentals are located where the road ends at the beach and are a calming and private alternative to the cookie-cutter, highway-side cabins that dominate the area.

The various-sized housekeeping units are all set up and decorated differently, and are spaced nicely. Some are steps from the sand, while others require a five-minute walk to the beach. They are somewhat casual in a clean and functional way, but are also enjoyable and quiet. All of the cottages have cable television, laundry facilities, decks, patios, picnic tables, and grills. Some have heat.

© BETHANY ERICSON

The sandy beach here is pristine. It is a calm bay beach, good for beach-combing at low tide, and beach games at high tide. There are only 10 rental units and a lodge with apartment rentals here, so the area never feels overrun. And all of the units are well situated for the beach. The whole area is well groomed and relaxing.

Nearby you have the rest of the cape's ocean and freshwater beaches, as well as hiking at Nickerson State Park. Boating and bird-watching are possible, and kayak and canoe rentals are available. The nearby Cape Cod Rail Trail is great for biking, and whale-watching and fishing trips can be arranged. The Natural History Museum and Cape Cod National Seashore Visitor's Museum are also nearby.

Facilities: There are 10 housekeeping cottages. Three of the cottages are a five-minute walk to the beach, while the other seven are next to it. The cottages accommodate 3–8 people.

Bedding: Linens are provided.

Reservations and rates: Rates for the cottages vary with the season and location of the cottage and range $830–1,850 per week. Call early for reservations. The cottages are rented weekly in high season, while shorter stays are possible in the low season. Open mid-April–December 1.

Directions: From Boston, take Route 93 south, or Route 128 south, to Route 3 (Cape Cod). Drive along Route 3 south to the Sagamore Bridge. Driving over the bridge automatically puts you on Cape Cod (Route 6). Follow Route 6 to Exit 12, the Route 6A Brewster/Orleans exit. Turn left at the end of the ramp onto Route 6A and drive for approximately 2.25 miles. Turn right onto Linnell Landing Road. Landmarks to watch for are Nickerson State Park on your left and Crosby Lane on your right, which is the road just before Linnell. Cobies, a hot dog/ice cream stand, is opposite Linnell Landing Road. The Linger Longer office is at the end of Linnell Landing Road on the left.

Contact: Linger Longer by the Sea, 261 Linnell Landing Road, Brewster, MA 02631, 508/240-221 or 508/896-3451, website: www.capecodtravel.com/lingerlonger.

25. PINE HILLS COTTAGES

Brewster

Luxury rating: ★★☆☆☆   **Recreation rating:** ★★★★☆

Pine Hills Cottages are a 1940s cabin colony that has been well preserved in its original form. The identical gray-and-maroon painted cabins offer single rooms with small kitchens and baths, one double bed, a twin bed, a cot, a small table, and a dresser. The furnishings and linens are simple, and you'll find vintage paint colors, floral table coverings, and classic breadboxes.

© BETHANY ERICSON

Rosalie and Nick Wherity took over the business from Nick's parents and are the third owners. They like to tell guests what you won't find at Pine Hills: televisions, telephones, and air-conditioning. You won't find it a good place for indoor privacy for groups of more than two people either: There is only a curtain that can be pulled between the double bed and the twin bed.

This is a traditional Cape Cod cabin experience, and unlike most current cabin colonies, this one remains an inexpensive place to stage your cape explorations. This is a place for small families or couples comfortable with staying in lodgings a step above camping. It's a good launching spot rather than a destination, and it sees a high percentage of repeat guests.

From here you can take a short walk to swim in the bay, hike in Nickerson State Park, rent kayaks or canoes, bike to the Cape Cod Rail Trail, golf, or fish. The Natural History Museum is directly across the street.

Facilities: There are four cottages accommodating up to four people.

Bedding: Linens are provided. Bring your own towels.

Reservations and rates: Cottage rates range $300–400 per week, and are $70 per night for an overnight stay. Call early. People often book a year ahead. Open June 15–September 15. No credit cards accepted. Well-behaved dogs are allowed.

26. THE COTTAGES AT THE BOAT BASIN
on the wharves of Nantucket Harbor

Luxury rating: ★★★★★   **Recreation rating:** ★★★★★

Rank: Top 10 for Boating, Top 10 Most Unusual

The Cottages at the Boat Basin (formerly the Wharf Cottages) are three sets of fun cottage locations under common management: Old South Wharf, Swain's Wharf, and Harborview. The two wharf locations are directly on the water, and the Harborview cottages are up the street on land. The cottages out on the wooden docks are right in the middle of the boat action, but are also private, casually elegant lodgings.

The Boat Basin (same ownership) rents the boat slips in front of the cottages—you can cruise right up to your door. You can also launch canoes and kayaks from here and fish from the docks. Nantucket is a perfect island for exploring its many beaches by bike.

The Cottages at the Boat Basin are newly renovated, with studio to three-bedroom configurations. The interiors are decorated in nautical colors, and have sisal rugs on pine floors. They have modern, eat-in kitchens. The beds are often under sloping ceilings or by dormer windows, and the bathrooms have slate floors. Some cottages have private balconies or terraces. Be sure to specify if you want a direct waterfront location.

Celebrities are rumored to rent these cottages for long periods of time, so be sure to get your reservation in quickly. The pier is loud with boat activity, but it's very festive to be here, jutting out into the middle of the action. All cottages have telephone and cable television.

Facilities: There are 33 cottages, ranging from studios to three-bedroom cottages. Many of them are wheelchair-accessible. If you are traveling with a pet, inquire about *The Woof Cottages,* which are specially designated one- and two-bedroom cottages that have special amenities for dogs and cats—even litter boxes. For boat slip rental, call the Boat Basin, 508/325-1350.

Other Cabins and Cottages Nearby

• The Wauwinet, P.O. Box 2580 Wauwinet Road, Nantucket, MA 02554, 508/228-0145 or 800/426-8718, website: www.wauwinet.com.

• Harbor Cottages, 71 Washington Street, Nantucket, MA 02554, 508/228-4485, website: www.nisda.org/cottage.html.

27. THE SUMMER HOUSE INNS & COTTAGES

Siasconset in Nantucket

Luxury rating: ★ ★ ★ ★ ★   **Recreation rating:** ★ ★ ★ ★ ★

Rank: Top 10 for Romance, Top 10 for Biking, Top 10 for Ocean Beach Activities, and Top 10 Most Luxurious

Nantucket's well-photographed, rose-covered cottages are found here in 'Sconset, and you can rent one of your own. There is nothing cozier than entering a tiny, weathered, seaside cottage and smelling the honeysuckle and roses. Though small, these are upscale romantic hideaways, where you can find antique furnishings, marble whirlpool tubs, skylights, and fireplaces. Some have kitchens, but continental breakfast is included and can be delivered to your door in the morning. The inn also has dining facilities.

The only things in 'Sconset are a few restaurants, a market, a liquor store, a post office, and a chapel. The old "Casino" was never a place for betting, but in the summer it's a good place to see movies. This area was founded as a place for fishermen, and later their wives, to live. In the late 1800s, when the railroad extended to the ferry, actors from New York formed a colony here that still thrives. The Cagney Cottage is named after the actor who stayed here in the 1930s, and the cottages are popular during the Nantucket Film Festival. This is a place of privacy, where the pounding Atlantic can mesmerize you. The cottages have a lovely flower garden, and each have Adirondack chairs for you to contemplate the day ahead over a cup of coffee.

Here, on the eastern side of the island, there is nothing between you and Portugal, and the surf-shows make that clear. 'Sconset beach has lifeguards and a playground. To the north, the Sankaty Lighthouse guides your night walks on the beach. At the inn is an idyllic beachside pool with umbrellas, and a dining tent is by the dunes.

Nantucket is a beautiful place to pedal. There is a bike path between the main village and 'Sconset that runs about seven miles. Although not the most scenic of the paths on the island, it's a good way to get to and fro, and it connects to some of the other lovely paths that traverse the island, like the Polpis Road path, with its hundreds of springtime daffodils.

Facilities: There are seven one-bedroom cottage rooms and suites, and three two-bedroom cottages. The two-bedroom units are the free-standing cottages. The two-bedroom cottage facing the ocean's bluff is the one named after Jimmy Cagney. Four cottages have galley kitchens. Penrose Cottage has a working fireplace. Continental breakfast is included. Lunch and dinner are served daily on-site in July and August.

Bedding: Bedding is provided.

Reservations and rates: Book by early spring, even earlier for a two-bedroom. There are occasionally last-minute openings. Nightly rates range $575–650 for a one-bedroom, $700–900 for a two-bedroom, and about half price in the shoulder seasons. Minimum stays are required at certain times. Children are welcome, and smoking is permitted.

Directions: Drive 7.5 miles east of Nantucket (the town) to the village of Siasconset

Contact: The Summer House Inns & Cottages, P.O. Box 880, Siasconset, MA 02564, 508/257-4577, website: www.thesummerhouse.com/sconset.html.

Other Cabins and Cottages Nearby

- Wade Cottages, Shell St, Siasconset, MA 02564, summer 508/257-6308, winter 212/989-6423, website: www.wadecottages.com.

28. CHATHAM BARS INN

Chatham

Luxury rating: ★ ★ ★ ★ ★   **Recreation rating:** ★ ★ ★ ★ ★

Rank: Top 10 for Ocean Beach Activities, Top 10 Most Luxurious

---

© BETHANY ERICSON

Chatham Bars Inn is an old-school Cape Cod resort. This is a place to pack your khakis and tennis racket, not your sleeping bag. Chatham is the definition of a quaint Cape Cod village, and the inn is located about a 10-minute walk from downtown. The inn's multitude of rooms is in the sprawling main building and throughout numerous cottages. Most of these cottages house several inn rooms, but there are two standalone accommodations: the Bayview and the Holly Cottage.

The Bayview is situated beside the main inn building, while Holly Cottage is in the far corner of the property, by the golf course. The Bayview is one of the inn's "master suites," with fabulous furnishings, a wet bar, and fireplace. The Holly Cottage has a more secluded location and also is beautifully decorated, with hand-painted furniture and nice views.

The impressive, yet warm, main inn building was opened in 1914. It is set on a hill, and the grounds and gardens are immaculate. Summer brings staircases flanked with flowers and endless beach time. Christmas at Chatham Bars brings copious decoration. They are known for delivering on their reputation of fantastic service. Within the inn are a tavern, a main dining room, and a beachside restaurant, all open to the public. There are often special author programs, celebrity chefs, bands, and dancing.

The beach is the main center of activity. It's a beautiful wide, sandy beach dotted with striped cabanas. There's also a pool on the beach for when you want the atmosphere without the salt. Beside the beach are tennis courts and a golf course (the latter doesn't belong to the inn). Activity programs are designed for all age groups and include kayak tours, nature programs, crafts, and even a Children's Etiquette Program.

For some easy hiking along the water, take a boat shuttle across to the barrier beach or visit the Monomoy Wildlife Sanctuary, an important bird area in Massachusetts. At certain times of year, this is a fabulous area to kayak and see gray seals. The Cape Cod Rail Trail, a relaxing place to ride a bike, travels through Chatham.

Facilities: There are over 100 luxury rooms in 25 cottages, with two (Bayview and Holly) single-unit cottages. Meals are served in the inn. Pets are not permitted.

Bedding: All linens provided. Laundry is available for a fee.

Reservations and rates: The Superior Cottage Suites (Holly) range in price $360–670 a day, while the Master Cottage Suites (Bayview) range $740–1,600 a night, depending on the season. June 13 to September 13 is the very popular summer season. Open year-round.

Directions: From the Boston area, take Route 93 south to Route 3 and cross the Sagamore Bridge. Drive across the Cape Cod Canal onto Route 6 (the Mid-Cape Highway). Drive on Route 6 east to Exit 11 marked for Route 137 Chatham. Turn left onto Route 137 and drive south for three miles to the Route 28 intersection. Turn left onto Route 28 and proceed to the small rotary (three miles). Continue driving through the rotary onto Main Street, Chatham, passing the Chatham Hardware Store on the left. Take the next left onto Seaview Street. The entrance to Chatham Bars Inn is just beyond the golf course on the right. Enter at the "Lobby Level Entrance" sign on the right.

Contact: Chatham Bars Inn, Shore Road, Chatham, MA 02633, 508/945-0096 or 800/527-4884, website: www.chathambarsinn.com.

29. PILGRIM'S VILLAGE

along White Pond in Chatham

Luxury rating: ★★★☆☆   **Recreation rating:** ★★★★☆

Pilgrim's Village has a main house on busy Route 28, but then, tucked away down a long driveway and a hill, you will find a quaint colony of well-hidden cottages in a wooded, hilly lot on White Pond. The centerpiece of the cottages is a large perfect lawn.

This well-kept colony started in the late 1930s. Owner Peter Swenson's family vacationed there before the family bought it in 1944. At that time, Peter says, you could rent a two-bedroom cottage without a bath or kitchen for $7 a week. Peter and his wife bought Pilgrim Village from his uncle in the 1970s and have put in new cottages (with bathrooms) since. The business has grown, as neighboring rental-property owners have left the area

© BETHANY ERICSON

and sold their properties to Peter. His son owns the Eider Duck colony up the street.

At Pilgrim Village, they say that if you've got kids and you lay eyes on the place, they've won you over. It's the kind of place where impromptu games spring up on the lawn, and parents and kids fish and swim together in the lake. Rowboats and a swimming dock are provided. Families tend to meet and form friendships, and their kids instantly form teams. For saltwater swimming, Harding Beach is just 1.5 miles away.

The shingled cottages have knotty-pine paneled interiors and screened porches. They all have combined living and dining rooms, with televisions, bathrooms with shower stalls, and fully equipped kitchens. A short walk up the street will find you a seafood market, a deli, and other stores.

Facilities: There are 31 one- and two-bedroom cottages and one three-bedroom house. They can accommodate 2–4 people in each. The cottages are not heated. There are laundry facilities and food stores within walking distance. Small sailboats are permitted.

Bedding: No linens are provided.

Reservations and rates: Cottage rates range $400–800 per week. The rate for the small house ranges $850–1,250 in season. Call in January for the few openings not already taken by repeat guests. There is a 10 percent discount for stays of two weeks or longer. Open June–mid-September. No credit cards accepted. Pets are not permitted.

Directions: From Boston, take Route 93 south, or Route 128 south, to Route 3 (Cape Cod). Drive on Route 3 south to the Sagamore Bridge. Driving across the bridge automatically puts you on Cape Cod on Route 6. Continue driving for 31 miles on Route 6 to Exit 11, Chatham (Route 137). Turn left onto Route 137 and proceed three miles to Route 28, passing through two intersections. Turn left on Route 28 toward Chatham. Continue two miles and you should find Pilgrim Village on your left.

Contact: Peter and Judy Swenson, **Pilgrim's Village**, 1370 Main Street, Chatham, MA 02633, 508/945-0041, website: www.pilgrimvillage.com.

Other Cabins and Cottages Nearby

• Eider Duck Cottages, 1470 Main Street, Chatham, MA 02633, 508/945-1976.

30. MORGAN'S WAY BED & BREAKFAST

between Orleans and Chatham

Luxury rating: ★ ★ ★ ★ ☆   **Recreation rating:** ★ ★ ★ ☆ ☆

Morgan's Way is an upscale, but not stuffy, bed-and-breakfast with breathtaking gardens. The contemporary main building is hidden away off the beaten track on one of the cape's rare hills, amidst impeccable landscaping and woodlands. The poolside cottage is a romantic getaway about 20 feet from the main house, connected to it by a wooden deck.

© BETHANY ERICSON

This is a frequent honeymoon cabin. Couples tend to stay in the cottage, as it is a one bedroom; kids under 12 are not permitted, but non-walking infants are allowed (there is a steep staircase). Though next to the pool, it feels secluded and has its own private deck. It has both heating and air-conditioning.

Cottage dwellers do not participate in breakfast at the main guest house. Instead, there is a fully equipped kitchen with a dishwasher. The living/dining room has a cathedral ceiling and glass walls, with panoramic views of the wooded grounds and the pool area. It also has a television and telephone. The 2nd-floor loft has a queen bed.

There is a 20- by 40-foot heated swimming pool. The pool is situated in the sun and is bordered by more gorgeous gardening. After a very short drive, you'll find yourself exploring the dunes of the Cape Cod National Seashore, hiking at Nickerson State Park, playing in the waves at Nauset Beach, or biking the Cape Cod Rail Trail. Golfing is possible, or you can go swimming or fishing in local ponds. Consider chartering a boat out of Provincetown for sailing, fishing, or whale-watching.

Facilities: There is one poolside cottage.
Bedding: All linens are provided.

Reservations and rates: The cottage rates range $700–1,100. Open year-round. No credit cards accepted.

Directions: From Boston, take Route 93 south, or Route 128 south, to Route 3 (Cape Cod). Drive on Route 3 south to the Sagamore Bridge. Crossing the bridge automatically puts you on Cape Cod (Route 6). Drive approximately 35 miles on Route 6 to Exit 12. Turn right at the end of the exit ramp onto Route 6A and drive to the traffic light. Turn right onto Eldredge Parkway. Drive to the first traffic light and turn right onto Route 28. Drive one mile; watch on the left for Morgan's Way. Turn left at Morgan's Way and drive about 400 feet to Morgan's Way Bed & Breakfast, which is the large complex on the right.

Contact: Page McMahan and Will Joy, **Morgan's Way Bed & Breakfast**, 9 Morgan's Way, Orleans, MA 02653, 508/255-0831, website: www.capecodaccess.com/morgansway.

31. NAUSET BEACH-SIDE

Nauset Beach

Luxury rating: ★ ★ ☆ ☆ ☆   **Recreation rating:** ★ ★ ★ ★ ★

Rank: Top 10 for Ocean Beach Activities

The traditional cape cottages of Nauset Beach-side are located on a bluff above the parking area on a mellow street, looking out across the bay over grand Nauset Beach. There's the 1970s-style motel near the driveway, and then duplexes and cottages to the side and behind the motel on seven acres of grass, pine trees, and woods.

The cottages are basic, pine-paneled, heated two-bedroom units with kitchens, bathrooms with tubs and showers, cable televisions, fireplaces, and outdoor showers. But don't plan on spending your time in the cottage. This place is one minute from one of the best beaches on the Atlantic Coast.

Nauset Beach is a wide, relatively uncrowded, gorgeous sandy beach with good sunrise, surf (for the East Coast), and swimming. There are lifeguards during the summer, and it's a popular place to ride the waves. This is also a popular place to surf cast for striped bass and bluefish.

Nearby at Rock Harbor you can go deep-sea fishing. If you're a birder, come in the fall and you'll have the beach nearly to yourself

Here in Orleans you are minutes from the Cape Cod Rail Trail, a 25-mile bicycling trail. There are many sheltered areas in Pleasant Bay for canoeing. Monomoy Island is a National Wildlife Refuge and an excellent bird-watching location.

Facilities: There are four two-bedroom cottages.

Bedding: No linens or table silverware provided.

Reservations and rates: Rates range $800–1,140 per week. Weeks run Saturday–Saturday. There is a two-week minimum rental in the high season. Open April–October.

Directions: From Boston, take Route 93 south, or Route 128 south, to Route 3 (Cape Cod). Drive on Route 3 south to the Sagamore Bridge. Crossing the bridge automatically puts you on Cape Cod (Route 6). Continue driving on Route 6 to Exit 12, turn right at the traffic lights, and follow the signs to Nauset Beach

Contact: Nauset Beach-Side, P.O. Box 121, East Orleans, MA 02643, 508/255-3348, website: www.capecodtravel.com/nausetbeachside.

32. COTTAGE GROVE

on Route 6 in Eastham

Luxury rating: ★★★☆☆   **Recreation rating:** ★★★★☆

If you'd rather escape the strong sun and bustling families at the end of a day at the cape, Cottage Grove offers a wooded setting a couple of miles from the beach. Separated from busy Route 6 by a fence and a parking lot, the property feels somewhat private. The cabin closest to the road has a common eating area, and all the cabins have air-conditioning, which cuts down on traffic noise.

The colony is made up of small, shingled cottages ringing a small yard. They're on three acres of land and back up to pine and oak tress. They have knotty-pine walls, with mission-style furnishings, high-end mattresses, and wool rugs. They are comfortable and stylish and are best suited for couples. They offer telephones with voicemail, cable television, and VCRs. Chris Nagle and Greg Wolfe took over the business in the early 2000s and have updated it considerably.

One of the changes they made to Cottage Grove is that now it is run

like a bed-and-breakfast and has more of a focus on retreats. Chris's mother and sister also contribute to the business and can often be found leading kayaking outings or women's retreats. Wine retreats and other programs are typically scheduled.

The cottages are in Eastham, and the ocean beaches, fresh-water ponds, Cape Cod National Seashore, bike path, and more are all within a very short drive. Eastham doesn't have much of a town center, but most amenities and equipment rentals can be found just five minutes away in Orleans.

Facilities: There are eight cabins, accommodating 2–5 people in studio, one-, and two-bedroom cottages. Children over 12 years old are welcome. All units but one have kitchenettes, and continental breakfast is provided.

Bedding: All linens are provided.

Reservations and rates: June 15–September 15 is the high season. Prices range $85–260 per night, and $650–1,700 per week. Open mid-May–late October. Pets are allowed in four of the cabins.

Directions: From the Boston area, pick up Route 93 south, then take Route 3 to the Sagamore Bridge. Cross the Cape Cod Canal onto Route 6 (the Mid-Cape Highway). Proceed on Route 6 until you reach the Orleans Rotary. The cottages are 1.5 miles beyond Orleans Rotary, on Route 6, on the left.

Contact: Chris Nagle and Greg Wolfe, **Cottage Grove**, 1975 Route 6, Box 821, Eastham, MA 02642, 508/255-0500 or 877/521-5522, website: www.grovecape.com.

33. WHALEWALK INN

Eastham

Luxury rating: ★ ★ ★ ★ ★   **Recreation rating:** ★ ★ ★ ★ ☆

Rank: Top 10 Most Luxurious

The Whalewalk is a luxury inn that has been created out of what was originally a whaling captain's house in an unexpectedly rural location in Eastham. If you are looking for privacy in an upscale setting while exploring the waters and sands of the cape, the Salt Box Cottage, set behind the inn, may be for you.

Originally home to a cow and a horse, the little white cottage has come a long way. These days, it is appointed similarly to the inn. It has a white, queen-size, cottage-style bed with a wood-burning fireplace and a full bathtub and shower.

© BETHANY ERICSON

A small kitchenette is provided. There is also a television, VCR, and a telephone. Visitors coming in May to enjoy less-crowded walks on the beach will find the cottage surrounded by blooming lilacs.

The inn's common areas and dining rooms are richly decorated with 19th-century country antiques from Europe and Waterford crystal. The back patio has white wrought-iron tables on a stone patio. Other guests staying at the inn are divided among rooms in the main building, the renovated barn, and the carriage house.

Wake up with your sweetheart in your private cottage, then stroll over to the patio to enjoy a breakfast of pecan waffles, or pancakes with blueberries and Cape Cod cranberries. Then take one of the inn's bicycles to Marconi Beach or to the Cape Cod Rail Trail, or take a leisurely walk to the shore.

Facilities: There is one standalone single unit cottage that accommodates two people. Breakfast is provided.

Bedding: Linens are provided.

Reservations and rates: The Salt Box cottage rates range $200–225. There is a two-night minimum on weekends. Call early. Open year-round. Pets are not permitted.

Directions: From Boston, take Route 93 south, or Route 128 south, to Route 3 (Cape Cod). Drive on Route 3 south to the Sagamore Bridge. Driving across the bridge automatically puts you on Cape Cod (on Route 6). Continue driving on Route 6 and go past all 12 exits. You will come to the Orleans Rotary, approximately one mile after you pass Exit 12. Take the third exit off the rotary, which will be Rock Harbor Road. Turn left as you come off the exit (Rock Harbor Road). Drive approximately .25 mile to Bridge Road on your right. The drive approximately .25 mile down Bridge Road and you will see the Whalewalk Inn sign on your right.

Contact: Whalewalk Inn, 220 Bridge Road, Eastham, MA 02642, 508/255-0617 or 800/440-1281, website: www.whalewalkinn.com.

34. CRANBERRY COTTAGES

Eastham

Luxury rating: ★ ★ ☆ ☆ ☆   **Recreation rating:** ★ ★ ★ ★ ☆

The same family has run these traditional, roadside, gray-shingled cottages for about 40 years. They are a clean and convenient place to sleep after a sandy day of swimming, sunbathing, surfboarding, or surf casting at nearby Nauset Light Beach.

The cottages are on busy Route 6, but they are set back from the road. There are woods around the cottages, but few trees within the colony. The single-room cabins include microwaves, coffeemakers, and mini-refrigerators, while the two-bedroom cottages have fully equipped kitchen areas. All have air-conditioning, heating, and cable television.

While not directly on the beach, Cranberry Cottages is in a particularly central location for exploring Nauset Light Beach, Coast Guard Beach, and the National Seashore. Boats can be rented a short distance away in Town Cove, where you can also fish for flounder. Whale-watching trips, golf, tennis, and bicycling are popular activities. Birders will want to be sure to enjoy the Audubon Sanctuary. The entrance to the Cape Cod National Seashore Visitors' Center and Museum is close by.

Cranberry Cottages also rents two little two-bedroom houses. One, called Sleepy Hollow, is a five-minute walk to a private-association beach. It is rented weekly June–September, and for a three-night minimum other months. It has a fireplace, a large deck with a grill, and both indoor and outdoor showers.

Atlantic View at Nauset Light is a ranch cottage overlooking the beach, with two decks, a fireplace, and more. Nauset Lighthouse is across the street.

Facilities: The Cranberry Cottage and colony cottages accommodate up to four people. Sleepy Hollow and Atlantic View both hold five people comfortably. Children are welcome. The colony two-bedroom units have kitchens, the one-bedroom units have kitchenettes, and the one-room nonhousekeeping units have mini-refrigerators, microwaves, and coffeemakers. Both small houses are fully equipped. No food is served. There are no telephones in the cottages, but both small houses do have telephones.

Bedding: Linens provided. Bring your own beach towels.

Reservations and rates: Housekeeping cottages range $395–750 weekly. Non-housekeeping cottages (maid service included) are rented daily for $50–100 per night for two people. Sleepy Hollow is rented weekly June–November, and Atlantic View is rented for $850–2,000 per week, year-round. Call in January to reserve your summer cottage. The main colony is open April–November for nonhousekeeping units, and year-round for housekeeping units. No pets are allowed.

Directions: From the Boston area, pick up Route 93 south and drive to Route 3, to the Sagamore Bridge. Drive across the Cape Cod Canal onto Route 6 (the Mid-Cape Highway) and proceed to the Orleans Rotary—do not go off on 6A. Cranberry Cottages are one mile beyond the Orleans Rotary, on Route 6. There is a sign on the left.

Contact: Guy and Lisa Grant, **Cranberry Cottages**, 785 State Highway, Eastham, MA 02642, 508/255-0602 or 800/292-6631, website: www.sunsol.com/cranberrycottages.

35. GIBSON COTTAGES

Pondside in Eastham

Luxury rating: ★★★☆☆   **Recreation rating:** ★★★★☆

The typical Cape Cod tourist won't ever find this perfect colony of charming, shingled cottages on a private beach on Depot Pond. The property is wooded and grassy, and the cottages are nicely spread out. This is a family setting, perfect for relaxing after a day of salt and sun. It's a place where you can return to cook a beachside barbecue while the kids mess about in boats and inner tubes, or it's a place to never leave.

The Gibsons have owned this business for nearly 40 years. They've a friendly, repeat clientele, and it's a well-kept secret. Only a larger five-bedroom rental is advertised online. The place is a bit hard to find at first; you'll travel down a well-hidden dirt road lined with tall trees and shrubs, that opens up to expose a tranquil hillside dotted with cottages by a freshwater pond. It's one block from a general store and next door to a small library.

Though you're hidden off the beaten path here, you're still just two miles from the ocean beaches and Cape Cod National Seashore, the Cape Cod Rail Trail (bike path), kayak and canoe rentals, fishing, and boating trips. Downtown Orleans is only five minutes away.

Alongside the cottages, there is also the five-bedroom rental house. It has two queen beds and five twin beds, a glass-enclosed wood stove, three full baths, a washer and dryer, and an enclosed porch with two decks.

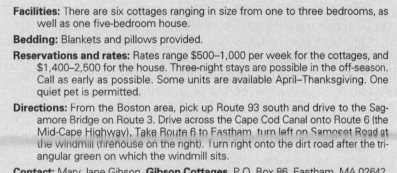

Facilities: There are six cottages ranging in size from one to three bedrooms, as well as one five-bedroom house.

Bedding: Blankets and pillows provided.

Reservations and rates: Rates range $500–1,000 per week for the cottages, and $1,400–2,500 for the house. Three-night stays are possible in the off-season. Call as early as possible. Some units are available April–Thanksgiving. One quiet pet is permitted.

Directions: From the Boston area, pick up Route 93 south and drive to the Sagamore Bridge on Route 3. Drive across the Cape Cod Canal onto Route 6 (the Mid-Cape Highway). Take Route 6 to Eastham, turn left on Samoset Road at the windmill (firehouse on the right). Turn right onto the dirt road after the triangular green on which the windmill sits.

Contact: Mary Jane Gibson, **Gibson Cottages**, P.O. Box 86, Eastham, MA 02642, 508/255-0882, website: www.capecodtravel.com/gibson.

36. EVEN'TIDE RESORT

South Wellfleet

Luxury rating: ★ ★ ☆ ☆ ☆   **Recreation rating:** ★ ★ ★ ★ ★

Rank: Top 10 for Biking, Top 10 for Family Activities

The Even'tide Resort is tucked back off of the main road. Behind the two-story motel and tucked into the woods are eight cottages, named after birds. They are all very different, ranging from single-story Capes to A-frames with spiral staircases.

The resort is located directly on the 25-mile Cape Cod Rail Trail bike path and has a .75-mile path to Marconi Beach on the National Seashore. Your kids will soon be running about the grounds with new friends, playing miniature golf, horseshoes, riding bikes, playing basketball, badminton, and table tennis, and even hula hooping.

© BETHANY ERICSON

The Even'tide also sells Wellfleet beach stickers for three days or a week. These allow you to go to all nine of the town's ocean, bay, and freshwater beaches. Faced with bad weather? Relax, the Even'tide has the biggest indoor motel pool on the Cape.

The Even'tide is not only family-friendly, it is family-operated, and even family-built, right down to some of the furniture. The cottages range in size, but all have outdoor barbecue areas and picnic tables, as well as cable television. All but one unit have full kitchens and outdoor decks. The A-frames have woodstoves. The phones are not modem compatible.

Facilities: There are eight cottages, accommodating up to six people. Four of the two-bedroom cottages and two of the one-bedroom cottages are housekeeping units. The other two cottages have maid service. These two cottages are the only units with air conditioning. There are coin operated laundry facilities on-site.

Bedding: Linens are provided.

Reservations and rates: The rates range $515–1,400. Mid-May–mid-September the cottages are rented weekly. Open May–October. Pets are not permitted.

Directions: From the Boston area, pick up Route 93 south and drive to the Sagamore Bridge on Route 3. Drive across the Cape Cod Canal onto Route 6 (the Mid-Cape Highway). Drive on Route 6 until you reach the Even'tide Motel and Cottages at Mileage Marker 98.

Contact: The Even'tide Resort Motel and Cottages, P.O. Box 41, Route 6, South Wellfleet, MA 02663, 508/349-3410 or 800/368-0007, website: www.eventidemotel.com.

37. MAURICE'S CAMPGROUND

South Wellfleet

Luxury rating: ★★☆☆☆   **Recreation rating:** ★★★★☆

If you like the idea of a simple cabin or cottage located in a campground setting next to busy Route 6, across from a drive-in movie theater, with direct access to the 25-mile Cape Cod Rail Trail bike path, Maurice's is for you.

© BETHANY ERICSON

The Rail Trail runs directly behind the forested campground, and you can bicycle to Marconi Beach on the Cape Cod National Seashore with ease. The Wellfleet Bay Wildlife Sanctuary, with its scenic trails and great variety of songbirds and shorebirds, is also nearby.

The campground is mainly an RV haven, run by three brothers and their wives. It has many seasonal campers, and there are usually lots of kids playing there. It also has a handful of housekeeping cottages that sleep 4–6 people, and some smaller cabins with maid service that sleep three with a cot.

The cabins and cottages are exceptionally clean. They have one or two bedrooms with a television and refrigerator, but the smaller maid-service cabins closer to the road do not have cooking facilities. The store at the campground offers a full deli and even lobsters, and it has a liquor license.

Facilities: There are five small, one-bedroom cabins with maid service and four two-bedroom housekeeping cottages with kitchens.

Bedding: Bring your own linens.

Reservations and rates: Rates range $300–500 weekly and $55–85 nightly for two people. There is a two-night minimum stay for reservations. Minimum stays may be required during holiday weekends and during July and August. Open mid-May–mid-September. No pets are permitted.

Directions: From Boston, take Route 93 south, or Route 128 south, and drive to Route 3 (Cape Cod). Follow Route 3 south to the Sagamore Bridge. Driving

across the bridge automatically puts you on Cape Cod (on Route 6). Continue driving on Route 6 and follow the signs to Wellfleet and Provincetown. In Orleans you will come to a rotary. From the rotary, drive for six miles on Route 6 east toward Provincetown. At the Eastham/Wellfleet town line, the Wellfleet Drive-In Theater is on the left. Look to the right. You'll see Maurice's Market and Maurice's Campground is the next driveway on the right.

Contact: Maurice's Campground, 80 Route 6, Unit One, Wellfleet, MA 02667, 508/349-2029: website: www.mauricescampground.com.

38. FRIENDSHIP COTTAGES AND LODGE

on Herring River

Luxury rating: ★★★☆☆   **Recreation rating:** ★★★★★

Friendship Lodge and its three cottages are in a fabulous seaside location in a residential area of Wellfleet. Cottages 1 and 2 are fairly basic and are located next to each other, which is convenient for extended families traveling together. They look across the road to the water. Cottage 3 is more modern, up the hill, and separate.

The view from the cottages looks across the Herring River, which is a nice, protected spot to take a kayaking course. Just across the river is the National Seashore and Great Island, where the National Park Service and the National Audubon Society run nature programs and tours. (The entire eastern half of Wellfleet is now a part of the National Seashore.)

The cottages have two bedrooms, each with a full bed in one and two twin beds in the other. Cottage 3 sports a lovely, renovated sleeping loft at the top of a companionway-style staircase, as well as two first-floor bedrooms. It also has a cozy, private, second-floor deck that overlooks the bay and harbor.

All of the cottages have decks or patios, outdoor grills, outdoor (and indoor) showers, televisions and VCRs, heat, and full-size kitchens.

The shingled cottages are just yards from Powers Landing Beach, and only .25 mile from the Yacht and Golf Club. Wellfleet also has a few fresh-

© BETHANY ERICSON

water ponds for swimming, and the town still boasts one of the few drive-in movie theaters. From the lodge and cottages you can watch sailboats, pick up shells on the beach, and admire a truly outstanding sunset view.

Facilities: There are three cottages that hold 4–6 people. Cottage 3 has a washing machine in a shed behind the building.

Bedding: Linens are not provided.

Reservations and rates: The rates for cottages 1 and 2 range $400–1,200 a week. The rates for Cottage 3 range $800–1,575 per week. Multiple week discounts are available. Open January–October, but call for winter weekends. Credit cards are not accepted. Pets are permitted.

Directions: From the Boston area, pick up Route 93 south and drive on Route 3, to the Sagamore Bridge. Drive across the Cape Cod Canal onto Route 6 (the Mid-Cape Highway). Take the exit for Wellfleet Center, and turn onto the first left. Keep along the shore on Commerical Street past the marina. Turn left at the first fork (Chequessett Neck Road). The cottages are on the right.

Contact: Friendship Cottages and Lodge, 530 Chequessett Neck Road, Wellfleet, MA 02667, website: www.wellfleetcapecod.net. Between July 1 and Labor Day, call Charles Currier at 202/722-0185; after Labor Day through June, call Kristin Frazier at 508/349-3390.

39. GREEN HAVEN

in Wellfleet on Cape Cod

Luxury rating: ★ ★ ☆ ☆ ☆   **Recreation rating:** ★ ★ ★ ★ ☆

Green Haven's pleasant cottages are positioned very close to each other, across the parking lot from busy Route 6. They are more of a place to land after a full day of Cape Cod sun, salt, and shopping than a destination spot.

© BETHANY ERICSON

The owners, Mark and Mary, met while Mary was visiting on the cape, and they ought to have some tips for those looking for a remarkable vacation.

Despite the closely situated quarters, this section of Route 6 has a much more rural feel, and these are organized, affordable, and tidy lodgings surrounded by trees, situated very close to the Cape Cod Rail Trail, and less than a mile's walk to the Cape Cod National Seashore.

Marconi Beach is the nearby historic beach, in South Wellfleet. It looks out to the Atlantic Ocean. It's said to be where Marconi sent the first transatlantic message to the King of England in 1903. There is also a wonderful nearby nature trail that goes through the Atlantic Cedar Swamp. Wellfleet also has three large freshwater ponds.

The cottages are one- and two-bedroom units with fully equipped kitchens, heat, cable television, and outdoor grills. They are fairly basic, but clean.

Facilities: There are five buildings with eight units. Three of the cottages are duplex units, and two are large two-bedroom standalone cottages.

Bedding: Linens rentals are offered.

Reservations and rates: The cottages range in price $400–900 per week, or $80–110 per night in the off season. There is a 5 percent discount for stays of two weeks or more. Open May–November. Pets are welcome in the fall only.

Directions: Take Route 93 south (or Route 128 south) to Route 3 (to Cape Cod). Drive on Route 3 south to the Sagamore Bridge. Driving across the bridge automatically puts you on Cape Cod (on Route 6). Stay on Route 6 and follow the signs to Wellfleet and Provincetown. In Orleans, you will come to a rotary. Drive halfway around the rotary, staying on Route 6. Proceed for another seven miles and you will see Green Haven Cottages on the left side, one mile past the Wellfleet Drive-In Movie Theatre.

Contact: Green Haven Cottages, P.O. Box 486, South Wellfleet, MA 02663, 508/349-1715, website: www.greenhavencottages.com.

40. DAYS' COTTAGES

North Truro

Luxury rating: ★ ★ ☆ ☆ ☆   **Recreation rating:** ★ ★ ★ ★ ★
Rank: Top 10 for Value

Days' Cottages are the icon of Cape Cod beach cottages. You may have seen paintings or photos of these cottages, which were built during the Depression, when the beach was wider and the road was not a major cape highway. They are visually striking as you wind your way up Route 6 toward the tip of the cape: 23 identical cottages in a precise line next to the road with a thin strip of beach behind them. They are known as the Cape Cod Flower Cottages, due to each being named after a different flower.

The accommodations are very basic. They are two-bedroom cottages facing away from the road toward the ocean, which surges just a few steps outside the cottages' doors. The cottages have survived some major hurricanes over the years, and there is now a seawall to prevent any further beach erosion. There is also a ramp for boat launching, but no personal watercraft are allowed, in order to foster a peaceful and safe swimming environment.

The cottages have a decent amount of space inside, if not between them. Each has a living room, two bedrooms, a fully equipped kitchen, and a bathroom with a shower stall. They all are heated. Noise from the road and other families is inevitable, but the cottages see a very high rate of repeat guests who have gotten to know each other over the years.

Provincetown is only 10 minutes away, and opportunities for biking, boating, fishing, hiking, playing tennis, and swimming on the cape are close by. However, once you've had your own private slice of beach just outside your door, you may never want to join the crowds at public beaches again.

Facilities: There are 23 two-bedroom cottages. No personal watercraft are permitted.

Bedding: Linens are provided.

Reservations and rates: Rates range $70–120 per night, and $490–840 per week, depending on the month. Open late April–late October. No credit cards are accepted. No pets are allowed.

Directions: From the Boston area, pick up Route 93 south and drive to Route 3 to the Sagamore Bridge. Drive across the Cape Cod Canal onto Route 6 (the Mid-Cape Highway), and continue driving until you see the signs for Route 6A Shore Road. On Route 6A, continue driving for another 2.5 miles. Days' Cottages is located midway between North Truro and Provincetown on Shore Road (Route 6A).

Contact: Days' Cottages, 271 Shore Road, Route 6A, P.O. Box 157, North Truro, MA 02652, 508/487-1062.

41. EAST HARBOUR

on Cape Cod Bay

Luxury rating: ★★★☆☆   **Recreation rating:** ★★★★★

This is a very pleasant motel with family-oriented cottages set on Beach Point in North Truro, on Route 6A. Most of the tidy cottages are placed away from the road. They encircle a yard and are angled to provide guests with extra privacy. The gardening and grounds at East Harbour are very lovely. There is a play area and an enticing boardwalk to the back of the property, leading to the bay beach. The cottages face Cape Cod Bay on one side and Pilgrim Lake and sand dunes on the other.

Each unit has a wallpapered living room with cable television and a fully equipped kitchen. There are two bedrooms (one with a queen bed and one with two twin beds) and a joining bathroom with a shower stall. All the cottages are heated.

The cape offers endless beach activities, ranging from swimming and boating to fishing and whale-watching. Here, on the point in Truro, there are notable sand dunes to walk and explore. You also have the Highland nine-hole golf course and the Cape Cod National Seashore nearby.

Like many cottage colonies on the lower cape, this set is located right on busy Route 6A. However, unlike many places, you can get a cottage positioned a little farther from the road. The nearby grasslands add to a spacious feeling, and the beach's play area for children is located away from the road.

Facilities: There are seven two-bedroom cottages that accommodate a maximum of four people. There are coin-operated laundry facilities on premises.

Bedding: Linens are provided.

Reservations and rates: Rates range $600–1,000 per week. Call early for reservations due to a high number of repeat guests. Waterview cottages (1, 6, and 7) are rented Saturday–Saturday, and Beachfront cottages (2 to 5) are rented Sunday–Sunday. Open April–October. No pets are permitted.

42. KALMAR VILLAGE

on the beach in North Truro

Luxury rating: ★ ★ ★ ☆ ☆   **Recreation rating:** ★ ★ ★ ★ ★

Rank: Top 10 for Family Activities, Top 10 for Ocean Beach Activities

Kalmar Village is an expansive family resort with landscaped lawns leading to a big, private, sandy beach. The village of cottages is set farther off the road than most in the area. Cars are kept in a lot, separate from the neatly similar black-and-white cottages, which adds to the visual charm of the place.

© BETHANY ERICSON

This is a favorite repeat-visit destination for many families, and there is no lack of kids here. The beach is on the southerly side of the cape and has great views of the rolling dunes of the Cape Cod National Seashore to the north. Kalmar Village also has a large swimming pool, picnic tables, and grills.

Buses to Provincetown and other ocean beaches run frequently, so you may never even have to get in your car. There are 36 cottages that may be full on a hot summer day, and kids tend to form their own communities with new friends during their stay.

Two-room cottages have two full beds or a full and a twin in the bedroom, and two sofa beds in the living room. Three-room cottages have a full bed in one bedroom, two twin beds in a second bedroom, and one sofa bed in the living room. Some cottages are on the waterfront. All have cable television. All come with fully equipped kitchens and private outdoor areas with a grill. All have heating, and some have air-conditioning.

Facilities: There are 36 cottages that can accommodate up to six people in each. Daily housekeeping services are provided.

Bedding: All linens are provided.

Reservations and rates: Cottage rates range $550–2,050 per week. Some daily rates are available off-season. Open mid-May–mid-October.

Directions: Take Route 93 south (or Route 128 south) and drive to Route 3 (Cape Cod). Follow Route 3 south to the Sagamore Bridge. Driving across the bridge automatically puts you on Cape Cod (on Route 6). Follow Route 6 (toward Provincetown). Go into Truro and continue driving for 8.1 miles on Route 6. Turn left at the "Beachpoint, Route 6A" sign, and then turn right onto Route 6A. Kalmar Village is 1.5 miles up on the left side.

Note: There are numerous turnoffs to get onto Route 6A. If you turn off onto 6A before passing highway mile marker 112 on Route 6, you will be driving the slower route to Kalmar.

Contact: Kalmar Village, 674 Shore Rd, P.O. Box 745, North Truro, MA 02652, 508/487-0585, winter address: Kalmar Village, 246 Newbury St., Boston, MA 02116, 617/247-0211, website: www.kalmarvillage.com.

43. HIDEAWAY HILL

Provincetown on Cape Cod

Luxury rating: ★★★★☆   **Recreation rating:** ★★★★☆

Provincetown is a tightly populated area, but those lucky enough to be heading to Hideaway Hill will drive up a hidden forest hillside and feel tucked away on a private mountain. The Cottage and Studio units are near the owners' round, self-built home, and the Barn is across the street.

© BETHANY ERICSON

The privacy and space found here, just a 10-minute walk from downtown Provincetown and a few minutes walk to the beach, are very unusual. The cottages are decorated with original artwork and rustic architectural details—metal beams in the studio and exposed wood around the window frames. An old truck is purposefully in your view. If you can appreciate this kind of rustic, unfinished style, you will adore Hideaway Hill.

The Cottage is behind the parking area and was originally a work space for Jonathan, the owner. It is good for couples and includes a tub with jets. His workspace is now under the Studio, which feels like a tree house with its leafy views. The Barn, across the street, was Jonathan's mother's art studio. It overlooks a professionally groomed garden with pergolas and walkways. You can see the ocean if you look between the houses behind the garden lot, and you can walk to Race Point in five minutes. Fishing, boating, and whale-watching opportunities are within a short walk downtown.

These are cottages with a high attention to detail, ceramic tiles, and fabulous artwork, and they retain a strong feeling of homeyness, making this less a place for those seeking mass-produced polish and more of an eclectic oasis.

Facilities: There are three separate, open-format cottages with full kitchens accommodating 2–4 people.

Bedding: All linens provided.

Reservations and rates: Rates range $850–1,600 per week and $135–275 per night. Units are rented weekly only in July and August. For the rest of the year there are length-of-stay minimums. Open year-round. No pets permitted.

Directions: Hideaway Hill's well-guarded location will be revealed when the Sinaikos email your directions to you.

Contact: Jonathan and Camille Sinaiko, **Hideaway Hill**, Provincetown, MA 02657, 508/487-7264, website: www.hideawayhill.com.

44. THE MASTHEAD RESORT

Downtown Provincetown

Luxury rating: ★ ★ ★ ☆ ☆   **Recreation rating:** ★ ★ ★ ★ ☆

If you're heading out on fishing, boating, or whale-watching trips with outfits based in Provincetown, you can stay right in town in a cottage at the Masthead. This collection of shingled buildings is located off Commercial Street, the main drag that goes through the very busy center of town, but by the time you arrive at the Masthead, the street is narrower and more residential.

There is a bit of lawn between the buildings, and 450 feet of private sandy beach. The beach is rather narrow at high tide, but the resort has a raised boardwalk with seating. There are showers and cast-iron grills on the beach. Deep-water secure moorings and launch service can be provided.

The close cluster of well-kept, weathered buildings includes a motel and multiunit cottages, as well as two stand-alone rentals: Richard's Cottage and the Isabella Rossellini Cottage. All of the units are decorated somewhat differently, but most are paneled and include kitchens. All are reasonably spacious, and all have big living room picture windows looking out across the water.

© BETHANY ERICSON

Richard's Cottage (No. 35) is a three-bedroom with two floors. The living room has a 12-foot glass door facing the bay, and the kitchen is new. One of the bedrooms has a skylight. The Isabella Rossellini Cottage (No. 39) is a little smaller, with two bedrooms. The living room has a cathedral ceiling, and there is a private porch by the water.

Facilities: There are two standalone cottages and numerous inn and apartment rooms. Cottages are cleaned weekly, and daily maid service is optional at an additional charge.

Bedding: All linens are provided. Bath and kitchen linens are changed three times a week.

Reservations and rates: Rates range $1,967–3,541 per week in the summer, and lower rates and shorter lengths of stay are available in the off season. No cancelations are allowed on single-unit cottages, so book carefully. There is no charge for children under 12 years of age. Open year-round. No pets are permitted.

Directions: From Boston, take Route 93 south (or Route 128 south) and drive to Route 3 (Cape Cod). Follow Route 3 south to the Sagamore Bridge. Drive aross the bridge and continue on Route 6 for 70 miles to Provincetown. You'll pass a sign that reads "Welcome to Provincetown." Continue driving through a set of traffic lights, and take the next left at a blinking yellow light onto Shank Painter Road. Follow this road to the end, and then turn right at the stop sign onto Bradford Street. After driving for .25 mile on Bradford, turn left onto West Vine. Follow West Vine to the end and turn right onto Commercial Street. Follow this street for about .25 mile and the Masthead will be on the left.

Contact: The Masthead Resort, 31–41 Commercial Street, P.O. Box 577, Provincetown, MA 02657, 508/487-0523 or 800/395-5095, website: www.themasthead.com.

© BETHANY ERICSON

Chapter 9

Connecticut

CHAPTER 9—CONNECTICUT

The country's third-smallest state packs a lot into its boundaries. Connecticut is a wealth of academics, art, history, and outdoor fun. You won't find many cabins and cottages along the southwestern coast. This is Connecticut's Gold Coast, home to many a New York expatriate, business executive, and movie star. Commuter rail stations, corporate headquarters, upscale restaurants, and private mansions line the shore that once housed the Fitzgeralds.

From Norwalk, home of the Maritime Aquarium, travel north of the southwest coast on Route 7 to Wilton, where you'll find the J. Alden Weir farm. Here many famous American Impressionists visited and painted. This is a National Historic Site that can be compared to Giverny, Monet's estate in France.

Traveling further north still, you'll find the Housatonic Valley, where the wealth is tucked behind white picket fences on tree-lined streets in picture-perfect colonial towns. Antique dealers, fine artists, and craftspeople populate this area. The highway continues north into the Litchfield Hills, an absolutely stunning drive during the peak colors of autumn.

The Litchfield Hills area is full of quaint, New England village greens. This is a land for antiquing, canoeing and kayaking on the Housatonic and Farmington Rivers, exploring flea markets, hiking the hills, horseback riding across rolling meadows, and swimming in Lake Waramaug and the Twin Lakes. Many people continue on this pretty drive into the Berkshires of Massachusetts and on into Vermont. The Appalachian Trail travels 53 miles through this northwestern corner of Connecticut. It's a lovely area to hike, with some mountains sharing summit ownership with neighboring states in places like Mount Riga State Park. The trail goes through Housatonic Meadows State Park, a good fly-fishing spot.

Hartford, Connecticut's big city, is home to insurance companies, as well as to the historic, neighboring houses of Samuel Clemens (Mark Twain) and Harriet Beecher Stowe. It also lays claim to the nation's oldest public art museum, the Wadsworth Athenaeum.

The northwestern corner of Connecticut is called the Quiet Corner. It has no major cities, and in the late 19th century, it was a summer-estate spot for rich New Yorkers and Bostonians. World War II took a toll on this area. During the Depression, the economic base of the area—the textile mills—moved south. You can still see derelict, red-brick mills in the area. Today, this area has become a National Heritage Corridor. It has Connecticut's largest forest (in Voluntown) and the longest village common (in Lebanon). The area has textile-history exhibits and even a museum of puppetry. Putnam, a former mill town, has become a huge antiquing hotspot. There are several scenic byways for touring the area.

The southeastern coast of Connecticut has a long history of shipbuilding and whaling. There are long beaches, homey cottages, fried clams, and lobster. Hammonasset Beach State Park is a great spot for bird-watching, and Mystic is the place to get a salty taste of maritime history, environment, and culture. Meanwhile, Old Lyme is a quaint town of American Impressionist artwork at the Florence Griswold Museum and neighboring school. These harbors have housed warships and whalers, and continue traditional boatbuilding today.

From beachside cottages to hideaways in the forests and hills, Connecticut is likely to evoke a feeling of pastoral calm with its peaceful colonial villages and rambling paths.

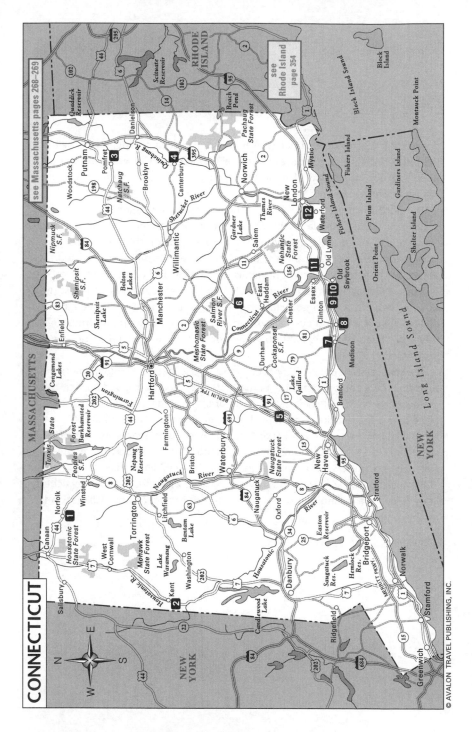

CHAPTER 9
CONNECTICUT

1. BLACKBERRY RIVER INN

on Route 44 in Norfolk

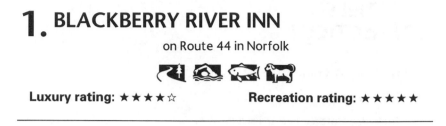

Luxury rating: ★ ★ ★ ★ ☆   **Recreation rating:** ★ ★ ★ ★ ★

The Blackberry River Inn first welcomed guests in the 18th century. Today, these Colonial Williamsburg buildings have been restored, and it's easy to imagine another era as you relax in the grand sitting parlors, or by the fire in the cherry library.

The Cottage is on the second floor of a two-story building next to the inn, where it looks over the 27-acre property. The first floor is simply storage space for the inn. The one-room unit has a king bed, whirlpool tub, television, refrigerator, and fireplace. Many inns skimp on the decor of their associated cottages, but not here, where you'll find the same warm, country furnishings as in the rest of the inn.

There are no cooking facilities in this unit, but there are many restaurants in the area, and the owners are happy to share menus and recommendations with you. They also know a local traveling chef who delivers made-to-order meals right to the inn.

There is a pool and a tennis court on-site, and you can fish for trout in little Blackberry River. You can cross-country ski from the property or at Maplewood Farm, downhill ski at Butternut Basin, picnic by the cascades at Campbell Falls State Park, explore Norfolk hiking trails, or ascend Dennis Hill or Haystack Mountain. You can even try your hand at curling with the Norfolk Curling Club.

The inn, with a large tent out back, often hosts parties and weddings. Complimentary afternoon tea is served in the library. Breakfasts, in a sunny room in the main inn, are also included and might consist of orange waffles or apple-stuffed pancakes.

Facilities: There is one cottage intended for a couple.

Bedding: Bedding and towels are provided.

Reservations and rates: The Cottage rate ranges $175–205. May–October there is a two-night minimum on weekends and holidays. Additional person(s) in the room are $25 each. Inquire about AAA discounts. Open year-round. Pets are sometimes accommodated, call for permission.

Directions: From Boston, take the Massachusetts. Turnpike (I-90) west to Exit 2 west to Route 201 west. From here, drive on Route 7 South to Canaan. Drive on Route 44 east to Norfolk. Blackberry River Inn will be on your left on Route 44.

Contact: Blackberry River Inn, 536 Greenwoods Road, Route 44 West, Norfolk, CT 06058, 860/542 5100 or 800/414-3636, website: www.blackberryriverinn.com.

2. CLUB GETAWAY

off Route 7 in Kent

Luxury rating: ★★☆☆☆   **Recreation rating:** ★★★★★

Rank: Top 10 Most Unusual

Club Getaway, on a lake at the edge of the Berkshire Mountains, is like a sports-camp resort for adults. There is a seemingly endless array of sports, great food, and nightly entertainment. Situated between New York and Boston, this is a big singles' spot on most weekends, with reservationists keeping an eye on gender ratios. Nobody under 21 is invited to stay, but there are also special family-vacation weekends.

The cabins overlook the lake and hill. They are camp style, with twin beds and no telephones, televisions, or radios. You're here to be active and outside of your cabin. Unlike summer camp however, there are daily housekeeping services.

A typical weekend package might include mountain biking, tennis, waterskiing, sailing, rock climbing, basketball, golf, volleyball, in-line skating, and fitness classes, as well as meals, wine, and entertainment (if you're still standing). Schedules are often devised around various events and weekend themes. If this is not enough for you, you can also water-ski, sea kayak, skydive, rock climb, canoe, play paintball, and even drive a race car.

If you feel like taking it easy while your friends get out there and sweat, you can take yoga classes, make crafts, listen to live music on the beach, or take a massage class. And if the weather has the poor grace to rain, there are still dance and self-defense classes, bowling, and indoor in-line skating.

Both hot and cold buffet breakfasts are served, and lunch is served under a white canopy, with an assortment of international themes. Dinner is served at eight-person tables with a great deal of free wine.

Facilities: There are 98 cabins; two are wheelchair accessible.

Bedding: Bedding is provided.

Reservations and rates: There are special summer-share and member-reward deals for guests returning several times a season. Inquire if you are considering booking for more than one weekend. (Hint: booking earlier saves you more money.) Special deals are sometimes posted on the website, and an annual membership fee will get you special mailings. All of the special Camps and Programs are free, with a few exceptions that carry $5–50 extra fees. An all-inclusive weekend at Club Getaway ranges from as little as $239–399. The price per person is based on four people per cabin. Add $9 per person per night for triple occupancy. Add $15 per person per night for double occupancy. Cabins with couples have no double-occupancy charge, but they have limited availability. Open June–August.

Directions: Directions are mailed to registered guests. There is a Getaway bus that leaves every Friday afternoon from First Avenue and 63rd Street at 5:30 P.M. in Manhattan. On holiday weekends there is bus transportation that leaves from Washington Baltimore and Boston. Please call the reservation office for more details.

Contact: Club Getaway, 59 S. Kent Rd., Kent, CT 06757, 860/927-3664 or 800/6-GETAWAY, website: www.clubgetaway.com.

3. CHICKADEE COTTAGE BED AND BREAKFAST

on Airline Trail in Pomfret

Luxury rating: ★★★★☆   **Recreation rating:** ★★★★★

This cute, antique-filled place has two accommodations. One is a room in the main house, and the other is the Carriage House—a separate, cozy hideaway with its own deck. Chickadee Cottage is a private retreat right on the Airline Rail Trail, a former railroad line that is now a footpath.

The separate, sophisticated Carriage House cottage is furnished in old style, with antique pine. It has a double bed with a canopy, a small kitchen with a big table, and a gas woodstove in the sitting area. You can eat breakfast in the main house, or make your own morning meal in comfortable privacy.

The Airline Trail goes right through the property and leads to the 700-acre Connecticut Audubon Bafflin Sanctuary, which is a good place to bike, walk, or cross-country ski. The trail runs unbroken from Windham to Putnam and offers relatively easy mountain biking. It's hoped that one day the Putnam-to-Willimantic section of this rail trail will eventually be part of the East Coast Greenaway, a multiuse trail proposed to run from Maine to Florida. Also in Pomfret is the Mashamoquet Brook State Park, which has swimming, fishing, and some nice hiking trails. Pomfret has its own winery, and there are numerous restaurants in the area.

If the weather keeps you off the trail, Putnam is famous for its more than 400 antique dealers. The town is named after Israel Putnam, who local lore credits with crawling into the den of the last wolf in Connecticut and shooting her, which rendered the area safe for shopping.

Facilities: The Carriage House holds 2–4 people. Children more than four years of age are welcome.

Bedding: Bedding is provided.

Reservations and rates: The Carriage House rate is $195 per night for two. Additional guests are $35. Corporate and short-term rates are available. Open year-round. Pets are allowed.

Directions: From Boston, take the Massachusetts Turnpike (I-90) west to Auburn, Exit 10. After the tollbooth, follow the signs to Route 395 south. Drive into Connecticut and take Exit 97 (Route 44). Follow Route 44 west, driving through the town of Putnam, past Day Kimball Hospital, to the second blinking light (Vanilla Bean Cafe & Martha's Herbary). Turn left onto Route 169 south (which is also Route 44 west). Continuee past Pomfret School and take the right fork onto Route 44 west/Averill Road. The Chickadee Cottage is the last house on the right, immediately before Putnam Savings Bank. Park facing the bank.

Contact: Chickadee Cottage Bed and Breakfast, 70 Averill Road/Route 44, Pomfret, CT 06259, 860/963-0587, website: www.chickadeecottage.com.

4. LITTLE RED SCHOOLHOUSE

in Quiet Corner

Luxury rating: ★★★☆☆   **Recreation rating:** ★★★☆☆

Tucked away in pastoral Canterbury is a lovely, three-room country cottage that was built in 1849 as the one-room Frost District Schoolhouse. There are neighbors, but this rural area has houses on 2- to 10-acre lots, so your closest neighbor will likely be a visiting bunny on the wide half-acre lawn. Most guests come here to enjoy the outdoors, as well as the plethora of antiques in Putnam.

The cottage retains its original hardwood floor and has some other intriguing nods to its past. There is a framed reading cue card, a neighbor's 1929 diploma, and the minutes from the meeting where it was decided to build the schoolhouse in 1849. In the living room is a reproduction of an old student desk.

The cottage is otherwise decorated in very nice, comfortable, country decor. It has one bedroom with a queen bed, a fully equipped kitchen, a living room with a full-sized futon, and a washer and dryer. There is a television, VCR, and telephone. Outside, there is a grill, a picnic table, a fieldstone fire pit, and a very popular hammock.

In the area you'll find great fishing in nearby streams and rivers, including on the Natchaug, Willimantic, and Moosup Rivers. You can hike in nearby Mohegan State Forest in Scotland. You can swim at Hopeville Pond State Park or drive less than an hour to Ocean Beach in New London, or Misquamicut Beach in Westerly, Rhode Island. Many people take day trips to the state's largest forest, Pachaug State Forest, in Voluntown, or to the seaport of Mystic.

If your weather doesn't hold, you are near the region's great antique center in Putnam, and you're about half an hour from casinos. There are also a great number of historic homes in the area, as well as the interesting Ballard Institute and Museum of Puppetry in Storrs.

Facilities: The one cottage can accommodate up to four adults.

Bedding: Bedding and towels are provided.

Reservations and rates: Rates range $400–500 per week. The cottage is available by the week, month, or season. Most rentals are from Saturday to Saturday. A security deposit is required. Open year-round. Pets and smoking indoors are not permitted.

Directions: The schoolhouse is about 90 minutes from Boston. Take the Massachusetts Turnpike (I-90) to Exit 10 (Routes 395/12/290). Turn left at the fork onto Route 395 south and continue into Connecticut to Exit 91 (Route 6). Drive west on Route 6 to Brooklyn, and then turn left onto Route 169 south. Bear right at the intersection with Route 205 to stay on Route 169. Continue on Route 169 until you reach the stop sign in Canterbury, then turn right on Route 14 West. After two mini-malls, turn left on Lisbon Road at Cackleberry Farm Antiques. At the first stop sign, the schoolhouse will be on your right.

Contact: Bob and Jackie Desrochers, **Little Red Schoolhouse**, 75 Lisbon Rd., Canterbury, CT 06331, 860/546-6238, website: http://home.mindspring.com/~rfd2.

5. HIGH MEADOW BED AND BREAKFAST

Wallingford

Luxury rating: ★ ★ ★ ☆   **Recreation rating:** ★ ★ ★ ☆

© BETHANY ERICSON

Nancy Charles returned as an adult to her father's dairy farm, where she and her brother now own 70 acres. Nancy and her husband, Bob, moved the lovely 1742 Jonathan Towner Half Way Tavern here and reopened it as a bed-and-breakfast. They also built Nancy's mother an upscale cottage on the grounds, using pieces from old houses. This comfortable escape is now rented out to guests year-round.

The Brae Cottage is in a meadow overlooking the pond. It has beautiful woodwork: a cherry floor; maple, pine, and cherry paneling; and floorboards radiating out from the fireplace in an arc. Family and friends have painted much of the artwork on the walls. The antique furniture and quilt-covered bed are inviting.

The modern full kitchen includes a dishwasher. You can enjoy a gourmet breakfast in the inn, or you can be supplied with all you need to make one yourself. There are endless nice touches here, from a large coat closet to the cathedral ceiling to jets in the tub. There is a washer and dryer, and a blue-slate patio lined with herbs.

Some of the less obvious touches are the most special. The entire house is wheelchair-accessible; even the fireplace is built at a convenient height. And hidden folded in the living room wall is a queen Murphy bed for curling up by the fire.

You can swim in the private pond, and this is good country for walking. There is fishing and boat rentals in the area. The Metacomet Trail leads up to picturesque Castle Craig on Hubbard Peak; the Mattabesett Blue Trail, on its way from Chauncy Peak to Lamentation Mountain, is just a mile from the door. Wallingford is home to Wharton Brook State Park, which holds more fishing and swimming opportunities, and the town has a good rock-climbing gym for rainy days.

Facilities: There is one cottage that sleeps 2–4 people. Kids are accepted with permission. Small weddings can be arranged under the wisteria-covered archway and in the field.

Bedding: Bedding is provided.

Reservations and rates: The Brae Cottage rents for $250 per night, $1,100 per week, and $3,600 per month. Call early; note that it is popular with parents of students enrolled at nearby Choate Rosemary Hall. Open year-round.

Directions: From Boston, take the Massachusetts Pike (I-90) to I-91 south and take Exit 14. Turn left (east) off the exit onto East Center Street. You'll drive across a bridge over I-91, and then railroad tracks. After driving for 75 miles and round a sharp curve, you will see Mackenzie Reservoir on the right. Turn right onto Whirlwind Hill Road, which divides the reservoir. Continue up two hills and watch for the mailbox on the left marked 1290. Turn onto the gravel drive.

Contact: Bob and Nancy Charles, **High Meadow Bed and Breakfast**, 1290 Whirlwind Hill Road, Wallingford, CT 06492, 203/269-2351, website: www.highmeadow.com.

6. SUNRISE RESORT

on Salmon River

Luxury rating: ★ ★ ☆ ☆ ☆   **Recreation rating:** ★ ★ ★ ★ ★

Rank: Top 10 for Family Activities, Top 10 for Value

Sunrise Resort is a family-run camping resort with a large number of cabins scattered about the property in clusters. The family summer-camp atmosphere is contagious here; it's the kind of place where parents play with their kids rather than dropping them off with counselors. This is also the site of the fun Great Connecticut Cajun/Zydeco Music & Arts Festival, held on the first weekend in June.

There are a variety of traditional pine and brand-new cabins and cottages on the hillside and waterfront. You could host a reunion for 100 people here, or you can just bring your family for some outdoor fun. The newly refurbished waterside cottages are mostly double units that can be opened up as one. They're farther away from some activities, but they are closer to the dining room and have the best views. The others are more convenient to the activities and to the pool.

All of the rooms have bedroom furnishings, bathrooms with showers, heating, air-conditioning, and daily housekeeping service. None of the rooms have telephones or televisions.

The Salmon River is a tidal river that you can walk across at low tide. At high tide you can launch a kayak, canoe, rowboat, or paddleboat—or you can take one of the organized pontoon boat rides. You can fish for bass, trout, carp, and catfish here.

There are countless activities at Sunrise, such as aerobics, dancing lessons, basketball, boating, boccie, horseback riding, kids' games, miniature golf, mountain biking, sand volleyball, shuffleboard, sitting in a whirlpool, softball, swimming, and tennis. There is nightly entertainment and a weekly luau. If that's not enough, there's also a 300-acre nature preserve next door. The owners recommend that above all else you bring a camera and a beach towel in order to be happy here.

Facilities: There are 200 guest rooms overall at Sunrise, split between motel rooms, the cabins, and the double-unit waterfront cottages. Breakfast, lunch, and dinner are provided. Each week there are four meals with live music and a different theme in a lovely outdoor setting.

Bedding: Bedding is provided.

Reservations and rates: The cabins and cottages range $85–108 per day and $352–540 for five-day and weeklong stays. Rates include three meals per day. The rates are based on newness and facilities rather than on the season. Kids 14 years old and under get one-third off the adult rate. Kids 4 years old and under get two-thirds off the adult rate. Kids must be with adults. Almost 90 percent of the guests return, so be sure to book early. Open May–September. Pets are permitted.

Directions: From Boston, take the Massachusetts Pike (I- 90) to Exit 9 for Hartford–NY. Drive for 42 miles on I-84 to Exit 55 (marked Route 2 east, Norwich–New London). Turn onto Route 2 and drive for 14 miles to Exit 13. Turn right onto Route 66 west and drive for four miles, then turn left onto Route 196 south and drive for six miles. Bear left on Route 151 south and continue for one mile to Sunrise, which will be on the right.

Contact: Sunrise Resort, Route 151, Moodus, CT 06469, 860/873-8681 or 800/225-9033, website: www.sunriseresort.com.

7. TIDEWATER INN

on Route 1 in Madison

Luxury rating: ★ ★ ★ ★ ☆   **Recreation rating:** ★ ★ ★ ★ ☆

Hidden behind a privacy hedge behind the main inn, the cottage at Tidewater Inn is a cute hideaway for couples. It has high-quality antique furniture and a high level of attention to detail. The guest book is full of comments like "Everytime we looked for something, we opened a drawer, and there it was!"

There is a bedroom and sitting room with 1930s furniture, cable television, a VCR, a king bed with a carved teak headboard, and a two-person whirlpool tub. The cottage is just minutes from romantic walks on the beach, and has witnessed more than one wedding proposal.

Hammonassett State Park is two miles down Route 1. It is a popular birding spot, with 2.5 miles of beach and protected wetland. Ask about birding trips at the Audubon store down the street. In the winter, there are often cruises down the southern part of the Connecticut River to see bald eagles.

The inn provides passes to the town beaches on Long Island Sound, and you can bike or hike on back roads and numerous state parks in the area. Chatfield Hollow, off of Route 80, has a forest pond for swimming.

The inn provides a full breakfast, and there is a range of restaurant options in the area. Madison is a wealthy, educated town with an art cinema and a fantastic independent bookstore. The downtown is a short walk from the cottage.

Facilities: There is one cottage intended for a couple.
Bedding: Bedding is provided.
Reservations and rates: Rates for the cottage range $165–185. Call at least six months ahead.

Directions: From Boston, take I-95 south to Exit 62. Turn left off the exit ramp onto the Hammonasset Connector. Drive about one mile, and turn right onto Route 1. The inn is about 1.5 miles on the right.

Contact: Jean Foy, **Tidewater Inn B&B**, 949 Boston Post Road, Madison, CT 06443, 203/245 8457, website: www.thetidewater.com.

8. A VICTORIAN VILLAGE

Shoreline Route 1 in Clinton

Luxury rating: ★ ★ ★ ☆ ☆   **Recreation rating:** ★ ★ ★ ★ ☆

Rank: Top 10 Most Unusual

Patricia was a retired opera singer and a negotiator for construction outfits in Frankfort when she met Al LePera, a very accomplished contractor, at a party. Things progressed, and they decided to build something that would last.

© BETHANY ERICSON

The couple bought a handful of cottages by the ocean and totally rebuilt them. Then they began adding new units, keeping everything Victorian. (If you want to see Patricia's eyes light up, talk to her about cupolas, gables, and turrets.) Eventually, Al bought Patricia her own power tools so that she could start making her own gingerbread trim for the cottages.

The result is a safe, growing neighborhood village of charming Victorian cottages tastefully decorated in individual themes ranging from flowers to Alice in Wonderland. Some have fireplaces, restored chandeliers, oriental carpets, or whirlpool tubs, and all have full kitchens, air-conditioning, wood floors, and Victorian antiques.

The cottages are just two blocks from Grove Beach, and guests can use passes to go to fun Clinton Town Beach, just 1.5 miles away. Hammonasset State Park is a five-minute drive away and is good for barbecues and bird-watching. You can fish for striped bass off the nearby docks or rent a space at a local marina for your boat. This coastal route is popular with touring cyclists. In the winter, the towns in this area have delightful light displays.

While the village layout of the cottages and the welcoming pet policy create a very open and friendly community of guests, the LePera's have also taken steps to ensure it is safe and private. They often have some long-term guests—from people relocating, to traveling medical professionals—and they've created a homey atmosphere conducive to business travelers and vacationers alike.

Facilities: There are 16 cottages, and more on the way. They can accommodate 1–4 people.

Bedding: Bedding is not provided. They will loan linens to guests traveling from afar.

Reservations and rates: Rates for the cottages range $325–1,000 per week (Friday–Friday). Call in April for reservations.

Directions: From I-95, take Exit 64, Horse Hill Road, toward the beach. Turn right where the road stops at a T intersection. Drive about .25 mile and go over a small bridge on an inlet. At the next left turn onto Grove Beach Road. Drive a couple of miles and turn right onto Shoreline Route 1 (known in Clinton as Main Street). The cottages will be on your right, about 100 yards past the Fish Tail Restaurant.

Contact: A Victorian Village, 345 East Main Street, Clinton, CT 06413, 800/895-9588, website: www.avictorianvillage.com (mailing address: 24G West Main Street, Box 112, Clinton, CT 06413).

9. WESTBROOK INN BED AND BREAKFAST

on Route 1 in Westbrook

Luxury rating: ★ ★ ★ ☆   **Recreation rating:** ★ ★ ★ ★ ☆

Glenn and Christine Monroe are the best kind of people for running a romantic Victorian inn. True to the period decor surrounding them, they are hardworking people who even grind their own organic wheat when baking for the guests. The thoughtful attention to quality and detail found here does not go unnoticed.

© BETHANY ERICSON

Glenn put a great deal of work into the cottage, replacing fir with yellow pine that looks aged to match the inn. He used cedar beams in its basement and attic. Christine is responsible for the beautiful interior decorating and the elegant garden.

The cottage has two floors and two bedrooms, a full bath, and a full kitchen with modern appliances. There is air-conditioning and a television and VCR on each floor, but no telephone. The cottage is clean and spacious, and the wood floor glows in the sunlight. A hammock made for two is in the yard.

The property extends to the Patchogue River, where guests can fish or catch crab from the inn's small dock. Beach passes, bicycles, towels, blankets, chairs, and umbrellas are provided for a day at the beach. There is also a large marina nearby at Pilot Point.

The common rooms of the inn are decorated with leather and antique furnishings, Victorian wallpaper, lace curtains, candles, and beautiful rugs. There are 250-year-old chestnut floors in the library and foyers, and you'll be served a full breakfast in the old ballroom, with its large fieldstone fireplace.

Facilities: There is one cottage that accommodates 2–4 people. Kids, while not accepted in the main inn, are welcome in the cottage.

Bedding: Bedding and towels are provided.

Reservations and rates: The rates for the cottage range $226–260 per night. Extra guest charges and minimum-stay requirements may apply.

Directions: From Boston, take I-95 south to Exit 65. Turn left on Route 153. After .3 mile, bear right onto Route 1 and drive for .5 mile. You will see the inn on your right.

Contact: Glenn & Chris Monroe, **Westbrook Inn Bed and Breakfast**, 976 Boston Post Road, Westbrook, CT 06498, 860/399-4777 or 800/342-3162, website: www.westbrookinn.com.

10. SAYBROOK POINT INN AND SPA

on Saybrook Point

Luxury rating: ★ ★ ★ ☆ ☆   **Recreation rating:** ★ ★ ★ ★ ★

Rank: Top 10 for Boating, Top 10 Most Unusual

Once a fabulous 1950s institution (known as Terra Mar to guests like Frank Sinatra, Tom Jones, and Jayne Mansfield), the Saybrook Point Inn and Spa is now a modern, updated resort complete with a restaurant and wide-ranging spa facilities. An associated marina with numerous boat slips has an office in a small working lighthouse at the end of the docks. Hidden upstairs is a special place to stay. Surrounded by water on all sides, the lighthouse lodging has a living room, a bedroom with a queen bed, and a kitchen with a microwave and dishwasher (but no stove)—decorated in a more modern

style than the 18th-century furnishings in the inn. A balcony and a whirlpool tub are planned additions.

The marina is popular in the summer, and people arrive and rent slips for the night, sometimes on their way to Block Island. There is a trolley into town if you arrive by boat. It can be somewhat loud in the lighthouse in the mornings, when the boats refuel, but that is also part of the charm.

There are complimentary bikes at the inn, and there are beaches nearby in Old Saybrook and Westbrook. If you arrive by boat, be sure to try for a striper on your way. Lighthouse dwellers have full use of the inn's facilities, including a pool, a spa, and a fitness center. You can even order room service to your perch above the docks. The restaurant is known for its seafood.

Facilities: The Lighthouse has a sofa bed and can accommodate 2–4 people. There are laundry facilities on-site.

Bedding: Bedding is provided.

Reservations and rates: Rates range $399–429 per night. Call a couple of months ahead. Weekends are very busy. The inn is open year-round; the lighthouse is open April–October.

Directions: From I-95, take Exit 67 to Route 154 South. Turn left at the third traffic light. Follow the signs to Saybrook Point or Shore Points. When you come to a three-way stop sign, the inn will be in front of you, on the right.

Contact: Saybrook Point Inn & Spa, 2 Bridge Street, Old Saybrook, CT 06475, 860/395-2000 or 800/243-0212, website: www.saybrook.com.

11. BEE & THISTLE INN

Riverside in Old Lyme

Luxury rating: ★ ★ ★ ★ ☆   **Recreation rating:** ★ ★ ★ ★ ★

Old Lyme is an incredibly charming New England town tucked off the highway on Route 95. It is best known as the seat of American Impressionism. The cozy Bee & Thistle Inn was built in 1756 on the Lieutenant River. It has a commanding circular drive and wonderful landscaping. The lawn stretches down to the river, where Adirondack chairs line the shore.

Behind the inn is an exceptional cottage. Built like a small house in the woods, it is very private. It has a wood-burning fireplace, a glass sunroom, a large living area, and a full kitchen. It's a favorite with couples and with folks visiting Yale, Wesleyan, and Connecticut College.

A good trip to Old Lyme might include launching a kayak about a minute from the inn and exploring the Lieutenant River as it flows into the Connecticut River and then into Long Island Sound. Another day could be spent exploring the state parks in the area, such as Rocky Neck, Hammonassett, and Devil's Hopyard State Parks, just 10 minutes north. Fishing for bass and trout in the river is also possible.

Your trip won't be complete without strolling over to the Florence Griswold Museum. Old Lyme was an art colony in the early 20th century and is now home to the Lyme Academy College of Fine Art, a four-year accredited college focused on painting and sculpture. You may see students from the college or local art association painting on the lovely grounds of the inn.

Facilities: There is one cottage that can hold two couples. Kids more than 12 years old are welcome. The inn is home to an award-winning restaurant. The restaurant is closed for lunch and dinner on Tuesdays.
Bedding: Bedding is provided.

Reservations and rates: The rate for the cottage is $210 per night. Call at least three or four months in advance for weekend reservations.

Directions: From I-95 take Exit 70. Turn right at the end of the ramp, and the inn is the third house on the left.

Contact: Marie and Philip Aberham, **Bee & Thistle Inn**, 100 Lyme Street, Old Lyme, CT 06371, 800/622-4946, website: www.beeandthistleinn.com.

Other Cabins and Cottages Nearby

- The Island Campground and Cottages, 20 Islanda Ct., East Lyme, CT 06333, 860/739-8316.

12. THE LIGHTHOUSE INN

on Long Island Sound in New London

Luxury rating: ★★★☆☆   **Recreation rating:** ★★★★★

Steel magnate Charles Guthrie built this extravagant country mansion in 1902, and it became an inn in 1927. The opulent lobby and richly decorated dining room and pub are a testament to the days when the Connecticut Shore was known as a playground for the rich and famous. Today, it is still a popular, upscale destination, and families, groups, and even couples have discovered the flexibility of the inn's more casual Watchman's Cottage.

The cottage is located back behind the inn. It has a meeting-room feel when unoccupied, but this is partly because the cottage gets reconfigured to meet the needs of various guests. A group might have a holiday celebration in the room, beds might be lined up to sleep a small football team, or a couple might just want the extra privacy of a separate dwelling.

There is a microwave, a sink, and a two-burner stovetop. You can use the mini-refrigerator or request a larger one. There is wall-to-wall carpeting and daily maid service. The bathroom is tiled in 1940s pink-and-gray tiles and has a tub. There is cable television, two telephone lines, and a private patio that looks out over the lawn and woods.

The Lighthouse Inn is the only hotel in this section of Connecticut that has a private beach, and most of the guests take advantage of this. There is a popular local kayaking club, and the inn is .5 mile down the Thames River from a yacht club. If you love experiencing the grandeur of the inn, but not soaking in it, staying in the cottage allows you that option. You can play by day, visit the inn to enjoy lobster bisque and a whiskey-voiced lounge singer by evening, and then escape to your private cottage on the Great Lawn by night.

Facilities: There is one cottage with multiple configurations possible. It generally sleeps 1–6 people.

Bedding: Bedding is provided.

Reservations and rates: The cottage rates range $150–395 per night. Inquire about AARP and AAA discounts. Open year-round. Pets are permitted with permission and a small fee.

Directions: From Boston, take I-95 to Exit 84 south, and keep left at the fork in the ramp to Route 32, which becomes Eugene O'Neill Drive. Follow Eugene O'Neill Drive to the end. At the intersection, turn left, then turn right at the next light onto Bank Street. At the first light, turn left onto Howard Street. At the first traffic circle take the third exit. This will take you to a second traffic circle, where you will turn off at the first exit (Pfizer Offices is on the left) onto Pequot Avenue. Continue for 1.5 miles to Guthrie Place, and you will see the inn at the end of the street.

Contact: The Lighthouse Inn, 6 Guthrie Place, New London, CT 06320, 860/443-8411, www.lighthouseinn-ct.com.

Chapter 10

Rhode Island

CHAPTER 10—RHODE ISLAND

There is more to Rhode Island than the Bella Epoque mansions of Newport and the America's Cup. The tiny state has more than 400 miles of coastline (with more than 100 public beaches), and it is 60 percent woodlands (with at least 18,000 acres of parklands). It's also home to the Great Swamp and Block Island, a true haven just 13 miles from the shore. You can bike on paths across the state and around Block Island, kayak in beautiful Narragansett Bay, and canoe on numerous ponds and rivers—all in the country's smallest state.

Western Rhode Island has a notable hiking trail that traverses the entire state. The North South Trail is a multiuse trail that navigates 72 miles of seven different state forest areas. You cannot bike the entire trail, as it has sections that are limited to hikers only. However, Rhode Island has made great progress participating in the East Coast Greenway, the proposed traffic-free bike path from Florida to Maine. Here, the path may go from western Coventry through West Warwick, Warwick, and Cranston to the Blackstone River Bikeway.

The Blackstone River Bikeway is the first three-mile section of a path proposed to link the Blackstone Valley National Heritage Corridor with Worcester County in Massachusetts. The Blackstone Valley was the location of Samuel Slater's cotton mill on the Blackstone River in Pawtucket. Its opening in 1793 is said to have sparked the Industrial Revolution. For years, this area, like the Quiet Corner of Connecticut, was home to immigrant textile mill workers (many from Quebec). Today, the area has been revitalized by artists and factory-store outlets.

Nearby, the capital of Providence is filled with cultural attractions and restaurants. The re-routed rivers downtown have been edged with landscaped walkways and link College Hill and the East Side with Venetian-style bridges.

Thirty miles south, in Newport—a land of mansions and yachts—you can tour the palatial homes of the rich and famous residents of the Gilded Age along the

Cliff Walk. You can also tour by kayak the fine boats moored in the harbor. These days, Newport may be gaining more waterfront concertgoers than new blue blood, but it is still home to world-class yachting and the International Tennis Hall of Fame. The word "cottage" has a more posh meaning here.

Northeast of Newport, East Bay has recently become a more popular place to visit. The 14-mile East Bay Bike Path runs along Narragansett Bay here. Nearby Blithewold Mansion has 33 acres of gardens to tour. Six America's Cup winners were built at the Herreshoff Marine Museum. However, if it's a pure ocean lifestyle that you desire, you may want to go to the south shore.

Rhode Island's beaches have been a popular vacation spot for more than a century. You can enjoy birding, boating, fishing, hiking, swimming, and whale-watching all along the coast. At Smith Castle there is even a charming Theatre-by-the-Sea. You can often buy lobsters from roadside vendors or dig for clams on the beach and cook them in a beach cottage.

Trustom Pond is one of the areas notable for bird-watching, and Arcadia Management Area has trails for mountain biking and horseback riding. The Great Swamp in South Kingston is home to holly trees and osprey. On the beach, the Ninigret Conservation area is a great walking place that is often empty in the shoulder seasons.

Off the shore, Block Island offers 25 miles of walking trails across bluffs, hills, meadows, and moors. It's sometimes likened to Ireland and other times is said to be the Bermuda of the North. Wherever it reminds you of, with its long beaches, 365 freshwater ponds, and ideal roads for cycling, you're likely to enjoy it.

The ocean truly defines Rhode Island. Every summer there are more than 100 boating-related events on the Rhode Island and Block Island Sounds and on Narragansett Bay. The sea is truly the heart and soul of the state.

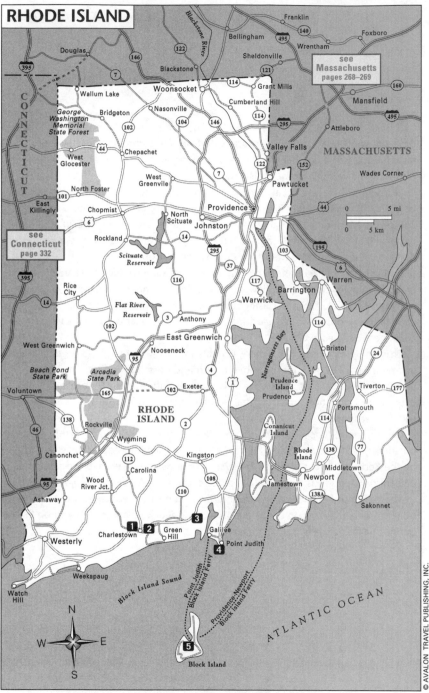

RHODE ISLAND

CONNECTICUT

MASSACHUSETTS

see
Massachusetts
pages 268–269

see
Connecticut
page 332

Douglas

Blackstone River

Franklin

Bellingham

Sheldonville

Wrentham

Foxboro

Wallum Lake

Woonsocket

Grant Mills

Mansfield

Bridgeton

Nasonville

Cumberland Hill

George
Washington
Memorial
State Forest

West
Glocester

Chepachet

West
Greenvile

Valley Falls

Wades Corner

North Foster

Pawtucket

Attleboro

East
Killingly

Chopmist

Providence

Rice
City

North
Scituate

Johnston

Rockland

Warren

Scituate
Reservoir

Flat River
Reservoir

Anthony

Warwick

Barrington

West Greenwich

East Greenwich

Nooseneck

Bristol

Tiverton

Beach Pond
State Park

Arcadia
State Park

Exeter

Prudence
Island

Voluntown

RHODE
ISLAND

Prudence

Portsmouth

Rockville

Narragansett Bay

Canonchet

Wyoming

Kingston

Conanicut
Island

Middletown

Wood
River Jct.

Carolina

Rhode
Island

Newport

Ashaway

Jamestown

Sakonnet

Westerly

Charlestown

Green
Hill

Galilee

Point Judith

Weekapaug

Watch
Hill

Block Island Sound

Point Judith
Block Island Ferry

Providence–Newport
Block Island Ferry

ATLANTIC OCEAN

N
W E
S

Block Island

0   5 mi
0   5 km

© AVALON TRAVEL PUBLISHING, INC.

CHAPTER 10
RHODE ISLAND

1. BURLINGAME STATE PARK

on Watchaug Pond in Charlestown

Luxury rating: ★☆☆☆☆   **Recreation rating:** ★★★★★

© BETHANY ERICSON

The 3,100-acre Burlingame State Reservation was opened in the early 1930s and named after the chairman of the former Metropolitan Park Commission. It has an enormous campground, with five simple camping cabins on the far side of the sites from the entrance, nicely positioned on the shores of Watchaug Pond. The cabins are clean, basic, pine camping cabins on the water, with two wooden bunk beds, louvered blinds, and tiny porches. No utilities, baths, kitchens, mattresses, or heat are included, just a fire pit and a picnic table.

Burlingame is a pretty campground dotted with evergreens. It offers numerous bathroom facilities, a playground, a swimming beach on the pond, and a bathhouse. The beach has lifeguards on duty, and in the summer Red Cross Swimming Lessons are offered.

The park is only a 10-minute drive to the large coastal beaches. There are hiking trails, and the park hosts more than 80 species of birds. The area north of Buckeye Brook Road is mostly used as a hunting area. The pond is a popular place to boat and fish, and the Audubon Society's Kimball Wildlife Sanctuary borders the south side of the pond.

If you're looking for a roof over your head while enjoying the pond and exploring the nearby shore, this is a basic facility for centering your activities. There is a lot to keep both kids and adults busy, and it's a pleasant place to just relax.

Facilities: There are five camping cabins. There is a camp store and a coffee shop on-site.

Bedding: No bedding is provided.

Reservations and rates: Cabins are rented for $35 per night. Memorial Day–Labor Day, a minimum stay of five nights and a maximum stay of 14 nights are required for reservations. The reservation form is available on the park's website and must be mailed in. A fee equal to a two-day stay will be deducted for each reservation canceled. Open April–October. No pets are permitted.

Directions: From Boston or Providence, take I-95 south to Exit 1. At the top of the exit, turn right onto Route 3 south. Follow Route 3 to Route 78 east. At the stoplight, get into the left lane to make a left turn onto Route 1 north and follow the road to Burlingame State Park.

Contact: Burlingame State Park, Charlestown, Sanctuary Road (Route 1), Charlestown, RI 02813, 401/322-7994 or 401/322-7337, website: www.riparks.com/burlingastatepark.htm.

2. HATHAWAY'S GUEST COTTAGES

in Charlestown

Luxury rating: ★★☆☆☆   **Recreation rating:** ★★★★☆

This sweet row of compact beach cottages is off a very charming road on a rise. The old farmhouse in the center of the property is the office and is registered with the Charlestown Historical Society. The cottages are a well-maintained and peaceful base for you to explore the beaches and wildlife areas of southern Rhode Island. They are comfortably furnished, and there are efficiency cottages as well as simple standard cottages with no cooking facilities. These are cozy alternatives to motels for the adventurous visitor who is looking for an activity-filled region.

Charlestown is halfway between Mystic, Connecticut and Newport, Rhode Island. It's also a short drive to the daily ferries to Block Island. Staying in Charlestown gives you an early-bird start to get a parking space at East Beach, a three-mile barrier beach, or to go birding or windsurfing at Ninigret Pond. Ninigret Park is also host to the Big Apple Circus and the annual Chamber of Commmerce Seafood Festival.

The Breachway, added in the 1950s at the end of Charlestown Beach Road, offers a dramatic wraparound view of Block Island Sound and is a popular destination for surf casting. Nearby Burlingame State Park and Forest is populated with a

© BETHANY ERICSON

remarkable multitude of birds and wildlife, and encircles Wautchaug Pond, where a federal study of yearly cycles in the pond's environment has been running since the 1990s.

The ocean lurks around every corner. Local shops outfit scuba divers, the Snug Harbor Marina runs a well-known fishing-tournament series, sailors and paddlers set out from the shores and beaches, sightseeing cruises sail round the points, and the annual Highland Games even pay tribute to coasts on the opposite side of the Atlantic. Maritime history awaits you at Mystic Seaport, or the Block Island Ferry can take you out even further into the spray.

Facilities: There are nine cottages.

Bedding: No linens are provided.

Reservations and rates: The rates are $150 per night, double occupancy, for the efficiency cabins, and $120 per night for the smaller cabins without kitchens, with a $15 fee for extra guests. Reservations are always a good idea, but they are required only if you're staying for more than one night.

Directions: Hathaways is located right on Route 1A, east of Mystic, Connecticut or west of Newport, Rhode Island.

Contact: Hathaway's Guest Cottages, Jeff and Donna Yorty, 4470 Old Post Road, Charlestown, RI 02813, 401/364-6665, website: www.hathawaysguestcottages.com.

3. WAKAMO STATE RESORT

on Potter Pond in South Kingston

Luxury rating: ★★☆☆☆   **Recreation rating:** ★★★★★

Located on Potter Pond, close to Matunuck Beach and the rest of the southern Rhode Island coast, Wakamo State Resort is a very well-developed area that is mostly designed around RV use. There are a wide variety of cottages that are rented through the resort, and they range in quality and offerings. Be sure to ask a lot of questions when you call, but don't hesitate to reserve yourself a decent cottage located just a .25-mile walk from the ocean.

Wakamo has a boat launch and dock space on Potters Pond, which has ocean access. On a hot summer day you can go bicycling, boating, fishing, swimming, or waterskiing. If that's not enough, you can also play tennis, or even dig for your own clam dinner. If you don't have any luck, there are restaurants within walking distance of the cottages.

People return to Wakamo year after year and participate in planned activities, like cookouts and bingo, resulting in long-lasting friendships. It has an all-ages summer-camp atmosphere. There is a basketball court and horseshoes. The

© BETHANY ERICSON

resort gives free rides on pontoon boats, and has paddleboats, kayaks, and canoes that can be rented.

Nearby, there are biking and hiking trails at Great Swamp Management Area in South Kingston. Ninigret Pond and the Trustom Pond National Wildlife Refuge in Charlestown are great spots for bird-watching, and autumn fishing for striped bass and bluefish at Trustom Pond is not to be missed.

Facilities: Wakamo Park rents over 20 cottages owned by Shore Line Realty, as well as a number of private cottages.

Bedding: No linens are provided.

Reservations and rates: Weekly rates range $625–950; daily rates run $900–140. Most cottages are rented weekly in the summer, daily off-season. Some cottages are rented by the season; call for more information. Discounts are given for stays of more than two weeks. Open April 15–October 15. Pets are not permitted.

Directions: From Boston/Providence, take I-95 south to Route 4 south. Drive on Route 1 south to the East Matunuck Beach exit. Succotash Road and Jerusalem are on the right. Continue driving for approximately .5 mile. Wakamo Park will be on the right.

Contact: Wakamo State Resort, 697 Succotash Road, South Kingstown, RI 02879, 401/783-6688, website: www.cottages.org/properties/RI_South Kingstown_WakamoParkResort.htm.

4. KAGEL'S COTTAGES

on Point Judith in Narragansett

Luxury rating: ★★☆☆☆   **Recreation rating:** ★★★★★

Kagel's is a lovely set of private-ly spaced, unique cottages in a grove by a salt pond. The site was previously known as Ken-yon Farms and Indian Rock Farm, both of which have been in the Kenyon family since 1911. The property is a very quiet, undeveloped setting with incredible views.

© BETHANY ERICSON

The cottages are built on a 230-acre area of farmland, on Point Judith, on the east side of the pond, facing the sunset. There is a dock for small boats. Across the pond is Ram Island, an undeveloped bird sanctuary. The cottages are about three miles from the access to Block Island Sound in Galilee, near Salty Brine State Beach and the ferry to Block Island.

There are hiking and biking trails nearby at Great Swamp Management Area in North Kingston, charter fishing boats in Galilee, and beaches with protected harbors, as well as those with big waves. Bikes and kayaks can be rented in Narragansett.

The cottages at Kagel's are all different, and they are frequently snatched up for the season by repeat guests, so be sure to call early. They all have kitchens, some have televisions, and some have convenient out-door showers. They are very clean, and they are near all of the outdoor possibilities of southern Rhode Island.

Facilities: There are six traditional, standalone cottages. Two have one bedroom, three have two bedrooms, and one has three bedrooms.

Bedding: Linens are not provided.

Reservations and rates: The rates range $950–1,450. Cottages are rented week-ly. Call very early, by January at the latest. Cancelations are nonrefundable unless the unit is re-rented. Open June–September. Credit cards are not accepted. Well-behaved pets are permitted.

Directions: From Boston/Providence, take I-95 south through Providence. (You may want to take Route 295 around Providence during rush hours.) Drive for about 10 miles south of Providence, and you will pass where Route 295 merges back into Route 95. Drive past the next exit for Apponaug (Exit 10). Take the next exit (Exit 9), a left exit, to Route 4. Drive on Route 4 all the way to the end (about 10 miles), where it merges with Route 1 south. Continue driving for about eight miles on Route 1. You will pass an exit for Wakefield and one for Narragansett. Take the next exit to Route 108, Point Judith and Scarborough. Turn right at the end of the ramp. Drive to the second traffic light and turn right onto Route 108. At the fourth light (where you would turn left to Scarborough Beach), turn right onto Indian Rock Farm Road, a gravel road. After about .5 mile, turn right at the fork in the road. If the signs are up, just follow the signs to Kagel's. Otherwise, drive for another .25 mile, and the main road takes a sharp right turn around a pond on your right. Take this right and then the next left up the hill. The Kagel's house is the large blue house at the top of the hill, a little to the right.

Contact: Kagel's Cottages, 91 Kenyon Farms Road, Narragansett, RI 02880, 401/789-9983 or 978/927-3860 (winter phone), website: www.kagels.com.

5. BLUE DORY INN

on Crescent Beach on Block Island

Luxury rating: ★ ★ ★ ★ ☆   **Recreation rating:** ★ ★ ★ ★ ★
Rank: Top 10 for Biking

The four cottages of the Victorian Blue Dory Inn in Old Harbor are located right by the rolling surf of Crescent Beach and the historic district of Block Island. They offer lavish antique decor, wall-to-wall carpeting, and a continental breakfast in the main inn's breakfast area each morning.

Known as honeymoon cottages, these are a romantic escape from the mainland. Whether you are reconnecting or honeymooning, the cottages are a swank place to stay while exploring the 17 miles of beach or 350 freshwater ponds of Block Island.

Block Island has at least 25 miles of walking trails, as well as dirt roads that are suited for off-road biking. Fall is a great time for birders to visit, and the island is much less busy then.

Fishing, parasailing, charter boats, kayaking, beachcombing, playing tennis, surfing, taking a moped for a spin, and admiring the North Light and the 250-foot bluffs are all as popular activities as taking a well-deserved nap on the beach. After all, the Blue Dory Inn's cozy one-room cottages, like The Doll House and The Tea House, take romance seriously, so don't tire yourself out too much.

Facilities: There are four cottages that can accommodate 2–8 people. Continental breakfast is included.

Bedding: All linens are provided.

Reservations and rates: The private cottages range $245–590 per night on summer weekends. A two-night minimum is required in the high season. Lower rates are available midweek and off-season. Call at least two months ahead in the high season. Open year-round. Pets are permitted in some cottages.

Directions: Blue Dory is located near the Point Judith ferry terminal. For interstate navigation from Point Judith, call 401/783-4613. For a schedule, visit the website www.block-island.com/binfo/fsched98.html.

Contact: Ann Law, **Blue Dory Inn**, Dodge Street, P.O. Box 488, Block Island, RI 02807, 401/466-5891 or 800/992-7290, website: www.virtualcities.com/ons/ri/b/rib35010.htm.

INDEX

Page numbers in **bold** *represent maps.*

ACKNOWLEDGMENTS

I am deeply grateful for the ideas, help, support, and advice from the following people: Susan Aaron, glenn mcdonald, Jerry Weinstein, Bob Ericson, Donna Ericson, Walter Nye, J. Samatha Gould, Tom Maloney, Andrea Jones, Michele Babineau, Delani Quintal, and Joe Christian.

My heartfelt thanks to all.

ABOUT THE AUTHOR

Bethany Ericson, a widely published and televised writer, has been propelling herself through New England with all manner of sporting equipment since she was a child. You may find her playing on Mount Washington in any season, yodeling from the Knife's Edge of Mount Katahdin, watching storms on the coast of Maine, biking (sometimes successfully) over boulders, swimming in the Lakes Region, fishing at North Woods camps, maple sugaring in Vermont, cooking venison stew in a yurt, canoeing the Saco, rafting the Kennebec, or kayaking with gray seals on Cape Cod. She calls the coast of Massachusetts home, insists that lobster be cooked for only 13 minutes, and occasionally slows down enough to read email at outdoors@infinitesea.com.

© glenn mcdonald

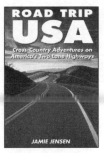